EDUCATION
AND
AGING

**DAVID A. PETERSON, JAMES E. THORNTON,
and JAMES E. BIRREN, Editors**

Andrus Gerontology Center
University of Southern California

and

Donna E. Deutchman, Editorial Coordinator

Prentice-Hall, Inc., Englewood Cliffs, New Jersey 07632

Library of Congress Cataloging-in-Publication Data

Main entry under title:
Education and aging.

   Includes index.
   1. Aged—Education—United States. 2. Adult
education—United States. 3. Gerontology—United States.
I. Peterson, David Alan II. Thornton, James E.
III. Birren, James E.
LC5471.E38 1987   370'.880565   86-18750
ISBN 0-13-235698-8

Editorial/production supervision: Eva Jaunzems
Manufacturing buyer: Barbara Kelly Kittle

© 1986 by Prentice-Hall
A Division of Simon & Schuster, Inc.
Englewood Cliffs, New Jersey 07632

Printed in the United States of America

10 9 8 7 6 5 4 3 2 1

ISBN 0-13-235698-8   01

Prentice-Hall International (UK) Limited, *London*
Prentice-Hall of Australia Pty. Limited, *Sydney*
Prentice-Hall Canada Inc., *Toronto*
Prentice-Hall Hispanoamericana, S.A., *Mexico*
Prentice-Hall of India Private Limited, *New Delhi*
Prentice-Hall of Japan, Inc., *Tokyo*
Prentice-Hall of Southeast Asia Pte. Ltd., *Singapore*
Editora Prentice-Hall do Brasil, Ltda., *Rio de Janeiro*
Whitehall Books Limited, *Wellington, New Zealand*

CONTRIBUTORS

James E. Birren, Ph.D. (Foreword) is the Dean Emeritus of the Ethel Percy Andrus Gerontology Center, Director of the Andrew Norman Institute for Advanced Study in Gerontology and Geriatrics, and the Brookdale Distinguished Scholar at the University of Southern California. Dr. Birren is also currently a member of the World Health Organization's Expert Advisory Panel on Health of Elderly Persons. He is a past president of the Gerontological Society of America, the Western Gerontological Society, and the Division on Adult Development and Aging of the American Psychological Association. In addition, he is a Fellow of the American Psychological Association, the Gerontological Society, the American Geriatrics Society, and the American Association for the Advancement of Science. His many awards include the Brookdale Foundation Award for Gerontological Research, an Honorary Doctorate from the University of Gothenberg, Sweden, and the Gerontological Society Award for Meritorious Research.

James P. Henry, M.D., Ph.D. (Chapter 6) is currently Professor of Psychiatry at Loma Linda University Medical School, and Staff Physician at the Jerry L. Pettis Veterans Hospital. He is also an Associate Fellow of the Andrew Norman Institute for Advanced Study in Gerontology and Geriatrics at the Andrus Gerontology Center, University of Southern California. His area of special interest is the mechanism by which emotional arousal can lead to disease. Publications include *Stress, Health and Social Environment,* and related articles in professional journals.

Huey B. Long, Ph.D. (Chapter 1) is Professor of Adult Education, University of Georgia. His research and teaching interests include the adult as a learner, the history of adult education, and free and reduced tuition provisions for older adults. He is a former president of the Adult Education Association of the U.S.A. and is internationally recognized for his research and leadership contributions in adult education. He has been visiting professor/lecturer at Dalhousie University, Halifax, Nova Scotia; Penn State University; the University of British Columbia, Vancouver, B.C.; and the University of Surrey, Guildford, Surrey, United Kingdom. Professor Long's awards include the Cyril O. Houle International Award for Literature in Adult Education, 1984; an Andrew Norman Institute Fellowship; and a Florida State University Graduate Fellowship. He has served in numerous editorial positions for adult education and gerontological publications.

Priscilla Gilliam MacRae, Ph.D. (Chapter 8) is an Assistant Professor of Sports Medicine at Pepperdine University in Malibu, California. She received her degree in Physical and Health Education at the University of Texas at Austin where her research focused on motor control and aging. Currently, Dr. MacRae is

Director of the Motor Behavior Laboratory at Pepperdine where she is continuing her research on the interactions of aging and exercise on physiological function. Dr. Gilliam MacRae has published in the areas of aging, motor function, and brain neurochemistry.

John McCallum, Ph.D. (Chapter 6) is currently Visiting Fellow at the Ageing and the Family Project, Research School of Social Sciences, The Australian National University, Canberra, Australia. His doctorate, from Oxford University, England, involved a critical analysis of social gerontological theory, and he has written articles on retirement and retirement income using Australian and British data. Dr. McCallum is currently involved in empirical and theoretical research on retirement, retirement income, and late-life role change.

Harry R. Moody, Ph.D. (Chapter 5) is presently Deputy Director of the Brookdale Center on Aging of Hunter College (City University of New York). Among his other publications, he serves as Editor of the *Human Values & Aging Quarterly* and his book, *Aging Society,* will appear in 1986. His current research interests include bio-medical ethics, autobiography, and social policy in aging. Dr. Moody is a graduate of Yale and received his Ph.D. in philosophy from Columbia University.

David A. Peterson, Ph.D. (Chapter 2) is Director and Professor of the Leonard Davis School of Gerontology and Associate Dean of the Andrus Gerontology Center. During the 1984–85 year, he was on sabbatical and served as a Fellow and Seminar Coordinator of the Andrew Norman Institute. He is a past president of the Association for Gerontology in Higher Education. He has published in the areas of the education of older people, *Facilitating Education for Older Learners,* and the teaching of gerontology, *Gerontology Instruction in Higher Education* (with Christopher Bolton). He is currently conducting research on the growth and change of gerontology instructional programs in American colleges and universities.

Penelope L. Richardson, Ph.D. (Chapter 7) is Associate Professor of Higher and Postsecondary Education at the University of Southern California. As Director of the Department of Health, Education and Welfare's Lifelong Learning Project, she wrote *Lifelong Learning and Public Policy,* an analysis of federal, state, and institutional policies in lifelong learning. Her current research interests are instructional strategies for adult distance learners and the role of higher education in the psychosocial development of re-entry women. She serves on the editorial board of *Continuum,* the journal of the National University Continuing Education Association.

Gerald A. Straka, Ph.D. (Chapter 4) is Professor of Education at Bremen University, Federal Republic of Germany. His research is in the area of learning and teaching on a cognitive basis, as well as the evaluation of the learning/teaching process. In 1983, he published an article entitled "Features of a form of didactics based upon teaching-learning theory" in the journal *Education.* His latest book contributions are *Lernen, Lehren und Bewerten (Learning,*

Teaching, and Evaluation, 1983) and *Lehren und Lernen in der Schule (Teaching and Learning at School,* 1979) (with G. Macke). He has presented papers on media and the elderly at the annual meetings of the American Educational Research Association and the International Congress of Gerontology (1985) and recently toured Brazil, China, Czechoslovakia, Hungary, and Poland to present invited lectures on related research topics.

James E. Thornton, Ph.D. (Chapter 3) teaches Adult Education in the Department of Administrative, Adult and Higher Education, Faculty of Education, and is Coordinator of the Committee on Gerontology, Faculty of Graduate Studies at the University of British Columbia. He received his Ph.D. in Adult Education from the University of Michigan. In 1984–85 Dr. Thornton was a visiting research scholar in educational gerontology at the Departments of Geriatric and Long Term Care Medicine, University of Gothenberg, Sweden, and Adult Education, Kyoto University, Japan. His research interests concern the impact of educational activity on the development and well-being of the elderly.

Gwen C. Uman, R.N., Ph.D. (Chapter 7) is a partner in Comp-U-Stat, a research consultation firm, and a visiting lecturer at UCLA School of Nursing, teaching evaluation research. In a broad program of examining adult education in its various contexts, she recently completed a series of measurement and treatment studies of incontinence in nursing home residents (with J. G. Ouslander and H. N. Urman). She is currently conducting training evaluations in business and industry with H. N. Urman; and, in preparation for a treatment intervention study with K. Dracup, is developing an instrument to measure the functional status of people with severe congestive heart failure.

CONTENTS

CHAPTER 2

AGING AND HIGHER EDUCATION

Older Students, Older Faculty, and Gerontology Instruction, **30**

By David A. Peterson

CHAPTER 3

LIFE SPAN LEARNING AND EDUCATION

A Conceptual Progression in the Life Course, **62**

By James E. Thornton

CHAPTER 4

TELEVISION AND THE ELDERLY
From Broadcasting to Narrowcasting, **93**

By Gerald A. Straka

CHAPTER 7

APPLICATION OF CLASSROOM HEALTH EDUCATION TO HEALTH BEHAVIOR IN DAILY LIFE, 185

By Gwen C. Uman and Penelope L. Richardson

CHAPTER 8

THE EFFECTS OF PHYSICAL ACTIVITY ON THE PHYSIOLOGICAL AND PSYCHOLOGICAL HEALTH OF THE OLDER ADULT

Implications for Education, **205**

By Priscilla Gilliam MacRae

FOREWORD

Currently, two strong forces are affecting the nature of education in America. One is the increased technology of what is often called "postindustrial society." The other is the changing demographic picture of this society, in which the fastest growth is occurring in the oldest portion of the population. There are many implications for education in this changing American scene, and not all of them can be dealt with, or even foreseen, in one book. However, this volume does attempt to bring to the surface some of the issues that are latent in the topic of education and aging.

Earlier in this century, no one would have expected that one of the tasks of education was going to be the fostering of personal growth in middle-aged and older adults. Therefore, to meet this obligation, education now must study the psychology of development in adults with the same intensity as child development was studied in the first half of the century. Higher education will have to foster research on the development of the individual over the life course. This research should include matters of health, motivation and interests, learning, emotions, values, and the attainment of life satisfaction. Our ideal is the self-constructing individual, the person who can transcend the bruises and limitations of the environment and exercise creativity in finding a pathway that is both productive and satisfying. Environmental opportunity is often limited and many persons do not transcend their environments; instead, with age, they become victims of the environment. It is at this point that education must intervene.

Older adults have a need to develop strategies for good health, management of personal resources, finding durable interpersonal relationships in the face of family changes, and maintaining self-esteem in the face of change and stress.

In the past decade, many middle-aged and older workers have been "given" early retirement as their employers seek ways of reducing costs and increasing output. Set back on their heels by losing jobs they had counted on for their work life, they engage in a search for self-respect while trying to learn new marketable skills. In addition to those who may *be retired,* there are those who choose to retire early, possibly because life has been a stressful and sometimes boring foot-race with the two companions of income and obligation. Since many persons can live 25 years beyond their age at retirement, this presents the issue of finding useful roles and tasks for the years after leaving the work force. Mature and older adults are not only interested in the job opportunities or advancement that increased skills may bring; they are also interested in the pursuit of meaning in life beyond that generated by employment.

In the past we have not allocated much in the way of resources to studying and serving the adults of our society through education. Children in earlier centuries were looked upon as little adults; likewise, we had assumed until recently that development ceased early in life and that adults were but grown-up adolescents. Both of these assumptions relieved us of the obligation to look in depth at individuals over the life course. However, if older persons are not to become a large-scale social concern, we must now create a broad educational climate within which they can contribute to society and find fulfillment. Research demonstrates that there are older adults who refuse to become victims of the technological change that can trivialize their contributions and feelings of worth. The question now becomes: How can we increase the number of these older, productive adults?

There is no doubt that matters of adult development and aging must be high on the agenda of educational institutions for the decades ahead if we are to realize fully the human-resource potential of America. In this regard, this volume is the product of a year-long seminar designed to provoke the research, thoughts, and services of education in and for a maturing society.

James E. Birren

PREFACE

Education, both as anticipation of and adjustment to personal and social change, is universally accepted in the developed world. However, the concept of education for older people and as a means for gaining a more complete understanding of an aging society is only now gaining general recognition. Thus, there remains much to learn about the effects of education on aging and vice versa.

This book identifies several aspects of education and aging. The first two chapters consider the historical and philosophical setting in which today's educational institutions function, and examine the role of higher education in an aging society. Chapters 3, 4, and 5 examine the social resources that may facilitate instruction and lifelong learning, and explore television and the numerous other mechanisms of the information society. The three final chapters deal with the potential outcomes of education, the lifestyle and health implications, the transference of learning from the classroom to the living room, and the effects of physical instruction.

The book is not intended as a definitive reference work; rather, it selects representative and important topics to examine critically, suggests some new models, and indicates profitable directions for future research and policy. It is primarily intended for use by researchers, professionals, policy makers, and graduate students from many disciplines who are interested in education and older people.

This volume is the fourth in an annual series devoted to special topics in the field of aging, produced by scholars from the United States and other countries who are fellows of the Andrew Norman Institute for Advanced Study in Gerontology and Geriatrics at the Andrus Gerontology Center, University of Southern California. Other volumes include: *Cognition, Stress, and Aging; Age, Health, and Employment;* and *The Dementias: Policy and Management.* This series reflects a multidisciplinary approach to complex issues related to aging. The 1984–85 year of study which produced this volume involved fellows from the disciplines of adult education, psychology, medicine, physical education, philosophy, and history, and from the countries of the United States, Canada, Japan, and the Federal Republic of Germany.

The Andrew Norman Institute for Advanced Study in Gerontology and Geriatrics was established in 1981, funded by an initial grant from the Andrew Norman Foundation. Fellows of the Institute spend ten months at the Andrus Center doing work related to the year's special topic, meeting in a weekly seminar, and preparing papers for the annual book, as well as pursuing individual research projects.

The goals of the institute include furthering research in gerontology and geriatrics, and encouraging the exchange of information and the development of collaborative research. The "aging of societies" is one of the most important issues facing all nations in the world today; and the field of gerontology will benefit greatly from cross-cultural and multinational exchanges of information and approaches to issues related to aging.

It is our pleasure to acknowledge the generous support of the Andrew Norman Foundation and the Andrew Norman Charitable Trust, whose original gift created and continues to support the Andrew Norman Institute for Advanced Study in Gerontology and Geriatrics, and of Dr. Armand Hammer, who each year has provided financial assistance through fellowships. We are grateful for the support of the Ernest J. Billman Fellowship from the Andrus Center Associates and the National Institute on Aging training grant, "Training in Health, Behavior, and Aging."

We would like to thank Christopher Bolton, Lydia Bronte, Richard Clark, Thomas Cole, Bradley Courtenay, Herbert deVries, Roger Hiemstra, Sharon Merriam, David Merrill, Morris Okun, Leonard Syme, James Thorson, Paul Torrens, Charles Wedemeyer, and Stuart Wolf for their assistance in reviewing chapters for this volume. Ms. Jessie M. Drew assisted in the production of the manuscript. Our special thanks to Ms. Donna Deutchman, for her extensive assistance in the editing and preparation of this book.

D.A.P.
J.E.T.
J.E.B.

A BRIEF HISTORY OF EDUCATION IN THE UNITED STATES

With Some Implications for the Public Education of Older Adults

Huey B. Long

Equal access, equal opportunity, and the need for formal education for adults are controversial topics. Despite the optimism of some educational gerontologists (e.g., Peterson, D., 1983) the need for, or appropriateness of, education for older adults is not universally recognized (Brookfield, 1984; Subcommittee on Post-Secondary Education, 1977). One factor that confounds discussion of older adults' education is the nature of its provision, i.e., personal and private or social and public. Discussions of personally—and privately—provided education generally raise little or no concerns in regard to costs since they are borne by the participant. The main concern seems to be associated with the question of the need or purpose of education for older adults. In contrast, discussion of socially—and publicly—financed education of older people raises questions of both costs and purposes or need. Consequently, it *seems* as if there is a recognition that older adults have a personal right to provide for their own education, just as they can spend their money for travel or other activities, but the idea of public responsibility for providing such education is debatable (Subcommittee on Post-Secondary Education, 1977).

Until the last decade or so the question of education for older adults was more academic than practical. However, two great trends have changed the status of this problem. First, deep, rapid, and pervasive social, technological, and epistemological changes occurring in the past twenty years have altered the relationships of all age groups to information and life style. Second, the aging of the

American population has dramatically altered the traditional population curve. The percentage of individuals 65 years of age or older has increased from 4 percent in 1900 to 11 percent in 1980. (Figure 1-1 illustrates the changes in proportions of the population less than 25 and more than 55 years of age for selected periods in this century.) Furthermore, the proportion of older adults will continue to increase at least until the year 2040. Thus these two changes encourage, if not require, a reconsideration of educational policy concerning older Americans.

Consideration of publicly-provided education for older people is perceived to be complicated by numerous diverse variables including difficult philosophical issues. These issues include questions of values, such as concepts of social justice and rights and responsibilities, that are not easily or casually addressed. In this regard, history and philosophy appear to be particularly instructive when struggling

FIGURE 1-1 Proportion of population less than 25 and 55+.

Sources: *Historical Statistics on the United States, Colonial Times to 1970,* Washington, D.C., 1975, pp. 15–16. *Statistical Abstract of the United States* (104th edition), Washington, D.C., 1983, p. 31.

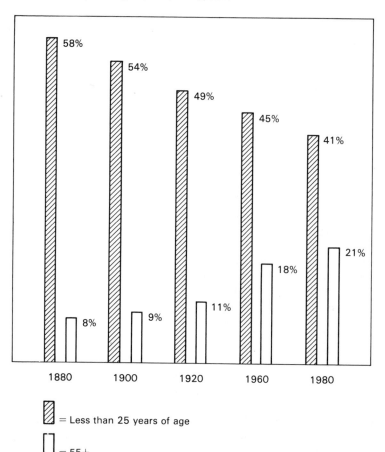

with concerns about educational provision for older people. This chapter provides a capsule overview of the history and philosophy of education in the United States. In addition, some conclusions and implications concerning public issues in education for older adults are presented. Three explicit purposes of this inquiry into history and philosophy are (1) to identify and comment upon governmental roles in the provision of education; (2) to identify and discuss structural and organizational changes in American education; and (3) to identify some major philosophical issues in public education for older adults. The traditional public education establishment, including grades K–12 as well as higher education, is the focus of the study. As a result, this essay is not concerned with other equally important issues such as which social agencies should provide educational services for older adults.

Two key concepts are used in the present chapter which may require definition: *older adults* and *older adults' education.* Older adults are defined in this chapter as individuals 55 years of age or older. Older adults' education, education for older adults, and similar terms are used to connote public education, i.e., governmentally-sponsored or provided programs of instruction; they are not necessarily free, but a percentage of the costs of these programs is paid by governmental (local, state, or national) funds. Educational programs of health and welfare agencies are not included in this definition; neither are privately-sponsored activities such as the Elderhostel.

HISTORICAL AND PHILOSOPHICAL OVERVIEW

History and philosophy are perceived to be profitable sources of information concerning educational views, including views on the appropriate clientele and aims of education. General historical trends concerning educational philosophy and educational practice also may be useful to the scholar seeking answers to questions concerning the prospects for governmentally-sponsored education programs for older people.

Historical Views of Education

Hillway (1961) stated the importance of historical knowledge in understanding American education when he said "without knowing its history, one cannot really know American education" (p. 8). He also noted that most Americans do not really know what their schools are like or what the schools are doing. The history of American education is a mystery to these people. This essay is based upon the above assumptions as well as the speculation that history is not only helpful in understanding the present but is also useful in discerning the future. Therefore, in this context the discussion of the history and philosophy of education has two underlying purposes: (1) to briefly describe important selected historical events and philosophical developments; and (2) to search for trends in the organization, support by governmental means, clientele, and changing purposes of education, as suggested by history and philosophy.

Hillway (1961), apparently following an older work of Cubberly (1919), devised the following historical periods in American education: 1640 to 1800, 1800 to 1860, 1860 to 1890, and 1890 to the present. For the purposes of this essay, historical periods slightly different from those described by Hillway have been identified to better reflect other social and philosophical developments: 1620 to 1799, 1800 to 1879, 1880 to 1919, 1920 to 1959, and 1960 to 1985. Comments on each of the above time periods address two major historical topics: (1) major social contextual phenomena, and (2) educational developments.

Three kinds of phenomena are discussed in the educational development sections. First, broad general perceptions of the basis of education are noted. Second, ideas concerning public or governmental authority and responsibility for education are reported. Third, major structural modifications that are believed to signal social attitudes concerning education are discussed. Discussion of purposes of education is necessary in this historical section to observe relationships among the purpose, providers, and structure of education. Yet comments are purposely limited to reduce overlap with the discussion of purposes of education included in the philosophical section of the chapter. Whenever appropriate, the section on educational developments also contains specific reference to education of adults. The content included in each historical period and each topical section is of necessity selective and summative, and suffers the limitations thereof. Furthermore, of necessity, events cited usually are included for discussion in one historical period even though their genesis or termination may have been in another period.

1620-1799: The Formative Period

Social context. This rather lengthy era can be described as a formative period in the nation's history. The coastal frontier was settled, cities built, and commerce expanded during the first 180 years. The Age of Enlightenment spread from Europe to America as commerce in ideas contributed to changing views of humanity, politics, economics, and religion. Puritan and Congregational determinism and idealism weakened as deism and rationalism increased in strength. Thus a new nation embodying a range of views was faced with establishing governmental and social structures and priorities. Despite the religious basis of education in New England, Pierce (1979) identifies political forces as the *sine qua non* of the American experience.

Educational developments. Puritan attitudes concerning education expressly focused on the spiritual basis of education (Soltow and Stevens, 1981). The purpose and content were firmly based upon salvation of souls. Thus it is not surprising that the Puritans, whose heritage placed a heavy emphasis on education, should be responsible for the first socially legislated requirements for education in the United States (Morrison and Commager, 1956). The famous Massachusetts Bay Colony laws of 1642 and 1647 are often cited as the beginning of the public educational system in the United States. In 1642 the General Court passed a law instructing officials of every township to see that parents and masters of apprentices gave children in their care sufficient education to ensure "their ability to read and understand the principles of religion and the capital laws of the country" (Wright, 1971, p. 137). The 1647 legislation warned everyone against the wiles of "that old deluder Satan," whose purpose was "to keep men from the knowledge of the Scriptures" (Wright, 1971, p. 137). Hence, the designs of the devil were to be defeated by requiring every town with fifty households or more to hire a teacher who would instruct all the children of the town in reading and writing.

The spiritual basis of education was not to go unchallenged during the colonial period, however. Increasing commerce of ideas among the people of the colonies and Europe opened dialogue based on materialism and rationalism. The rationalists, identified with the Age of Enlightenment, held views that differed from the spiritualists and idealists. As a result, even though education of children remained in a spiritual context it was increasingly secularized to include economic and cultural goals. Commager (1970) notes that while these goals did not equate with the religious ones, they were not perceived to be contradictory.

Beginning about 1750, however, American merchant men began to express dissatisfaction with the nature of the curriculum of education on the grounds that it focused too heavily on professional preparation for the clergy. A "practical" and applied approach to education was desired by the business community (Cremin, 1970). Subsequently, a practical curriculum, identified with Franklin and the Academy of Philadelphia, was developed to be conceptually different from that of the Latin Grammar School (Long, 1976).

Thus the foundations of public authority and responsibility for education were laid during this historical period (Pierce, 1979). The laws of 1642 and 1647 were the first of several legal steps taken to establish governmental *authority* for education. Even though the seventeenth and eighteenth century did not witness the creation of a public education system (Hillway, 1961), the principle of social *responsibility* was clearly affirmed. The early educational legislation in New England is important for a number of reasons, not least among them being the recognition that responsibility for education extended beyond the family. Some, such as Bailyn (1960), suggest that the change in the locus of responsibility and authority for education from parents to society was a result of the stress in the family structure caused by wilderness hardships. Even though Bailyn's position has been challenged and the exact cause of the shift from family to society is debatable, the effects are apparent.

Another elementary but important step was taken by the national government when the Land Ordinance of 1785 was adopted. This action, among other things, encouraged education by setting aside one section of land (640 acres) for the maintenance of public schools (Faulkner, 1954). (See Morrison and Commager [1956] for more information on this and the Northwest Ordinance of 1787.) According to the Land Ordinance, education remained in the religious context, yet the justification was increasingly secularized during this time period to include economic and cultural goals that were neither contradictory nor equated with the religious objectives (Commager, 1970). Furthermore, the nature of the curriculum was modified to make education more utilitarian (Cremin, 1970).

Gradually, over the first 100 years following the initial laws in Massachusetts, private systems of education emerged in the colonies. In New England, New York, and Pennsylvania these private systems frequently included dame schools, Latin Grammar Schools, and colleges. In the mid-Atlantic states and the South private systems were mostly limited to plantation schools, including tutors for the sons and daughters of plantation owners, and grammar schools in the larger cities. Sons of the wealthy occasionally went to Great Britain or to Northern colleges (Wright, 1971).

Structural and social elements and ideas concerning the purposes of education for older youths and adults are also identifiable in this period. A range of structural provisions existed; noteworthy examples include apprenticeship, public lectures, intellectual clubs, and proprietary schools. Apprenticeship, especially in the Northeast, provided a traditional entry into many of the important crafts and trades of the seventeenth and eighteenth centuries (Seybolt, 1969). Isaiah Greenwood began his lecture series in 1721 and by the end of the century every seaport city of any size hosted lectures on a variety of subjects from electricity to phrenology (Long, 1976).

Franklin's Junto and the American Philosophical Society are the quintessential examples of the intellectual clubs or organizations of the century. They were not alone, however, as Cotton Mather, a generation earlier, had created a number of neighborhood clubs in Boston similar to the Junto (Long, 1984).

Proprietary schools under the direction of private-school masters provided a range of instruction for adults, as well as children, in both day and evening classes. Literacy, navigation, surveying, and accounting were frequently available in these schools (Long, 1976).

In addition to the practical business and trade orientation of apprenticeships and the evening school curricula, adults continued an interest in piety and liberal studies. Thus this historical period reflects a number of contrasting elements. Structurally, the provisions expanded but the responsibility for adult education was personal. Objectives included spiritual aims, practical purposes, and rationally-based liberalizing reasons.

1800–1879: Nationalism

Social context. The social history of the second major period in American education is more complex than in the first period. Nationalism increased as the young republic faced a number of challenges including tumultuous international relations that twice led to foreign wars: the War of 1812 and the Mexican War. Intersectional conflict, westward expansion, immigration, and democratization also presented formidable challenges (Nevins and Commager, 1956). These and other developments served to stimulate views concerning humanity and education. Thus, significant changes affecting education occurred during this period.

Educational developments. Due to the radical differences in educational thought and structure that can be noted across this eighty year time span, Hillway (1961) and Cubberly (1919) divide this period as follows: 1800 to 1860, and 1860 to 1880. The free public school, supported by *ad valorem* taxes and sometimes hailed as the genius of American education, was created during the middle years of this period; and by 1850 the battle to institutionalize such schools essentially had been won even though a few skirmishes were yet to be fought (Hillway, 1961).

Ideas concerning the purposes and procedures of education were introduced from Europe as academics learned of the work of individuals like Herbart, Pestalozzi, and Froebel. Pestalozzi's ideas of faculty psychology gained a foothold only to be challenged by Herbart's more modern views. Both, however, contributed to changed attitudes concerning the nature of student-teacher relationships as encouragement and support supplanted harsh classroom discipline.

Views concerning the purposes of education during this period included a mixture of European and American ideas. Spiritualism was not completely removed, but among the intellectuals it was influenced by a more sophisticated form of idealism. Goals associated with nationalism, cultural transmission, and utilitarian concepts emerged as increasingly important. Social authority *and* responsibility for education was more strongly affirmed with the emergence of the free public school. Free schools supported by *ad valorem* taxes became a reality that was firmly fixed in American society by 1850 even though, as already noted, a few minor battles remained to be fought (Hillway, 1961).

The free common school of the nineteenth century provided the foundation for many of the contemporary views concerning education. Three important trends in American education can be traced to concepts of state authority and responsibility for education: (1) support of the schools by public funds derived through taxation; (2) egalitarian access to educational opportunity; and (3) compulsory education. Individually and collectively the above trends contribute to other educational policies and procedures such as increasing differentiation and specialization of the school program curriculum and extension of the school term. The development of kindergarten and the evening school illustrates these points.

Evening schools, which during the seventeenth century had been proprietary, were provided in a number of states. The first public evening school was opened in Louisville in 1834. By the middle of the century a number of states and cities had permissive legislation enabling school districts to provide evening schools for both boys and girls. The first evening high school was opened in Cincinnati in 1856 and by 1916 there were 458 in the nation (Cubberly, 1919).

Expansion of educational opportunity was not limited to children during the first 80 years of the 19th century. Major developments in the education of adults included the establishment of Mechanics Institutes in cities as diverse as Boston, St. Louis, and San Francisco. The American Lyceum was established with local chapters in 3,000 communities (Bode, 1968). Near the end of this era the Chautauqua was founded. However, except for the evening high schools, adults continued to be primarily financially responsible for their participation in the above organizations.

1880–1919: Industrialization

Social context.   Different time frames may be used by different historians to determine the beginning of the era known as the Age of Enterprise. Most agree, however, that it began after the War Between the States and before 1900. Starting about 1880 a transformation in America was underway. The American landscape was literally and figuratively changed between the great intersectional war and the end of World War I. Walker (1971) credits the Age of Enterprise with settling the wilderness and founding towns, and with constructing a new physical environment from steam, electricity, coal, and other resources. Simultaneously, the nation was wrapped with railroad lines and telegraph cables resulting in what Frederick Jackson Turner called the closing of the American frontier.

From 1880 to 1919 the United States changed in radical ways. Fortunes were amassed under the banner of "social Darwinism" and apologies were provided for injustice and social irresponsibility by Spencerian naturalism. The law of the jungle was applied in business and politics until excesses gave way to Progressive reaction (Commager, 1970). A voice for reform emerged in politics, religion, welfare, economics, and education. The likes of Lincoln Steffans and Upton Sinclair typified the muckrakers of the period; the city-manager form of government represented a major political reform; the social gospel was preached as religion responded to social conditions; and John Dewey emerged as the first major American philosopher of education.

In reality, like other historical eras, this period is characterized by contradictory movements. Industrialization and a traditional individualism were counteracted by a welfare ethic and the growing labor movement. Monopolies led to anti-monopolistic legislation. Religious fundamentalism and liberalism in the form of a social gospel coexisted, and educational ideals changed (Commager, 1970).

Educational developments. As life became more complex and knowledge more specialized in the 19th century, Spencer developed a classification of knowledge according to its value (see Table 1-1). Accordingly, he identified knowledge as being most valuable in five areas of life: (1) self-preservation; (2) securing the necessities of life; (3) rearing and disciplining offspring; (4) proper social and political behavior; and (5) pursuing leisure activities that gratify tastes and feelings (Hillway, 1961). Spencer, like his European predecessors, Froebel, Herbart and Pestalozzi, was among the important contributors to American thought on education. Americans like John Dewey, William James, and Charles Pierce added their thoughts to the expanding dialogue as the educational system gradually evolved in the last half of the nineteenth century. But as they were writing and reflecting, their America was vanishing.

TABLE 1-1   Educational Objectives for Childhood Education,
Adult Education, and Late Life Education

CHILDHOOD			
19TH CENTURY	SPENCER—LATE 19TH CENTURY	1918	1926
Perpetuate Culture	Self-Preservation	Health	Social
Train the Mind	Securing Necessities	Command of	Communication
Preparation for	of Life	Fundamental	Physical Fitness
Adulthood	Rearing and	Processes	Citizenship
	Disciplining	Worthy Home	Meeting
	Children	Membership	and Mingling
	Proper Social and	Vocation	Amusements
	Political Behavior	Citizenship	and Recreation
	Pursuing Leisure	Worthy Use	Mental Fitness
	that Gratifies	of Leisure	Religion
	Tastes/Feelings	Ethical Character	Parental Duties
			Nonvocational
			Practical Activities
			Vocational
			Development

Two extremely important changes in education, revealing transitions in American values, occurred almost simultaneously during this period. Both were rooted in the growth and consequences of industrialism. One was the realization that education could be employed as a social tool. The other was the fashioning of education as an economic tool. These developments are not as different as they seem to be on the surface: both arose out of industrial expansion and related social change, and both required philanthropic support and encouragement before they were integrated into the public school establishment (Cremin, 1964).

As noted earlier, since about 1750 a segment of American society had favored utilitarian goals for education. Their aspirations were finally realized during the final years of the nineteenth century in the form of manual or vocational education. The evolution of vocational education provides an interesting case study in educational development. First, the school curriculum was criticized. Second, spokesmen and leaders in the manual school philosophy emerged. Third, some curricula in some highly visible schools were changed to provide manual arts education. Fourth, the school community debated the issue. Fifth, separate manual arts schools were established with the sponsorship of business and industry. Sixth, vocational education became a part of the accepted school curriculum; and, seventh, governmental support for vocational education was obtained (Cremin, 1964).

It is interesting to observe that national security was introduced in the debate concerning the value of what was referred to as "practical arts, industrial, manual training or other technical schools" (Cremin, 1964, p. 38). The challengers to American economic well-being were then perceived to be Germany and the United Kingdom. Proponents also justified manual training as a means to achieve a variety of social goals. The social goals to be attained by vocational education were related to provision of greater opportunity for the foreign-born and for unskilled youth. Conflicts immediately arose among labor, the manual schools, and industry, however (Cremin, 1964).

	ADULT			LATE LIFE	
1938	1936 (BRYSON)	1984 (LONG)	1978–1982 (McCLUSKY)	1978 (THORSON)
Self-Realization	Remedial	Americanization	Copeability	Adapting
Human	Occupational	Application	Adult Basic	Growing
Relationships	Relational	Personal	Independence	Perpetuating
Economic	Liberal	Liberation	Health	Culture
Efficiency	Political	Literacy	Political	Putting
Civic		Social	Economics	Life Into
Responsibility		Improvement	Transportation	Perspective
			Estate Planning	Self-
			Leisure	Acceptance
			Personal	Social
			Fulfillment	Integration
			Expressive	Control and
			Contributive	Avoidance of
			Influencing	Helplessness
			Transcendent	

A more specific social approach to education was taken by the settlement house movement. Settlement houses originated in England during the 1880s and were quickly embraced in large American cities like Boston, Chicago, and New York in response to the negative impact of industrialism and urbanization. Education was a primary instrument of the settlement house movement to change all kinds of conditions from health problems and housing to work-related difficulties (Cremin, 1964).

The social and educational context was thus ripe for the philosophy of John Dewey who believed philosophy should be used to solve problems in areas such as education, hence his use of the term "instrumentalism." Following James' pragmatism, Dewey's instrumental philosophy was soon identified as either pragmatism or progressivism. While Dewey's philosophy influenced thought on the goals of education and appropriate curriculum, others, such as William H. Kilpatrick, translated similar principles into classroom activities.

Until about 1900, the goals of education were not expressly of an occupational or specifically social nature. Jeffersonian ideals concerning the role of education in a democracy continued to persist. The three dominant 19th century aims of education were to perpetuate the culture, train the mind, and prepare children for adulthood. Even though he wrote after 1900, Bertrand Russell's aims of education reflect the essence of pre-1900 thought on the topic. Russell noted that the aims of education were to produce an ideal character: vitality, courage, sensitiveness, and intelligence (Russell, 1970). Likewise, Kant's influence was still visible. He believed there were five aims of education: discipline, culture, discretion, morality, and the ability to think (Kant, 1970).

The economic or occupational importance of education was at the personal and individual level. Change was already underway, however, as in the first decade of the 20th century industrialists and farmers began to lobby the federal government for support of vocational education. Following the debates of this period, the education of children was increasingly discussed in economic and social terms (Cremin, 1964).

Equally important, Parker, Spaulding, and others introduced concepts of efficiency management into educational decisions, policies, and practices (Callahan, 1962). The federal government began its support of vocational education with the passage of the Smith-Hughes Act of 1919 (Long, in press). Psychological testing also emerged as an educational factor in this period. State literacy campaigns, the strengthening of immigrant education, and the creation of the Cooperative Extension Service by the Smith-Lever Act of 1914 were significant advances in adult education programs during the second decade of the current century.

New developments in the school system during this period were significant. It was an important period devoted to reform and to developing administrative structure and control. Cubberly (1919) provides an interesting chart that reveals how the originally simple, common school structure had been extended and modified by 1900. Important events occurred that would have lasting effects on both the practice and philosophy of education during the 40 years between 1880 and 1920. Progressive education also developed healthy roots during these years.

Education for adults continued to receive increasing attention as the evening high school, junior college, vocational high school, and university extension developed. It is important to note that the above institutions were unlike the Mechanics

Institutes, Lyceum and Chautauqua of earlier periods. In contrast to the latter, the former were associated with formal educational establishment and reflected increasing recognition of the role of the state in the education of adults. Thus 1880–1919 was a watershed era for both segments of the educational establishment, the grade schools and higher education.

1920-1959: Internationalism

Social context.   A variety of memorable incidents including the emergence of the United States as a major power in world affairs influenced education in this forty-year period. The first ten years were years of affluence, optimism, and expansion. Ten years of economic hardship and political unrest followed. The third decade included the advent of World War II for the United States and postwar recovery. The final decade is sometimes known as "the Eisenhower Years" or the tranquil years; but the latter sobriquet is misleading. The Cold War exerted stress within the political and social systems and the Korean War was a source of national frustration. The industrial strength of the United States became a source of security as well as economic and political pride.

Educational developments.   Spiritual goals, the basis of colonial education, had not been completely excised from educational objectives by this period. Yet they were seldom mentioned in the various lists of educational objectives published between 1920 and 1959. (See the discussion of educational objectives in the second major section of this chapter for more detailed information.)

During this period, issues concerning public authority and responsibility for education generally involved questions of extent of control and of which governmental bodies (local, state, or federal) would make educational decisions. Compulsory education; support based on property taxes; and increasing regulations of the curriculum, textbooks, and personnel confirmed the authority of the state in educational matters.

Educational gains achieved in the previously discussed historical periods were solidified in the 1920 to 1959 period. Management principles were increasingly applied to public education. The states increased their control and standardized curricula among the diverse school districts, and accrediting agencies became more visible. The concept of governmental authority and responsibility in education was extended and the federal role in education became more active. The opportunity for a high school education was broadened as a high school diploma became the basic educational credential.

All was not peaceful on the educational front, however. Illiteracy continued to cast a shadow over much of the nation and conflicts over state versus federal governmental responsibility increased, particularly regarding racial segregation. Also, a dramatic change occurred in educational leadership between the first historical period and the end of this one. For most of the time since the colonial period, education and philosophy were the province of the clergy. However, between 1920 and 1959, a transformation that began late in the 1800–1879 period was completed. Educational leadership generally had been assumed by professional educators and politicians. Even higher education, which had maintained a close relationship with the church, was no longer dominated by religious leaders. In contrast to the state of education in 1840, when the president of every important college was a clergyman or someone trained to the clergy, a century later no clergyman occupied the presidential office of any of the leading institutions of learning in the United States (Commager, 1970).

Perhaps the major event affecting childhood schooling and college education came at the very end of the period as a result of the Russian satellite, Sputnik. Following the Russians' successful launch of the earth-orbiting satellite, the public schools and colleges received intense scrutiny as questions of educational goals and curriculum were hotly debated. (More is said on this point in the philosophical section of this chapter.)

Yet another major development concerning education for adults is associated with this historical period. Even though education of adults had been a continuing element in American intellectual history from the seventeenth century, it was not customarily distinguished by the adjective "adult" until this period. Americanization education and education provided by business enterprises and professional groups were not uncommon phenomena by the third decade of the twentieth century when the American Association for Adult Education was formed (Bryson, 1936). It was also the time when the first graduate curriculum in adult education was offered by an American university, and graduate degrees in adult education were available at a growing number of universities (Knowles, 1977). Thus education of adults gradually emerged in both public recognition and in the institutionalization of the educational system.

1960–the present: Postindustrialism

Social context.   The current period is the shortest and most recent historical era in this scenario. Recency and complexity contribute to difficulty in identifying and choosing from among the many events now impacting upon education in what is called the postindustrial period. Some of the more salient social developments in this period include the development of a high-tech society and concomitant structural changes in the economy; the changing roles, status, and consciousness of women; and attitudes concerning minorities based on race, ethnic origins, age, and sex. Other major developments having educational implications include electronic communications (computers, radios, and television), increasing polarization of special interest groups, and stresses in politics and education.

As a nation, the United States experienced significant trauma beginning with the Vietnamese War, weakened relationships with foreign governments, increasing terrorism, and frustration with impotence while simultaneously being a world power. Science, technology, engineering, and math became "king of the hill" while disciplines in the arts and letters languished.

Educational developments.   Purposes of education during this period were increasingly expressed in pragmatic terms. Efforts to develop consensus on the purposes of education, as conducted in the two previous historical periods by the NEA and other groups and as discussed in the second section of this chapter, ceased. But even though formal statements of purpose are lacking, inferences are possible. Accordingly it appears that educational goals are expressed in increasingly pragmatic terms and are identified with economic (occupational skill development), nationalistic (national defense), and social purposes (Spring, 1976).

The idea that educational purposes are not limited to the young was affirmed during this period as the free- and reduced-tuition programs of colleges and universities were debated. A review of the purposes of education for older adults reveals a salient pragmatic justification. Oppenheimer (Subcommittee on Post-Secondary Education, 1977) listed 15 reasons for senior adults' enrollment in postsecondary education. Five of those reasons illustrate the pragmatic nature of the entire list: to enable elders to do more for themselves; to enable elders to do more for their peers; for personal growth and self-realization; to prepare for retirement; and to develop better uses of leisure time.

Governmental authority and responsibility for education was extended into the prekindergarten and postsecondary areas during this period. States such as California, Florida, and Texas developed extensive community college systems that extended greater public support to postsecondary education. Many states also developed a similar system of vocational–technical schools. A college education for the majority of young men and women was envisioned early in the period. Simultaneously, federal laws concerning education for handicapped children provided funds for the support of education for all of the very young. Free kindergartens for children five years of age became commonplace by the 1980s.

Debates concerning governmental authority seem to focus on questions of civil rights (racial and sexual discrimination) and parental authority and responsibility for education. Some states have challenged or withheld certification of certain religious schools and the educational practices of some religious sects in order to ensure separation of church and state in the educational arena.

Major developments concerning authority and responsibility for the education of adults include certification and relicensure laws and permissive legislation for free and reduced tuition for older adults. Beginning midway into this period, states began adopting laws and policies that permitted older people to attend higher education classes, on a space-available basis, without paying the normal tuition fees (Long, 1980; Long and Rossing, 1979). By 1980 free and reduced college tuition programs existed in most states for individuals 62 years of age or older (Long, 1980).

Both of the above developments are consistent with the historical development of educational provision in the United States. The relicensure action extends state authority for standards of practice, and is based on the idea that education increases the probability of improved practice in professional areas. Free and reduced tuition programs follow a trend in permissive legislation that has provided initial access to and opportunity for education.

The most provocative contemporary development is the emergence of the lifelong learning or lifelong education concept. Even though the concept remains variously defined and frequently vague, the term is increasingly found in both popular and scholarly literature (see Thornton, this volume). Lifelong learning was given official sanction by the education establishment in 1976 with the adoption of the Lifelong Learning Act. Even though the federal legislation could be described as abortive, support for the concept may follow the traditional historical development sequence noted by Cubberly (1919) and discussed later in this section. Awareness and acceptance of state responsibility for education of citizens regardless of age can also be discovered at the state level. For example, legislation known as the Louisiana Learning Incentive Fund was introduced, but not adopted, in 1984. Among other things, that act says "all citizens have the right to learn as long as they are alive and it is the duty of the state to provide and to support opportunities for learning for all segments of the population" (Senate Bill 865, 1984, pp. 1–2).

Following the 1971 White House Conference on Aging the idea of education for older people became even more visible. Increasing attention to the topic is noted in the literature of the 1970s. DeCrow (n.d.) identified 3,500 programs for older adults in a range of public settings including schools, universities, and community colleges. At about the same time, the California Department of Education added a staff position to assist with public school programs for older adults (Marshall, 1978).

Summary

This first major chapter division discusses selected historical events and developments. In the process, certain trends in organization and structure of education, governmental support, clientele of public education, and underlying foundations or justifications of education are noted.

Four consistent and significant trends are observable in the historical development of education in the United States over the past 300 years. They are trends toward increased secularization of education, increased governmental responsibility for education, increased use of educational institutions and programs as means toward social ends, and increased vocationalism. Stated in another way, it can be suggested that spiritual and individualistic attributes that often characterized American education during its first two hundred years have been replaced by secular vocationalism designed to achieve broad social purposes.

These trends are noted throughout the educational systems of the United States, including postsecondary education. Modifications of historical positions concerning the role and responsibility of the government for education have been much greater and more rapid since 1920.

Three of the above trends support speculations concerning the eventual provision of education for older adults by the state. The trends toward increasing governmental responsibility for education and expanding educational opportunities for social goals support the likelihood of further governmental policies supporting such educational provision. Indeed, almost three-quarters of a century ago Cubberly (1919) noted a five-step sequence in the development and extension of public education:

1. securing permissive legislation;
2. securing mandatory legislation;
3. establishing organizational and administrative machinery to supervise the schools;
4. creating a public belief in education for democratic ends; and
5. creating sentiment for support of additional programs.

Evidence can be found indicating that all of the above steps, except step 2 and to some degree step 3, are being addressed currently regarding the education of older adults. As the expansion of educational opportunity and provision in this century has gradually, but increasingly, included young adults, eventual acceptance of public responsibility for education of older people can be hypothesized. Rapid acceptance of the idea may encounter some difficulties, however. Some obstacles preventing early acceptance of state responsibility for education of older people are discussed in the next section.

Philosophical Considerations

Given the historical characteristics of education in the United States as outlined in the previous section, we note a trend that may indicate education of older adults will eventually become an accepted governmental service. The four major trends of secularization, governmental responsibility, education as an instrument of social policy, and vocationalism are not necessarily sufficient for such an eventuality, however. Just as there were a number of philosophical issues involved in public acceptance of the idea of free schools for children, there are arguments opposed to the notion that society, i.e., government, should provide educational services for older adults. Philosophical support for, or opposition to such provision appears to be influenced by one's orientation to older people, conceptualization of education, conceptualization of adulthood, ideas of social justice, economics, and concepts of educational goals. Each of these important factors is discussed in the following pages.

Orientation Toward Older People

Moody (1978) has identified a four-part typology of basic philosophical orientations toward older people that in turn influence attitudes concerning the appropriateness of education for them. The typology ranges on a continuum from the most primitive view to what might be called the most enlightened philosophy. The first philosophical model is based on rejection, an idea that involves avoidance, repression, neglect, isolation, and expendability; it provides no rationale for educating older adults. According to this view, it would be a waste of valuable resources to provide expensive services for older adults because of the perception that they are nonproductive, parasitic, and weakened competitors for scarce goods and resources. This orientation is sometimes discovered in primitive cultures. Michener (1974) illustrates it in his story of Blue Leaf, the Indian woman who is left to starve and freeze after the death of her husband, Lame Beaver. Likewise de Beauvoir (1972) presents numerous incidents including an anecdote from a Japanese novel which presents two characters who behave differently as they face the "mountains of death" where old people are abandoned to whatever kind of death awaits them: one, a grandmother named O'Rin, voluntarily and cooperatively seeks her fate; the other, a man called Matayan, violently attempts to foil the efforts of his son to take him to the mountains. He escapes only to be recaptured and thrown over a cliff.

The second orientation proposed by Moody often represents the views of liberal political activists and proponents of the welfare state. This view is a social-services model that, although more humane than the first orientation, also has some degrading elements. According to this second view, educational opportunities and other services *are* provided for the elderly; yet it seems that these are justified on questionable grounds. Educational services are here perceived as a kind of entertainment that keeps older people occupied and may reduce the pressure for more expensive services.

The third orientation is based on an activity concept; its adherents believe in the value of life among the aging and believe that evidence of this value is partially related to activity. As a consequence, education is designed to introduce older people to, and maintain them in, leadership development, second career preparation, and other activities to keep them in the mainstream of life.

The fourth orientation is an extension of the third. It could be called the self-actualization model because it represents human life as having unlimited potential for development. Maturity is believed to be an especially productive time for achievement built upon earlier periods of life. More than the others, the fourth model romanticizes later life. The goal of the September years is perceived as an objective psychological development across the life span. Education is conceived as an appropriate element in the attainment of the highest psychological goal of fulfillment in the last stage of life.

Three of the four orientations described by Moody include a provision for educational services for older people. Despite the near unanimity on the desirability of education for older adults there are differences in justification that reflect views of both aging and the aims of education. More is said about aims and purposes later in this chapter.

Conceptualization of Education

A second consideration in philosophical discussions of education for older adults includes the conceptualization of education. The term "education" is one of the most frequently used words in the English language. It means many things. It is frequently used as a synonym for propaganda, for processing information, for adhering to the party line, and so forth. It is used as both a noun and a verb. It is a process and it is a product. Hence, it is no surprise that disagreements exist concerning the definition of education.

Conceptual difficulties are serious impediments to the support of education for older people. Education, in its recent historical usage, almost automatically conjures up visions of childhood. *Education* is derived from the Latin word *educere,* meaning either "to lead out," "to train," or "to mold according to some specifications" (Peters, 1970). All these uses connote a process appropriate to, if not peculiar to, childhood. Education as traditionally defined in terms of the *developing* human being connotes a biological, psychological movement from childhood to adulthood. In the process of evolving, the concept of a *complete* or *developed* human being emerged out of childhood. Hence education primarily has been associated with transformation of the child into an adult. Accordingly, "man can only become man by education. He is only what education makes of him" (Kant, 1970, p. 180). It is not what people are at eighteen, it is what they become afterwards that matters (Whitehead, 1967). According to this view, to speak of the *education of adults* is almost as incongruous as using the word *swim* to refer to locomotion across an area of land, or to speak of a square circle.

Blakely (1971) criticizes the concept of education that is characteristic of the industrial era. Particularly challenging is the need to refocus education from a schooling concept, where education is isolated from society, and to alter the dominant regard for education as schooling for the young. Blakely cites Margaret Mead whose concept of lateral learning contrasts with traditional linear learning. If we are living in a new environment, as Blakely suggests and a variety of data implies (see Moody, this volume), education must shift from an orientation toward the past to one toward the future where the *process of knowing* is more important than the static notion of *knowledge.*

Current conceptualization of adulthood correctly represents the human adult as an unfinished product. Individual adults continue to change physically, mentally, and socially. If education was beneficial to the child, arguments for education of the adult do not seem to be inappropriate unless the following assumptions are true: (a) children learn all they will ever need to learn; (b) children master skills that enable them to be successful lifelong learners; (c) learning is limited, by psychological and biological factors, to childhood.

Conceptualization of Adulthood

Another possible source of opposition to public provision of educational services to older adults emerges out of the concept of adulthood. Until about 1600, adulthood was conceptualized as a progressive series of biological, sociological, religious, and legal capabilities and rights. By the late nineteenth century, childhood from birth to 21 was perceived to be the most complex life period, while adulthood was perceived as a less dynamic one. To the degree that the perception of adulthood as static and unchanging exists, opposition to education for older people is also likely to exist.

Demographic and scientific phenomena are likely to bring about an adjustment in concepts of adulthood. The changing demographic profile of the United States has focused new energy and interest upon older adults. As their numbers and proportions in the population increase, the complexity and dynamism of adulthood will receive greater scientific attention. A rich body of knowledge concerning life-span development (Gould, 1978; Levinson et al., 1978) and biological and psychological development (Baltes and Schaie, 1974; Clayton and Birren, 1980; Londoner, 1971; McCoy, 1977; Willis, 1985) already exists.

Social Justice

The concept of social justice is a fourth potential source of philosophical consideration in the debate concerning education for older adults. To oppose educational opportunity or access for older adults on this basis, however, requires an assumption that other age groups in society are disadvantaged relative to older adults. They may be perceived to be disadvantaged in terms of available resources to purchase educational services; or they may be believed to be disadvantaged in terms of their greater needs. Or a third such proposition would hold that other age groups (who would benefit more) would be denied access to educational services that were provided to older adults.

Issues of social justice in some educational programs include (1) denial of access based on age, such as sometimes happens in graduate programs and some professional schools; and (2) special tuition waiver programs for adults beyond certain minimum ages, usually age 62. Both of these practices raise philosophical questions.

To appeal to social justice is to invoke concepts of fairness, equality, liberty, and morality. When applied to the issue of public responsibility for educating older adults in the United States, the concepts of fairness, equality, and morality seem to dominate the discussion. Fairness calls for policies that avoid distinctions while obtaining a proper balance between competing claims (Rawls, 1957). Judgments of individual fairness will be determined by whether institutional arrangements are just or unjust. In his theory of social justice, Rawls (1971) developed a priority ordering of two basic principles: (1) each person is to have an equal right to the most extensive system of basic liberties compatible with a similar system of liberty for all; and (2) social and economic inequalities are to be arranged so that they are both to the greatest benefit of the least advantaged, and attached to offices and positions open to all under conditions of fair equality or opportunity (Rawls, 1971). As a consequence, Rawls' idea of social justice calls for equal distribution of social primary goods (including education) unless an unequal distribution of any or all of these goods is to the advantage of the least favored.

Thus, denial of older adults' access to education, according to Rawls' concept of social justice, must be based on evidence that older adults are more favored than other age groups. However, even this method is flawed because of the great range of assets among older adults. As a group they may be more advantaged than other groups, but as individuals, a sizable minority may be less advantaged. Thus, policy decisions must consider inequities within the older age group.

Economics

Yet another philosophical point of departure includes economic issues. Economic justification for limiting public educational services to childhood derives from the first of Moody's (1978) orientations.

Proponents of economic justification perceive that the purpose of education is primarily to train the worker. Educational expenditures are thus reduced to the level of a social investment that will return tangible economic benefits to society. Programs of education and populations to be served by them are chosen according to the net returns of contributions to the nation's economic welfare. The justification of expenditures for childhood education on economic grounds, however, is becoming increasingly controversial. Previously, it was believed that increases in the Gross National Product (GNP) directly flowed from increases in educational expenditures. However, there is now speculation suggesting the flow is reversed, i.e., increases in educational expenditures follow increases in the GNP (Spring, 1980).

Educational Goals and Purposes

One of the most interesting issues in philosophical discussions of the role of government sponsorship of education for older adults concerns educational goals and purposes. Included are questions such as: Are the goals and purposes of education different for adults and children, for young adults and older adults? Why are they different, if they are? Should they be different? And are differences general or specific, generic or particular? Still, how the answers to questions such as these may eventually influence one's position on the issue of governmental support for older adults' education is not always clear.

Definitive discussion on this point is beyond the purposes of this chapter. Therefore, the debate will not be resolved here. However, the following comments address questions of differences or similarities in goals and purposes of education for children, young adults, and older adults.

Consequences of education are sometimes stated at three levels: (1) goals or aims; (2) purposes; and (3) objectives. When the above typology is used consistently, goals and aims are the most abstract, and general objectives the most specific. However, only two levels are used in this chapter: goals or aims, used interchangeably to refer to the consequences of education at the general abstract level; and purposes and objectives, used as synonyms to refer to the more pragmatic results of education. The major philosophical goals or aims of education and the pragmatic purposes of education according to age groups are discussed in the following pages.

Goals and Aims

General philosophies of the nature of the human being have existed for centuries as we have sought to understand and interpret life. These philosophies frequently addressed the development of the individual and the roles of education in his or her development. Philosophers such as Comte, Hegel, Kant, Locke, Plato, and Rousseau provided philosophical foundations for early American education. American philosophers had little impact on educational thought until the 20th century.

John Dewey—influenced by Europeans such as Frederick Froebel, Johann Herbart, Johann Pestalozzi, and Herbert Spencer, and Americans such as Charles Pierce and William James—developed his philosophy of pragmatism that provided a basis for the philosophical movement known as progressivism. As noted earlier, Dewey's impact on early 20th century educational thought and practice is significant. A number of additional educational philosophies were stimulated by progressivism, and existing positions were more systematically developed. As a consequence, 20th century philosophical educational goals usually have been influenced by one or more of the following philosophies: eclectism, essentialism, perennialism, progressivism, reconstructionism, or metaphysical positions such as Thomism (Gruber, 1961; Maritain, 1970).

Space limitations preclude any effort to analyze and describe the different educational philosophies here. However, after careful review of the differences and similarities, it was concluded that *educational aims based on these philosophies do not differ according to the age of the student.* As general philosophies, the aims of education suggested by essentialism, perennialism, progressivism, and reconstructionism do differ—but not by age. (See Table 1-1 for a tabular presentation of the aims, content, and learning activities recommended by these philosophies.) Admittedly, the tabular presentation obscures differences such as the ones that exist between essentialism and reconstructionism concerning social change. In a similar manner, differences between progressivism and existentialism concerning emphasis on the individual are blurred. Yet the purpose of this section is not to describe these philosophies, but rather to report the result of an analysis of them in terms of older adults.

In this regard, the important conclusion to be drawn from the analysis of philosophical aims of education is that one cannot justify limiting education to youth strictly in terms of philosophical goals of education without defining education strictly as a childhood phenomenon.

PRAGMATIC PURPOSES OF EDUCATION AND AGE

The pragmatic purposes or objectives of education are usually written on a more concrete level than the philosophical aims. Also, the literature contains separate lists of educational objectives for youth, adults, and older adults. Therefore, these lists are reported in the following pages to illustrate the agreement among educational purposes that exists at this level.

Childhood. Table 1-1 (pp. 8-9) identifies the pragmatic purposes of childhood education, adult education, and education for older adults as identified in the literature. The 1938 NEA list of objectives is the last major national effort to reduce the mission of education to a short list of objectives. Since then, some efforts have been made at other levels. For example, the New York City school system has a list of nine objectives (Board of Education, 1965). But perhaps the California experience best illustrates the current difficulty of reaching agreement on educational purposes. In California the individual teacher has the responsibility for establishing educational objectives (Walker, 1980). Walker expresses the situation succinctly but boldly when he observes that "formal education is experiencing an unprecedented confusion of purpose" (1980, p. 26).

Nevertheless, while numerous statements of educational objectives can be found in the general education literature, less numerous are the published objectives of education for adults and older adults. Some of the major ideas concerning the 20th-century purposes of education are noted in the following paragraphs.

In 1918, the NEA Commission on Reorganization of Secondary Education identified what has become known as The Seven Cardinal Principles of Secondary Education in the United States. The commission indicated that the high school program should contribute to students' (1) health, (2) command of the fundamental processes, (3) worthy home-membership, (4) vocation, (5) citizenship, (6) worthy use of leisure, and (7) ethical character.

Using a different approach, Franklin Bobbit's (1924) analysis of modern human activity suggested a curriculum that contributes to (1) social communication (language), (2) physical fitness, (3) citizenship, (4) meeting and mingling (social activities), (5) amusements and recreation, (6) mental fitness, (7) religion, (8) parental duties, (9) nonvocational practical activities, and (10) vocational development.

Nevertheless, the above formulations were not altogether satisfactory. As a result, another NEA commission, The Educational Policies Commission (1938), set out to describe the well-educated American. They proposed that the educational system should produce an individual with certain achievements in four areas of conduct: (1) self-realization, (2) human relationships, (3) economic efficiency, and (4) civic responsibilities. These areas of conduct were further described as follows.

Self-realization reflects an appetite for learning, the ability to speak the mother tongue (English) clearly, the ability to read and write efficiently and effectively, and an ability to deal with numerical calculations. This area of conduct also includes skills in listening and discussing. The individual should understand basic facts concerning health and disease. The individual also protects personal health and the health of dependents while contributing to community health. The individual is both a competent participant and observer of sports and recreational pastimes. The individual also should possess mental resources necessary for leisure, to appreciate beauty, and to give direction to life.

The area of human relationships includes placing priority on human interactions while being able to enjoy a rich, sincere, and varied social life. The individual should have knowledge of how to work and play with others. The individual observes the amenities of social behavior, appreciates the family as a social institution, and helps to preserve it and its ideals. Finally, the well-educated American, according to the 1938 Educational Policies Commission, should have homemaking skills that include a mastering of democratic relationships.

The third area of conduct was identified as economic efficiency. Accordingly, the individual knows the satisfaction of good workmanship; e.g., as producers, individuals understand the requirements and opportunities found in various jobs and thoughtfully select their vocation. The individual is able to succeed in his or her chosen profession while mastering and improving occupational efficiency. The social value of work is appreciated. As consumers, individuals should plan the economics of their own lives, and should be informed and skillful buyers with the ability to safeguard their personal economic interests.

Civic responsibilities were included by the Educational Policies Commission as the fourth area of conduct. Accordingly, it states that well-educated Americans should be sensitive to the disparities of human circumstance and act to correct unsatisfactory conditions; that they should seek to understand social structures and social processes; that they should be capable of defending themselves against propaganda. Respect for honest differences of opinion is also valued. The Commission further indicates that well-educated persons should have regard for the nation's resources and should measure any scientific advancement by its contribution, actual or potential, to the general welfare. Well-educated people are, according to the Commission, cooperating members of the world community who respect the law, and who also understand economic problems and principles. Lastly, they should accept civil responsibility and be loyal to the nation and to democratic ideals.

Other formulations of the purpose or goals of the education of children can be found. It is doubtful, however, that many new objectives will be noted. Generally, it can be noted that different goals appear in differing order, while a few lists are longer than others. The ones cited here share in common academic, civic, economic, and leisure objectives. Some important differences are also obvious. The 1918 list places a priority on ethics that is not specific to the other two lists, while only Bobbit's list includes religion. The 1938 goals imply reformists' behavior in the political arena and focus on social goals.

Adults.   Up to this point, discussion of the pragmatic purposes of education has focused on childhood education. The literature of adult education, including gerontological education, that discusses either general philosophical aims and goals or specific pragmatic purposes, is less developed. A few writers such as Apps

(1973), Bergevin (1967), Cotton (1968), Elias and Merriam (1980), and Kallen (1962) have directly addressed philosophical goals of education for adults. Others, such as Bryson (1936) and Long (in press), have written about the pragmatic purposes of education of adults. An even more recent document (Commission on Higher Education and the Adult Learner, 1984) has identified five goals of adult learning: "Developing or renewing employability for the unemployed; maintaining and enhancing occupational skills in the face of technological change; eliminating adult illiteracy; providing equal access to education for all adults; and developing knowledgeable citizens in an information-technological world" (p. 4). These sources indicate limited differences between the educational goals or educational purposes of adults and children.

Slightly different conclusions emerge from the less developed work that addresses educational purposes of education for older adults. McClusky (1978, 1982) and Thorson (1978) have provided lists of purposes for such education. (See Table 1-1, pp. 8-9, for a list of the ideas they have identified.)

Yet another approach indicates that there are greater differences in the ultimate ends of education for older adults than the above sources reveal. This approach is based on the concepts of needs and wants that may be associated with developmental factors. Using this approach based on the work of scholars such as Havighurst (1952), Peck (1968), Gould (1978), Levinson et al. (1978) and others, some researchers, such as McCoy (1977), have developed educational programs. This approach seems to emphasize cohort differences that are believed to be associated with needs at particular stages or phases of life.

As a consequence, different impressions are associated with the above approaches. If one uses the general philosophical approach and looks for differences in the aims or goals of education between children, adults, and older adults, fine distinctions are blurred and it can be concluded that there are really no major differences. The same conclusions seem to be supported by the approach that investigates the pragmatic purposes of education as reported in the literature. However, different conclusions are suggested by the needs literature based on developmental concepts. The validity of the conclusions, however, remains questionable (Merriam and Mullins, 1980).

The possibility that the purposes of education for adults and children differ only in degree, i.e., specific topical treatment or in content and process, indicates policymakers and others must distinguish between them either in terms of degree or in some other way. It appears that the distinction has been made more often within a two-step process that includes perceptions of relative value of the different educational goals, and perceptions of the relative importance or the priority of these goals to society. For example, self-realization may be perceived to be of less value than economic efficiency. Then it is additionally concluded that education for economic efficiency, defined as work skills, is more important in childhood education than in adult or late–life education defined, for example, as managing one's retirement income. Importance may be determined by diverse criteria such as relative contribution to the GNP, length of productive life, financial status of the target group, and so on.

Note that the above procedure does not imply within itself that self-realization is unimportant. It does suggest that it is perceived to be less important than economic efficiency. Furthermore, it indicates that the goal of economic efficiency as defined to be achieved through childhood education is more important than the same objective for adult education.

DISCUSSION

Even where agreement exists concerning the desirability or importance of education for older adults, there may be disagreement upon the appropriate institution. For example, Midwinter (1985) indicates that such confusion exists in Great Britain. Is education for older adults a responsibility of educational institutions or is it a matter for health and welfare agencies? To restrict educational services for older adults to the health and welfare agencies would limit the kinds of educational programs available. Such an approach may be justified by the economic model that would posit the health and welfare variables as the ones most likely to affect the net social investment. This approach is also supported by some philosophical orientations. The second orientation is noted by Moody (1978) but it begs the question of social justice and the philosophical goals of education.

Based on the historical and philosophical overviews provided here, certain important ideas concerning the historical and philosophical foundations of education in the United States emerge. First, it is apparent that education has been a highly valued item in the American culture. Commager (1970) has emphasized this point by referring to education as an American religion. Second, it is an important prerogative of the state. Third, it has increasingly become an instrument of the state for achieving social goals (Martel, 1984). Fourth, concepts of education including goals, purposes, populations to be served, and finance are subject to change.

Despite the dynamic attributes of education, the education establishment is very conservative. Change occurs slowly and contemporary attitudes are frequently the residue of the thinking of authorities of an earlier era (Callahan, 1962). Only educational agencies that lie outside the traditional educational core (Moses, 1971) have the flexibility to respond quickly to contemporary needs. The core institutions, in contrast, have tremendous inertia to overcome as well as conflict generated by pluralistic expectations of education.

Given those circumstances, it is not surprising that policy positions concerning governmental support of education for older adults are unclear and tentative. Yet there are reasons to believe that state support for education of older adults will gradually become more available. The historical trend favors such a development; the increasing social complexity also justifies support of education for all ages in society. And finally, the dramatic demographic shift and the resulting attention to adulthood (Graubard, 1976) also point in that direction.

SUMMARY AND CONCLUSIONS

It was noted in the introduction that the idea of social and public provisions of education for adults is more problematic than the idea of personal and private education. Because of the social responsibility for self-support of older adults, there is less enthusiasm for public education for old people than for young people. Yet the reasons for limited support of free education for old people are not always clear. Thus, philosophical and historical information that may help in understanding some of the justifications for supporting and opposing education for older adults was provided. In addition, some other explanations that might be associated with philosophical and historical positions were discussed.

Important changes are observable in the historical development of the social context, educational developments, and philosophy of education. It is readily apparent that the social context of the United States today is significantly different from that of the original British colonies; therefore further comment here is not required. Educational changes are less well known, but they include changes in the basis of education (from a spiritual basis to a secular one, from a concept of education based on salvation of the soul to the notion of education as a means for social ends). Changes are also noted in ideas concerning governmental authority and responsibility for education. An evolution of the structure of the educational establishment is also revealed in the historical analysis.

Similarly, changes are revealed in the analysis of philosophical concepts associated with education. Even though idealists and realists continue to contend with each other, idealism has become more secular in its focus. Pragmatism, transcendentalism, and existentialism have emerged to challenge the older philosophies.

In addition to the above general observations, nine specific conclusions are suggested by the historical and philosophical material reviewed. They are as follows:

1. Governmental authority and responsibility for education have expanded continuously since 1642.
2. Public provision for free schooling has expanded dramatically since 1830.
3. Educational opportunities for adults have multiplied since 1920; and an increasing number of adult education opportunities have been publicly financed.
4. Some educational programs, such as manual education, were tested outside the traditional school establishment before becoming a common element of the educational structure.
5. The trend in educational provision has been to obtain permissive legislation before mandatory legislation. In the interim, however, support for mandatory provision has developed.
6. Prospects for free education for older adults are complicated by complex currents of public and professional opinion concerning the abstract ends or pragmatic purposes of education. These conditions are similar to those existing when manual education was emerging in the nineteenth century.
7. Historical precedents for failing to provide public education for older adults are extensive. However, the prominence of adult education and the level to which it has been publicly supported seems to be associated with increasing awareness of the importance of education beyond preoccupational education. As the complexity of society increases and the proportion of adults increases, support for education further into adulthood is predicted.
8. There are some philosophical sources of opposition to education for older adults such as a negative orientation to older people as defined by Moody (1978), and social justice based on the premise that older adults are a more favored social group. Philosophical aims of education, however, do not seem to be age-related, unless education is defined in a restrictive manner.
9. Six related factors confuse the issue. They include orientation toward older people, conceptualization of education, conceptualization of adulthood, social justice, economics, and educational goals and purposes.

IMPLICATIONS

Some rather diverse implications for the education of older adults are contained in the conclusions previously noted. This diversity is associated with the philosophical confusion and inconsistencies that have been identified, and the model of educational development that is inferred from the history of education in the United States.

Implications concern the following topics: (1) goals and objectives of education for older adults, (2) frequency of educational opportunity for older adults, and (3) providers of education for older adults. Each of the above topics is discussed in the following pages.

Goals and Objectives of Education

Conclusions one, two, eight, and nine in the previous section are a mixed bag indicating that, while the American mind favors an egalitarian approach to education, the focus has been on childhood education. The final ends of education do not necessarily limit attention to childhood education, but historical concepts of pragmatic purposes favor childhood preparation for adult roles. As long as the human capital ideal guides educational thought, public education for the older person will depend on the ability to make a case for it on the basis of economic benefit.

Frequency of Educational Opportunities

Conclusions three, four, and five, based on the historical review section, imply that educational opportunities for adults may be available more frequently in the future. The reasoning on which this implication is based assumes that the historical American precedent of extending educational opportunities to adults will be continued. As a result, educational opportunities will be broadened to include a broader spectrum of adults and will be lengthened to include a longer age span. Conclusions four and five reveal that educational provisions have often followed a kind of pattern that includes public acceptance of an educational program such as manual or vocational education. Subsequently, such educational programs have become formalized through the use of permissive legislation. Implications concerning providers also relate to this conclusion.

Providers of Education for Older Adults

Conclusions six, seven, and eight imply that public provision for the education of older adults will encounter a number of obstacles. There are problems of justification and clarification as suggested in implications one and two above. It could be speculated that education for the elderly will eventually become the province of the helping agencies such as welfare, health, and religious organizations or some combination thereof as discussed by Niebuhr (1984). On the other hand, success with educational programs by these agencies may stimulate greater interest in older populations by the traditional educational institutions. Either way, it appears that the providers might be expanded and thereby increase the availability of a range of educational opportunities.

Thus, while the possibility of immediate expansion of publicly provided education for the elderly is questionable, it appears the potential for increased educational opportunities are great. The prospects for public education provided by higher education and the traditional public school sector may not be as great as some would wish; the historical and philosophical review conducted here implies that the obstacles are primarily associated with public education of an academic nature. Other kinds of educational provision may have fewer obstacles and, as such, may provide the stimulus for more free or reduced-cost scholastic education as currently provided through the tuition-reduction programs in most states.

REFERENCES

ADAMS, J. T. (1944). *The frontiers of American culture.* New York: C. Scribner's Sons.

APPS, J. W. (1973). *Towards a working philosophy of adult education.* Syracuse, New York: Syracuse University Publications in Continuing Education.

BAGLEY, W. C. (1907). *Classroom management.* New York: The Macmillan Company.

BAILYN, B. (1960). *Education in the forming of American society.* New York: Random House, Vantage Books.

BALTES, P. B., and SCHAIE, K. W. (1974). Aging and I.Q.: The myth of the twilight years. *Psychology Today, 1*(10), 35–40.

BERGEVIN, P. (1967). *A philosophy for adult education.* New York: The Seabury Press.

BLAKELY, R. J. (1971). *The new environment: Questions for adult educators.* Syracuse, New York: Syracuse University Publications in Continuing Education.

BOARD OF EDUCATION, CITY OF NEW YORK (1965). Educational specifications as viewed by a local school board. In H. J. Carter (Ed.), *Intellectual foundations of American education.* New York: Pittman Publishing (pp. 475–476). (Original work published 1955–56, excerpts from *Curriculum development in the elementary school,* Curriculum Bulletin no. 1, 2–3.)

BOBBIT, F. (1924). *How to make a curriculum.* Boston: Houghton Mifflin Co.

BODE, C. (1968). *The American Lyceum: Town meeting of the mind.* Carbondale: The Southern Illinois University Press.

BRIM, O., and WHEELER, S. (1966). *Socialization after childhood: Two essays.* New York: American Book Company.

BROOKFIELD, S. (1984). *Adult learners, adult education and the community.* New York: Teachers College Press.

BRYSON, L. (1936). *Adult education.* New York: American Book Company.

CALLAHAN, R. E. (1962). *Education and the cult of efficiency.* Chicago: The University of Chicago Press.

CLAYTON, V. P., and BIRREN, J. E. (1980). The development of wisdom across the life span: A reexamination of an ancient topic. In P. B. Baltes and O. G. Brim, Jr. (Eds.), *Life-span development and behavior in the context of the human life-span.* New York: Academic Press (pp. 103–135).

COMMAGER, H. S. (1970). *The American mind.* New York: Bantam Books.

COMMISSION ON HIGHER EDUCATION AND THE ADULT LEARNER (1984). *Adult learners: Key to the nation's future.* Columbia, Maryland: The Commission.

COTTON, W. E. (1968). *On behalf of adult education.* Boston: Center for the Study of Liberal Education for Adults.

CREMIN, L. A. (1964). *The transformation of the school: Progressivism in American education.* New York: Vantage Books, Random House.

CREMIN, L. A. (1970). *American education: The colonial experience, 1783–1876,* 1st edition. New York: Harper and Row.

CUBBERLY, E. P. (1919). *Public education in the United States.* Boston: Houghton Mifflin Co.

de BEAUVOIR, S. (1972). *The coming of age.* New York: G. P. Putnam's Sons.

DeCROW, R. (n.d.). *New learning for older Americans.* Washington, D.C.: Adult Education Association of the U.S.A.

DEWEY, J. (1916). *Democracy and education.* New York: The Macmillan Company.

EDUCATIONAL POLICIES COMMISSION (1938). *The purposes of education in American democracy.* Washington, D.C.: The National Education Association.

ELIAS, J. L., and MERRIAM, S. (1980). *Philosophical foundations of adult education.* Huntington, New York: Kreiger.

FAULKNER, H. U. (1954). *American economic history,* 7th edition. New York: Harper and Brothers.

GOULD, R. (1978). *Transformations: Growth and change in adult life.* New York: Simon and Schuster.

GRAUBARD, S. R. (1976). Preface—Adulthood. *Daedalus, 105* (2), v–viii.

GRUBER, F. C. (1961). *Foundations for a philosophy of education.* New York: Thomas Y. Crowell Co.

HAVIGHURST, R. J., and ORR, B. (1965). *Adult education and adult needs.* Chicago: Center for the Study of Liberal Education for Adults.

HILLWAY, T. (1961). *Education in American society.* Boston: Houghton Mifflin Co.

KALLEN, H. M. (1962). *Philosophical issues in adult education.* Springfield, Illinois: Charles C. Thomas.

KANT, I. (1970). Thoughts on education, from *Kant on education* (A. Churton, trans.). London: Routledge & Kegan, Paul. In S. M. Cahn (Ed.), *The philosophical foundations of education.* New York: Harper and Row (pp. 179–197). (Original work published 1899.)

KNOWLES, M. S. (1977). *The adult education movement in the U.S.* Huntington, New York: Krieger.

LEVINSON, D. J., DARROW, C. N., KLEIN, E. B., LEVINSON, M. H., and McKEE, B. (1978). *The seasons of man's life.* New York: Ballentine.

LONDONER, C. A. (1971). Survival needs of the aged: Implications for program planning. *International Journal of Aging and Human Development, 2,* 113–117.

LONG, H. B. (1975). The education of girls and women in colonial America. *Journal of Research and Development in Education, 8* (4), 66–82.

LONG, H. B. (1976). *Continuing education in colonial America.* Syracuse, New York: Syracuse University Publications in Continuing Education.

LONG, H. B. (1980). Characteristics of senior citizens' educational tuition waivers in twenty-one states: A follow-up study. *Educational Gerontology, 5,* 139–149.

LONG, H. B. (1984). Searching for the roots of Franklin's Junto. *The Journal of Continuing Higher Education, 32* (3), 16–20.

LONG, H. B. (In press). Postcompulsory education in the United States.

LONG, H. B. (In press). Purposes of adult education in the United States: An historical analysis. In H. Long, *New perspectives on the education of adults in the United States.* London: Croom-Helm.

LONG, H. B., and ROSSING, B. E. (1979). Tuition waiver plans for older Americans in post-secondary public education institutions. *Educational Gerontology, 4*, 161–174.

MARSHALL, M. E. (1978). State Education Department enters gerontology field. *Generations, 3*(1), 27–28.

McCLUSKY, H. Y. (1978). Learning opportunities abound. *Generations, 3*(1), 25.

McCLUSKY, H. Y. (1982). Education for older adults. In C. Eisdorfer, et al. (Eds.), *Annual review of gerontology and geriatrics,* Vol. 3. New York: Springer (pp. 403–428).

McCOY, V. R. (1977). Adult life cycle change. *Lifelong Learning: The Adult Years, 1*, 14–21.

MARITAIN, J. (1970). Education at the crossroads. New Haven: Yale University Press. In S. M. Cahn (Ed.), *The philosophical foundations of education.* New York: Harper and Row. (Original work published 1943.)

MARTEL, L. D. (1984). The nation at risk. A challenge for continuing education. *The Journal of Continuing Higher Education, 32*(1), 9–11.

MERRIAM, S., and MULLINS, L. (1980). Havighurst's adult developmental tasks: A factor analysis. In G. C. Whaples and D. M. Ewert (Eds.), *Proceedings: Lifelong Learning Research Conference.* College Park, Maryland.

MICHENER, J. A. (1974). *Centennial.* New York: Fawcett.

MIDWINTER, E. (1985). The social determinants of educational policy in the United Kingdom and their likely effects on the provision of educational opportunities for the elderly. *Educational Gerontology, 10*(3), 197–206.

MOODY, H. R. (1978). Education and the life cycle. A philosophy of aging. In R. H. Sherron and D. B. Lumsden (Eds.), *Introduction to educational gerontology.* Washington, D.C.: Hemisphere (pp. 31–48).

MORRISON, S. E., and COMMAGER, H. S. (1956). *The growth of the American republic, Vol. I,* 4th edition. New York: Oxford University Press.

MORRISON, S. E., and COMMAGER, H. S. (1958). *The growth of the American republic, Vol. II,* 4th edition. New York: Oxford University Press.

MOSES, S. (1971). *The learning force.* Syracuse, New York: Syracuse University Publications in Continuing Education.

NEVINS, A., and COMMAGER, H. (1956). *The pocket history of the United States.* New York: Pocket Books, Inc.

NIEBUHR, H., JR. (1984). *Revitalizing American education.* Belmont, California: Wadsworth.

PECK, R. C. (1968). Psychological development in the second half of life. In B. Neugarten (Ed.), *Middle age and aging.* Chicago: The University of Chicago Press.

PIERCE, W. (1979). Education's evolving role. In J. A. Johnson, H. W. Collins, V. L. Dupis, and J. H. Johansen (Eds.), *Foundations of American education readings.* Boston: Allyn and Bacon. (Originally published in *American Education,* May, 1975, 16–29, 189–196.)

PETERS, R. S. (1970). Must an education have an aim? From *Authority, responsibility and education.* New York: Paul S. Erickson (pp. 83–95). In S. M. Cahn (Ed.), *The philosophical foundations of education.* New York: Harper and Row (pp. 375–396). (Originally published in 1959.)

PETERSON, D. A. (1983). *Facilitating education for older learners.* San Francisco: Jossey-Bass.

PETERSON, R. (1979). *Lifelong learning in America.* San Francisco: Jossey-Bass.

RAWLS, J. (1957). Symposium, justice as fairness. *The Journal of Philosophy, 54* (October), 653.

RAWLS, J. (1971). *A theory of justice.* Cambridge, Massachusetts: Harvard University Press.

RUSSELL, B. (1970). *On education.* London: George Allen and Unwin, Ltd. (excerpted pages 15–65). In S. M. Cahn (Ed.), *The philosophical foundations of education.* New York: Harper and Row (pp. 287–301). (Originally published in 1926.)

SENATE BILL 865, Regular Session of the 1984 Louisiana Legislature. SRSX84-1415.

SEYBOLT, R. F. (1969). *Apprenticeship and apprenticeship education in colonial New England and New York.* New York: Arno Press and The New York Times. (Originally published by Teachers College, Columbia University, 1917.)

SOLTOW, L., and STEVENS, E. (1981). *The rise of literacy and the common school in the United States.* Chicago: The University of Chicago Press.

SPRING, J. (1976). *The sorting machine: National educational policy since 1945.* New York: David McKay Co.

SUBCOMMITTEE ON POST-SECONDARY EDUCATION OF THE COMMITTEE ON EDUCATION AND LABOR. HOUSE OF REPRESENTATIVES, 95TH CONGRESS (1977). Hearing on H. B. 3542, June 11, 1977. Washington, D.C.: U.S. Government Printing Office.

THORSON, J. A. (1978). Future trends in education for older adults. In R. H. Sherron and D. B. Lumsden (Eds.), *Introduction to educational gerontology.* Washington, D.C.: Hemisphere (pp. 203–228).

WALKER, D. F. (1980). The problem of purpose in American education. In L. Rubin (Ed.), *Critical issues in educational policy: An administrative overview.* Boston: Allyn and Bacon (pp. 26–38).

WALKER, R. H. (1971). *Life in the age of enterprise.* New York: Capricorn Books, G. P. Putnam's Sons.

WHITEHEAD, A. N. (1967). *The aims of education and other essays.* New York: Macmillan Company. In S. M. Cahn (Ed.), *The philosophical foundations of education.* New York: Harper and Row (pp. 265–285). (Originally published in 1929.)

WILLIS, S. (1985). Towards an educational psychology of the older adult learner: Intellectual and cognitive bases. In J. E. Birren and K. W. Schaie (Eds.), *Handbook of the psychology of aging,* 2nd edition. New York: Van Nostrand Reinhold, Inc.

WRIGHT, L. B. (1971). *Life on the American frontier.* New York: Capricorn Books, G. P. Putnam's Sons.

2

AGING AND HIGHER EDUCATION

Older Students,
Older Faculty,
and Gerontology
Instruction

David A. Peterson

Higher education functions in a continual state of flux. Change has become a way of life as external pressures, faculty or student unrest, and budgetary constraints demand adjustments in the purposes, programs, and outcomes of universities, colleges, and community colleges.

The aging of American society is one of the external pressures which is only beginning to be recognized and the impact of which is yet to be fully felt. Four aspects of this demographic trend are now impacting on institutions of higher education. First, the number of traditionally aged students (18 to 24) is declining and will continue to do so for the remainder of this century. Institutions have anticipated this decline and have begun to struggle with the accommodations needed to maintain enrollment in an increasingly difficult market. Second, the number of middle-aged and older adults is rapidly increasing, so higher education institutions are seeking to develop new missions in serving this group of potential participants. Third, the median age and tenure density of faculty are increasing, resulting in higher costs and reduced flexibility. Fourth, knowledge about aging processes has grown rapidly as intellectual and social interest in aging has increased and the conditions of older persons have been studied in a variety of disciplines.

Sensing the implications of these trends, higher education institutions have begun to modify their traditional approaches. To maintain a viable student body, student recruitment activities have been intensified, admission standards have been relaxed, and curriculum has been reoriented to reflect the career interests of current students. Nontraditional and older students have been attracted through evening courses, off-campus workshops, and noncredit programming. New faculty roles and early retirement have been initiated in some institutions. And gerontology instruction and research have been developed emphasizing the generation and dissemination of information on the processes of aging and the condition of older people in contemporary society.

The purpose of this chapter is to explore the current status of institutions of higher education and to show that although they currently face the need for substantial modification of traditional practices in order to survive, most have successfully accomplished this in the past and, hopefully, can do so again. The concern here, however is not totally with these institutions. The present chapter also explores how the needs of the institution and those of older persons can form a symbiotic relationship that will achieve a modification of the mission of higher education, help increasing numbers of middle-aged and older people acquire the learning that they desire, and meet contemporary social goals. The aging of American society is not only one cause of a current problem for higher education; it is also at least one part of the solution to that problem.

This chapter is divided into seven parts. The first provides a brief introduction to higher education in the United States emphasizing its traditional functions and its continuing change. The second describes the decline in the number of traditionally aged students and the heightened attempts at recruitment and retention. The third deals with institutional modifications that have been made to accommodate the needs of nontraditional, middle-aged students—primarily women, employees seeking retraining and skill upgrading, and persons exploring personal development experiences. The fourth topic is the arrival of the older person on campus and the accommodations (or lack of them) made to serve this new clientele. The fifth section shifts to the aging of the faculty and the implications that this will have for the productivity, quality, and operation of institutions of higher education. The sixth describes the development of gerontology as a multidisciplinary field of research and instruction in higher education; and the final part looks toward the future, focusing on the adaptations that will be required if educational institutions are to serve the learning and/or education needs of an aging society and to be helped by it.

THE ORIENTATION OF HIGHER EDUCATION IN THE UNITED STATES

Higher education is a major undertaking in America today. With an annual budget of nearly $100 billion, it includes community and junior colleges; four-year, primarily liberal arts institutions; regional colleges and universities, many of which had a teacher-education history; and research universities which emphasize graduate instruction. It is distinguished from, and is a subcategory of, postsecondary education which includes the institutions listed above, as well as proprietary schools, business and industrial training, technical schools, and other instruction offered to high school graduates (Carnegie Foundation, 1975).

The orientation of American higher education has changed over time from its original role of preparation for the ministry and teaching, with an emphasis on the Bible and the classics; to preparation for the early professions, law and medicine; to preparing leadership for agricultural and industrial production; to an emphasis on science, engineering, and business administration (see Long, this volume).

Since 1870 enrollments in higher education have grown at a compound annual rate of five percent, nearly three times as fast as population growth (Carnegie Council on Policy Studies, 1980). After World War II growth was even more pronounced. In 1946 there were two million students enrolled in all American colleges and universities, a number which increased to 12 million in 1980 (Bowen, 1982) and 12.4 million in 1983-84 (Evangelauf, 1984). Nearly half of each age cohort in America now enters college, and more than 25% of each receives a baccalaureate degree (Bowen, 1982).

The cost of higher education since 1930 has grown at an annual rate of inflation plus three percent (Kerr, 1972). Although this may sound modest, from 1870 to 1980 the cost of higher education increased from 0.1 to 2.1 percent of the Gross

FIGURE 2-1   Points of acceleration and deceleration in higher education enrollments.

Sources: Carnegie Council estimates based on U.S. Bureau of the Census (1975) and U.S. National Center for Education Statistics, *Fall Enrollment,* appropriate years. *Carnegie Council,* 1980, p. 33. Reprinted by permission.

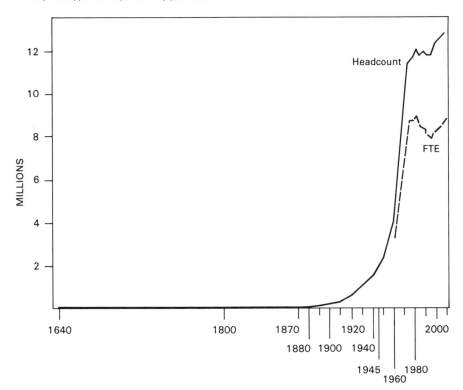

POINTS OF ACCELERATION AND DECELERATION

National Product (plus costs of construction) (Carnegie Council on Policy Studies, 1980).

Before 1940, a college education was typically available only to a small percentage of the total population. This elite group resided on campus and attended courses full time. They generally assumed that the benefits from their education would accrue to them personally through the development of culture, understanding, and values. The G.I. Bill of Rights changed this exclusive orientation and allowed 2.2 million returning servicemen to seek education and vocational preparation at the college level (Henry, 1975). During this period, access to higher learning became a major goal, and the institutions of higher education became increasingly available to all qualified persons regardless of their income, sex, ethnic origin, religion, or handicaps (Bowen, 1982). The number of students from new clientele—minorities; women; middle-aged persons, handicapped persons, and low-income groups; and those seeking part-time education—grew rapidly as total enrollment exploded. Institution-building occurred at all levels: existing institutions were expanded, former teachers' colleges converted into universities, and new community colleges were built in over 500 cities. This encouraged college attendance by nearly half of each age cohort and provided continuing education opportunities to an increasing number of older persons.

However, growth was not evenly distributed across all segments of higher education. The public sector grew much more rapidly, especially community colleges which doubled between 1960 and 1980. Good economic times encouraged state legislatures to provide increased funds, and the federal government assisted with student financial support, aid to disadvantaged groups, and research funding.

TABLE 2-1. Institutions of Higher Education: Estimated Number, Enrollments, and Expenditures for Research and Development

	1950	1960	1970	1980[e]
Number of institutions[a]				
Four-year	1,345	1,451	1,639	1,810
Two-year	518	508	886	1,030
Total	1,863	1,959	2,525	2,840
Enrollment (in millions)[b]				
All students	2.3	3.8	8.6	12.0
Full-time equivalents	2.1	2.9	6.7	9.0
Expenditures for organized research and development (billions of 1967 dollars)[c]	0.3[d]	0.7	2.0	2.2

[a] U.S. Bureau of the Census, *Historical Statistics of the United States* (1975, Vol. 1, p. 382); National Center for Education Statistics, *Digest of Education Statistics* (1980, p. 115).

[b] National Center for Education Statistics, *Digest of Education Statistics* (1980, pp. 87, 89).

[c] National Science Foundation (1977).

[d] 1953.

[e] Estimated by author.

Source: Bowen, 1982, p. 4. Reprinted by permission.

The result was that private sources, especially endowment, contributed a much smaller portion of the costs of higher education, and the federal government provided a much higher proportion.

Although private higher education did grow during the 1970s, it did so at a rate much slower than public institutions. This resulted in a decline in the proportion of student enrollments in private higher education, from half the students in 1950 to only one-fifth in 1980 (Carnegie Council on Policy Studies, 1980).

The curricula expanded, especially interdisciplinary areas, as many new fields

FIGURE 2-2   Changes in sources of income of institutions of higher education for educational and general purposes, 1929/30 to 1976/77.

Indicates current income received for educational and general purposes, including research. Does not include such items as sales and services of educational activities, sales and services of auxiliary enterprises, and sales and services of hospitals and institutions. Tuition represents gross tuition and includes, especially since 1969–70, tuition expenses met from student aid.

Source: *Carnegie Council*, 1980, p. 17. Reprinted by permission.

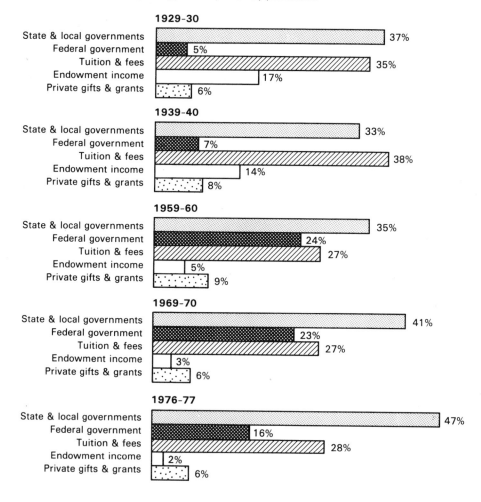

attained departmental/degree status. Faculty interests became more specialized, and those who could taught small numbers of advanced graduate students rather than the hosts of undergraduates on campus. Faculty rewards were directed to those most heavily involved in research and publication, resulting in fewer instructors concerned about the overall education of the individual. This occurred partly because of the increasing role played by large institutions. Campuses with 10,000 or more students accounted for one-quarter of all enrollments in 1955, but one-half in 1977. Campuses with fewer than 500 students accounted for 8 percent in 1955 and only 1.5 percent in 1977 (Carnegie Council on Policy Studies, 1980).

Another change in higher education has been the rapid growth of the community college and the general involvement in community and continuing education. Courses have moved away from the campus and are regularly offered in business and industry, community centers, and storefronts. Television instruction has continued to expand, and access to education has been greatly facilitated by moving the instruction to closer proximity with the clientele.

Higher education has grown sufficiently so that it is now subject to substantial buffeting and pressures from society such as inflation, energy problems, litigations, alleged lack of national leadership, world interdependence, and environmental damage (Stauffer, 1981). During the 1960s and 1970s, every state established some kind of multicampus university system or a special state agency to plan for future growth and to assure coordination among the various campuses. Advisory committees were established not only for individual programs, but for schools and campuses in order to assure the responsiveness of the expanded instruction to the perceived needs of the community. The institutions of higher education modified their scheduling and curriculum and cited these adjustments in their public relations response to outside criticism. Funding sources and the public generally began to demand more accountability as the cost of higher education rose and social benefits were not immediately visible. The purpose of higher education began to shift from an emphasis on individual development (liberal arts and sciences) to social value (job training, professional service orientation, and civic literacy) (Beattie, 1978).

Higher education has struggled to redefine its mission consistent with the needs of society and its own tradition. The accommodation has not come easily, but it is important for colleges and universities to provide a number of very important services, such as socializing the young, preparing persons for professional and technical careers, expanding the level and sophistication of knowledge, and acting as the commentator on and critic of the general society. In the past, higher education has served society well; its contributions will be needed to support the nation in the future.

THE EFFECT OF DEMOGRAPHIC CHANGE
ON HIGHER EDUCATION

The current "academic revolution" involves institutions striving to find their niche in the current marketplace. Survival is now the theme, and in order for colleges to achieve it, sufficient students must be attracted to support existing faculty, staff, and facilities. Since most states now use a formula based on enrollment to determine the level of financial support provided to academic institutions, student registrations have become the key to their survival and prosperity. However, many states have placed a cap on enrollment which restricts the total number of students to some arbitrary number which the legislature is willing to support.

Population growth has traditionally resulted in enrollment increases in higher education, and the baby boom of the 1950s and 1960s provided the students for the massive expansion in higher education enrollments during the 1960s and 1970s. However, the number of births peaked in 1961 and declined thereafter. These smaller cohorts began reaching college age in 1979, and institutions of higher education began to experience the enrollment decline that had been widely predicted. Table 2-2 shows the change in the birth cohorts (add 18 years to determine when the cohort will reach college age).

The number of 18- to 24-year-olds has been projected to decline by 23% between 1979 and 1997. However, the number of college registrations may not fall as rapidly, perhaps only by 5 to 15% (Carnegie Council on Policy Studies, 1980), because the 18- to 24-year-olds only comprise 80% of the total student body and the decline of that cohort is expected to be offset to some extent by the increasing enrollment rates of persons over the age of 25. As can be seen in Figure 2-3, the decline will occur in two parts separated by a period of stability. The first, from 1983 to 1989, will result in 40% of the reduction, and then from 1991 to 1997 the rest of the decline will occur.

Graduate enrollments, on the other hand, are not expected to decline sub-

TABLE 2-2. Number of Births, United States, 1930 to 1976 (in thousands)

1930	2,618	1954	4,102
1931	2,506	1955	4,128
1932	2,440	1956	4,244
1933	2,307	1957	4,332
1934	2,396	1958	4,279
1935	2,377	1959	4,313
1936	2,355	1960	4,307
1937	2,413	1961	4,317
1938	2,496	1962	4,213
1939	2,466	1963	4,142
1940	2,570	1964	4,070
1941	2,716	1965	3,801
1942	3,002	1966	3,642
1943	3,118	1967	3,555
1944	2,954	1968	3,535
1945	2,873	1969	3,630
1946	3,426	1970	3,739
1947	3,834	1971	3,556
1948	3,655	1972	3,258
1949	3,667	1973	3,137
1950	3,645	1974	3,160
1951	3,845	1975	3,144
1952	3,933	1976	3,165
1953	3,989		

Source: United States Department of Commerce, Bureau of the Census, *Current Population Reports,* Series P-25, Nos. 521, 541. Bowen, 1980, p. 24.

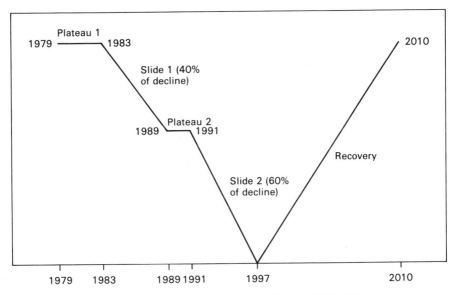

FIGURE 2-3 Generalized view of enrollments, 1979–2010.

Source: *Carnegie Council,* 1980, p. 47. Reprinted by permission.

stantially. Although doctoral graduates are experiencing employment difficulties and enrollments in Ph.D. programs are declining, doctoral students comprise less than 10% of all graduate enrollments. Therefore, this decline is not likely to have a major impact on total graduate registrations. Masters and professional degree programs, especially those leading to employment fields with high demand, are expected to remain stable or even to increase slightly during the rest of the century.

The decline in undergraduate enrollments is not expected to be evenly distributed across the entire range of higher education. Research universities, liberal arts colleges that are able to be selective in the students they admit, and public community colleges are likely to be the least vulnerable to decline. Their adjustments will be primarily internal; some may use the opportunity to increase quality while others may expand research and service activities. On the other hand, institutions of average or above average vulnerability will include doctorate-granting universities with modest research activities, and those with multiple programs below the Ph.D. level. These include the many institutions that were formerly teachers' colleges which have grown to graduate institutions but never developed strong research traditions. The most vulnerable will be liberal arts colleges which have a reputation for lower selectivity, especially those in the East and the Midwest where outmigration is occurring, and private two-year colleges which have experienced declining enrollments for several years (Carnegie Council on Policy Studies, 1980).

This demographic change and the resultant search for students has resulted in power shifting to the students (Riesman, 1980). This power shift has not resulted because of demonstrations and demands for more student input in the curriculum. Rather it is because state reimbursement is directly tied to enrollment in public institutions and the tuition paid is currently the only source of institutional income that is controlled by the colleges and universities. At many private institutions, tuition income comprises over half of all revenue, so it is carefully monitored. Thus the curriculum has often been adapted to student interests in order to secure adequate enrollment.

The emphasis on enrollment has resulted in a type of contemporary non-intellectualism that is manifested by interest in grades and degrees but not learning; by cheating and compromise in integrity, less interest in extracurricular activities, and loss of curiosity (Ellis, 1981). As entering full-time freshmen, three-quarters of the students indicate that they are anticipating vocational majors. At graduation, 61% receive vocational majors, and, if community college degrees and dropouts are considered, the proportion is probably higher.

Attracting and retaining students has become a major goal; admission requirements have been lowered, emphasis has been placed on the retention of students, grade point averages have risen, popular subjects have been expanded, and there has been a turn toward vocationalism. As the Carnegie Council on Policy Studies in Higher Education (1980) pointed out: "Students will be recruited more actively, admitted more readily, retained more assiduously, counseled more attentively, graded more considerately, financed more adequately, taught more conscientiously, and placed in jobs more consistently. They will seldom, if ever, have had it so good on campus" (p. 53).

Overall, the past twenty-five years has been a time of concern for the consequences of growth, both the problems of building a system large enough to accommodate the demand, and the maintenance of that system when demand declines. The concerns have been practical ones of finances, facilities, and faculties, not those of quality, outcomes, or purposes. The 1960s included new institutions, curricular approaches, teaching methods, and financing arrangements. The 1970s and 1980s are seeing less innovativeness in response to the problems of enrollment decline. The tradition of diversity in higher education is now dissolving as every institution creates a center for management development or an institute for computer sciences. As the Carnegie Council has pointed out: "The diversity of American higher education used to be found between and among institutions with conformity within each of them; now diversity is more often found within institutions, with the institutions in their entirety being more alike" (Carnegie Council, 1980, p. 22).

NEW AND NONTRADITIONAL STUDENTS

In addition to recruiting and retaining traditional 18- to 24-year-olds, colleges and universities have been searching for new clientele. These fall into three categories: (1) the new 18- to 24-year-old—the employed lower-income, minority individual—who has traditionally not attended college (this type of student is not the focus of this chapter); (2) the student between the ages of 35 and 55 who is part-time, employed, female, and/or a member of a minority group; and (3) the older student, the person over age 55 who typically is not seeking credentials as a means of achieving an employment goal, but rather is more interested in social interaction or personal development. The latter two groups have different educational needs and interests and will be discussed separately, one in this section of the chapter and one in the next.

To aid in the recruitment of nontraditional students, course scheduling and location have been modified to make education more easily accessible to working persons, women with young children, and those without transportation. The new nontraditional student groups (as well as many of the traditional students) are now highly oriented toward vocational outcomes from their education. Jobs are the key measure of success, and instructional programs that currently have good job prospects (business, medicine, engineering, and computer science) are in great demand while humanistic and liberal arts areas are struggling to attract students. The public has made its support of vocational outcomes from higher education known, but faculty remain more committed to the academic outcomes of personal development, civic responsibility, and aesthetic cultivation.

Higher education is now more accessible to nontraditional student populations, most of whom attend part-time. Their presence has kept enrollments stable, although a few institutions have closed and as many as 4,000 of the 490,000 faculty positions have disappeared (Scully, 1983). As Table 2-3 shows, between 1972 and 1982 the number of students under age 35 increased by 32% and the number of students over age 35 increased by 76% (Crimmins and Riddler, 1985).

During this 10-year period, total enrollment in higher education increased from approximately 9 million to approximately 12 million. Nearly 19% of this increase was the result of the enrollments of people over 35, the vast majority being women. Many of these women are returning to school once they no longer have young children; and both men and women participate in professional upgrading, maintaining the skills necessary to be competitive and productive. Career change and technological advancement are now the allies of higher education, as is the tendency for persons with higher levels of education to continue learning throughout their lives. Both career goals and self-fulfillment have encouraged the middle-aged person to pursue further education, and have been a factor in ameliorating enrollment declines that were expected with the end of the baby boom.

By the year 2000, the modal student will have changed from the young, male, full-time student, to a female who is as likely to be a part-time student as a full-time one. One-quarter of all enrollments will come from minority group members. As Figure 2-4 shows, the change is expected to be very significant between 1960 and 2000. By the year 2000, roughly half of all students in the classroom would not be there if the composition of 1960 had been continued (Carnegie Council on Policy Studies, 1980).

The growth of the nontraditional student population has caused some changes in the admissions and student-services emphases on campuses. High school grade-point averages from many years ago are no longer as useful in predicting college performance; academic counseling is expected to have a clear vocational orientation; student services deal less with entertainment and more with child care, shared transportation, personal counseling, study skills, and job placement services (Kasworm, 1980); offices must be open evenings to serve this clientele; and faculty schedules must include teaching and holding office hours in the evenings and on weekends (Chelsvig and Timmermann, 1982).

Thus, the nontraditional student is one who has had some previous experience with higher education, but whose learning was interrupted or incomplete because of family needs, work pressures, or personal preferences. Nontraditional students are likely to be very focused in their pursuit of a career—the degree is a means to an end, and learning is not the primary reason for college enrollment—

TABLE 2-3 Distribution of Numbers Enrolled in College and Percent of All Students, by Age and Sex: October 1972 and 1982

	OCTOBER 1972			OCTOBER 1982			PERCENT CHANGE, 1972–82		
	TOTAL	MEN	WOMEN	TOTAL	MEN	WOMEN	TOTAL	MEN	WOMEN
A. Numbers (in thousands)									
Totals, all ages	9,096	5,218	3,877	12,309	5,899	6,410	35.3	13.1	65.3
Less than 35 years old	8,307	4,850	3,457	10,920	5,409	5,510	31.5	11.5	59.4
35 years old and over	789	368	420	1,389	490	900	76.0	33.2	114.3
B. Percent group is of all students of all ages									
Totals, all ages	99.9	57.3	42.6	100.0	47.9	52.1			
Less than 35 years old	91.3	53.3	38.0	88.7	43.9	44.8			
35 years old and over	8.6	4.0	4.6	11.3	4.0	7.3			

Source: Crimmins and Riddler, 1985.

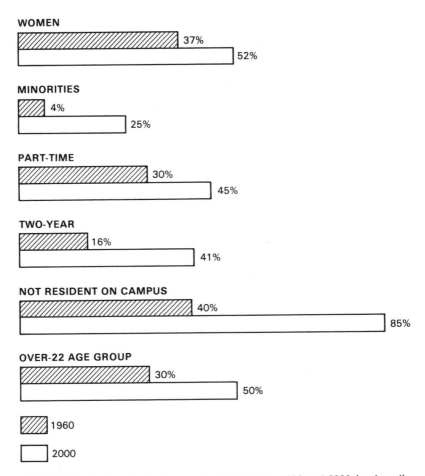

FIGURE 2-4 Undergraduate student characteristics in 1960 and 2000 (projected).
Sources: U.S. Bureau of the Census (1964): U.S. NCES (1972). *Carnegie Council,* 1980, p. 54. Reprinted by permission.

an orientation that is having a pervasive and cumulative impact on the functioning of institutions of higher education.

It is possible to place the enrollment change in a more positive light. Bowen (1980) has pointed out that the United States has always been committed to becoming "a nation of educated people," one that desires the appreciable cultural advantages of education for a substantial portion of the entire population. In a period of sluggish growth or excess capacity in higher education, there is an opportunity for substantial advancement toward that goal.

In order to gain some perspective, it should be noted that there have been three other occasions in this century when higher education had excess capacity, during the Great Depression (when enrollment fell 9%), during World War II (a decline of 23%), and in the early 1950s after the GIs had departed (a 13% decline) (Bowen, 1980). In none of these cases was the higher education system dismantled.

Rather, the typical reaction was to maintain faculty, slow the growth of current expenditures moderately, and reduce plant expenditures substantially.

For the coming period of anticipated excess capacity, resources could be profitably directed toward the improvement of quality, the expansion of research and service to the community, and/or the involvement of new clientele. There are currently 85,000,000 American adults who have had no college at all (78% of those over age 25) and 100 million who have not graduated. These adults could be the major beneficiaries of the coming period of change in higher education (Bowen, 1982).

THE OLDER STUDENT ON CAMPUS

In the past few years, older persons (those over the age of 55) have begun partaking of educational offerings in increasing numbers. Although institutions of higher education are not the principal providers of educational services for older learners (Peterson, 1981), they have experienced a good deal of the growth and have begun to recognize their responsibility to serve this new clientele. This is occurring in Western Europe and Japan just as it is in the United States (Missinne, 1983; Nusberg, 1982). Table 2-4 shows that in 1969 a total of slightly more than one million persons over age 55 attended educational programs. By 1981 that number had increased to more than 2.5 million with 25% of these enrollments in institutions of higher education (Harris et al., 1981). The total enrollment of older students is expected to continue to grow because each cohort reaching age 55 has a higher level of formal education than the preceding ones (see Table 2-5), and participation in adult education is highly correlated with educational attainment (Peterson, 1983). Moreover, subsequent cohorts of "young old" (between ages 55 and 75) (Peterson, 1983) are more likely than their predecessors to be healthy, considering career changes, and positively predisposed to returning to the college campus.

Education for older learners is typically viewed as simply an extension of nontraditional programming. It is often assumed that the accommodations of format, content, and purpose for nontraditional students discussed previously will serve the older learner just as effectively, so further program modifications are not believed to be necessary.

Unfortunately, however, the accommodations made for nontraditional learners are not totally appropriate for meeting the educational needs of older learners, who are as different from those in middle age as that group is from the traditional, 18- to 24-year-old student. Differences can be pinpointed in terms of the purpose for enrolling, the content selected, the format preferred, the setting chosen, the fees charged, the attitude of the faculty, and learning characteristics.

Purpose. The older population (those from 55 to 85) is very diverse, including the total range of educational interests found in the younger and middle-aged populations. However, it is clear that there are differences in the modal interests and reasons for participation by older learners. Of this group, the 55- to 65-year-olds typically pursue education as a means to enter or further a career, the primary motivation for the nontraditional learner (Goodrow, 1975; Ventura and Worthy, 1982). Approximately one quarter of the older students, generally men, seek a vocational outcome from their education (Cross, 1979). Personal or social satisfaction is cited by 66% of older students as their principal motivation (Ventura and Worthy, 1982).

Older learners often participate in learning activities for intrinsic reasons, that is, they enjoy the learning and have relatively minor expectations for applying the knowledge in employment or their daily lives (Covey, 1980). A number of studies have examined the perceived reasons for participation, and although they use slightly different terms, their conclusions are reasonably consistent. Older people participate in education for intellectual stimulation, interest in the subject, or desire for more education (Kingston, 1982); they view self-initiated goals as the most relevant (Dellmann-Jenkins and Papelia-Finlay, 1983); personal growth, pursuit of an academic interest, or the desire to remain mentally active are frequently stated motivators (Perkins and Robertson-Tchabo, 1981); wishing to contribute to society, to become cultured, or to gain a general education are often reported (Daniel, Templin, and Shearon, 1977), as is the desire to learn something new, to gain some new experience (Romaniuk and Romaniuk, 1982). The older learner has been found to be motivated more by cognitive interest and drive for knowledge than younger and middle-aged students (Boshier and Riddell, 1978).

A second major motivator for educational participation after age 55 involves the desire for an interpersonal relationship. Studies showed that frequently this had nothing to do with the content of the course that was offered but involved a desire to meet people (Daniel, Templin, and Shearon, 1977; Fisher, 1979; Peterson, 1981; Romaniuk and Romaniuk, 1982). This social motive, typically reported as the second most important reason for participation, indicates a major human need in later life and one which can be effectively supplied when the instructional process involves discussion and shared experience.

The purposes that older learners seek, then, are frequently content-oriented or social, and less often instrumental and vocational such as those typically attributed to middle-aged learners. This distinction is important in terms of the course content that is offered and the orientation which is given to that content.

Content selected by older students. While middle-aged students are likely to choose educational content perceived to help them acquire or progress in employment, older learners typically prefer courses that can be characterized as leading to personal and social satisfaction (Ventura and Worthy, 1982). This content is frequently found in the humanities, religion, social sciences, arts, or current history and geography, although there is a substantial amount of interest in topics which may be of instrumental usefulness such as money management, health care, diet, exercise, estate planning, or retirement preparation (Peterson, 1983; Ventura and Worthy, 1982).

Examples of this can be seen in the Elderhostel Program, established in 1975 and now being conducted on over 700 campuses each year. It involves one-week liberal arts courses offered on campus with living accommodations provided for the older students (Knowlton, 1977). Similar undertakings, without the residential aspect, are found in several other colleges such as the Institute for Retired Professionals of New York City's New School for Social Research (Lipman, 1985), the Academy of Senior Professionals at Florida's Eckert College (Nussbaum, 1984), the UCLA Plato Society, the Academy of Lifelong Learning at the University of

TABLE 2-4: Numbers and Proportions of Participants in Educational Activities*

YEAR	TITLE OF SURVEY/ REPORT	NUMBERS (IN THOUSAND) AND PERCENT INVOLVED IN EDUCATIONAL ACTIVITIES							
		PERSONS 17-34 YEARS OLD		PERSONS 34-54 YEARS OLD		PERSONS 55-64 YEARS OLD		PERSONS 65+ YEARS OLD	
		TOTAL NO.	% OF TOTAL POP. 17-34	TOTAL NO.	% OF TOTAL POP. 34-54	TOTAL NO.	% OF TOTAL POP. 55-64	TOTAL NO.	% OF TOTAL POP. 65+
1969	Participation in adult education (NCES)	17,500	36	5,037	11	774	4.5	274	1.4
1972	Participation in adult education (NCES)	20,246	37	5,727	13	985	5.5	378	1.8
1975	Participation in adult education (NCES)	29,313	34	6,161	13	1,165	6.0	498	2.3
1978	Participation in adult education (NCES)	21,317	33	6,445	13.8	1,382	6.8	573	2.5
1981	Participation in adult education (NCES)	29,991	42.4	7,605	15.6	1,738	8.0	778	3.1

NUMBERS (IN THOUSAND) AND PERCENT INVOLVED IN EDUCATIONAL ACTIVITIES

YEAR	TITLE OF SURVEY/ REPORT	PERSONS 18-39 YEARS OLD		PERSONS 40-54 YEARS OLD		PERSONS 55-64 YEARS OLD		PERSONS 65+ YEARS OLD	
		TOTAL NO.	% OF TOTAL POP. 18-39	TOTAL NO.	% OF TOTAL POP. 40-54	TOTAL NO.	% OF TOTAL POP. 55-64	TOTAL NO.	% OF TOTAL POP. 65+
1974	*Myth and Reality of Aging;* NCOA/Harris & Assoc.	15,320	22.5	1,762	5.0	975	5.0	436	2.9
1981	*Aging in the Eighties;* NCOA/Harris & Assoc.	37,254	44.3	8,616	25.0	2,387	11.0	1,277	5.0

*Because of different breakdowns used in defining age groups, the NCES and NCOA Louis Harris survey results have been kept separate.

Sources: NCES Participation in Adult Education, 1969, 1972, 1975, 1978, 1981. Harris et al., 1974 and 1981.

Ventura and Worthy, 1982, p. 10. Reprinted by permission.

TABLE 2-5 Educational Attainment of the Population 65 Years Old and Over and 25 Years Old and Over: 1952 to 1990

	MEDIAN SCHOOL YEARS COMPLETED		PERCENT HIGH SCHOOL GRADUATES	
	65 YEARS OLD AND OVER	25 YEARS OLD AND OVER	65 YEARS OLD AND OVER	25 YEARS OLD AND OVER
1952	8.2	10.1	18.4	38.4
1959	8.3	11.0	19.4	42.9
1965	8.5	11.8	23.5	49.0
1970	8.7	12.2	28.3	55.2
1975	9.0	12.3	35.2	62.6
1980	9.7	12.4	37.9	65.4
1985	10.9	12.5	44.0	70.2
1990	11.9	12.6	49.4	74.2

Source: *Current Population Reports,* Series P-20, Nos. 45, 99, 158, 207; and Series P-25, no. 476.

Ventura and Worthy, 1982, p. 4. Reprinted by permission.

Delaware (Grimble, 1985), the Institute for Learning in Retirement at American University (Young, 1985), and many others (see Peacock and Talley, 1984). These programs have few courses that involve occupational preparation; rather the curriculum typically responds to the variety of humanistic, scientific, and applied interests of the older clientele.

Format. Older learners are dissimilar from middle-aged learners in their preferences for format as well. While the middle-aged student is likely to have major commitments during the working day, principally employment or a family, the older learner is less likely to have these constraints in seeking education. Thus, the older learner generally does not prefer the evening, weekend, or condensed format courses sought by nontraditional students.

Most older learners prefer midday course scheduling since travel at night is perceived to be hazardous, both because of the fear of crime and because the decline in visual acuity is especially troublesome when driving or walking in poorly lighted areas. Most older drivers seek to avoid peak traffic periods (8-9 A.M. and 4-6 P.M.) because of the street congestion. Thus, the middle of the day becomes the preferable time to schedule events, especially when social interaction can be facilitated by inclusion of a meal.

Weekend schedules seem to fit the preferences of working persons, but they are not as desirable to older learners. For reasons that have not been examined (perhaps habit or the desire to avoid crowded areas), the older person seems more likely to stay at home during the weekend and to schedule regular undertakings, such as a class, during the weekdays.

Preferred length of instructional sessions also differs. Most older persons find that long sessions are not as comfortable as shorter ones, scheduled in several parts. Thus, one two-hour session every week for a month is preferable to an all-day program. For working persons, scheduling and transportation are the problems, so a day-long schedule may be easier to handle.

Setting. Older students also have a series of concerns about the physical environment in which they learn. These include easy access, e.g., few stairs and close parking (Kingston, 1982); need for increased illumination and a high quality audio system (Goodrow, 1975); and the availability of other services such as personal and career counseling (Hildreth, Dilworth-Anderson, and Rabe, 1983). Although only a few institutions of higher education have developed special services for older persons, most older students are unfamiliar with the various student services that are typically provided, and therefore are unlikely to utilize them (Chelsvig and Timmermann, 1982).

Older students are likely to participate in programs of organizations with which they are familiar (Hooper and Marsh, 1978; Peterson, 1981). For instance, alumni of a college are more likely to return for continuing education programs than are those who have had no previous contact with the school. Even vicarious contact, through a child who was a student there, is frequently sufficient to encourage participation.

Thus, the setting preferred by older people is one that is accessible and familiar. Often this is a college campus that is close to home or, as in the case of Elderhostel, is approved as appropriate by a national organization which the older learner has come to trust. In most cases, the older learner will be more careful than others about choosing the setting, and additional accommodations will be required beyond those needed by middle-aged learners.

Fees. One major accommodation that many public institutions of higher education have made is the reduction or elimination of fees for older persons who choose to participate in the regular course offerings of the institutions. Typically this special consideration is made only if the older student registers for no-credit (audit), and is limited to classes which have space available after the normal enrollment period. Chelsvig and Timmermann (1979) reported that in 1979 half the American institutions of higher education offered free or reduced tuition. Community colleges and public institutions were more likely to have this policy than private schools. Long and Rossing (1979) found that 19 states had enacted legislation creating such policies, and eight had similar accommodations implemented by state higher education agencies. In a later study, Long found that 43 states had some provision for reduced or free tuition (Long, 1982).

Tuition waiver policies, though common, do not appear to be widely used by older persons. Since many schools keep no records of such registrations, the total number of older students who use these opportunities is unknown, but it does not appear to be large (Long, 1983). The reason for this may be that some older people are hesitant to request financial assistance while others may be unaware of these special considerations. Romaniuk (1983) reported that in a survey of older persons in Virginia only 44% of the respondents had heard of the free tuition and only 29% of older people enrolling in these institutions took advantage of it. She concluded that the institutions of higher education were not advertising the opportunity because they were not reimbursed for any costs involved, so had no incentive to increase enrollment.

Although some programs for older adults such as the Plato Society or the Institute for Retired Professionals charge fairly large fees ($300 per year), most programs do not. This is in contrast to career education for middle-aged persons in which both credit and non-credit instruction typically costs much more than the few dollars charged for older adult education. At the present time, there does not seem to be a desire on the part of older persons to pay substantial sums for instruction, regardless of the quality or topic.

Instructors. Many of the instructional programs for older people involve peer teaching. The Institute for Retired Professionals (Lipman, 1985) has become a model in which membership in the Institute brings with it the expectation of an active role in carrying out the program, frequently operationalized in the form of coordinating a course or giving a lecture. This is much different than programs for middle-aged learners in which regular faculty conduct the instruction.

In courses where regular faculty are used, such as the Elderhostel program, the attitude of the instructor is very important in determining the success of the instruction. Although some instructors have been found to be wary of older students in their regular classes, expressing concern that older people would dominate the discussion or would deal exclusively with their personal experience, these concerns have generally not proven to be major problems. Most older students report that they are well accepted by their teachers (Kingston, 1982), and most teachers' attitudes toward aging improve after having older learners in their courses (Barnes, 1982). In a study by Covey (1980), older persons did not seem to have difficulty in adapting to the student role, young people were perceived to be supportive and friendly (Perkins and Robertson-Tchabo, 1981), and good relationships developed between the age groups (Long, 1983). In a study of performance, older people did as well as or better than younger students but typically wanted lectures and discussion to proceed a little slower (Long, 1983). In sum, the instructors who succeed are not only knowledgeable but are conscious of the learning preferences and limitations of their older students, a concern that is less frequently evidenced by instructors of middle-aged students.

Learning characteristics. A large number of experimental studies have examined the learning abilities and performance of adults and older persons. In general they show that older people learn less efficiently, and benefit more than younger persons from specific accommodations in the design and conduct of instruction. This chapter provides insufficient space to offer a complete review of this research, but a number of good summaries do exist (for instance, see Botwinick, 1978; Willis, 1985; Schaie and Parr, 1981; or Arenberg and Robertson-Tchabo, 1977).

The studies show that the learning performance of older people can be enhanced through a number of actions on the part of the instructor. Although these studies are set in laboratories, many of them have direct implications for the instructor of older adults. These include the reduction of interference; allowing for self-pacing or, if this is not possible, slow pacing of the material; providing some assistance in organizing the material that is presented, such as outlines and note-taking guides that help identify the important points; enhancing motivation by making the subject matter relevant to the interests of the older learner, concrete, and useful; reducing any anxiety generated by the learning setting through the provision of a comfortable, supportive atmosphere; using both visual and verbal means of communicating information; and providing feedback as soon as possible to reduce the possibility of incorrect understanding.

Thus, the accommodations that educational institutions need to make for older learners are quite different from those made for nontraditional students. Liberal arts content, scheduling during the day, heightened social interaction, an emphasis on learning for its own sake, reduced costs, and a modified instructional process are all common to the older learner but not to the middle-aged nontraditional student.

The role that higher education can play in education for the older person is yet to be completely developed. The traditional areas of higher education—the arts and humanities, the sciences and professions—do seem appropriate, but conscious attempts to design learning environments specifically for older persons have been slow in developing and have not yet had a significant impact on the perceived mission or behavior of the institutions of higher education.

AGING OF THE FACULTY

The aging of American society has not only affected the number of traditionally aged students and the growth of the nontraditional and older student population, but is also having an impact on faculty age in institutions of higher education. Concerns about faculty layoffs, high tenure density, lack of jobs for recent Ph.D.s, and faculty obsolescence have become widespread in colleges and universities.

The median age of faculty in American institutions of higher education, the professoriate, has increased from 39 in 1968-69 to 45 in 1978-79 (George and Winfield-Laird, 1984) and is expected to continue rising throughout the rest of the century. By 1990 35% of the faculty will be over age 55, and by 2000, half will be over 55 (Claxton and Murrell, 1984). Although the aging of American society (of which college faculty are a part) explains some of the increase in median age, the aging of the professoriate will be much more pronounced because of limited opportunities for young Ph.D.s to enter the field. Similarly, increased age has meant greater seniority and higher tenure density. In 1975 more than half of the faculty were at the associate or full professor rank, and tenure density increased from 50% in 1969 to 64% in 1978 (Carnegie Council for Policy Studies, 1980).

This situation, of course, has been caused by the rapid growth of the professoriate in the 1960s and early 1970s which accompanied the massive increase in the student body. At the peak of growth, approximately 20,000 new faculty positions were added annually (Carnegie Council on Policy Studies, 1980). Since the growth of higher education ended in the late 1970s, new faculty positions declined to zero as only replacements were needed for those lost through attrition (retirement, departure for a new job, and death).

New job openings in higher education are expected to remain at a low level since it will be at least twenty years before the faculty who joined the professoriate in the 1960s and 1970s reach retirement age. Likewise, movement of faculty among institutions of higher education is at a very low level. For instance, the annual turnover rate in tenure track positions dropped from 8% in the 1960s to 2% in the 1970s (Clark, Boyer, and Corcoran, 1985). With stability or decline in enrollments and a reduction in federal government support for research, few new positions are presently being created, resulting in a period of employment stability with limited openings for new Ph.D.s. This may have some positive consequences such as allow-

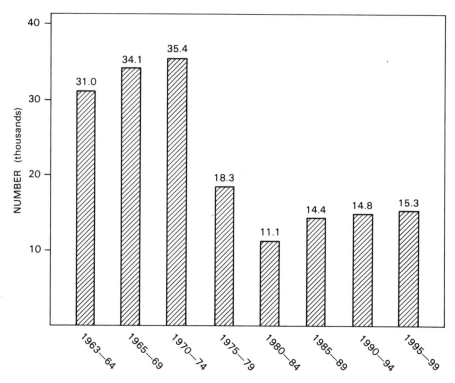

FIGURE 2-5 Estimated new hires of FTE senior faculty members (instructor and higher ranks) in all institutions of higher education, fall 1963 to fall 1999.

Note: These data assume a constant student-faculty ratio from 1940 to 1999.

Sources: Adapted from data in U.S. National Center for Education Statistics, Projection of Education Statistics, and from projections prepared by L. Fernandez based on enrollment projections.

ing smaller and less affluent institutions to hire faculty from prestigious Ph.D. programs, thus upgrading their faculty and spreading the available "talent."

Although the research is somewhat limited and does not adequately deal with all the relevant variables, there is little support for the general assumption that academic productivity declines in a linear fashion with increased age. The best general description of faculty productivity seems to be that it is bimodal, peaking about 10 years after receipt of the Ph.D. and again just before retirement (Reskin, 1985). There are also indications that faculty members of different ages have differing levels and types of productivity. Older professors may be likely to travel more than younger ones, to be on more boards and commissions, to speak outside their own institutions more often, and to be involved more heavily in the faculty governance of the institutions. Younger professors, at least until they achieve tenure, are likely to do more research and publishing, to be more concerned about increasing competence in their field of expertise, and to be active in seeking outside funding (McKeachie, 1979).

However, too many administrators and board members still hold to the simplistic view that younger faculty are more productive, and the contributions of older faculty members through community and professional service as well as institutional maintenance are frequently depreciated. Approaches are increasingly sought which would encourage older faculty to leave the institution. However, each group may provide a great assistance to the institution and the community through doing well those tasks that they have chosen.

There are several implications that result from an aging faculty, most of which have been carefully explored by many institutions of higher education. Although positive results could occur, such as increased stability, experience, and loyalty, the emphasis is typically placed on the potential negative outcomes. First, costs rise because senior faculty members are paid higher salaries than junior members, frequently as much as two-and-a-half times higher. This fact alone has been sufficient to motivate some institutions to reduce the number of older faculty regardless of their contribution.

Second, with an aging faculty, administrative flexibility is reduced; there are fewer opportunities to accommodate to social and institutional changes. New student interests cannot be responded to as quickly because new faculty positions are unavailable; tenured faculty cannot be terminated as quickly or easily when the demands of the institution no longer require their services; and curriculum is more difficult to revise when few new faculty members have joined the department since the previous review.

Third, an inadequate flow of ideas results when few new faculty members are added to the institution. This may mean that the faculty falls behind the cutting edge of technology or ideas; but it may also simply mean that the richness of some fields is not fully sampled because there are no funds to recruit persons with differing ideas and values. This is especially important in the sciences where obsolescence occurs quickly, and the impact of an outdated faculty can be devastating.

Fourth, members of minority groups and women are disadvantaged in their attempts to gain seniority and tenure. The present situation frequently results in a smaller percentage of persons being promoted and tenured. Since many minority group members and women have only recently joined the professoriate, they are the ones who bear the brunt of the promotion limitations and who must meet the rapidly rising standards for continued employment.

All of this is viewed by some potential faculty as a situation in which there are few chances for the new entrant. Undoubtedly, some of the best will choose careers in industry or business, passing up the opportunity to teach and conduct research in higher education. Likewise, there is some evidence that the quality of persons entering Ph.D. programs (and ultimately the professoriate) is declining and that this career is not as attractive as it had been in the past (Mehrotra, 1984). To the extent that this is true, the quality of higher education will suffer as a generation of potential scholars is lost.

However, there are at least three areas which suggest that having an older faculty is not automatically an insoluble problem. First, studies of adult cognition over the past several years have shown that intellectual decline occurs much slower and later than had been previously believed (Willis, 1985). A stimulating environment and interpersonal contact play a major part in enabling all older persons, including faculty, to maintain their abilities. Verbal skills are the last to decline, and since these are the skills most used by faculty, the decline is not likely to be too serious. With years of experience and the ability to compensate for any deficits, older faculty only need the will to learn in order to remain current on the developments in their fields and to enhance their continued productivity.

Second, the negative implications of an aging faculty are all based upon the assumption that developmental processes are at work which make older faculty less valuable and productive than younger ones. There is another possible explanation for the data that show differences between young and old faculty: cohort socialization. From this perspective, faculty in an older cohort can be expected to concentrate their energies on institutional maintenance, teaching, and community service not because of their age but because they were socialized during their graduate training and early careers to see these as their most valued roles. In exploring this area, Lawrence (1984) found no correlation between age and the number of publications, a common and valued measure of productivity. Only faculty members facing the tenure decision were clearly more likely to publish. She speculated that current young faculty tend to publish more than current older faculty because that is the way they were socialized, not because older faculty gave up rigorous intellectual pursuits.

The implication of this perspective is that the current large cohort of middle-aged faculty are more likely than preceding cohorts to be productive in terms of research and publishing throughout their careers. While those who are currently old are less likely to do so, those who will grow old in the next 20 years have been socialized in a different time and are more likely to maintain their scholarly productivity throughout the remainder of their academic careers. Thus they are not likely to be viewed as a negative influence on the quality of higher education, at least as measured by publications.

Third, there are a variety of approaches currently being contemplated or used by colleges and universities that can minimize the perceived negative implications of an aging faculty. These include: inducements to early retirement, frequently with a generous lump-sum payment or partial salary and fringe benefits for several years; phased retirement or part-time employment, allowing the faculty member to adapt gradually to increased leisure or to secure other employment; withholding of salary increases from those who are deemed the least productive; decreasing the wage differential between senior and junior faculty; and retraining for career change (George and Winfield-Laird, 1984). Although each of these approaches has some value, they tend to be either not very effective (financially or in terms of faculty morale), or quite expensive.

The one approach that does appear to offer promise is that of retraining older faculty for new administrative or teaching responsibilities. A good deal of experience has been gained in retraining within business and industry (Belbin and Belbin, 1972), and this knowledge could be applied effectively to higher education. Most colleges and universities offer faculty development programs, but these typically have been directed toward helping younger faculty develop better instructional techniques (Baldwin, 1984). A program aimed at older faculty will need to include both a counseling function and a content element. The counseling is needed to help faculty members consider midcareer change and dispassionately assess individual strengths and weaknesses. The establishment of long-term goals, and development of plans to achieve those goals, will be necessary in order to encourage an organized approach to revitalization of middle-aged and older instructors.

Once a clear path is identified, the institution can create workshops and support that will lead to the acquisition of knowledge necessary to implement the plans. Although most faculty probably will choose to remain in their own content areas, some will decide to focus on other disciplines and acquire knowledge in one of the developing fields related to their backgrounds. One example of this can be found in the academic study of gerontology, a field which is rapidly growing because of the aging population and increasing interest in understanding both what occurs in normal aging and how to provide human services to individuals who are experiencing normal senescence or pathological difficulties.

GERONTOLOGY INSTRUCTION AND RESEARCH
IN HIGHER EDUCATION

Gerontology instruction and research deal with the generation and transmission of knowledge and skill that have been acquired on the processes of aging and the condition of older people in contemporary society. The motivation for and purpose of these gerontology instruction and research activities in higher education have derived from at least two different strains of development.

One strain has involved researchers initially responding to the growing visibility of the older population by making aging a topic of scientific investigation. Physiological studies have examined the normal and pathological aspects of aging; psychological studies have sought to determine the extent of cognitive change over the life span; and sociological studies have examined adjustment to the changing roles of later life, such as retirement, new and different family relations, and widowhood. These disciplinary studies were undertaken primarily as a scientific endeavor to understand the multiple and interrelated processes of aging. They were largely successful and much knowledge has been generated, organized, and incorporated into several disciplines (see for example the Handbooks on Aging: Binstock and Shanas, 1985; Birren and Schaie, 1985; Finch and Schneider, 1985).

The second developmental strain has involved surveys and descriptive research which provided data on the current social and physical characteristics of older persons, such as their income situation, health condition, social supports, housing, mobility, and morale. These data were typically used in the public policy process as justification for urging various levels of government to create programs to help dependent and disadvantaged older people. They were also incorporated into the curriculum of the helping professions and are included in the preparation of professionals in social, health, and educational fields.

Gerontology instruction has rapidly expanded and now typically results in one of three distinct outcomes: (1) generalized understanding of the processes of human aging, (2) skills and knowledge necessary for professional employment with the elderly, or (3) specialized knowledge and skills preparatory to a career in scientific research. These outcomes frequently are combined, but the first is commonly emphasized at the undergraduate level, the second at the master's or professional level, and the third at the doctoral level of instruction.

The earliest gerontology education was within the disciplines of biology, psychology, and sociology, with doctoral students taking a specialized course or two and then completing their dissertations on a gerontological topic. The number of dissertations in aging was very small for many years, totaling 694 from 1856 to 1968, then growing rapidly to 1,113 from 1969 to 1975, and to 2,526 from 1976 to 1982 (Moore, Mueller, and Birren, n.d.).

Liberal and professional gerontology courses have been developed around a multidisciplinary base since no single discipline covers the interrelated and complex processes of human aging. This instruction has expanded until today it is available in numerous departments and at all levels of higher education. It is typically offered as an adjunct to a traditional major, but in a growing number of colleges and universities is available as a separate degree or certificate program primarily aimed at providing knowledge and skill appropriate to persons seeking employment in services and programs for older persons and their families.

The extent of instruction in gerontology is currently difficult to assess since no comprehensive national survey has been conducted since the publication of the first *National Directory of Educational Programs in Gerontology* (Sprouse, 1976). Bolton et al. (1978) developed tabulations from that directory and reported that 607 colleges and universities offered at least one credit course in gerontology, 402 offered at least two such courses, and 219 reported a program of study leading to a specified outcome such as a major, minor, emphasis, specialization, concentration, sequence, or degree in gerontology.

Although comprehensive data are not available, two examples can be used to suggest the rapid growth of the field. Recent surveys of graduate schools of social work showed that gerontological concentrations increased from 23 (36% of respondents) in 1980 to 47 (50% of respondents) in 1983 (Nelson and Schneider, 1984); and the American Personnel and Guidance Association reported that counselor education and counseling psychology departments offering course work in gerontology increased from 18 (6%) in 1975 to 114 (37%) in 1981 (Myers, 1983).

Of the approximately 3,000 accredited institutions of higher education in the United States, as many as 700 to 800 may have aging-related instructional programs, some consisting of only a few courses, but at least half resulting in a gerontology credential. This estimate is derived from adding the membership of the Association for Gerontology in Higher Education (approximately 275 colleges and universities) to an extrapolation of a recent random sample of 300 institutions of higher education that were surveyed by telephone. Of these, 50 were found to have four courses in gerontology. If responses from this sample are generalized to the 2700 institutions that are not AGHE members, that would suggest that 450 schools offer this level of course work in addition to those affiliated with AGHE (Peterson, in press).

However, a simple tabulation of the number of colleges and universities offering gerontology instruction masks a clear understanding of the field. Many large universities now have several instructional programs on the same campus, for instance in a Gerontology Center as well as in schools of social work, public administration, medicine, nursing, or allied health, or in departments of counselor education, psychology, sociology, or humanities. Gerontology instruction is growing very rapidly and can be expected to become a part of most liberal arts curricula as well as a scientific and professional specialization at the graduate level.

As a new field of study, gerontology instruction does not have a universally recognized curriculum, but rather has developed differing forms in various institutions. Only a few studies have compared curricula at various levels (associate, bachelor, master's, doctoral) in order to determine the extent of agreement on program length, required courses, and field experience. Van Orman (1984) examined curricula of undergraduate programs listed in the 1982 AGHE directory (Sullivan, 1982) and reported a good deal of consistency in the gerontology courses that were required. Peterson's (1984) study compared gerontology master's degree curricula and found them to have similar requirements and length. However, there are no studies of program consistency for other instructional outcomes, such as programs that result in a minor, specialization, concentration, or certificate.

Two national projects have suggested standards for gerontology instruction that could be used by faculty designing new gerontology instructional programs. The Association for Gerontology in Higher Education, in cooperation with the Gerontological Society of America, sponsored the Foundations for Gerontological Education Project (Johnson, 1980) and the Western Gerontological Society's Education Committee developed Standards and Guidelines for Gerontology Programs (1978). Another contribution has been made by a statewide task force on curriculum objectives for service providers in Virginia (Arling and Romaniuk, 1980). However, there does not exist any set of guidelines or standards for the extent or quality of professional gerontology instruction that is generally accepted, so the development of course work in the area is typically based on individual faculty interests or available text material.

Gerontology instruction, then, is in a state of rapid development paralleling the growth of the older population. It has become widely recognized but has not yet developed the infrastructure to assure consistency and quality in its many applications. As new faculty gravitate toward the field, there is increasing interest in the development of greater consistency and national guidelines that would enhance instructional quality, providing assurance to the public that persons prepared for professional roles with older people are knowledgeable and competent. As this work is accomplished, gerontology instruction can be expected to become more widely accepted and to gain increasing respectability as an interdisciplinary field of study and practice.

IMPLICATIONS AND CONCLUSIONS

The impact of an aging society on institutions of higher education is just beginning to be felt, and predictions of imminent disaster still exist. However, the beginnings of an adaptive process can be seen, one that typically occurs in three stages (Peterson and Birren, 1981). First, institutions realize that the societal, technological, or demographic change will have a real impact on them. This frequently does not happen immediately but only becomes real after a period of hesitation and delay. Second, a reexamination is initiated in which the institutions establish committees, commissions, and study groups to examine the implications of the change. It is not unusual for this to result in the conclusion that the institution must become more efficient and more productive in order to regain prosperity. It stresses a return to the basics of the past, to a resurgence of former values. Third, there occurs the development of a "new goal" stage in which the institution slowly reexamines its purposes in light of the changes, and eventually reaches consensus on appropriate modifications in order to achieve continued viability. It would appear that many institutions of higher education are still in stage one or two, while a few have begun actively pursuing new solutions to the issues facing them.

Higher education has survived for nearly 1,000 years and in so doing has changed radically. Since World War II, it has experienced the influx of GIs, the decline when they left, the baby boom, student unrest of the 1960s, the new vocational orientation of students, and the aging of the faculty. There is no reason to believe that the institution will not adapt, albeit slowly and with reluctance, to the situation of the 1980s.

There are also some indications that the end of the baby boom may not have as disastrous results as has been anticipated. Enrollment in American colleges and universities, though not maintaining the growth of the 1960s and early 1970s, has not experienced the precipitous decline that was expected. The 23% decline in the number of high school graduates between 1979 to 1997 was expected to have a cataclysmic impact on all levels of higher education, but to date the impact has been relatively minimal. Total enrollment peaked in 1983–84 at 12,464,661, and for the 1984–85 year was estimated to be only slightly less (Evangelauf, 1984). Although freshman enrollments have declined, graduate enrollments have increased, leaving the total virtually unchanged. The demographic peak occurred in 1978–79; five years later only stability, not decline, is evident in total college enrollment.

This is consistent with the enrollment projections that have been made by Ahlburg, Crimmins, and Easterlin (1981). They suggested that declining enrollment growth in the 1970s was caused partly by unusually high enrollments in the 1960s due to the draft. They showed that smaller cohorts, such as will be experienced in the 1980s and beyond, are likely to result in higher enrollment rates thus reducing the demographic impact. Their predictive model included cohort size, financial stress of the household, and marriage rates. When taken together, these variables result in several predictions which at the lowest rates suggest that enrollment of 18- to 24-year-olds will remain stable until 1995 and then increase between 1995 and 2000, and at their highest rates suggest that enrollment will increase by 25 percent between 1976 and 2000.

The positive enrollment picture is enhanced by the nontraditional student. The rapidity of technological change, the movement of women into the labor market, and the number of role and career transitions made by most adults has led to a much greater interest in education throughout the adult years. As Aslanian and Brickell (1980) have shown, education is the means by which 83% of adults prepare for or adjust to the transitions of adulthood. This is especially true for persons with higher levels of formal education, who are also more likely to enroll in both adult education offerings and formal college classes. Thus, the total enrollment by adults can be expected to continue to grow both in numbers and in significance, assisting adults to make the transitions throughout their adult lives.

The older population is also likely to be increasingly served by institutions of higher education in the future. Although not primarily as degree students, older people will increasingly seek out opportunities for learning in order to maintain social contacts, develop coping skills, increase their awareness of options, seek personal fulfillment, and increase their understanding of the historical and contemporary world. The major issue here is who will pay for this education. New mechanisms will be needed to provide colleges and universities with reimbursement for the services provided. Free tuition on a space-available basis will be insufficient motivation for institutions to develop modified format and content, and older people will not register unless some of the aforementioned accommodations are made.

To enroll substantially increased numbers of older persons, it will be necessary to develop age-segregated programs such as Elderhostel or the Institute for Retired Professionals. These programs are designed around the content and methods preferred by older learners; they eliminate the required assignments and formal evaluation which most older learners dislike; and they allow for the increased social participation desired by older learners. These programs will not be of sufficient size to save institutions of higher education if the regular student base erodes substantially, but they can be used to reduce the underutilization of facilities and to provide new and attractive teaching activities for faculty members in the humanities and social sciences.

The aging of the faculty will remain a concern for at least 20 years, but if enrollment does not decline as much as anticipated, and if colleges and universities begin to take seriously their responsibilities to serve all adults regardless of whether they enroll in traditional liberal arts or professional programs, there will be roles for many faculty members. Faculty development opportunities will be required if these new audiences are to be taught well. If this is successfully achieved, such instruction will provide a valuable service to society, bring the faculty into closer touch with the communities they have traditionally claimed to serve, and provide a model for human capital redirection that can be emulated in other sectors of society.

The growth of gerontology instruction will provide another option for faculty retraining. As the demand continues to increase, there will be opportunities for faculty from many disciplines to adapt their fields of expertise to instruction on gerontology. Student audiences, both younger and older, seem likely to desire more learning opportunities in this area; it will offer possibilities for faculty involvement while serving adult students, meeting manpower needs, and providing community service.

Overall, the adaptation of higher education to the aging of society and to the interests of adults and older people in the opportunities offered by higher education seem mutually compatible. The natural affinities of the two will support each other and with effective planning could result in a modification of higher education's goals to respond to the needs and interests of our aging population, providing an opportunity for older persons to explore new options for growth, coping, and skill development.

REFERENCES

AHLBURG, D., CRIMMINS, E. M., and EASTERLIN, R. A. (1981). The outlook for higher education: A cohort size model of enrollment of the college age population, 1948–2000. *Review of Public Data Use, 9,* 211–227.

ARENBERG, D., and ROBERTSON-TCHABO, E. A. (1977). Learning and aging. In J. E. Birren and K. W. Schaie (Eds.), *Handbook on the psychology of aging.* New York: Van Nostrand Reinhold.

ARLING, G., and ROMANIUK, J. G. (1980). *Final report of the task force on gerontology in higher education.* Richmond, Virginia: Virginia Commonwealth University.

ASLANIAN, C. B., and BRICKELL, H. M. (1980). *Americans in transition: Life changes as reasons for adult learning.* New York: College Entrance Examination Board.

BALDWIN, R. G. (1984). The changing development needs of an aging professoriate. In C.M.N. Mehrotra (Ed.), *Teaching and aging. New directions for teaching and learning, no. 19.* San Francisco: Jossey-Bass.

BARNES, C. M. (1982). Experience and faculty attitudes toward older learners. Paper presented at the 8th Annual Meeting of the Association for Gerontology in Higher Education, Washington, D.C.

BEATTIE, W. M. (1978). Major concerns and future directions in gerontology and higher education. In M. M. Seltzer, H. Sterns, and T. Hickey (Eds.), *Gerontology in higher education.* Belmont, California: Wadsworth.

BELBIN, E., and BELBIN, R. M. (1972). *Problems in adult retraining.* London: Heinemann.

BINSTOCK, R. H., and SHANAS, E. (Eds.) (1985). *Handbook of aging and the social sciences.* New York: Van Nostrand Reinhold.

BIRREN, J. E., and SCHAIE, K. W. (Eds.) (1985). *Handbook of the psychology of aging.* New York: Van Nostrand Reinhold.

BOLTON, C. R., EDEN, D. Z., HOLCOMB, J. R., and SULLIVAN, K. R. (1978). *Gerontology education in the United States: A research report.* Omaha, Nebraska: University of Nebraska at Omaha.

BOSHIER, R., and RIDDELL, G. (1978). Educational participation scale factor structure for older adults. *Adult Education, 28,* 165–175.

BOTWINICK, J. (1978). *Aging and behavior.* New York: Springer.

BOWEN, H. R. (1980). *Adult learning, higher education, and the economics of unused capacity.* New York: College Entrance Examination Board.

BOWEN, H. R. (1982). *The state of the nation and the agenda for higher education.* San Francisco: Jossey-Bass.

CARNEGIE COUNCIL ON POLICY STUDIES IN HIGHER EDUCATION (1980). *Three thousand futures: The next twenty years for higher education.* San Francisco: Jossey-Bass.

CARNEGIE FOUNDATION FOR THE ADVANCEMENT OF TEACHING (1975). *More than survival.* San Francisco: Jossey-Bass.

CHELSVIG, K. A., and TIMMERMANN, S. (1979). Tuition policies of higher educational institutions and state government and the older learner. *Educational Gerontology, 4,* 147–159.

CHELSVIG, K. A., and TIMMERMANN, S. (1982). Support services for older adult tuition programs. *Educational Gerontology, 8,* 269–274.

CLARK, S. M., BOYER, C. M., and CORCORAN, M. (1985). Faculty and institutional vitality in higher education. In S. M. Clark and D. R. Lewis (Eds.), *Faculty vitality and institutional productivity.* New York: Teachers College, Columbia University.

CLAXTON, C. S., and MURRELL, P. H. (1984). Developmental theory as a guide for maintaining the vitality of college faculty. In C.M.N. Mehrotra (Ed.), *Teaching and aging. New directions for teaching and learning, no. 19.* San Francisco: Jossey-Bass.

COVEY, H. C. (1980). An exploratory study of the acquisition of a college student role by older people. *The Gerontologist, 20,* 173–181.

COVEY, H. C. (1983). Higher education and older people: Some theoretical considerations, Part 1. *Educational Gerontology, 9,* 1–13.

CRIMMINS, E. M., and RIDDLER, E. W. (1985). College enrollment trends among the population thirty-five and older: 1972–1982 projections to 2000. *Educational Gerontology, 11*, 363–385.

CROSS, K. P. (1979). Adult learners: Characteristics, needs, and interests. In R. E. Peterson and associates, *Lifelong learning in America.* San Francisco: Jossey-Bass.

DANIEL, D. E., TEMPLIN, R. G., and SHEARON, R. W. (1977). The value orientation of older adults toward education. *Educational Gerontology, 2*, 33–42.

DELLMANN-JENKINS, M. M., and PAPALIA-FINLAY, D. E. (1983). Older adults' participation in university classes: Cognitive, morale, and family correlates. *Educational Gerontology, 9*, 501–509.

ELLIS, D. W. (1981). Should education be useful? In T. M. Stauffer (Ed.), *Beyond the falling sky: Surmounting pressures on higher education.* Washington, D.C.: American Council on Education.

EVANGELAUF, J. (1984). Enrollments stable this fall; faculty salaries up 7 pct., outpacing inflation rate. *Chronicle of Higher Education, 29*, 1 and 14.

FINCH, C. E., and SCHNEIDER, E. L. (Eds.) (1985). *Handbook of the biology of aging.* New York: Van Nostrand Reinhold.

FISHER, J. C. (1979). Educational attainment, anomie, life satisfaction and situational variables as predictors of participation in educational activities by active older adults. Unpublished doctoral dissertation, University of Wisconsin, Milwaukee.

GEORGE, L. K., and WINFIELD-LAIRD, I. (1984). Implications of an aging faculty for the quality of higher education and academic careers. In C.M.N. Mehrotra (Ed.), *Teaching and aging. New directions for teaching and learning, no. 19.* San Francisco: Jossey-Bass.

GOODROW, B. A. (1975). Limiting factors in reducing participation in older adult learning opportunities. *The Gerontologist, 15*, 418–422.

GRIMBLE, R. W. (March 17, 1985). Successful model programs. Presentation at the national workshop on organizing college level educational programs for retired persons, Newark, Delaware.

HARRIS, L., and associates (1974). *The myth and reality of aging in America.* Washington, D.C.: National Council on the Aging.

HARRIS, L., and associates (1981). *Aging in the eighties: America in transition.* Washington, D.C.: National Council on the Aging.

HENRY, D. D. (1975). *Challenges past, challenges present.* San Francisco: Jossey-Bass.

HILDRETH, G. J., DILWORTH-ANDERSON, P., and RABE, S. M. (1983). Family and school life of women over age fifty who are in college. *Educational Gerontology, 9*, 339–350.

HOOPER, J. O., and MARSH, G. B. (1978). A study of older students attending university classes. *Educational Gerontology, 3*, 321–330.

JOHNSON, H. R., BRITTON, J. H., LANG, C. A., SELTZER, M. M., STANFORD, E. P., YANCIK, R., MAKLAN, C. W., and MIDDLESWARTH, A. B. (1980). Foundations for gerontological education. *The Gerontologist, 20*, 1–61.

KASWORM, C. E. (1980). Student services for the older undergraduate student. *Journal of College Student Personnel, 21*, 163–169.

KERR, C. (1972). Policy concern for the future. In D. W. Vermilye (Ed.), *The expanded campus.* San Francisco: Jossey-Bass.

KINGSTON, A. J. (1982). Attitudes and problems of elderly students in the university system of Georgia. *Educational Gerontology, 8*, 87–92.

KIRK, C. F., and DORFMAN, L. T. (1983). Satisfaction and role strain among middle-aged and older reentry women students. *Educational Gerontology, 19*, 15–29.

KNOWLTON, M. P. (1977). Liberal arts: The Elderhostel plan for survival. *Educational Gerontology, 2*, 87–94.

LAWRENCE, J. H. (1984). Faculty age and teaching. In C.M.N. Mehrotra (Ed.), *Teaching and aging. New directions for teaching and learning, no. 19*. San Francisco: Jossey-Bass.

LIPMAN, H. T. (March 18, 1985). Curriculum, instruction, and program development. Presentation at the national workshop on organizing college level educational programs for retired persons, Newark, Delaware.

LONG, H. B. (1982). Analysis of research concerning free and reduced tuition programs for senior citizens. *Educational Gerontology, 8*, 575–584.

LONG. H. B. (1983). Academic performance, attitudes, and social relations in intergenerational college classes. *Educational Gerontology, 9*, 471–481.

LONG, H. B., and ROSSING, B. E. (1979). Tuition waiver plans for older Americans in postsecondary public education institutions. *Educational Gerontology, 4*, 161–174.

McKEACHIE, W. J. (1979). Perspectives from psychology: Financial incentives are ineffective for faculty. In D. R. Lewis and W. E. Becker, Jr. (Eds.), *Academic rewards in higher education*. Cambridge, Massachusetts: Ballinger Publishing Co.

MEHROTRA, C.M.N. (1984). Responding to institutional concerns and faculty needs. In C.M.N. Mehrotra (Ed.), *Teaching and aging. New directions for teaching and learning, no. 19*. San Francisco: Jossey-Bass.

MISSINNE, L. E. (1983). Will gerontology change our educational system? *Gerontology and Geriatrics Education, 4*, 25–35.

MOORE, J. L., MUELLER, J. E., and BIRREN, J. E. (n.d.). An analysis of doctoral dissertations on aging written in institutions of higher learning in the United States, 1976–1982. Mimeo.

MYERS, J. E. (1983). Aging and counseling. *Gerontology and Geriatrics Education, 4*, 67–73.

NELSON, G. M., and SCHNEIDER, R. L. (1984). *The current status of gerontology in graduate social work education*. New York: Council on Social Work Education.

NUSBERG, C. E. (1982). Educational opportunities for the elderly in industrialized countries outside the United States. *Educational Gerontology, 8*, 395–409.

NUSSBAUM, L. L. (1984). The academy of senior professionals at Eckerd College. In C.M.N. Mehrotra (Ed.), *Teaching and aging: New directions for teaching and learning, no. 19*. San Francisco: Jossey-Bass.

PEACOCK, E. W., and TALLEY, W. M. (1984). Intergenerational contact: A way to counteract ageism. *Educational Gerontology, 10*, 13–24.

PERKINS, H. V., and ROBERTSON-TCHABO, E. A. (1981). Retirees return to college: An evaluative study at one university campus. *Educational Gerontology, 6*, 273–287.

PETERSON, D. A. (1981). Participation in education by older people. *Educational Gerontology, 7*, 245–256.

PETERSON, D. A. (1983). *Facilitating education for older learners*. San Francisco: Jossey-Bass.

PETERSON, D. A. (1984). Are master's degrees in gerontology comparable? *The Gerontologist, 24*, 646–651.

PETERSON, D. A. (In press). Extent of gerontology instruction in American institutions of higher education. *Educational Gerontology*.

PETERSON, D. A., and BIRREN, J. E. (1981). The impact of aging on institutions of higher education. In M. Boaz (Ed.), *Issues in higher education and the professions in the 1980s*. Littleton, Colorado: Libraries Unlimited.

PETERSON, R. E. (1981). Opportunities for adult learners. In A. W. Chickering and associates, *The modern American college*. San Francisco: Jossey-Bass.

RESKIN, B. F. (1985). Aging and productivity: Careers and results. In S. M. Clark and D. R. Lewis (Eds.), *Faculty vitality and institutional productivity*. New York: Teachers College, Columbia University.

RIESMAN, D. (1980). *On higher education*. San Francisco: Jossey-Bass.

ROMANIUK, J. G. (1983). Educational tuition-waiver policies: A secondary analysis of institutional impact in Virginia. *Educational Gerontology, 9,* 279–292.

ROMANIUK, J. G., and ROMANIUK, M. (1982). Participation motives of older adults in higher education: The Elderhostel experience. *The Gerontologist, 22,* 364–368.

SCHAIE, K. W., and PARR, J. (1981). Intelligence. In A. W. Chickering and associates, *The modern American college*. San Francisco: Jossey-Bass.

SCULLY, M. G. (1983). 4,000 faculty members laid off in 5 years by 4-year institutions, survey shows. *The Chronicle of Higher Education, 27,* 21.

SPROUSE, B. (Ed.). (1976). *National directory of educational programs in gerontology*. Washington, D.C.: Association for Gerontology in Higher Education.

STAUFFER, T. M. (1981). Solving higher education's problems. In T. M. Stauffer (Ed.), *Beyond the falling sky: Surmounting pressures on higher education*. Washington, D.C.: American Council on Education.

SULLIVAN, E. (Ed.) (1982). *National directory of educational programs in gerontology*. Washington, D.C.: Association for Gerontology in Higher Education.

VAN ORMAN, W. R. (1984). Curriculum topics for baccalaureate gerontology: A research brief. Paper presented at the Western Gerontological Society Annual Meeting, Anaheim, California.

VENTURA, C. A., and WORTHY, E. H., JR. (1982). *Education for older adults: A synthesis of significant data*. Washington, D.C.: National Council on the Aging.

WESTERN GERONTOLOGICAL EDUCATION COMMITTEE. (1978). Draft standards and guidelines. *Generations, 3,* 43–51.

WILLIS, S. L. (1985). Towards an educational psychology of the older adult learner: Intellectual and cognitive bases. In J. E. Birren and K. W. Schaie (Eds.), *Handbook of the psychology of aging*. New York: Van Nostrand Reinhold.

YOUNG, K. E. (March 19, 1985). Securing institutional commitment. Paper presented at the national workshop on organizing college level educational programs for retired persons, Newark, Delaware.

3

LIFE SPAN LEARNING AND EDUCATION

A Conceptual Progression in the Life Course

James E. Thornton

INTRODUCTION AND PURPOSE

This chapter is about learning and education over the life span, and the biography of learning created over the course of one's life. During the life course individuals must learn new and complex things in order to develop and be competent. Recurrent or continuous episodes of learning and education assist individuals in planning their lives and in coping with life events. Ultimately, these episodes of learning and education offer a history of life-span developmental phenomena on which a biography of the learner is based. At any one point in time this biography is key to understanding subsequent developmental concerns.

We need to know *how* we know and experience the world, as well as how we derive meaning from these experiences and how they influence life-span development. Learning is essential to understanding experience, while education is a social activity designed to enhance learning and provide experience. This is the context for conceptualizing life-span learning and education.

The purpose of this chapter is to discuss learning and education as essential functions in life-span development and to provide a basis for increased social support of educational opportunity through the life span. The chapter develops four topics. First, learning is discussed as an inherent process in the development of the individual over the total life span. Although learning does not cease at a particular point in the life course, the focus of learning is qualitatively different throughout the life course. These qualitative differences in learning reflect changes in life-span developmental forces (physical, cognitive, emotional, social, and environmental). The necessity to learn changes as the forces of development introduce new tasks and resolve earlier tasks; but the need to learn does not cease. Learning is as much a part of development as is hunger, thirst, or physical movement. We ignore the learning imperative in our development, regardless of age, at great peril as individuals and as a society.

Second, a paradigm is proposed that characterizes life-span learning as a "history" of learning in the "biography" of the learner. This history and biography reflect idiosyncratic development and provide the background and context for developmental tasks and growth. At any one time or place, life-span learning will be involved in the transitions and transformations of new or as yet unresolved life events. Avoidance of life transitions and transformations aborts development since it is improbable that in this information-rich society, we can "bank" enough learned experience at one point in the life course to suffice for a whole lifetime. Houle (1984) used the biographies of such writers as Thoreau, Everett and Osler, among others, to illustrate how learning and education were central to their life history and life course.

Consequently, this history and biography of learning affects educative responses to emerging learning tasks in the life span, particularly in the later years. Thus, the third topic in the chapter describes a paradigm of life-span education that provides a developmental perspective for continuous educative opportunity, and less of an *add-on* and *age-graded* view (Wedemeyer, 1981). The proposed paradigm of life-span education offers a contextualistic perspective of learning, the person, and institutions, and suggests educative configurations involved in life-span learning for the later years.

Finally, the chapter discusses implications and future directions for policy and research in life-span education. A major policy question in educational gerontology and adult education involves the observed discrepancies between the elderly's under-utilization of educational opportunity and the imperative of continued learning in the later years.

DEVELOPMENT AND LEARNING

Our perceptions of human development are based on fundamental world views which Pepper (1970) described as mechanistic, organismic, and contextualistic models. These have been elaborated on in a life-span development perspective by Hickey (1974) and Hultsch and Deutsch (1981). If man is viewed as an "organ in the body of society," then a mechanistic metaphor and behaviorism dominate education. On the other hand, if man is viewed as having "free choice and self-direction," then an interactive metaphor dominates education. This is an essentially contextualistic view of learning and education: a view concerned with interactions between people and environments resulting in ongoing transactions or transitions over time. The contextualistic view provides the basic assumptions for life-span learning and education.

Current thought suggests that learning, as a process, is embedded in the development of the individual. Kegan (1982) characterized this embedded process as a *meaning-making conversation* between the maturational forces stimulating development within us and the social forces of the world in which we live. Our feelings and thoughts originate in this conversation and influence perception and knowledge. Kegan's thesis is that this meaning-making conversation never ceases in the human being; and that it is an essential part of the psychosocial forces in self-preservation and self-transformation, and ultimately to social-evolutionary processes. This is what Holmes called "the dialectic of limit and possibility" (cited in Kegan, 1982). Inherent in all of this are fundamental assumptions about development and learning, assumptions on which this chapter is based. Learning is essential for understanding and maximizing life-span developmental forces. Consequently, we need to look more closely at the linkages between development and learning, particularly their interactive, cumulative effects in and on late life experience.

Basic Assumptions about Development

Life-span development is characterized by three phenomena so inextricably intertwined that each must be understood by its interaction with the other two. Baltes (1979) identified these phenomena as (1) *normative age-graded (ontogenetic)*, (2) *normative history-graded (evolutionary)*, and (3) *non-normative* events. Normative age-graded events include biological maturation; physical development; and socialization, i.e., social competencies and roles within the individual's potential. Normative history-graded phenomena include general cultural and social events involving cohort effects and historic time; for example, the Great Depression, World War II, etc. Non-normative phenomena include significant events in the life of the individual which are not readily generalizable to other individuals: for example, family life, education, occupation, health, and life-style. According to Baltes (1979), there are both biological and environmental antecedents determining these phenomena, which shape general development. Havighurst (1972) proposed similar antecedents for the maturational, psychosocial, cultural, and environmental forces which shape developmental concerns across the life span.

Birren and Woodruff (1973) characterized development as a process of increasing differentiation from less complex to more complex, from a lower to a higher state of ability, skill, or trait. Their thesis is that the processes of cognitive and affective differentiation and development do not cease at some point in the life course, such as with physical maturation, but proceed throughout the life span. According to Reinert (1980), the realization that development does not end with adolescence is not new; however, a life-span viewpoint is essential to understanding the laws of ontogenetic development. Developmental theories focusing on particular segments of the life span (for example, childhood, adolescence, or adulthood) run the risk of incorrectly generalizing from one developmental period to others. For this reason, life-span development models assume large intraindividual plasticity and interindividual variability, making generalizations extremely difficult.

These views of development raise some fundamental questions regarding learning and education over the life span: What are the learning and educational concerns and strategies for a particular part of the life course? Which concerns are generalizable to the whole life course? What concerns and which strategies accommodate individual development (intraindividual plasticity)? Which accommodate differences among individuals and situations (interindividual variability)? How do normative age-graded and history-graded phenomena influence learning and education? What are the cumulative effects of learning and educational experiences (non-normative) in a life-span perspective?

Attempts to answer these questions are reflected in the growing educational gerontology and adult education literature (see, for example, Brown, 1978; Cross, 1981; Havighurst, 1972; Sherron and Lumsden, 1978; Wedemeyer, 1981). Learning and education are strategies for resolving developmental tensions and transitions in the life span, for deriving meaning from life experiences and events, and for understanding the flow of our lives and human history. Learning is the process of organizing meaning out of experience. According to Kegan (1982), "There is thus no feeling, no experience, no thought, no perception independent of meaning-making context in which it becomes a feeling, an experience, a thought, a perception, because we are the meaning-making context" (p. 11). The life-span development perspective provides the context for understanding the interaction among the endogenous and exogenous forces that shape development and influence learning, which subsequently influences further development. This perspective also provides the context for a "biography of learning" as the individual matures (see, for example, Rosenmayr, 1982).

Basic Assumptions about Learning

Not only is learning an inherent function of maturation and development, but as a social activity it is a necessary component for understanding and responding to growth as it occurs. A "push-and-pull" hypothesis explains the function of learning. That is, learning initiated by intrinsic factors, such as exploratory behavior, bonding, muscular development, and speech, "pushes" maturation and development forward. Learning initiated by external factors "pulls" development toward particular states of cognition, affect, language, etc. Although this hypothesis is far too simplistic in that it does not fully account for the interaction of these factors, it does provide an expanded and alternative view of learning currently conceived as an "add-on" educative process (Wedemeyer, 1981). It is an important contribution to our understanding of the learning process in that it draws attention to internal and external forces and to past and future influences on current learning. The life-span development perspective requires that we view learning within a context of time, place, antecedents, and events. Learning, as it is characterized here, should not be confused with educational activities or interventions which society develops to optimize learning, particularly in the "pulling" of development (see, for example, Birren and Woodruff, 1973; Thornton, 1967).

Learning occurs in response to intrinsic (endogenous) and extrinsic (exogenous) processes, and thereby changes behavior in a developmental and purposeful way. Learning is often defined as changes in behavior resulting from experiences. Conditions and states of the organism, as well as how the organism perceives and manages itself in a particular context, necessitate learning. Although the learning processes themselves are not observable, the outcomes of learning, in terms of acquisition of behaviors and performance, are observable. Learned outcomes include perceptions, affect, knowledge, skills, values, and sensibilities. Behavior changes resulting from altered states and fatigue are not considered learned as the word is intended here. Current educational psychology holds to fundamental laws of learning regardless of age.

The meaning of learning in the life span is difficult to assess, particularly in the later years. The meaning given to learning over an individual's life course depends on his or her learning capabilities, experiences as a learner, and social contexts in which thought and behavior have developed. Assessment is difficult because criteria are lacking in regard to what is to be learned or known in the later years. Furthermore, criteria based on normative standards and values in the present are not likely to adequately reflect the social-historical context of previous learning. For example, changing the diet and exercise of older people to current recommended standards is difficult because of social values involved in the acquisition of food and exercise habits. Thus learned behavior and previous learning experiences have a confounding effect on the acquisition of new behavior. This necessitates the use of strategies of learning which creatively accommodate this history of learning. Learning difficulties and interferences from existing repertoires have not been adequately studied in the elderly. Furthermore, in the later years it becomes more difficult to sort out age effects from history and cohort effects on learning (see, for example, Birren and Cunningham, 1985; Denny, 1984; Willis, 1985). As a consequence, paradigms of the conditions of learning for the later years need to accommodate this history of learning in the biography of a learner, integrating past with present, often in subtle ways (see, for example, Havighurst, 1968).

Life-span learning denotes all of the learning that occurs during the life course including learning which is intuitive, self-motivated, and self-directed, and learning which results from other-directed or contrived events (education). According to Wedemeyer (1981), life-span learning as a concept (1) includes learning from birth to death; (2) is a blend of formal, informal, traditional, and nontraditional modes and processes; (3) is a jumbled sequence of concurrent events in the life course; and (4) is more than schooling (p. 171). Wedemeyer sees life-span learning as inclusive of all purposeful behavioral changes that enable the person to achieve goals and satisfy needs. Life-span learning is idiosyncratic, personal, and largely self-directed from the perspective of the life course. Although learning can occur in social, interactive situations such as in groups and classrooms, social interaction per se is not learning (Wedemeyer, 1981, pp. 171-172). Learning is less likely to occur in drug-induced states without a therapist, and in states of fatigue.

Life-span learning is influenced by our assumptions about the meaning of life events. These events have to be understood in terms of their characteristics: type, time, attributes, sequence, mediating variables, significance, resolution, and consequences (Hultsch and Plemons, 1979). A learner is apt to attempt to understand the meaning of an event and how best to adapt to it, transform it, or even ignore it, at any point in time. During the life course it is appropriate to conceive of some learning as adding to existing knowledge for a life event. That is, the learning is new and supplemental to what is known, involving new knowledge, experiences, and affect; for example, a first job, a first marriage, and a first child. In contrast, other life events require transformation of knowledge, experience, and affect regarding an event; for example, children leaving home, divorce and remarriage, alcohol abuse and rehabilitation, retirement, and widowhood. Both examples provide a biographical perspective of learning in the life span—what Havighurst (1968) suggested as the task of integrating one's past into one's present. These tasks involve learning abilities that are quite stable in later life. There is nothing in our present knowledge about human development that precludes the ability to learn through the life span except for some limited types of neurophysiological difficulties which do not occur in the aged with great frequency (Eisdorfer, 1983; Schaie, 1973).

Learning Potential in Later Life

This section reviews recent research on learning potential in later life. Evidence mounts that the elderly's abilities to learn persist, particularly when challenged and with continued use, and when physical health is maintained. Learning deficits in the elderly often reflect social and environmental conditions and poor lifestyles.

Society imposes many of the learning deficits associated with aging through traditional age-graded arrangements and expectations, and the limitations of structured environments and roles. Gould's (1982) provocative study titled *The Mismeasure of Man,* a case in point, explored the thesis of biological determinism in studies of intelligence over the past one hundred years. The early studies imposed a "selection of the fittest" racial–cultural bias on our understanding of intelligence, an issue that remains unresolved. We must be careful not to impose a similar social deterministic bias on the learning potential of the elderly or, as a matter of fact, on their overall capacity to be productive.

Our measurement of learning over the life span, particularly for older learners, is in double jeopardy, however. Many age-graded social policies and programs are postulated on deficits of older adults' abilities as compared to younger adults' for tasks which are not equally salient for these two cohorts. The long-standing examples are speed of response and aspects of fluid intelligence. The double jeopardy results in two ways. First, we have not yet asked enough questions about the developmental differences between and within cohorts, and what the significance of these differences is in terms of learning and education in the later years. And second, we have not asked enough questions about the influence of life events on what is learned. We know far too little about learning and education as they influence life-span development.

What *do* we currently know about the learning potential and adaptive plasticity of the older adult? Cross-sectional, longitudinal, and cross-sequential research designs have contributed to the findings to date. According to Denny (1984), in cross-sectional and longitudinal studies older adults show declines in performance, with declines occurring later in the case of longitudinal studies. Willis (1985) noted different trends in cross-sequential studies. The following comments summarize the basic literature.

According to Denny (1979, 1984), there generally seems to be an increase in verbal ability throughout most of the life span with a possible drop in this ability for some adults in their late sixties and early seventies. There seems to be a decline in nonverbal ability (performance, perceptual-motor speed, etc.) that begins in early adulthood and continues throughout the balance of the life span. The point and rate of decline in verbal and nonverbal abilities depend on the type of ability tested and the "history" of the adult being tested. This history reflects continuing episodes of learning and education.

In an extensive review of literature of the older adult's intellectual and cognitive abilities, Willis (1985) presents the life-span developmental view. She reports that Schaie's (1983) cohort-cross-sequential studies demonstrate that the peak performance levels in verbal abilities, reasoning, word fluency, spatial orientations, and number skills continue to improve through the fourth decade. Furthermore, she reports that the data indicate that verbal abilities, spatial orientations, and reasoning continue to exceed those of 25-year-olds well into the sixth decade. Even in the eighth decade, older adults retain a full 80% of these capacities, except for number skills (see Figure 3-1).

Willis suggests that these data are the basis of an "index of educational aptitude" for adults who continue to pursue academic studies in traditional educational settings. Reflecting on these data, one can ask the question: What are the developmental purposes for the persistence of these cognitive abilities so late in the life span? Willis does not suggest that they are the abilities of exceptional older adults, but of those who have had access to and pursued learning throughout the life course. This seems similar to the "optimally exercised potential" Denny (1984) is testing.

Most studies to date suggest an age-effect and cohort-effect on changes in

FIGURE 3-1   Performance at various ages as a proportion of performance at age 25.

Source: Willis, 1984. Reprinted by permission of Van Nostrand Reinhold.

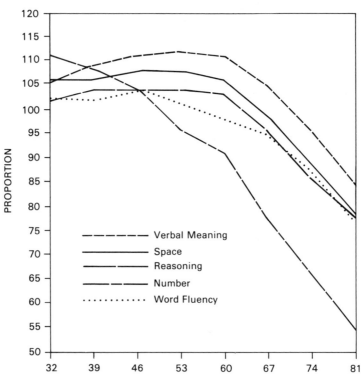

learning potential. The single variable most predictive of these changes is education. In the age-effect studies (cross-sectional), the number of years at school and sometimes measures of adult education represent education; while in the cohort-effect studies (longitudinal and cross-sequential) education means not only traditional schooling, but also adult education and the number of years since these experiences. Regardless of the type of learning intervention or training used to enhance cognitive abilities (modeling, direct instruction, feedback, practice, motivation, and the like), adults in the later years do learn. Modeling, direct instruction, and feedback are particularly effective interventions for the same type of problem-solving tasks that are ultimately used as criteria. Training studies tend to show that older adults learn more quickly and seem better able to generalize than younger ones (on some problem-solving tasks), thus suggesting that they may not be learning a new strategy but just "rediscovering" one that is already in their repertoire. If this is so, then we need to know more about skills for the incorporation of new and the transformation of existing abilities and knowledge in terms of recall and recognition. Regarding age- or cohort-effects, it is clear that adults living today and cohorts yet to enter adulthood will have received different types and amounts of education. Thus we need to know how these different learning histories affect life-span development.

Less obvious variables than education affect life-span learning: for example, reading, television viewing, traveling, social interactions, and other leisure-time pursuits. Other variables currently receiving considerable attention are nutrition, physical exercise, illness, and drug consumption. Not only do these variables influence learning abilities, but learning is essential to understand their influence and to accommodate lifestyle changes when that becomes necessary.

According to Sterns and Sanders (1980), a good deal is known about cognitive training potential in adulthood: (1) task analysis is helpful in the training of complex tasks; (2) basic and subordinate tasks must be learned or mastered before superordinate tasks can be learned; and (3) material must be organized and presented in meaningful ways. There is considerable literature on the presentation of information for effective learning. However, the comparative efficacy of alternate training methods and techniques is largely unexplored, particularly the durability and transfer of learning (see Uman and Richardson in this volume). Sterns and Sanders (1980) support the position that decline is neither universal nor generalizable to all older adults and all abilities; however, some form of decline is assumed.

The thesis of this chapter is that learned abilities and the processes of learning them are essential to life-span development. Both are necessary for the optimal functioning of the individual and must be continually challenged through use. A metaphor might be helpful here. The brain and the skeletal muscles are both a source of power and a place to do work. Their power is challenged by developmental tasks (work) of thinking, doing, and feeling. In turn the tasks they perform expand their ability as power sources to respond to future developmental tasks and demands. Thus, learning processes and learned abilities are essential for life-span development. However, the inherent power to learn is not necessarily maximized by biological forces of development but by the work that is done—it must be used. "Use it or lose it" is a simple but wise notion regarding learning processes and learned abilities in development. A paradigm of life-span learning is proposed in the next section which brings together the major concepts of development and learning theory as a way of illustrating the thesis and viewing the history of learning as a "biography" of the learner.

CONCEPTUALIZING LEARNING
THROUGH THE LIFE SPAN

Current literature on adult learning provides a rather static view of learning over the life span, a view based on the comparison of life stages rather than on the fluidity of the life course. Usually the phenomena and events that influence learning are treated as discrete and even competing conceptualizations. The position taken here regarding life-span learning is that it is a continuous and transforming process and an accumulative activity. Initial learning, whether cognitive or affective, should of necessity be continually examined by the learner and frequently transformed, particularly in subsequent learning. In this transformation, early learning does not necessarily disappear but becomes a part of the biography of the learner. Over the life span, learning expands one's horizons and potentials, psychologically and socially, "writing" a life history that needs to be "read." Frequently this history of learning may reveal missed learning opportunities of an earlier developmental period, for example, revealing the motivation for going to college at age 70. Or the history may reveal an unresolved personal concern about one's family roots. These are reasons that life review and autobiography activities are so popular in many educational programs for the elderly.

In this section a paradigm is proposed that brings together the major concepts and constructs of development and learning in the life span. The paradigm is intended to provide a more complete image of the factors that shape learning over the life course of individuals as well as a foundation for discussion of life-span education in the next section.

There is no attempt here to discuss the processes of learning *per se,* nor to conjecture whether in fact these processes change over the life span. However, life-span developmental phenomena are discussed that provide the motivation and contingencies for learning and change. For example, Schaie (1979) proposed a theory of cognitive development in a life-span context which implies changing applications for learned cognitive capacities and strategies from childhood to old age: acquisition, achievement, management and executive control, and reintegration; Schaie's theory will be referred to again in the discussion that follows. To illustrate learning over the life span, the next sections will discuss theories of learning, sources of guidance in learning, concerns of learning, social applications of learned abilities, and the "global" direction of learning outcomes. (Chart #1 sketches these phenomena in the life span.)

Life-Span Developmental Periods

Three developmental periods, suggesting the pathway of the life course, will be used to discuss learning over the life span: childhood, adulthood, and elderhood. These periods represent three developmental stages in the life span which can be characterized by major psychosocial forces shaping the course of one's life. They are not a conscious attempt to segment the life span into stages, *per se,* but on the

CHART #1
CONCEPTS OF LEARNING IN A LIFE-SPAN PROGRESSION

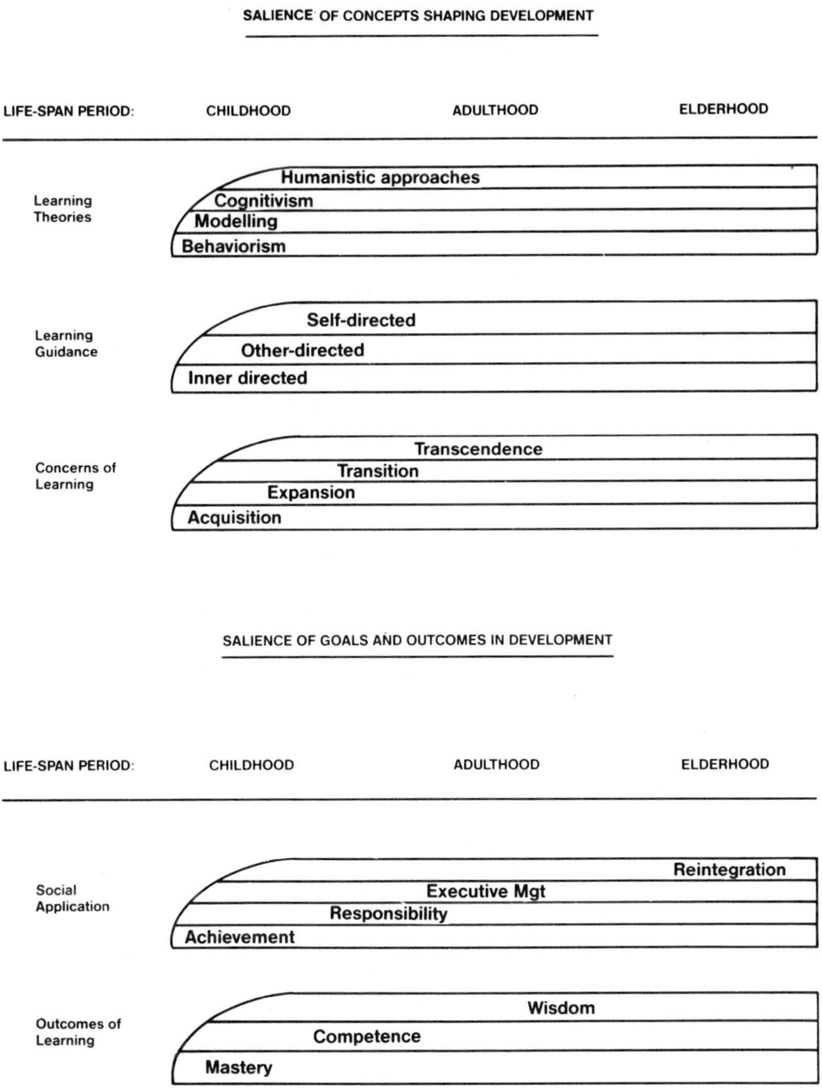

SALIENCE OF CONCEPTS SHAPING DEVELOPMENT

LIFE-SPAN PERIOD:	CHILDHOOD	ADULTHOOD	ELDERHOOD

Learning Theories	Humanistic approaches Cognitivism Modelling Behaviorism
Learning Guidance	Self-directed Other-directed Inner directed
Concerns of Learning	Transcendence Transition Expansion Acquisition

SALIENCE OF GOALS AND OUTCOMES IN DEVELOPMENT

LIFE-SPAN PERIOD:	CHILDHOOD	ADULTHOOD	ELDERHOOD

Social Application	Reintegration Executive Mgt Responsibility Achievement
Outcomes of Learning	Wisdom Competence Mastery

contrary to compress stages currently found in the literature; for example, childhood, adolescence, youth, adulthood, middle age, old age (young-old and old-old) (see Hareven, 1982).

These periods involve broad developmental themes and tasks which emerge and abate, becoming antecedents to subsequent forces of a later period. However, the timing of transitions across periods is influenced by interactions between the individual and relevant relationships (the context) as much as by individual development. An attempt is also made here to arrive at a perspective of old age—elderhood—that is understood and defined by these antecedent themes and tasks and their emergence, salience, and resolution as life events. The elderhood period is being shaped by our changing expectations of the later years and by social institutions concerned with older people (see, for example, Fitzgerald, 1983).

Childhood covers the period from birth and infancy to late adolescence. Adulthood covers the period after late adolescence to late middle age, while elderhood covers the period from late middle age to terminal decline and death. At the outset we must recognize that these developmental periods are not used to suggest mutually exclusive age-graded stages of life based on chronological age—there is much fluidity and openness in the life course and the timing of life events. Each developmental period in Chart #1 has its own unique life events, the exact timing of which may vary in individual lives. For example, one individual will marry and become a parent at 17 while another individual will marry and become a parent at 35, and a third might be a grandparent by 35. For this discussion, however, there is a need to simplify representation of the life span in order to make the main point: that learning through the life course offers a history of learning and a biography of a learner which provide a foundation for subsequent attempts to learn.

Nonetheless, childhood, adulthood, and elderhood can be reasonably demarcated by two developmentally significant rites of passage in our society: (1) the socially and legally determined "age of majority" between childhood and adulthood, and (2) the transition from work to retirement. It is not the exact age at which these occur that is significant, but rather the period of the life course and the psychosocial expectations and demands that come or go with transition and passage from one period to another. Both of these rites of passage, although somewhat arbitrary and idiosyncratic for each individual, are the two most relevant historical and culturally normative influences on development, learning, and education. They provide the basic expectations and sanctions shaping one's roles and social goals over the life span. For example, the linearity and exact timing of the youth-education-work-retirement paradigm, the linear life plan, is changing in most industrial societies. However, what is not likely to change are the developmental tasks associated with these events regardless of when they occur. As the linear life plan changes, there will be considerable change in when people learn and for what purposes. Thus, learning activities and educational efforts will be needed to maximize the use of human resources at all ages. According to Rosenmayr (1982), "A longitudinal view of life seems to be an appropriate method for establishing the prerequisites of retraining, of adjustments in later phases of life, preparation for retirement, and so on" (p. 28).

In Chart #1, word-concepts characterizing developmental phenomena are arrayed so as to suggest the general upward-sloping curve of the life span that typifies most diagrammatic representations (see, for example, Baltes, 1979; Denny, 1984; Schaie, 1979; Willis, 1985). In this regard, it is notable that initial and succeeding concepts continue to have salience over the life span to some degree, and set the stage for succeeding development, thereby characterizing both life span and life space dynamics. The uppermost word-concepts, for example "reintegration" and "wisdom" (Chart #1) represent the salient goals of growth (life space) in the life span.

Wedemeyer's (1981) discussion of life-span learning in part influences the chart. He named the foci of life span learning "survival learning" (infancy), "surrogate learning" (childhood), and "independent learning" (adulthood) within the context of traditional versus nontraditional learning situations. As terms characterizing learning over the life span, for purposes of this paper, they do not clearly differentiate it from concepts of education. Nonetheless, his formulation offers a starting point.

Learning Concepts Shaping Development

Learning theories. Numerous learning theories explain how the individual acquires information and becomes knowledgeable, develops complex physical and cognitive skills and strategies, and organizes feelings and belief systems. The major schools that characterize these theories are behaviorism, social learning or modeling, cognitivism, and the humanistic psychological approach. Each school claims its territory and its role in learning specific behaviors. No single theory can explain all learning although this has been attempted (see, for example, Skinner, 1971, 1976). In a life-span learning perspective, learning theory includes both intrinsic (endogenous) and extrinsic (exogenous) phenomena which cue either a readiness of the learner or a time imperative to learn. These "cues" might produce an ordering and staging of learning as proposed in Chart #1.

An infant's learning is mysterious since the infant must learn the most complex things: discriminating sounds and symbols, speaking, and gaining control of one of the most complicated bodies in the world. Much of this early learning is in response to maturational forces and environmental cues typically excluded from learning theory. However, learning during this period provides the essential *substrata of affect and experience* that will influence almost all subsequent learning behaviors and activities. This linkage of maturation, development, and learning continues through the life span. Thus, early life-span learning provides the foundation for the autobiography and "biography" of a learner (understanding of self and by others), a foundation which must be understood in physiological, psychological, social, and environmental phenomena which are transformed continuously through learning (see Rosenmayr, 1982).

During early infancy, operant theories of behaviorism along with social modeling theories respond to and effectuate the inner-directed forces to learn. The affective (bonding) relationship between parent and child further shapes significant early learning. Subsequently, cognitivist theories predominate in facilitating acquisition of complex intellectual skills and cognitive strategies (Piagetian formal operations). Humanistic psychological approaches predominantly facilitate interpersonal explorations, expansion of ego and moral development, and the assumption of responsibilities for self and others, particularly beginning in late adolescence.

In adulthood and elderhood learning is a very eclectic affair. Some learning episodes concern increasingly particularized needs of individuals while other episodes concern generalized development and growth. The determination of needs and goals is influenced by a normative paradigm of life-span development and dominated by the socialization and enculturation needs of society, particularly the assumption of social roles and behaviors. Developmental concerns are dominated by prescriptive tasks to be mastered by the increasingly competent individual: intellectual skills and knowledge, intra- and interpersonal social behaviors, esthetic sensibilities and affective behaviors (see, for example, Havighurst, 1972; Kohlberg, 1973; Piaget, 1972; Wedemeyer, 1981). During this long period it is expected that adults assume responsibility for their continuing learning needs for the balance of the life course: to become lifelong learners. Unfortunately, according to Overly et al. (1980), "What appears to be missing at present (in childhood education) in the innovations, projects, and programs reviewed is a conscientious effort to develop in students a commitment to learning throughout their lives" (p. 24). Without this foundation adults will find it difficult to acquire many of the skills of lifelong learning independently of educational opportunity. Tough's work (1978, 1982) indicates that adults do engage in many learning projects, but issues of motivation, efficiency, or effectiveness of intentional change strategies have not been completely studied in a life-span perspective.

Learning guidance. Early learning, that is, the inner-directed learning of infancy, largely occurs in response to maturational forces that are innate. Soon after this period, as the infant continues to grow, significant people and events externally stimulate learning; thus, learning cues are increasingly other-directed. For self-directed learning, the learner assumes control and responsibility for growth in ego and social maturity (achievement, responsibility, integrity, self-actualization, and wisdom). Self-direction is the ultimate expression of the learning potential for self-actualization. Self-directed learning dominates the adult's motivation to accommodate personal change and adapt to life events. Self-direction in learning is the most powerful force for mastering the maturing and differentiating forces of experience, for acquiring competence, and for acquiring the wisdom that comes with self-fulfillment and self-realization.

In all paradigms of change, taking responsibility for self is the essential motivator for growth. Self-direction is not to be confused with locus of control: self-direction is the basic strategy for characterizing the development of the individual over time, while locus of control provides basic tactics for dealing with life events. There is some evidence that internality does increase with age, supporting the idea of self-directing strategies as the major concern of learning through the adult years into elderhood (Birren et al., 1983). Perhaps self-direction is one goal of being human, essential for adaptation and social evolution.

Learning is the activity of the individual, although it occurs sometimes within conditions established by others. The learner is always the gatekeeper of what is to be learned. Teachers, curricula, programs, institutions, and media are all available means to facilitate learning either by self-directed events or other-directed instruction. The point is that learning and teaching are not synonymous; they do not involve the same operations and one is not irrevocably linked with the other (see, for example, Wedemeyer, 1981, pp. 37 and 207). Nonetheless, a great deal of time and money in education supports the assumption that learning and teaching *are* synonymous or at least interdependent. Thus, if adults have difficulty with self-directed learning and intentional change it is largely because they have been led to believe that learning is something that happens only when someone teaches.

Concerns of learning. When one looks at the human life course a perspective emerges of the major concerns of learning during particular periods. Early studies of individual biographies completed by Buhler (1953) clearly outlined these concerns. Subsequent research has identified the maturational, psychosocial, and socio-cultural forces which shape developmental concerns of individuals throughout the life course (see, for example, Erikson, 1963; Havighurst, 1972; Rosenmayr, 1982). In a life-span learning progression, the years of childhood are primarily concerned with acquisition of knowledge, skills, and affective repertoires which contribute to mastery of one's abilities to interact in socially appropriate ways. During the adult years acquisition learning continues as adults expand their social interactions into increasingly more complex social relationships. The extended period of adult-hood offers extensive learning tasks in the continuous transitions among social relationships and events, often transforming them (see, for example, Aslanian and Brickell, 1980; Gould, 1978; Peck, 1956; Sheehy, 1977). Typical examples of tran-sitional and transformational events are the continuous redefinition of parental and worker roles as individual, family, and work careers unfold (Elder, 1979). In later adulthood and elderhood, learning tasks emerge for retirement and alternative work-leisure patterns. During elderhood these tasks are directed toward integrating one's past with current experiences in order to resolve issues of fulfillment, worth, being-becoming, and transcending one's physical limitations and life-expectancy (Erikson, 1963; Havighurst, 1968; McClusky, 1971; Peck, 1956).

Salience of Goals and Outcomes in Development

Social applications. Schaie's (1979) theory of cognitive development pro-vides a framework for describing social applications of life-span learning. During transition phases of childhood and early adulthood the individual is expected to master effective social role behaviors (independence, responsibility) and placements (parent and family, worker and citizen, etc.). During adulthood there is sometimes a need to learn extraordinarily complex behaviors and, frequently, contradictory demands of managing complex social institutions and systems. In the later years, the imposed expectations for changes in work/retirement and the innate drive to refocus induces reintegration of cognitive and social repertoires. Havighurst (1968) described this as a refocusing of one's past into the present in order to derive a *meaning of life* for the present: the act of reviewing one's "biography" and, poten-tially, the emergence of wisdom (Clayton and Birren, 1980).

Each life-span period demands a qualitatively higher order of cognitive be-haviors and performance capacities: childhood demands achievement; adulthood, responsibility and executive management; and elderhood, reintegration. Funda-mental questions describing the cognitive development of the individual are: What should be known? How will it be used? And why should it be known? (Schaie, 1979). The content and conditions of learning for achievement, for assuming re-sponsibility and executive management, and, finally, for reintegration of one's "biography" are strikingly different. Nonetheless, Schaie's stage theory of cogni-tive development suggests that these are the essential prerequisites for subsequent mastery of life-course events, for a sense of competency and self-efficacy, and for the wisdom associated with "successful aging."

Outcomes of learning. In global terms the learning outcomes which each life-span period achieves are: for childhood, mastery; for adulthood, competence; and for elderhood, wisdom. To achieve mastery the child must learn fundamental social-personal skills and sensibilities. This mastery is the essential foundation for the adult to perform and adjust competently in ever-changing life events. In the later years, life-span learning outcomes involve extracting, reintegrating, and retelling the meaning of life experiences—this is the foundation of wisdom. The meaning of being human and becoming a person depends not only on increasing the capacity to know and perform, but also to become wiser in the process (see Moody, this volume).

In more specific terms, learning outcomes have been characterized as developmental concerns (Havighurst, 1972; Wedemeyer, 1981) and needs (McClusky, 1971). The intensity of a concern (motivational force) to influence learning depends upon: the stage of development, time, availability of resources, perception of task and formulation of goals and desired outcomes, as well as the interpersonal relationships in the situation.

A life-span developmental view increasingly interests educators because they greatly depend on "being protected from false assumptions" about what to teach and when, according to Reinert (1980). In particular, educators may view the developmental perspective as suggesting "the correct timing of education" (Reinert, 1980) or the "teachable moment" (Havighurst, 1972). Among the "false assumptions" to be avoided are: (1) Timing in the law of development is *not* dependent on learning. Change at any age is the product of *both* development and learning, each modifying the other. (2) Even though different individuals need to resolve a particular developmental task at the same time, the content of the task will *not* be the same. The course of development and the history of the individual modify and modulate these differences in developmental tasks (see Rosenmayr, 1982). These aspects of life-span learning for development must be understood if we are to establish educational policy appropriate to the concerns or needs of individuals and of an aging society. The next section discusses concepts shaping an expanded view of life-span education, and supporting the concept of life-span learning.

CONCEPTUALIZING EDUCATION
THROUGH THE LIFE SPAN

Educational Configurations

Fundamental to the imperative of learning through the life span is the idea that "educating" a person requires the efforts of many institutions; it is not the sole function of a single institutional group such as the schools. Learning opportunities exist in all social institutions—all can perform an educative function and contribute significantly to individual and group development (see, for example, Cremin, 1976; Essert and Spence, 1968; Heimstra, 1972; Houle, 1972; Verner and Booth, 1964; Wedemeyer, 1981).

Both other-directed and self-directed education efforts involve the social institutions, conditions, and processes created by the self or by others to influence and enhance an individual's learning. These educational efforts are the basis for dynamic growth and the innovativeness of a society. As such, education and educative processes are undertaken at almost any place by any person or group of persons who desire to learn something in a vast array of potential configurations (Cremin, 1976; Houle, 1972). Basic concepts that influence the configurations are outlined in Chart #2. [The charting conventions in Chart #2 are the same as those used in Chart #1 (see page 71).]

CHART # 2
CONCEPTS OF EDUCATION IN A LIFE-SPAN PROGRESSION

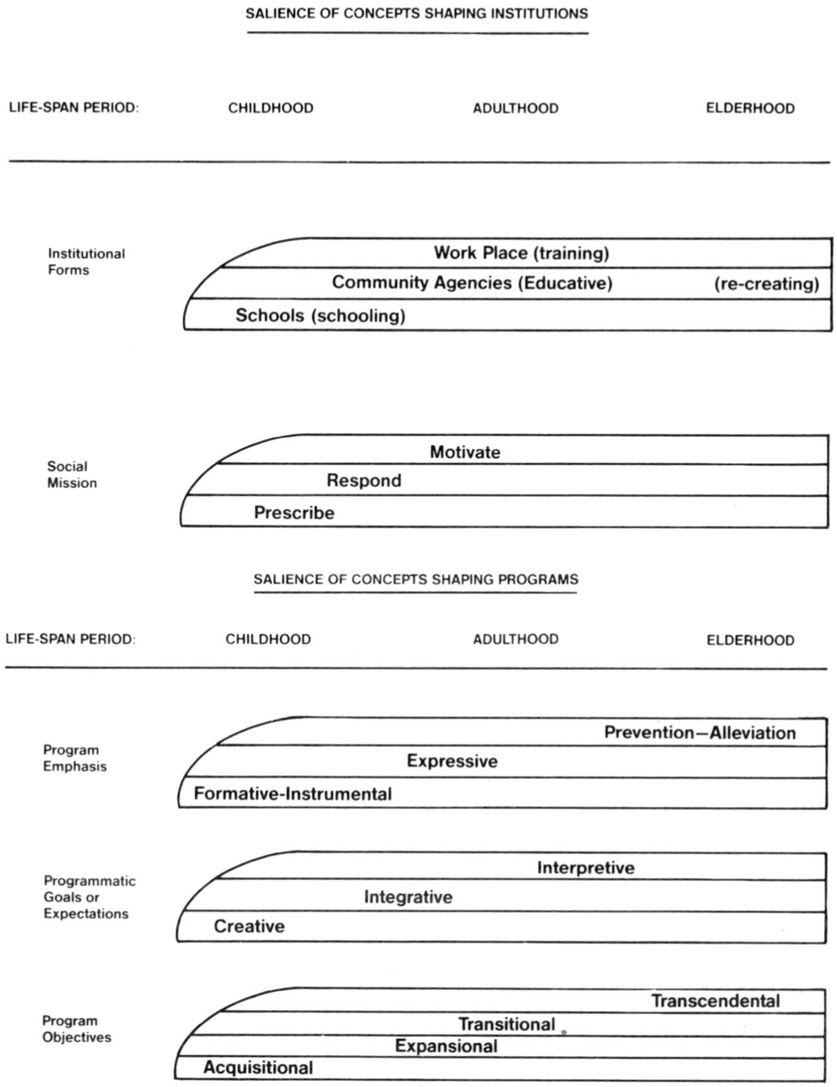

SALIENCE OF CONCEPTS SHAPING INSTITUTIONS

LIFE-SPAN PERIOD:	CHILDHOOD	ADULTHOOD	ELDERHOOD

Institutional Forms		Work Place (training)	
		Community Agencies (Educative)	(re-creating)
	Schools (schooling)		

Social Mission		Motivate	
	Respond		
	Prescribe		

SALIENCE OF CONCEPTS SHAPING PROGRAMS

LIFE-SPAN PERIOD:	CHILDHOOD	ADULTHOOD	ELDERHOOD

Program Emphasis			Prevention—Alleviation
		Expressive	
	Formative-Instrumental		

Programmatic Goals or Expectations			Interpretive
		Integrative	
	Creative		

Program Objectives			Transcendental
		Transitional	
		Expansional	
	Acquisitional		

The term *education,* as used in this chapter, "is the deliberate, systematic, and sustained effort to transmit, evoke, or acquire knowledge, attitudes, values, skill and sensibilities, as well as any outcomes of the effort" (Cremin, 1976, p. 27). In this definition, the phrase "to acquire knowledge" refers to educational activities and techniques and not the learning processes for acquisition of knowledge.

There are difficulties with this broad concept of education in terms of public policy and social resource allocation. These difficulties involve issues regarding:

(1) the *curriculum* or the *program* of the institutional group, (2) the extent to which the public accepts or places value on the content and its objectives and out-comes, and (3) funding mechanisms and public resources. These issues are most clearly discerned in the funding mechanisms that characteristically give higher priority to manpower training and employment and adult basic education pro-grams, as opposed to liberal adult education or retirement education. Public fund-ing supports the former because there is a discernible or imputed link with social and economic goals. On the other hand, it is more difficult to establish a similar direct linkage of education for continuing development in the later years with social and economic goals; consequently, such programs that do develop become far too altruistic. There is, however, greater attention being given to exercise and other health-promoting programs which ultimately impact on social and economic goals.

Life-span education beyond public schooling is an eclectic affair in terms of sequencing and rationalizing significant episodes of learning. Public schooling orga-nizes what is to be learned and in what order by its curriculum. However, after public schooling, life-span education must develop its programs from individuals' "unfolding careers" (family, work, and leisure) for which the timing and content of episodes is not easily established. Many of these episodes involve life-span learn-ing experiences outside of formal education. Thus, life-span education during child-hood is generally conceived of as adding to a limited experience base, while during adulthood and elderhood life-span education becomes a transformational activity: not only acquiring new knowledge, experience, and affect, but transforming what is already known in the process.

Salience of Concepts Shaping Institutional Forms

Institutional forms. Chart #2 suggests three major institutional forms of education: those associated with publicly and privately funded schools; those asso-ciated with the workplace; and those which are community-based and specific. In this analysis the first category, schools, includes: public and private elementary schools, junior- and senior-secondary schools, postsecondary schools, and higher education. Educative institutions in the workplace include: agencies and organi-zations where people work, and educational institutions that are proprietary. Community-based agencies are those primarily government-sponsored (such as pub-lic health agencies and recreation programs), or those sponsored by any number of special interest organizations (such as the YM/YWCA, churches, community cen-ters, and the Red Cross). Over the life span, individuals pursue their learning inter-ests and developmental concerns in any one or more of these institutions at the same time. These categories represent the *educative configurations* (Cremin, 1976) in the educative community (Essert and Spence, 1968; Heimstra, 1972; Verner and Booth, 1964).

The term *re-creating,* as used in Chart #2, means primarily renewal of the individual's potential which includes forms of recreation. For children and young adults, community agencies provide primarily recreation, for example, sports and social skills. For older adults, agencies should be working with the individual to re-create his or her potentials, for example, maintaining social networks, well-being clinics, and experiences in guided autobiography.

Social mission. Three words characterize the current social mission of educational configurations in the community throughout the life span: prescribe, respond, and motivate. Each concept attempts to capture the main social expectation and policy perspectives shaping life-span education and educative institutions. Most educative institutions share several goals, as Houle (1984) suggests, and diverse audiences; but their main social missions organize into a hierarchy of prescribe, respond, and motivate. These are not presented in Chart #2 as age-linked activities, *per se,* but are developmentally linked and are accumulative in the hierarchy. Childhood education and schools have legally mandated missions and their programs are prescribed. This prescription outlines what it is that the schooling is expected to accomplish. Adult education is sanctioned by legislative policy but financial support for it is minimal, except in the case of manpower training. Consequently, adult education responds to the expressed needs of individuals and groups of individuals in the community and in the workplace. A good deal of training and increasingly more human-potential education is accomplished, however, in the workplace. In elderhood, the major issue is not simply responding to the needs of older persons, but instead motivating them as learners toward greater participation in social and educational opportunity. Current programs, however, are directed to those elderly with less pressing psychosocial needs; most statistics of participation rates in organized adult education clearly delineate this problem (see Peterson, this volume). The adult education cliché is "those who need it least, get it most." If learning is considered essential for maximizing life-span development and optimizing the individual life course, then the imperative is to motivate many of the elderly to pursue learning in the community.

Life-span learning as a concept for life-span development implies that educative opportunities are accessible. Some opportunities can be provided by traditional organizations and others by nontraditional organizations, while many others are created by individuals as self-directed learners (Tough, 1978, 1982). However, agencies and programs able to respond to the life-span learning needs of older people must involve a broader spectrum and larger educative configuration of social support services, community centers, health care systems, church groups, community volunteer and self-help groups, etc., than those obtainable in the education sector (see, for example, Okun, 1982). The opportunities to maximize the "teachable moment" are numerous and require trained personnel who know how to capitalize on these opportunities in any setting. A clear understanding of the scope of life-span learning is essential for the development of a life-span educational policy.

Salience of Concepts Shaping Programs

Program emphasis. Instrumental and expressive orientations characterize most educative programs, the mix depending on the goals of the institution and the concerns of the learner. Havighurst (1976) noted that "the distinction between the instrumental and expressive aspects of education should not be carried too far. There is some intrinsic enjoyment in almost every instrumental form of education, at least if the learner is reasonably successful; and there is some instrumental or extrinsic outcome from almost every expressive form of education" (p. 42). This is the position being proposed here. Thus, a program may emphasize primarily one of these orientations, for example, exercise and nutrition programs which are largely instrumental; however, an expressive element is also necessary to sustain interest and motivation and to enhance success. The concept of program as it is used here refers to the general program of an institution, for example, schooling, recreation, or health education, and to specific activities and events (Thomas, 1964).

During childhood, the major developmental emphasis of educative programs is formative-instrumental. Program efforts are directed toward educating the child with a view to optimizing maturation and development (formative), and providing skills of learning (instrumental) for future benefit. The maturing learner during adulthood needs, in addition to that, the instrumental competencies for social role performance and expressive enrichment to derive success and enjoyment out of current educational activity. During the elderhood period, instrumental and expressive orientations become more diffuse as many older people require educational support with a preventative and alleviative emphasis (Birren and Woodruff, 1973).

Birren and Woodruff (1973) discussed program emphases for educational interventions in the life of older adults as immediate efforts to alleviate current deprivations, and long-term efforts at prevention and continuing enrichment. Peterson (1983) noted that many types of education (instrumental and expressive) for the elderly are of value and will continue to expand. However, he identified three major areas in which social need and collective preference encourage further educational development: financial independence, health maintenance, and community involvement. These are extremely relevant to general social policy (instrumental-preventative), but offer a limited educational formula for personal growth and enrichment (expressive).

Programmatic goals and expectations. During childhood, educational programs must maximize creative capacity by providing fundamental skills for thinking and doing (traditional reasoning and lateral problem-solving). In adulthood, most program goals concern integrating and consolidating role behaviors and social competencies. Finally, in elderhood, programmatic goals focus on interpretation, meaning, and self-fulfillment. These programmatic goals provide the umbrella under which learners can explore learning activities essential to their continuing development. None of these programmatic goals are successfully obtained at any age if the basic quality of life is poor or deprived.

There are many conceptions of how life-span education could best serve individuals and society. Houle (1984) identified at least five major goal patterns: (1) education as the entire purpose of life—the contemplative life; (2) education as a way of examining life—chiefly as a way to refine it; (3) education as an inherent part of a complex pattern of life—chiefly as an activity that in a variety of ways helps to achieve the diverse goals of human existence; (4) education as mastery of all knowledge—the renaissance man; and (5) education as a way of preserving or perfecting the state. According to Houle (1984), life-span learning suggests two designs of life-span education which he designates as the "stages of life" approach and the "sequential patterns of learning" approach. The first approach requires defining the kinds of education appropriate during each life stage, while the second approach requires analyzing how patterns of "learning shift (or can be made to shift) with advancing age" (p. 244). The sequential patterns of learning and education approach are fundamental to the position being developed here.

In more specific terms, Mc Clusky (1971) suggested five major goals for education in late life: (1) to help older people fulfill their lifetime potential; (2) to assist older people in contributing their wisdom to society; (3) to promote older people as models of lifelong fulfillment; (4) to help older people meet particular needs; and (5) to gain access to older people who are hidden or isolated from the mainstream of the community.

The concept of need is unfortunate in educational terms, not because it is not real but because need implies deficit, thus obscuring broader developmental concerns. The concept of need puts stress on providing education as compared to facilitating learning for growth and empowerment, an important distinction for the older adult. This is a fundamental problem in the education of older people: a problem of access and empowerment versus prescription and service. The emergence of educational concepts like andragogy (a problems orientation) and gerongogy (an aging orientation) is of little help. Neither of these conceptual approaches adequately incorporates a developmental-differentiating–reintegrative life-span and life-course perspective. Furthermore, these educational concepts reflect current social stereotypes and program modalities in human services (e.g., health care and education) responding to perceived social deficits of individuals when the deficits are often imposed by the social context in which individuals find themselves.

From a life-span developmental perspective, educational goals in the later years involve a significant effort to interpret one's experience and the meaning of one's life. The program goals proposed in Chart #2 capture Houle's (1972, 1984) and Mc Clusky's (1971) ideas.

Program objectives. There are general expectations regarding the content and the outcomes of education for children and young adults; however, there is limited consensus as to what adult education throughout the life span should accomplish. And there is *no* consensus about the desired outcomes of education for older adults, even though there is general consensus regarding their prescriptive and motivational needs. We need to rethink the functions of education as an investment in both social and individual terms as we move from an industrial to a postindustrial society. We need to adapt nineteenth- and early twentieth-century educational thinking to the new reality of aging in an information and learning society (see Long and Moody, this volume). We need to focus on education's role in changing social mores and expectations from a youth to an adult orientation, and technology's impact on human experience; we need a broader view of education as strategy for individual *and* social change.

INTERVENTION AND ADULT EDUCATION

The concepts of life-span learning and education are heavily laden with notions of intervention and planned change. Intervention and planned change are programmatic attempts to induce, stimulate, or anticipate growth and learning. At one level, society provides an educational system which undertakes systematic planned change in nearly everyone: schooling for social, cultural, and personal development during childhood and early adulthood. At another level, individuals engage in self-education and learning to accommodate efforts at intentional change, growth, and adaptation throughout adulthood (Tough, 1982). Life-span learning concepts discussed in Chart #1 identified developmental phenomena that cue and motivate these efforts at developmental change. Concepts of life-span education discussed in Chart #2 identified the educative configurations and social forces facilitating life-span learning and intentional change. This section will briefly deal with aspects of programmatic intervention and adult education that shape life-span education, particularly in the second half of life.

Interventions

Educational programs are interventions which contribute to the development, socialization, and resocialization of individuals and groups of individuals. Health care systems and social service programs are intervention strategies directed to physical and mental health concerns. Interventions are also found in sociopolitical and mass media programs of persuasion and propaganda. Whatever the institutional form, interventions are efforts to change people through learning, persuasion, or force.

Baltes (1973) suggested that the concept of intervention is "apt for the analysis of society's effect on the individual as well as the individual's effect on his own and society's development" (p. 4). According to this view, traditional public schooling and formal adult education and training ought to be used as interventions to enhance the ability of individuals to become lifelong learners, and become "self-directed" in these efforts (see, for example, Tough, 1978, 1982). So for self-direction to flourish, a democratic society provides people the skills, resources, and opportunities necessary to take control of their own destinies—both as lifelong learners and as self-constructing individuals. If we hold these views of education as intervention, then life-span learning and education become very powerful concepts for growth and change within individuals and society (Thomas, 1983).

Normative paradigms.   According to Looft (1973), there are intricate interactions of experience and behavior (biopsychological or neuropsychological) in the ontogeny of the aging phenomena in humans. Consequently, Looft suggests that our search for what might be termed *normal aging* is futile. One would expect, then, that the use of normative paradigms of education for aging people would be inappropriate—except on grounds of political philosophy, policy, regulatory requirements, and the like—irrespective of the aging experience. Perhaps normative paradigms of education (which delineate what "ought to be") are more useful to meet our professional expectations than are non-normative paradigms of the aging experience ("what is"). Certainly, a normative educational paradigm is programmatically simpler—that is, everyone gets the same learning experience. Education and learning in the later years, however, must be informed by the individual's idiosyncratic "history of learning," experience, and present social context. Because this will produce such a variety of individualistic life scripts, cues for learning and educational interventions are anything but normative for older adults. Furthermore, if learning results from experience, the learning activities must be informed by past and present experiences of the individual; and these experiential patterns, like fingerprints, are unique. A normative paradigm of education in the later years, applied irrespective of what we know about the individual's experience or present situation, is antithetical to the aging experience. Programmatic interventions are handy when based on norms because they are administratively convenient within a policy framework; but they generate programs likely to be ineffectual in practice. One example of this is suggested in Rosenmayr's (1982) discussion of the multifactorial nature of cumulative disadvantages and deprivations among the elderly.

> Differences among socioeconomic strata are thus greater among the elderly than among the younger- (childhood) and middle-age (adulthood) cohorts. This is because of greater differences in their *initial* social situations and of biographically created conditions that lead to a progressive reduction of chances of the deprived of coping with their aging processes (p. 46, parenthetical statements added).

The current interest in autobiographical activity for older people results in part from the flexible, non-normative approach of the educational activity. It can accommodate extremely variant life experiences among individuals seemingly from the same age and historical cohort.

Age irrelevance.   It has been argued that age *per se* is not very useful for understanding the demands of life-span development. This argument states that the older adult's needs (health care, education, social services) are not bounded by age in any significant way (Neugarten, 1982); i.e., children and young adults have the same needs. According to Schaie (1973):

> Adult psychological and physiological functions required to sustain socially significant behaviors are not subject to normal age decrements . . . . A mature and civilized society, which intends to stabilize its population at an optimal level, does not need to discriminate against any age group in the allocation of its resources, economic rewards and social roles (p. 33).

Schaie provides several corollaries to these two basic assumptions: (1) Age changes often occur from environmental insults and can be eliminated by adjustments in life support systems, (2) traumatic events impair functional capacities at all ages, (3) behavior decrements in the elderly are due to "perceived" age-graded role expectations, (4) rewards and roles should be assigned as a function of present contributions regardless of age, (5) compulsory retirement should be abandoned, and (6) adequate opportunities for leisure pursuits should be provided to all ages and should not be a special privilege of the young or old. When we have accomplished these social tasks, we will have a more liberating view of life-span education and learning. The information era and the technological revolution that spawned it may release people from categories bounded by chronological age, and provide adults of all ages with the tools to continue learning and contributing. Certainly access to information will become easier for those who possess these skills (see, for example, Quarton, 1968).

The point is that age is largely irrelevant for understanding the learning and educational concerns of individuals. These concerns when they emerge are to be understood in the context of the life course regarding such things as family, work, and leisure careers. At any point in the life span, changes in family, work, careers, and retirement, as developmental concerns, can serve as the bases of learning.

Technology. New technology is potentially very subversive in social terms. If the innovations in mass communications of the 1940s and 1950s created the *global village,* then the information technology of the 1980s and 1990s offers to transform us into *global citizens,* empowering and enfranchising those who have access to information in ways unimaginable to most of us today. Access in these cases is probably a solvable technological problem, but it very well may become a sociopolitical problem as well: information shared, possessed, withheld, or managed represents power. Management of information (withholding and sharing) represents opportunities to intervene as professionals, which in turn has significant ethical implications. The problem here for older adults will not be skills *per se,* but, rather, equal access to information and continued skill development.

Adult Education and Intervention

Verner and Booth (1964) offered a conceptual analysis of adult education as *means* and *ends* in response to the learning needs of individuals and institutions. If conceived of as means, adult education is an instrument for explicit social purposes. Examples are: (1) career preparation and advancement, (2) social role acquisition, (3) enhancement of human productivity in the workplace, (4) enhancement of informed consumerism, (5) facilitation of community development, (6) enhancement of physical and mental health among designated populations, and (7) socialization and resocialization in life-span development. If conceived of as an end in itself, adult education is an instrument for less explicit socially-valued but equally powerful expressive needs for development of human potential and transmission of culture. Examples are: (1) learning for learning's sake, (2) transmission of the collective culture, (3) enhancement of mental and physical well-being within a general concept of leisure, and (4) enhancing lifelong learning. Havighurst (1976) suggested that every educational activity provides both instrumental (means) and expressive (ends) opportunities to varying degrees.

As a means, adult education is discernible as social policy primarily in manpower development and consumer education, or as employee training. Only recently has it been considered as the basis of social policy in other sectors; for example, in health care. Whether as a means or an end, adult education is not guaranteed in most social institutions in any secure or enduring way. This is likely for two reasons: lifelong learning beyond the traditional schooling years has limited endorsement in social policy as essential for social stability or growth; and there are diverse images of what lifelong education should accomplish (see, for example, Houle, 1984). The adult population is expected to respond to problems that they as individuals have in work and career transitions, sometimes for retirement and sometimes for extra leisure time. The social necessity for life-span learning and for developing the lifelong learner has achieved greater recognition but not the mandate for funding commensurate with the changes occurring in our aging society (see, for example, Rubenson, 1982).

The point is that adult education, whether means or ends, must be seen as an essential strategy in the continuing development of individuals and groups, and ultimately society. This perspective of adult education is particularly crucial as knowledge expands and technology becomes more complex. The transition to an information or learning society means that learning must include information and skills about what to know, how to retrieve it, how to know, how to learn about learning, and how to accommodate to change. Thus, as social instrumentality, education in all of its configurations (Cremin, 1976) is both a means and an end.

Adult Education as Activity

All forms of adult educational activity in society are based on the concerns of individuals and groups of individuals to adapt to changes in their lives and situations. Implicit to this approach is the assumption that it is the individual's responsibility to seek out the activity most appropriately meeting his or her individual needs. Adult education programs that respond to these needs have been characterized as "reactive altruism" (Sterns and Sanders, 1980) and "problem oriented" (Knowles, 1980). Thus, programmatic approaches that respond to problems or needs of individuals dominate the literature of adult education far more often than proactive concerns. Consequently, the sociological and psychological rationale is supposedly normative but only in response to the conscious needs of individuals.

Part of adult education's mission is to be an active agent in social and technological change, and its activities ought to be proactive and anticipatory. It must help individuals and groups of individuals to become self-constructing architects of their own futures at all ages, and to shape the social opportunities that change provides.

FUTURE DIRECTIONS

Learning interventions can be developed that are effective in changing individual responses and capacities, as required by social and technological change (Stern and Sanders, 1980). But will these interventions in life-span education effectively maximize self-realization? Or will they be limited to ensure compliance and social control?

Most of the research in educational settings with older adults is anecdotal and descriptive. Certainly there is a need for carefully conceived research involving educational approaches that build on methodologies developed in cognitive intervention studies. However, these studies must be extended beyond the laboratory for a better understanding of cognitive functioning and its relationship to performance of everyday tasks. It appears that we know little about the adult, particularly the older adult learner, in more traditional educational situations; and we know only slightly more in nontraditional situations. We know little about the role of affect in late life and less about how the elderly derive meaning in life. Research has concentrated on characterizing the deficits of aging, but not its strengths. Educators are beginning to explore these themes in programs for older people. Sterns and Sanders (1980) quote the *Torah* for a common wisdom which, perhaps, we would have little difficulty accepting: "For as soon as he ceases to study he forgets." Too often we characterize forgetting as an aging deficit when it might better be considered a learning deficit resulting from discontinuous learning activities.

On a different level of concern, if we are to respond to the educational concerns of increasing numbers of individuals in an aging society, we must merge the
current dominant paradigm of behavioral aging into a contextual paradigm called
experiential aging (Sparks, 1973). This contextual view holds that we consider a
person's behavior (and its change) as a function of time and place. Thus, from a
contextual perspective, the behaviors of an aging individual are a necessary consequence of experience and situations over time. According to this view, intervention
strategies directed at experiences and situations which constrain the individual's
efficacy are more effective to enhance behavior than strategies directed only at
behavior (Schaie, 1973). The argument is that age-graded structures, as the context
of aging, and the organized nature of complex institutions are the major determinants of both experiential and behavioral aging. Social networking and self-help
groups among the elderly are examples of this contextualist experiential view.

If Toffler's (1980) *The Third Wave* and Naisbitt's (1982) *Megatrends* themes
are correct, we should see changes in most age-graded structures resulting from and
enhanced by technology. We are presently seeing these ideas emerge in the self-help
and "networking" movements. Self-help groups and networks are not necessarily
age-related or graded, *per se,* but will be need-related and interest-focused (see
Moody, this volume). And as Schaie (1973) implies, learning adaptive behavior
requires support during life-course transitions for all ages.

> In a complex society which changes very rapidly, however, it is likely that
> there will be at least several points in the life-span when an individual will lose
> his effectiveness, unless he manages to retool, change his job, or start a new
> career. Adaptive behavior is no more likely to occur in such mid-life crises
> than at retirement, if loss of effectiveness in a particular role is perceived as
> the consequence of personal inferiority, or as a natural and irreversible con-
> comitant of chronological aging (p. 34).

Several assumptions and observations Hickey (1974) outlined are pertinent
regarding life-span learning and educational interventions in the life span; i.e., scientific knowledge of what we know about adult learning and the art form of adult
education (see also Houle, 1972; Knowles, 1980). The sciences isolate the key variables in the learning process, and adult education provides the conditions for learning and instruction. The sciences and the art form collaborate in constructing the
methodological framework for program design, implementation, and evaluation.
The art form develops the craft of instruction for learning, and provides the pack-
aging and marketing. The difficulty lies in blending these two aspects—science and
art form—for the benefit of the vast majority of adult learners who are independent, self-directed, and increasingly proactive in their own learning. Furthermore,
social and technological changes increasingly demand an anticipatory approach to
learning at both individual and societal levels. There are far too few studies of the
translation of scientific knowledge regarding learning and aging into forms of proactive and anticipatory life-span education. We know far too little, for example,
of effective ways to prepare for the retirement transition, and of the productive
capacities that can be redirected to enhance the experience of aging over the balance of the life span.

Many older adult learners are being left out of educational opportunity not because they cannot learn or change, but because of prevailing myths and stereo-types about their potentials. There must be more than just a bridge built between the science and art of adult learning and instruction; it must lead to what is to be learned and the context for its use. Consequently, applied research and training in the community is a very real issue in the science and art of programming life-span education, particularly regarding life changes with age: exercise, nutrition, mental activity, and leisure. Programmers in older adult education and training must give greater attention to ensuring that educational activity enhances learning abilities which are, in turn, applied or transferred to everyday situations, behaviors, and per-formances (see Umen, this volume).

In many ways our major educational institutions and programs are focused on "rear-view mirror images" of society, to borrow a phrase from McLuhan. For adult education to become proactive and anticipatory, views of where we seem to be going and want to go must inform our perspectives of individual and social growth. Most educators, including adult educators, are not being trained to "think forward" and to "feed forward." When social and technological change do surface as themes in our deliberations, it is toward helping the individual "respond to" but not "an-ticipate" change. The most self-evident examples are programs for changing careers and retirement which are sporadic and ad hoc, lacking the systematic interventions and necessary social policy to support the significant adaptations and transfor-mation which changing careers and retirement induce (see George, 1980). As our society shifts in an information-driven economy the anticipatory paradigm, of necessity, will dominate most educational programs.

SUMMARY

This chapter has offered two paradigms conceptualizing life-span development, learning, and education. The paradigms characterized the basic role of learning and educative activity in the *push* and *pull* forces associated with development across the life course. The present literature of schooling and adult education does not provide such a paradigm; however, the philosophical, institutional, and psycho-social bases are currently being discussed (see, for example, Cross, 1981; Elias and Merriam, 1980; Long, this volume; Moody, 1976; Wedemeyer, 1981). Without such paradigms we impose concepts such as pedagogy, andragogy, or gerongogy on life-span learning and education for individual development without it being at all clear that any of them are appropriate approaches. Reinert (1980) cautions us not to develop educational concepts (pedagogy, andragogy, gerongogy, etc.) that seg-ment the life span, indicating that emerging models in life-span developmental psy-chology have the advantage of being "heuristically open" (p. 8). We need empirical studies to help us answer questions about how the life span and life course are ex-perienced, and to understand the function of learning and education throughout. We need to know more about methods of meeting the developmental needs of in-dividuals, informed by an awareness of the great degree of diversity among indi-viduals as they age. We need to know about the social meaning of being old in our society. And we need to know about the nature of the human "being" as a meaning–making organism in the context of aging. We need research that explores the linkages between learning and development. We need life-course studies about forms of intentional change and the transformation resulting from the accumulative effects of learning.

Public education in childhood and late adolescence is based on images of mastery of oneself and one's culture, and of behaviors and competencies believed to be individually and socially functional in adulthood. Educational activities are required with reasonably high predictive powers of obtaining these outcomes. Images of adulthood that shape adult education are those of competent adults who react to and solve problems presented by the circumstances of their daily living, life work, and career. This is a largely interpretative statement involving educational activities contributing to current "problem" resolution, although with limited predictive power. Because there are many potential images of aging throughout the life span to guide educational practice, the most frequent response, as noted earlier, can be characterized as "reactive altruism." On the other hand, however, we must not respond in a normative, behavioral modification mode where we—the professionals—intervene. Educative interventions must facilitate individual growth in an interactive social context. Learning and education in all their forms ought to be *anticipatory* and *self-constructing* since they are critical in the life span of individuals of any age. Consequently, the main focus of life-span education as intervention should be to enhance the context of aging so competent people can perform competently. Possibly both learning and education are the essential ratchets in the irreversible time clock of human development and aging because they release the energy and provide the information for change over time and throughout the life course.

We lack images of older people as *people* to guide our educational decisions and influence their life-span learning options (Keith, 1982). Unfortunately, without images we lack maps of the territory older people inhabit. We now know enough about aging and the experiences of old age to begin developing better educational guidelines to enhance the exploration. The question is not whether we can or cannot teach or retrain an older adult. Rather, the questions are "To what end? And why?" The questions are fundamentally social and philosophical. If we fail to support learning and educative opportunity throughout the life span, then the question becomes "What will be the cost in general social well-being, depleted human resources, and dignity for people of all ages, and for our own futures as an aging society?"

What is sketched in this chapter is a view of life-span learning and education fundamental to development of the life course. Present approaches to learning and education are largely dominated by social policy enhancing individual behaviors of the adolescent and adult as instrumental to social goals in increasingly more discrete life stages. Social policies must continually grapple with not only the lengthening life span and the learning this will require, but also the social programs and institutions needed to enhance the aging experience in a more heuristically open life-course perspective.

Although adult education has espoused lifelong learning and education as a social goal, until recently these efforts have lacked an adequate theoretical basis in life-span developmental terms, particularly for the later years. Thus, the view of life-span learning and education developed here attempts to conceptualize them as forces driving development even as they are responding to development. This view attempts to grapple with the "whys" of life-span learning and of life-span education.

REFERENCES

ASLANIAN, C. B., and BRICKELL, H. M. (1980). *Americans in transition: Life changes as reasons for adult learning.* New York: College Entrance Examination Board.

BALTES, P. B. (1973). Introduction: Strategies for psychological intervention in old age: A symposium. *Gerontologist, 13,* No. 1 (Spring), 4-6.

BALTES, P. B. (1979). Life-span developmental psychology. In P. B. Baltes and O. G. Brim, Jr. (Eds.), *Life-span development and behavior.* New York: Academic Press.

BIRREN, J. E., and CUNNINGHAM, W. R. (1985). Research on the psychology of aging: Principles, concepts and theory. In J. E. Birren and K. W. Schaie (Eds.), *Handbook of the psychology of aging.* New York: Van Nostrand Reinhold.

BIRREN, J. E., CUNNINGHAM, W. R., and YAMOMOTO, K. (1983). Psychology of adult development and aging. *Annual Review of Psychology, 34,* 543-575.

BIRREN, J. E., and WOODRUFF, D. S. (1973). Human development over the life span through education. In P. B. Baltes and K. W. Schaie (Eds.), *Life-span developmental psychology.* New York: Academic Press.

BROWN, M. (Ed.) (1978). *Readings in gerontology.* New York: Mosby.

BUHLER, C. (1953). The curve of life as studies in biographies. *Journal of Applied Psychology, 19,* 405-409.

CLAYTON, V. P., and BIRREN, J. E. (1980). The development of wisdom across the life-span: A reexamination of an ancient topic. In P. B. Baltes and O. G. Brim, Jr. (Eds.), *Life-span development and behavior, Vol. 3.* New York: Academic Press.

CREMIN, L. A. (1976). *Public education.* New York: Basic Books.

CROSS, K. P. (1981). *Adults as learners.* San Francisco: Jossey-Bass.

DENNY, N. W. (1979). Problem solving in later adulthood: Intervention research. In P. B. Baltes and O. G. Brim, Jr. (Eds.), *Life-span development and behavior, Vol. 2.* New York: Academic Press.

DENNY, N. W. (1984). A model of cognitive development. *Developmental Review, 4,* 171-191.

EISDORFER, C. (1983). Conceptual models of aging. *American Psychologist,* February, 197-202.

ELDER, G. H., JR. (1979). Historical changes in life patterns and personality. In P. B. Baltes and O. G. Brim, Jr. (Eds.), *Life-span development and behavior, Vol. 2.* New York: Academic Press.

ELIAS, J., and MERRIAM, S. (1980). *Philosophical foundations of adult education.* New York: Kreiger.

ERIKSON, E. H. (1963). *Childhood and society.* New York: W. W. Norton.

ESSERT, P. L., and SPENCE, R. B. (1968). Continuous learning through the educative community: An exploration of the family-educational, the sequential-unit, and the complementary-functional systems. *Adult Educational Journal, XVIII*(4), 260-271.

FITZGERALD, F. (April 25, 1983). A reporter at large: Interlude. *The New Yorker Magazine,* 54.

GEORGE, L. (1980). *Role transitions in later life.* Monterey, California: Brooks/Cole Publishing Co.

GOULD, R. (1978). *Transformations: Growth and change in adult life.* New York: Simon & Schuster.

GOULD, S. J. (1982). *The mismeasure of man.* New York: W. W. Norton.

HAREVEN, T. K. (1982). The life course and aging in historical perspective. In T. K. Hareven and K. J. Adams (Eds.), *Aging and life course transitions: An interdisciplinary perspective.* New York: Guilford Press.

HAVIGHURST, R. J. (1968). A social-psychological perspective on aging. *The Gerontologist, 8*(2), 67–71.

HAVIGHURST, R. J. (1972). *Developmental tasks and education.* New York: McKay.

HAVIGHURST, R. J. (1976). Education through the adult life span. *Educational Gerontology, 1,* 41–51.

HAVIGHURST, R. J. (1979). Older adults and learning activities. Paper presented to The Summer Institute for Educators in Gerontology, The University of B.C., Vancouver.

HEIMSTRA, R. (1972). *The educative community: Linking the community, school, and family.* Lincoln, Nebraska: Professional Educators Publications.

HICKEY, T. (1974). Eclectic model of adult education or (eclecticism deleted)? In R. W. Bortner, S. S. Dubin, D. F. Hultsch, and J. Withall (Eds.), *Adults as learners, Proceedings of a conference.* University Park, Pennsylvania: Pennsylvania State University.

HOULE, C. O. (1972). *The design of education.* San Francisco: Jossey-Bass.

HOULE, C. O. (1984). *Patterns of learning: New perspectives on life-span education.* San Francisco: Jossey-Bass.

HULTSCH, D. F., and DEUTSCH, F. (1981). *Adult development and aging: A life-span perspective.* New York: McGraw-Hill.

HULTSCH, D. F., and PLEMONS, J. K. (1979). Life events and life-span development. In P. B. Baltes and O. G. Brim, Jr. (Eds.), *Life-span development and behavior, Vol. 2.* New York: Academic Press.

KEGAN, M. (1982). *Evolving self: Problem and process in human development.* Cambridge: Harvard University Press.

KEITH, J. (1982). *Old people as people: Social and cultural influences on aging and old age.* Boston: Little, Brown and Co.

KNOWLES, M. S. (1980). *The modern practice of adult education.* New York: Association Press.

KOHLBERG, L. (1973). Continuities in childhood and adult moral development revisited. In P. B. Baltes and K. W. Schaie (Eds.), *Life-span developmental psychology.* New York: Academic Press.

LEVIN, J., and LEVIN, W. C. (1980). *Ageism: Prejudice and discrimination against the elderly.* Belmont, California: Wadsworth.

LEWIN, K. (1935). *Dynamic theory of personality.* New York: McGraw-Hill.

LONDONNER, C. A. (1978). Instrumental and expressive education: A basis for needs assessment and planning. In R. H. Sherron and D. B. Lumsden (Eds.), *Introduction to educational gerontology.* Washington, D.C.: Hemisphere Publishing Corp.

LOOFT, W. R. (1973). Reflections on intervention in old age: Motives, goals, and assumptions. *Gerontologist, 13*(1), 6–10.

MASLOW, A. (1968). *Toward a psychology of being.* New York: Van Nostrand Reinhold.

McCLUSKY, H. (1971). *Education: Background.* Washington, D.C.: White House Conference on Aging.

MOODY, H. R. (1976). Philosophical presuppositions of education for old age. *Educational Gerontology, 1,* 1–16.

NAISBITT, J. (1982). *Megatrends: Ten new directions transforming our lives.* New York: Warner Books.

NEUGARTEN, B. L. (1982). *Age or need? Public policies for older people.* Beverly Hills: Sage Publications.

OKUN, M. A. (Ed.) (1982). *Programs for older adults, Vol. 14. New directions for continuing education.* San Francisco: Jossey-Bass.

OVERLY, N. V., et al. (1980). *Model for lifelong learning.* Report of the Commission on Lifelong Learning. Bloomington, Indiana: Phi Delta Kappa.

PECK, R. (1956). Psychological developments in second half of life. In J. E. Anderson (Ed.), *Psychological aspects of aging.* Washington, D. C.: American Psychological Association.

PEPPER, S. C. (1970). *World hypothesis.* Berkeley: University of California Press.

PETERSON, D. A. (1983). *Facilitating learning for older people.* San Francisco: Jossey-Bass.

PIAGET, J. (1972). Intellectual evolution from adolescence to adulthood. *Human Development, 15,* 1–12.

QUARTON, G. (1968). Controlling human behavior and modifying personality. In D. Bell (Ed.), *Toward the year 2000: Work in progress.* New York: Houghton Mifflin.

REINERT, G. (1980). Educational psychology in the context of the human life span. In P. B. Baltes and O. G. Brim, Jr. (Eds.), *Life-span development and behavior, Vol. 3.* New York: Academic Press.

ROSENMAYR, L. (1982). Biography and identity. In T. K. Hareven and K. J. Adams (Eds.), *Aging and life course transitions: An interdisciplinary perspective.* New York: The Guilford Press.

RUBENSON, K. (October 1982). Interaction between formal and non-formal education. Paper presented to the ICAE Conference, *Towards an authentic development: The role of adult education.* Paris: (mimeographed).

SCHAIE, K. W. (1973). Reflections on papers by Looft, Peterson and Sparks: Intervention toward an ageless society? *Gerontologist, 13*(1), 31–35.

SCHAIE, K. W. (1979). Toward a stage theory of adult cognitive development. *Journal of Aging and Human Development, 8,* 129–138.

SCHAIE, K. W. (1983). The Seattle Longitudinal Study: A twenty-one year investigation of psychometric intelligence. In K. W. Schaie (Ed.), *Longitudinal studies of adult psychological development.* New York: Guilford Press.

SHEEHY, G. (1977). *Passages.* New York: Bantam Books.

SHERRON, R. H., and LUMSDEN, D. B. (Eds.) (1978). *Introduction to educational gerontology.* Washington, D.C.: Hemisphere Publishing Corp.

SKINNER, B. F. (1971). *Beyond freedom and dignity.* New York: Knopf.

SKINNER, B. F. (1976). *About behaviorism.* New York: Random House.

SPARKS, P. M. (1973). Behavioral versus experiential aging: Implications for intervention. *Gerontologist, 13*(1), 15–18.

STERNS, H. L., and SANDERS, R. E. (1980). Training and education of the elderly. In R. R. Turner and H. W. Reese (Eds.), *Life-span developmental psychology.* New York: Academic Press.

THOMAS, A. M. (1964). The concept of program in adult education. In G. Jensen, A. A. Liveright, and W. Hallenbeck (Eds.), *Adult education: Outlines of an emerging field of university study.* Chicago: Adult Education Association of the U.S.A.

THOMAS, A. M. (1983). Learning in society. In M. Hogue and C. Quinn (Eds.), *Learning in society: A new paradigm.* Ottawa: Canadian Commission for UNESCO.

THORNTON, J. E. (1967). *An exploratory study of the educational deficiencies of occupationally unstable economic-opportunity migrants.* Unpublished Master's Thesis. Ann Arbor, Michigan: University of Michigan.

TOFFLER, A. (1980). *The third wave.* New York: William Morrow and Co., Inc.

TOUGH, A. (1978). Major learning efforts: Recent research and future directions. *Adult Education, 28*(4), 250–263.

TOUGH, A. (1982). *Intentional changes.* Chicago: Follett.

VERNER, C., and BOOTH, A. (1964). *Adult education.* New York: The Center for Applied Research in Education.

WEDEMEYER, C. A. (1981). *Learning at the back door: Reflections on non-traditional learning in the lifespan.* Madison: The University of Wisconsin Press.

WILLIS, S. L. (1985). Towards an educational psychology of the older adult learner: Intellectual and cognitive bases. In J. E. Birren and K. W. Schaie (Eds.), *Handbook of the psychology of aging.* New York: Van Nostrand Reinhold.

4

TELEVISION AND THE ELDERLY

From Broadcasting to Narrowcasting

Gerald A. Straka

INTRODUCTION

Television rapidly penetrated the American society in the 1950s. According to Nielsen (1984), at that time 4.6 million households had television sets. This number increased to 83.3 million by 1982 (55 percent of these households having two or more sets). The total number of households in the United States at that time was 83.5 million; therefore, nearly all of them possessed a television set by 1982 (Bureau of the Census, 1983). There were 1,079 television stations on the air (802 commercial and 277 public) by 1983 (Nielsen, 1983); and that number increased to 1,152 television stations (869 commercial and 283 public) in January, 1984 (Nielsen, 1984).

However, the number of stations does not represent the amount of program variety. For the purposes of this chapter, we will define *broadcasting* in terms of its service, i.e., mass appeal and targeted audience; it is not defined in terms of its traditional, mechanical meaning. Excluding cable channels, the three major commercial networks in the U.S.—American Broadcasting Company (ABC), Columbia Broadcasting System (CBS), National Broadcasting Corporation (NBC)—and their affiliates control prime time UHF/VHF viewing. Nearly 80 to 90 percent of the viewing source between 8 and 11 P.M. (Nielsen, 1984) as well as much of the rest

Special thanks to Gustav A. Lienert, who greatly influenced my decision to do research in the field of gerontology.

of the day is dominated by these companies (Baldwin and McVoy, 1983). For these networks the major source of revenue is commercials. Since the amount of income depends on the number of viewers, the aim of these networks is to produce programs for a mass audience, to produce the so-called "lowest-common-denominator" programs (Baldwin and McVoy, 1983, p. 5). For this type of service the term *broadcasting* is adequate because, in addition to the specific concept of program construction, it is spread widely and scattered in all directions in order to reach the greatest number of viewers possible. As the networks and the individual stations tend to imitate each other's success, the broadcasted programs themselves become more and more similar (Baldwin and McVoy, 1983). However, broadcasting trends do not exclude the fact that there are certain segments of the audience which have specific tendencies in relation to television viewing. Older persons are one such group, and constitute an audience of "heavy viewers" (Comstock et al., 1978, p. 289). The question arises as to whether or not the programs and their messages portray a representative picture of the aged and the process of aging. This chapter will analyze these issues as well as explore alternative forms of televised messages and their implications for the elderly audience, both as learners and as consumers.

Currently, a variety of delivery systems and technologies developed for the home television set provide the viewer with increasing programming alternatives. For example, *cable television,* the most widespread of these alternatives in the United States, is characterized by programming brought to the viewer via a cable (*one-way cable television*). This system eliminates the problem of interference which can occur between messages televised over the air. One consequence of cable television technology is that now the number of channels is nearly unlimited. Another innovation with yearly growth rates of 50 percent and more is the *video cassette recorder (VCR)*. Recorders allow the viewer to replay, record, and, in combination with a video camera, produce a nearly unlimited variety of programs. These and other alternatives (see Figure 4-1) have become, over a relatively short period of time, a rapidly growing market. Their boundaries currently appear to be unlimited.

In 1981, consumer purchases reached 6.37 billion dollars; they were distributed as indicated in Figure 4-1 (Beardsley, 1982, p. 3). According to this figure, cable television (basic and pay cable which form 43.7% of the market share) as well as video cassette recorders, cameras, and video cassettes (27.6% of the market share) comprise nearly three quarters of the home video market. In addition, the speed of its implementation and the prognosis for cable television indicate that this type of television may have the same triumphal success in penetrating American society as did the broadcasting service. In 1983, 69.2 percent of the 83.5 million television households had access to cable, i.e., cable was made technologically available to them. At that time, 36 percent of those households were basic-cable subscribers, and 21 percent were pay-cable subscribers (note that the basic and pay subscriber can be one and the same). The estimates for 1990 are that 90 percent of all households having television will have access to cable—54 percent to basic, and 35 percent to pay cable (Cable Vision, 1985). Due to this estimated growth, one focus of this chapter will be on cable television and video recorders.

Since some systems are still in the developmental stage (e.g., interactive cable, and videotext) or have just entered the market, there is a great risk of making false

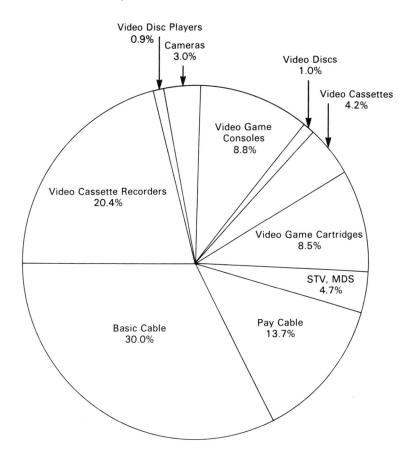

FIGURE 4-1 Consumer home video expenditures by segment, 1981.

Source: Reprinted from *The Home Video and Cable Yearbook, 1982–83.*
Published by Knowledge Industry Publications, Inc., 701 Westchester Ave.,
White Plains, NY 10604. © 1982 by Knowledge Industry Publications, Inc.
Reprinted by permission of the publisher.

predictions. These still have a small share and, therefore, they are not included in
the above-mentioned figures. For example, *two-way* or *interactive* cable television,
which allows an information flow both to and from the subscriber's television set,
is not mentioned. Possible applications of such a system would be home security
systems (e.g., alarm services), home shopping, or videotext (e.g., accessing *The
New York Times* on video with the possibility of recalling current and past articles
via a subject index). Another example is *low-power television (LPTV),* which covers
an area with a radius up to about 15 miles. LPTVs were admitted into the market
in 1980 by a decision of the Federal Communications Commission (FCC). With this
decision, a market for 4,000 new television stations was created, and by 1982 there
were 6,500 such applications on file (Beardsley, 1982).

One assumption regarding these new developments in home television is that
they will lead from broadcasting to narrowcasting (Naisbitt, 1982). *Narrowcasting*

TABLE 4-1 Average Hours of Television Viewing

		1981	1982	1983
55+ weekly	female	39.20	37.14	41.13
average hours	male	35.43	32.59	35.53
35–54 weekly	female	32.37	33.23	33.23
average hours	male	27.41	26.56	27.50

is programming for smaller audiences having specific backgrounds and/or interests in common (for example, older adults), and is concentrated in relatively small areas (for example, Leisure World, an older adult community in Southern California). Such areas are easily reached by low-power television stations or local cable channels. Another form of narrowcasting is a televised service for a specific subgroup, sparsely scattered over the country, reachable with specific programs stored on video cassettes or discs; for example, continuing education for physicians or nurses, or Jane Fonda's cassette on aerobics (Ames and Fabrikant, 1985). According to Toffler (1980, p. 164), these technological innovations have one thing in common: "They slice the mass television public into segments, and each slice not only increases our cultural diversity, it cuts deeply into the power of the networks that have until now so completely dominated our imagery" (see, for example, Nielsen, 1982-84; and Naisbitt, 1982).

The actual status of new developments in the field of television technology and the potential trend from broadcasting to narrowcasting raise some issues in regard to the older adult audience:

1. What are the roles of broadcast television in the lives of older persons?
2. What are the potential roles or implications of narrowcasting for this increasing group in the American society?
3. What is the actual and what may be the potential use of televised education for older persons?

THE ROLE OF BROADCASTED TELEVISION
IN THE LIFE OF THE ELDERLY

Watching television, listening to the radio, and reading are the most frequent activities of people aged 55 and older (Burrus-Bammel and Bammel, 1985; De Grazia, 1961; Schramm, 1969). The 1975 Harris study revealed that, among these activities, people over 65 spent most of their time watching television.

The Harris study (1975) also found that the socioeconomic status and educational level of older viewers have no or only minor influences on television viewing, unlike the effects on use of other media. Reviewing several studies, Kubey (1980) concluded that television viewing is the most time-consuming "leisure activity" of the elderly. Likewise, in a Canadian study which polled older adults it was found that, for the majority of older people, television is the most entertaining and relaxing activity, and is viewed as supplying more companionship than radio or newspapers (Adams and Groen, 1974 in Kubey, 1980).

Focusing specifically on television, the recent Nielsen reports find that per-

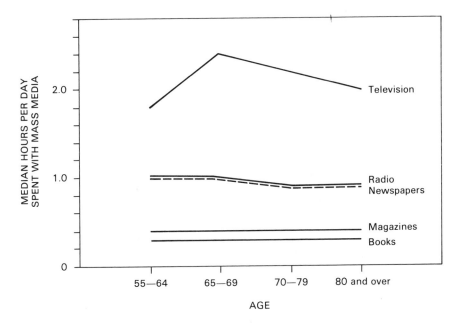

FIGURE 4-2 Pattern of media consumption with advancing age.

Note: For ages 55-64, N = 486; 65-69, N = 1033; 70-79, N = 1295; 80 and over, N = 469.

Source: Adapted from *A survey on aging: Experience of older Americans vs. public expectation of old age,* 1974. New York: Louis Harris and Associates, Inc., p. 208, by Comstock et al., 1978, p. 297.

sons age 55 and over spend more of their time viewing television than younger persons (age 2 to 54). For example, for the years 1981–1983 (Nielsen, 1982–84) the figures in Table 4-1 were reported.

These numbers also reveal that the elderly are by no means a homogenous group. For example, women generally watch more television than men (Comstock et al., 1978) and this pattern is maintained with increasing age. Referring to the Harris study (1975, see Figure 4-2), television consumption increases after the age of 55, reaches a peak at around the age of 70, and begins to decline slightly afterwards. Other studies, focusing on the elderly and using a variety of methods for measuring viewing time, led to different absolute figures; however the tendency remained the same as that reported by Nielsen (see Davis and Davis, 1985; Kubey, 1980). For example, although the actual number of hours spent watching television differed, older people were consistently found to watch more television than younger people.

In 1983, the average daily viewing time of the elderly (age 55+) was at least five hours. This amount is certainly influenced by factors such as the degree of general access, the cost, the variety of choices, the provision of visual and auditory stimuli, the delivery of information and entertainment, the parasocial experience of companionship, and the element of time demarcation of the daily schedule (Davis, 1980; Davis and Davis, 1985). Other factors that have been found to encourage television viewing by the elderly are sedentariness, sensory decline, isolation, and disengagement (Kubey, 1980). However, television can also promote social interaction by delivering topics for conversation, as well as promote changes in life style by presenting realistic behavior models to be imitated (Bandura, 1977; Comstock et al., 1978; Davis, 1971; Schramm, 1969).

Program Preferences

Studies by Bower (1973), Danowski (1975), Davis (1971), and Doolittle (1979) report that news and public-affairs programs are the first program choices of the elderly; and the consumption of news programs increases with age and educational level. The Long Beach study (Davis, 1971) found that the elderly ranked educational programs second and travelogues third in terms of desired viewing. The study was repeated in 1982 containing an East and West Coast sample of elderly persons (about 95 percent were 55+). The choices and ranks, based on a different list of program types, were: (#1) news, (#2) informative documentaries, and (#3) feature films (Davis and Davis, 1985).

As can be seen, the preferred programs above are not the whole program content of television, especially of commercial television where entertainment programs comprise the largest portion. Entertainment programs transmit values of the society in that, since television programmers know that messages threatening the collective value system are screened out, commercial television is designed to reinforce basic American values like self-reliance, man as a commodity, physical beauty, man as master, and future orientation (Davis, 1980). These values favor the middle-aged population where the greatest purchasing power is assumed. However, due to their focus on profit-oriented productivity and youthful appearance, they are disadvantageous for the elderly to a certain extent (Davis, 1978).

Furthermore, older adults' viewing is additionally affected by how the elderly are portrayed. Reviewing empirical research concerning this topic, Davis (1980), Davis and Davis (1985), Elliott (1984), and Kubey (1980) found that the proportion of older people appearing on television is not equivalent to their proportion in the society. Furthermore, women appear less often and in more passive roles; older men are powerful, successful in business, and physically and politically active; and older women advertise denture products, laxatives, and digestion aids, whereas younger and middle-aged women sell beauty products. The extremes of the elderly's range of health are portrayed; e.g., the very ill or extremely active are portrayed rather than the average healthy older adult. This result increases the likelihood of stereotyping the elderly, separating them from the rest of the society.

Programs Designed for the Elderly

Compared with television programs as a whole, programs for or about older adults are minimal. There have been some—for example, the 20-part 1977 NBC series "New Wrinkles in Aging"; the 1983 project "The Changing Family" of KHJ-TV, a Los Angeles station, which dealt specifically with aging themes; and the documentary "May to December" which dealt with aging, retirement, and social security. In addition, in the 1970s, several age-related series were broadcast by the public television system. One example was "Prime Time," presented by the Public Broadcasting System in the summer of 1979 (Davis and Fleisher, 1979). The issues discussed in this four-film series included central themes of the older adult lifestyle, such as coping with change, interdependent relationships, learning to enjoy life, and inner strengths. An evaluation of these films revealed they were "very much enjoyed," left "a very positive feeling about being old," and had more effect on the attitudes about aging of the younger groups of the sample than of the older ones (Davis and Fleisher, 1979). An evaluation of "Getting On," another series about aging, revealed considerable improvement in the impressions of adults about the elderly as a result of this program (Lieberman Research, 1977).

"Over Easy," a daily, half-hour magazine show aired on weekdays, was first shown in 1977. Targeted at the 55-years-and-older population in the United States, this program has been televised by nearly all public broadcasting stations (253 out of 256). The primary goals of this program were specifically designed to inform viewers about services and projects for the elderly, encourage positive attitudes about aging, and promote interaction among different generations. The magazine format combined information, entertainment, and social "messages." The format usually provided an opening monologue by the host concerning the content and theme of the day's program, live interviews with guests, a daily interview with an expert on some theme of interest to the target population, information of special interest to older people, presentations by the host, and a lifestyle segment showing older people and their successful and innovative approaches to the potentials and problems of aging (Office of Communication Research, 1981).

In a 1980 study, "Over Easy" was evaluated on the following dimensions: scheduling and viewing, awareness and general reactions to the program, impact, interaction of program and local institutions, and expert reactions to the program. It was found that the total audience in the spring of 1978 was about one million viewers. This viewing audience was considered low in relation to the target population of 43 million: 66% of the target group were unaware of the program at that time. The viewers watched about two episodes a week and each week there was a sizeable turnover in audience. The program had a strong appeal among viewers; 56% felt that this program was an excellent idea. The interview with the experts was the segment most positively received by the viewers, but was criticized on the grounds that it had a "patronizing" tone. This study resulted in a higher awareness of community services among viewers, and an increase in the number of requests for these services (Office of Communication Research, 1981). In sum, this example of television programming about aging and for the elderly met the program interests of this target group. However, only a small portion of this group actually watched these programs. A question therefore arises as to whether or not this type of program would be more feasible for narrowcasting.

THE POTENTIALS OF NARROWCASTING
FOR OLDER ADULTS

As mentioned earlier, the new technological advances of television which may lead to narrowcasting are low-power television (LPTV), cable television, video-cassette recorders (VCR's), and videocameras.

Low-power television. The techniques of low-power television (LPTV) are not new. In the past, such systems were generally used for retransmitting the programs and signals of television broadcast stations. According to the Federal Communications Commission's (FCC) regulations, such retransmittal is only permitted "without significantly altering any characteristics of the original signal other than its frequency and amplitude, for the purpose of providing television reception to the general public" (Baldwin and McVoy, 1983, p. 335). Recently new FCC regulations (1980) have allowed the use of this technology to provide original programming and have allowed satellite programs to be retransmitted without any limitatons (Baldwin and McVoy, 1983). The reason for this change is the FCC administration's desire to increase television services for rural areas and to establish a local television medium for smaller audiences previously not well covered by the broadcast system.

The number of applicants for licensing (6,500) suggests that LPTVs have a positive economic future. However, it is still not clear what type of program will be most feasible for this system. Everything is possible. In urban areas, with many more broadcast and cable facilities, LPTV might appeal to special interest groups. In rural areas and small towns, LPTV might supplement meager broadcast programming. Considering the underrepresentation of the elderly, the unrealistic portrayal of age in broadcasted television, and the growth of the elderly population, this segment of the population might become a major target group for this type of television. For agglomerations of older persons such as those in Sun City, Arizona or Leisure World, California, LPTV might be an option for programming for and by the elderly. The number of such stations is still small; by mid-1982, only forty-six companies had been approved for narrowcasting (Beardsley, 1982). Therefore, the development of programming in general and for the elderly in particular is an open field, but the research is still too limited to draw general conclusions. However, in this regard, research findings concerning cable television, especially via the open-access channel, may provide some ideas and devices for the use of LPTV.

Cable television.   Cable television is a "narrowcast system of distributing one or more television signals over a wired system to individual receivers in a given geographic area" (Cohen, 1984, p. 388). The origins of cable television go back to 1948 when broadcast television penetrated the United States and problems arose as certain geographic areas had difficulty receiving the signals because of mountains, tall buildings, or being slightly out of the broadcast area. At that time the community antenna-television system facilitated this access. With a master antenna the signals were received, reinforced, and distributed from house to house by cable. The exclusive goal was to receive and distribute the broadcast television programming. There was no vision of any additional services. The number of community antenna systems grew slowly and steadily. In 1971, there were 2,750 systems in the U.S. which linked nearly six million homes (Baldwin and McVoy, 1983).

> Cable television has exploded suddenly into a communication system of significance, viewed by cities as a major service medium, by businesses as growth investment in an otherwise dull economy, and by media and common carrier competitors as a major threat. All this happened over a few short months because of the discovery of what economists suggested many years ago was a consumer underinvestment in television. . . . And this newly discovered appetite for television, which is far beyond the dreams of the industry of just a few years ago, is based on presently available entertainment services that are only a fraction of the future entertainment and service potentials seen by industry visionaries (Baldwin and McVoy, 1983, p. 4).

What are the current promises and hopes associated with cable television? The increase in diversity takes first rank; there are now many channels available. The newest cable systems have 108 channels; and with the broadband and fiber-optic cable, this number is still increasing. Feeding these channels with software will inevitably lead to a greater variety of programming for more and more specific interest and target groups. This will also put an end to the quasi-monopoly of the broadcasting companies with a tight market for creative talents. There will be room for experimentation with new ideas, for more in-depth news instead of the traditional headline service of the networks, and fewer commercial interruptions. The "closed shop" of the broadcast market will be opened—not only by the number of available channels but by the *public access channel* as well, which allows for a two-way transmission of channels. This characteristic may contribute to television's becoming more interactive. New areas for community services and education will be set up (Baldwin and McVoy, 1983).

Davis and Miller (1983) mention the following possible uses of cable television which may be particularly valuable for older adults toward whom traditional forms are less directed:

1. *General information like news and public affairs.* Older viewers have an appreciation for this type of information. Assuming that several channels are transmitting public affairs programs, different types of approaches to news will be available. This might attract different groups of consumers, of which the elderly are one.

2. *Specialized information according to the needs and wants of older persons.* Kornbluh (1984), referring to the "Directory of Online Databases" (Fall issue 1983, published by Cuadra Associates, Inc. of Santa Monica), reported on databases to assist older persons. They have a range of information about services for the aging such as nursing homes, senior centers, preparing wills, and other medical and non-medical information. For example, since January, 1983 the Food and Drug Administration of the U.S. Department of Health and Human Services has offered an electronic bulletin board containing information which is of importance for the elderly. One such channel, the Cable Health Network, Los Angeles, broadcasts health-related programming all day (Davis and Davis, 1985).

3. *General entertainment via several channels.* This may create a diversity of, and specialization for programs far beyond those focusing on westerns, crime, and sex (e.g., see the Playboy Channel; Wirth et al., 1984). For example, movies that certain generations adored can be seen at any time and without commercials.

4. *Video music.* This is a growing market. However, these programs might not be very attractive for today's elderly because of the type of music actually produced.

5. *Ethnic and religious programming.* With the increase in the number of channels there may be more programming time available for the different ethnicities and religions in the United States. This may meet the needs and interests of the elderly since age is differentially experienced in the ethnic groups; and the homebound elderly would be able to participate in the practices of their congregations from home.

6. *Community news and local politics.* There is an increasing interest in this sort of information, especially for older adults (Kubey, 1980; Doolittle, 1979).

This list of potential uses by Davis and Miller (1983) refers mostly to one-way cable. An example for two-way, or interactive cable, currently offered but still in the stage of experimentation (Paisley, 1983), is the service *videotext,* a "system in which information is stored in a central computer and then transmitted to the home on phone lines or cable and is displayed on the home TV set" (Woolley, 1984, p. 123). The strengths of this system are that the users display only the information of interest to them, keeping it on the screen for as long as they want. The electronic storage of information can be constantly updated and is available to all users 24 hours a day. An example of such a system is VIEWTRON, developed in the late 1970s. Available services included updated news, weather, sports information, information for ordering merchandise from catalogues, the ability to transfer money from bank accounts, the ability to send messages to a public bulletin board, and educational programs like the Florida Driver's Test. Also, videotext is currently leaving the domain of information accessing and branching out to other areas like video games and business computing (Woolley, 1984).

Video-cassette recorders.   A great potential for future growth is predicted for *video-cassette recorders* (VCRs). In June, 1982 VCRs reached a market penetration of 3,860,000 (Beardsley, 1982). The prognosis is that there will be 25 million VCRs in U.S. homes by the end of 1985 (Ames and Fabrikant, 1985). VCRs can record audiovisual programming from the television set as well as play back existing cassettes; and, in combination with a video camera, an individual can make his or her own programming. Thus, video camera may replace the eight millimeter camera. The important advantage of this system is that the recording can be replayed immediately; there is no longer a time interval necessary for developing the film.

The VCR also may have some consequences concerning the transience of television broadcasts, and the "catch-it-or-miss-it" nature of the live broadcast or even LPTV (Levy and Fink, 1984). Everything that is available on television, over the air, or via cable or satellite can be stored with VCRs, although in some cases its value may be dependent on immediacy. The possibility of time-shifting and playback at any time may have slightly different functions in different media environments, population subgroups, and purposes. In television-rich programming environments (mostly urban), occasional programs of special interest not scheduled for replay can be stored and become part of a cassette library. In television-poor environments (many rural areas) video recordings can be used to fill up the usual viewing time with programs closer to the interests of the individual (Levy and Fink, 1984).

Research on the elderly's television consumption found that older persons, on the average, phase out an hour earlier (between 9:30 and 10:30 P.M.) than younger viewers (Davis and Davis, 1985). Sometimes programs for specific interest groups like the elderly are broadcast at a time unfavorable for them (like late night or early afternoon), when there is competition with other activities like shopping, visiting the doctor, walking in the park, or meeting with friends. Thus, the VCR might contribute to a more flexible lifestyle for older adults, allowing them to use daytime for active behaviors and social contacts.

For educational purposes this technique has another advantage compared with "live" televised instruction. The presentation stored on cassette can be interrupted and replayed whenever the student desires or needs it. This may be important considering the decreased speed of information processing with advancing age (Botwinick, 1978). Since the cassettes can be easily distributed, almost everything in television-rich environments is now also available in limited ones. Cassettes may create a market for highly specialized interests scattered across the country.

However, one problem remains; that is, the costs of recorded cassettes, VCRs, and video cameras are still prohibitive for many households (Baldwin and McVoy, 1983). Therefore, the relevant industry is planning to produce simpler and less expensive hardware (*Frankfurter Allgemeine,* February 14, 1985), and the prices generally will decrease. This means that this technology and its potential services and uses may become increasingly important for the life of the elderly.

Since VCRs, compared with other technologies like cable television, are actually used far less frequently by the elderly (see Kerschner and Chelsvig Hart, 1984), the focus of the remainder of this chapter will be on cable television.

Compared to broadcasting, these new narrowcasting technologies and services are relatively new. Therefore, not much survey data are available, particularly concerning older adults. The reasons for this failure may be because the segment of the elderly is still smaller than the younger population which has a higher consumption rate. In addition, marketing people assume that product purchase preferences are set up earlier in life and that the elderly are less likely to change consumption preferences and patterns than younger people (Danowski and Hannemann, 1980). However, some recent survey results and some case studies with the elderly are available, and will be reviewed in the following section. (See also Straka, *Project: Elderly and Cable Television—An empirical investigation with educational intervention,* starting July '86 for 2½ years.)

Attitudes of Older Adults toward the New Technology

A survey initiated by the National Retired Teachers Association and the American Association of Retired Persons concerning the use of and attitudes toward new technologies by the elderly was conducted in June, 1981 (Kerschner and Chelsvig Hart, 1984; Brickfield, 1984). A nationwide sample of 750 persons aged 45 and older was interviewed by telephone. The response rate was 81 percent. The results are indicated in Table 4-2. 32 to 40 percent of the sample use cable television (average, 37%), and 6 to 12 percent video recorders (average, 8%). An inverse relationship was found between age and use of modern technology, and additional correctional analysis revealed that income and educational level were positively related with use.

Part two of the survey was much less specific, focusing on the attitudes of older persons toward technology in general. Six statements were presented for agreement or disagreement. The results were as follows:

- —50 percent agreed "machines are doing too much that ought to be left for people to do";
- —87 percent agreed "machines make life too impersonal";
- —87 percent agreed "improvements in technology make it possible to get things done faster and more accurately than ever before";
- —34 percent agreed "life is going to be better when people are able to do banking, shopping, etc. from home by using telephones or cable television"·

— 50 percent agreed "using calculators, computers, and other electronic gadgets is usually too confusing to bother with"; and

— 50 percent agreed "improvements in technology really have not made life easier, just more difficult to deal with" (Kerschner and Chelsvig Hart, 1984, p. 139).

TABLE 4-2   Use of Technology by Age

	(N)	AGE GROUP		
		45–54 (206)	55–64 (204)	65 + (198)
Technology Used		%[a]	%[a]	%[a]
Calculator		75	65	39
Cable TV		40	39	32
Computer		37	29	18
Video recorder		12	7	6
Automatic teller machine		19	14	10
Video games		29	14	12

[a] Percents sum to more than 100 because some respondents used more than one type of technology.

Kerschner and Chelsvig Hart, 1984, p. 136. Reprinted with permission.

These responses to the questionnaire were combined with an index of attitudes toward technology ranging from "strong anti-tech" to "strong pro-tech." The overall result was that one third was "pro-tech"; one third, "anti-tech"; and one third, "neutral." More detailed data are listed in Table 4-3.

In the age group 45 to 64, 40 percent expressed a favorable attitude toward technology as compared with 20 percent in the age group 65 and older. Unfavorable attitudes were found in 27 percent of the age group 45 to 64 and 44 percent of the age group ·65 and older. Men had a more favorable attitude compared to

TABLE 4-3   Attitudes toward Technology by Age

	(N)	AGE GROUP		
		45–54 (206)	55–64 (204)	65 + (198)
Attitude toward Technology		%	%	%
Strong anti-tech		6	5	9
Anti-tech		21	26	35
Neutral		33	35	36
Pro-tech		24	21	16
Strong pro-tech		16	13	4
Total %		100	100	100

Kerschner and Chelsvig Hart, 1984, p. 140. Reprinted with permission.

women, and attitude was also affected by income, educational level, and residence. Interests of the elderly were smaller concerning services such as home shopping and expanded television channels compared to emergency alert systems.

Thus, a definite relationship between age and attitudes toward technology was determined. However, there are indications that the aged do not resist all technological development (La Buda, 1978). Brickfield (1984), in the NATO Conference on "Aging and Technological Advances," stated:

> For example, a home for the aged in suburban Washington won high favor with its residents by introducing computer games. Since most of the residents were over 80 and infirm, the games were adapted for poor vision and reduced manual dexterity. In playing the games, the older people felt they had a common interest to share with children and grandchildren (Brickfield, 1984, p. 37).

Another study, conducted in Los Angeles and Marin counties, concerned preferences for interactive cable services and investigated the following topics (Danowski and Hannemann, 1980):

1. visiting friends and relatives via two-way television from home,
2. performing civic and state functions (such as driver's license renewal and voting via two-way television), and
3. receiving information from newspapers and library documents (i.e., print information) via cable.

For Los Angeles residents there were significant positive relations between young (15 to 29), middle (30 to 59), and older (60+) adults' preferences for "two-way cable social visiting," "performing civic and state functions," and "receiving print information." The same relation was found for Marin County residents regarding "two-way cable social visiting"; however, "receiving print information" was not investigated (Danowski and Hannemann, 1980, p. 342). It is important to note that only the preferences for and not the use of these interactive cable services was investigated.

One of the most interesting developments in cable television regarding user preferences is the *public access channel*. Even though such a channel is no longer mandatory, the cable franchise companies are offering it in order to facilitate obtaining a license in certain areas. "The public access channel, under the American notion of freedom of speech, is available to any resident of the community on a first come, first served basis, to communicate whatever is desired" (Baldwin and McVoy, 1983, p. 95). An example is the Storer company application for Dallas-Fort Worth. In its 100-channel system are 24 access channels: "action clearinghouse/job bank, library, educational (6), government, interfaith, public, older citizen, black, Hispanic, health, women's, youth, fine arts, commerce, environmental, regional, public affairs, and college (2)" (Baldwin and McVoy, 1983, p. 100).

An example for the use of such a channel by the elderly is the project "Public Access Cabletelevision by and for Elders" (PACE). This project began in October, 1977, in San Diego. The intent of this project is to establish *user-controlled television programming* in an urban setting which has one of the largest concentrations of elderly in the United States. The assumption is that members of this target group know their own needs and wants best, a concept supported by Harrington's (1977) survey study concerning mass media use, preferences, and needs of the elderly in the San Diego area. That study found that 90.6 percent of the 1,411 individuals 55 years of age and over who were questioned would "like to have more information or programming about senior adult issues and interests" (Harrington, 1977, p. 44). It also confirmed that television was the preferred media (39.1%).

Eighteen months after the PACE project began, 95 older adults were trained in video production using a "How To" handbook produced for this purpose. Over 50 programs were produced covering a wide range of topics proposed by seniors; some examples of programs produced are as follows: "An introspective look at aging," "Age of the panthers," "Senior political advocacy," and "Learning doesn't stop at 21" (College of Extended Studies). These were recorded on tapes and are still available.

A survey of these self-producers found that approximately five percent of the target group had seen a PACE program (Real et al., 1980). Even if the number of viewers is small, and the numbers of the producers and "use controllers" are still smaller, this project demonstrated how the elderly can promote their interests. Perhaps this was one reason for the production of a small booklet by the Institute of Lifetime Learning in which advice is given regarding how to get access to stations or channels (AARP, 1983; Davis and Davis, 1985).

Another case study concerning a new form of community participation with and for older adults was first approved and evaluated in Reading, Pennsylvania with the two-way video cable system. It was one of 48 different projects summarized under the general topic "Social Services and Cable TV" (Kay and Gerendasy, 1976). This pilot experiment was financed by the National Science Foundation. The objectives of the project were: (1) to establish three neighborhood communication centers interconnected by cable television; (2) to train citizens to operate the system; (3) to link together older adults and public agencies; and (4) to produce a two-way public service program through which the elderly could communicate with each other and with service providers. A split screen was used with the effect that each discussant appeared on one half of the screen, thus producing a "face-to-face" contact between them. In addition, cable-connected receivers at home had access to communicating directly with participants and discussants through a telephone line.

Starting with 117 elderly, the program was subsequently carried to all 35,000 subscribers of the Berks Community Television. The program production was controlled for two hours a day by the elderly. One of the highlights during this experiment was the monthly, and later weekly, program "Meet the Mayor." In this program a two-way telecommunication took place between the three communication centers and members of the city council. Here, the telecommunication was not limited to the elderly and service agencies; there were also discussions between young and old viewers.

Moss (1978a) evaluated the project and found it impacted on three areas: "awareness of community problems, knowledge about social services, and involvement in social processes." Even though the Reading project was the first experiment in community access television with the elderly, the following principles seem to be applicable to other settings:

1. The role of citizens as initiators of programming.

2. The use of local neighborhood facilities as the origination sites for programming.
3. The reliance on spontaneous, interactive programs.
4. The aggregation of organizations to generate a diversity of public service programming.
5. The emphasis on programming to serve distinct sub-groups of the population (Moss, 1978, p. viii; see also Cohen, 1984).

THE POTENTIAL USE OF TELEVISED EDUCATION

Early Use

The advances in storing and transmitting information (see Haefner, 1982) have led to a new and increasing trend in the field of education. *Instructional technology, multimedia approach, computer-assisted instruction, audiovisual school, television university, the living room as the classroom,* and *distance learning,* terms created in the 1950s and 1960s, characterize this trend. As an example of the optimism of that time, the Carnegie Commission on Higher Education (1982) forecasted that "by the year 2000 it now appears that a significant proportion of instruction in higher education on campus may be carried out through informational technology" (p. 1).

Systems of this kind were to be designed:

1. to meet the rising demand for higher education (resulting from trends in the 1950s and 1960s) (Wiesner, 1983) and for adult education during a time of teacher and classroom shortage (Forman and Richardson, 1977);
2. to reach new students outside the regular educational system (e.g., working adults and homebounds) to increase the equality of educational opportunities (Forman and Richardson, 1977; La Buda, 1978) (to a certain degree this was also a reaction against the anticipated decline of college enrollment in the 1970s and 1980s) (Wiesner, 1983);
3. to provide substitute teaching activities like information delivery by these media and promote 'real' educational activities like guiding and counseling; and
4. to construct learning programs in accordance with the variety of the individual prerequisites of learning, like intellectual skills, cognitive strategies, and attitudes (Gagné, 1977). The mastery learning concept promoted by Bloom (1971) is an example of this (see Straka, 1981; Eigler and Straka, 1978).

These purposes initially received support on the basis of some assumptions about the characteristics of instructional technology: i.e., that instructional technology—like televised or multimedia instruction—is more effective than traditional teaching and that specific characteristics of media (symbol systems) require different classes of mental activities, construct different aspects of the world, and develop different intellectual skills (Olson, 1977; Olson and Bruner, 1974).

The optimism about the widespread application of these technologies has been revised, however. A study by Rockart and Morton (1975), sponsored by the same Carnegie Commission, suggested that the new technology would be for the most part an addition to, and not a replacement of, learning opportunities. The major improvements were designated as being an increased enrichment of target groups of students and access to universities formerly outside the traditional educational system.

One of these groups was considered to be the adult learner. As a result, telecourses for national distribution were produced for this target group by the Coastline Community College, the Dallas County Colleges, the University of Mid-America, the Miami-Dade County College, the Wayne State University, and the University of Maryland (Wiesner, 1983). This production of telecourses began new research into the educational applications of the new technology.

Existing Research

Focusing on longitudinal and cross-sectional research, findings concerning intellectual aging (e.g., Willis, 1985) show that there is some intellectual decline in later years but far less than most people assume (especially the elderly themselves) (Pratt and Wood, 1984). Thus, research has determined no natural limit for educability of older adults in general, or for the application of televised instruction in specific (Pratt and Wood, 1984). However, increasing cohort differences and, especially, the individual differences in the prerequisites of older learners may make individualized instruction far more important in adult education than in that of children or adolescents, where the discussion about this method originally arose (Bloom, 1971; Straka, 1981). Televised instruction may provide the much needed answer to these individualized needs.

The question thus arises: How much do we know about the learning–teaching process in televised instruction? Holberg (1975, p. 79) stressed the lack of research about the use of television in education:

> Apart from general statements about the evident value of radio, TV, audio and video recordings for illustration purposes and for bringing real life nearer to the study situation, little has been documented about the role of these media in distance education. Some practical experiences have been reported on, but no real guidelines seem to have been developed on how to create programs for these media as elements of distance education although some research work has been done.

Richardson (1980) reviewed nine investigations about the use of telecommunication for continuing education. She identified factors favoring the realization of these goals (e.g., learner-centered focus, quality of instructional materials), and criticized these projects on the following grounds:

> None of the studies undertook to establish explanatory principles or to break new ground in understanding the teaching–learning needs of adult learners. None of the studies made any attempt to build on concepts of the social sciences or to relate existing practices to a body of theory. Those steps must be taken if the field is to advance (Richardson, 1980, p. 39).

Wiesner (1983), reviewing telecourse research and the practices of distance learning, summarized that there is a lack of systematic studies of enrolled adults, that more attention has been paid to the technology than to the learners, and that the problems of distance education are still the same as when correspondence schools were first established in the 1920s. Therefore, it was concluded that this research will be consequent only when the development of a model of adult learning and teaching, both in general and under the specific "external condition" (Gagné, 1977) of distance learning, has been accomplished (see Richardson, 1983). In this regard, Cross (1981) has developed a conceptual framework for the Characteristics of Adults as Learners (CAL), an assessment measure derived from a review of the research findings in the field of adult learning. This model distinguishes *situational* and *personal* characteristics. The latter include physiological characteristics of aging, sociocultural characteristics, life phases, psychological characteristics, and developmental stages.

According to Cross's CAL model, the *situational characteristics* necessary for adult learning are that it be *part-time* and *voluntary*. Furthermore, the *motivational* dimension of the learning–teaching process (Straka, 1983) is more important than in institutional learning of children, the latter being full-time and compulsory (Cross, 1981). In terms of the motivational dimension, Cross (1981; for critical comments see Long, 1983) developed the Chain-Of-Response (COR) Model to identify relevant variables for the participation of adult learners. These variables are:

1. *Self-evaluation* as a relatively stable personality characteristic playing an important role in the achievement motivation.
2. *Attitudes toward education* as a result of the learner's own experience, and perceived attitudes of friends and "significant others."
3. *Importance of goals ("valence")* and *expectation that participation will meet goals ("expectancy")*. Valence is related to the attitudes; and there is also an interactive relation between self-esteem and attitudes. Expectancy is related to self-esteem (learners with high self-esteem have no doubts of being successful and vice versa).
4. *Life transitions* "as periods of change calling for adjustment to new phases in the life cycle" (Cross, 1981, p. 127). These are the periods of life which challenge the learner with the individually and socioculturally determined "developmental tasks" (Havighurst, 1972; Chickering and Havighurst, 1981). These tasks have certain valence for the learner.
5. *Opportunities* for and *barriers* to learning.
6. *Information* about educational offerings.

These variables and the relations between them are structured in the COR Model, Figure 4-3.

What does this model mean in regard to televised education for the elderly? Given that the elderly are heavy television viewers, a continuous presentation of representative models of successful older adult learners may contribute to a certain change in the attitudes toward education of older learners (see for example the life style segment in the program "Over Easy," Office of Communication Research, 1981). Another important element is the design of educational courses and opportunities close to the needs and wants of older persons (Peterson, 1983). However, the most important situational elements influenced by televised (broadcasted and narrowcasted) instruction are information, opportunities, and barriers. With these

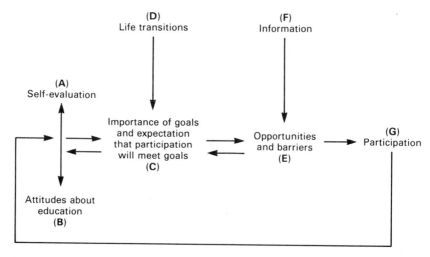

FIGURE 4-3 Chain-of-Response (COR) Model for understanding participation in adult learning activities.

Source: Cross, 1981, p. 124. Reprinted with permission.

new technologies and associated services, educational programs can be brought into the living rooms of the elderly, and these rooms may become classrooms. Also, if the educational program is stored on video cassettes, the elderly themselves can fix their individual learning speeds. In sum, with televised instruction, especially narrowcasting, a new delivery system for adult education is installed which may reduce the barriers and increase the opportunities, thus contributing to an increase in participation.

Another aspect of such educational systems is that progress in electronically storing and transmitting instruction may increase the likelihood of designing instruction according to the prerequisites of learning (Gagné, 1977). This might be one reason that the arguments used for the promoting of programmed instruction in the 1960s are now entering current discussions about telecommunication. For example, Kornbluh (1984) argues in favor of programmed instruction for the following reasons:

1. *Self-pacing.* Time to proceed and comprehend information is up to the speed of the individual learner without inconveniencing other persons and without losing the connection with the televised information.
2. *Little embarrassment.* Mistakes are made in complete privacy: only the computer recognizes them.
3. *Immediate feedback.* Feedback is immediately available in response to learners.
4. *Objective evaluation.* Objective evaluation is made solely on performance of the learner without considering the personal characteristics.
5. *Drill and practice.* The computer never gets tired.

Such advantages increase the likelihood of meeting the needs of the older adult as well as the goals of the instruction. Examples of such goals have been identified by Baldwin (1978) in his research on training adult firefighters using a two-way cable instructional program:

1. to force *attention and participation* by interactive items throughout the instructional program,
2. to *motivate* the learner, thus creating a good record through immediate feedback,
3. to *reinforce* the individual via feedback at each instructional step,
4. to create *competition* in the small learning groups in order to maintain interest and motivation,
5. to use interactive items as *teasers* when starting a new instructional segment,
6. to *pace* instruction by interactive question format,
7. to *drill* with frequent repetition of symbols and materials, and
8. to improve *administration and costs* once the system is installed (Baldwin et al., 1978, p. 184).

Due to the external condition of televised or generally mediated instruction, the attitude toward education (Cross, 1981) has to be further specified in order to assess the success in reaching these goals. Considering the process of education as a communicational activity, Salomon (1981) differentiates between the message, which is primarily informative, and its perceived intent. It may become communicative only as far as the learner perceives an intent to communicate. "This intent can be of three general kinds: an intent to entertain, or to convey information, or an intent to change" (Salomon, 1981, p. 52). In televised communication these intents seem to be important. For example, in a recent experiment with children comparing television and print media under instructional conditions, television was felt to be more efficacious and perceived as more realistic and easy. However, possibly due to the perceived intent of the media, the amount of invested mental effort correlated positively with print and negatively with television, and print led to better inference-making (Salomon, 1984). With regard to educative information delivered via broad- or narrowcasting, the likelihood of the perceived intent being restricted to entertainment may be particularly a problem for today's elderly due to their prior experiences coupled with the recency of alternative goals of the media. However, there is a need for empirical testing of these hypotheses with older adults in these educational settings.

The Function of Educators

With the increasing information technology, the importance of certain functions of existing adult-education institutions and their members will change. Generally, their importance in delivering education will decrease. In particular, well-designed audiovisual material may fulfill this function of information delivery far better and, in the long run, at lower costs. From the instructional teaching point of view instruction can be better designed in terms of learning theoretical principles because of the personal and material input a single instructor can never realize. The proficiency of information presentation may increase: for example, poetry can be presented by the author himself or by professional speakers.

However, a new market for entrepreneurial educators is also indicated: for example, in designing audiovisual self-instructional material and providing the elderly with the necessary instruction to use these potentials of the information technology. The recent book by Davis and Davis (1985), part two of which is a detailed guideline for how to get access to stations and channels and how to produce your own show, is another example of new educational activities in the field of telecommunication. The investigation of Kerschner and Chelsvig Hart (1984) revealed that these new technologies are avoided by a great number of elderly. Educators are needed who can provide the elderly with the skills necessary to approach this technology. For example, with the use of videotext, not only the hardware (typewriter, keyboard, screen, modem) is necessary; the readiness to approach the task from a computer vantage point is as well (Woolley, 1984, p. 124).

The function of guiding, counseling, facilitating, mentoring, and organizing the learning process may become increasingly important. Analogous to the supervision of students in the current educational system, there will be an increasing need for professionals familiar with the sea of learning software available via television or cassette, who can find those educational services or materials which optimally fit the learning needs, potentials, and interests of older adults. In this regard, Dale (1965; as cited in Davis, 1979) lists seven questions which have to be considered for selection of appropriate media:

1. Do the materials give a true picture of the ideas they present?
2. Do the materials contribute meaningful content to the topic under study?
3. Is the material appropriate for the age, intelligence, and experience of the learners?
4. Is the physical condition of the material satisfactory?
5. Is there a teacher's guide to provide a briefing for effective use?
6. Can the materials in question help to make students better thinkers and develop their critical faculties?
7. Is the material worth the time, expense, and effort involved? (Davis, 1979, p. 64)

Thus, the adult educator will become more and more *the organizer of learning opportunities* and far less *the instructor.* One such function, bringing people together, might involve initiating social networks for self-help analogous to the concept of "peer teaching" used in the traditional school. And when the network needs professional advice it can consult the professional or the supervisor of its choice. This all can be arranged via telecommunication.

In addition to these possible roles, it is important to note that while telecommunication and broadcasting deliver information about the world and how to behave in it, there are certain conditions necessary in order to adopt the presented behavior models—antecedent, intervening, and contingent conditions (Comstock et al., 1978). For example, most older adults know that smoking, alcohol abuse, and improper nutrition are health-threatening, but many individuals are negligent in transforming this knowledge into their own behavior (Haefner, 1982; Naisbitt, 1982; Rosenmayr, 1983). This might become a growing market for the educational activities of professionals, who might design therapies for behavioral changes where the learner's balance of expectations is positive (Straka, 1983) or the cost-benefit ratio is soon established. As Welford (1981, p. 107) points out:

From a human factors standpoint, an important implication of the effect of cost–benefit ratio on motivation lies in the fact that it is almost always more difficult, i.e., "costly," to work out and learn a new procedure than to apply one already known. . . . one can understand why changes are often resisted by older people and only accepted under extreme pressure or necessity.

SUMMARY AND OUTLOOK

Broadcast television is still the major media utilized by the elderly. Even if all the elderly have cable access in the future, it can still be assumed that broadcasting will not disappear. One example from the short history of telecommunication may verify this prognosis. The radio, the precursor of television, had its "golden age" in the 1930s and 1940s. The radio audience declined when television was introduced on a large scale in the 1950s. However, in this process, the radio did not lose its audience completely. Currently, there is a differentiation of functions between television and radio. What was in the past the *prime time* of radio has become the *drive time* catering to commuters. Also, for today's elderly, the radio is still an important information deliverer. In answer to the question "What is your primary source of news in the early morning? Is it TV, radio, or newspaper?" 60.3 percent of the elderly respondents identified the radio; and, for 71.2 percent, the radio was the primary source of weather information in the early morning (Davis and Davis, 1985, p. 178).

Thus, in reference to these new developments in telecommunication, the portion of broadcasting in telecommunication will probably decrease but will not be totally superceded by narrowcasting. "There will always be media events that will draw community and nation together for both serious purposes and less serious entertainment" (Baldwin and McVoy, 1983, p. 356), especially when they are delivered to the consumer cost-free.

Research about the relationship of the elderly to broadcast television increased considerably in the last decade (see Davis, 1980; Davis and Davis, 1985; Kubey, 1980). However, in comparison to the television research focusing on children, it is still minor (Pearl et al., 1982). A major problem remaining is that most of the research about television and the elderly is descriptive and correlative. Therefore more theory-oriented, explanatory research is needed in general. In addition, research should look at the impact of television on the elderly and the impact of television's portrayal of age on younger age groups (Comstock et al., 1978; Rubin, 1982). The latter seems to be particularly important since children are heavy television watchers. This must be realized due to the increasing dominance of the two-generation family. The televised world might become the predominant information delivery system about aging for children (see also Postman, 1983).

Far less research has been done about new technologies and their relation to the elderly. Kerschner and Chelsvig Hart (1984) have only made a first, preliminary step in this field. As the development of technology continues its rapid growth, more research and development *about* and *with* the elderly is necessary. Some fertile areas of research may be the needs and wants of the elderly concerning these technologies and their software, as well as models of participation and user control (see Jones, 1983). A clear understanding of the technologies, their potential uses, and the options and alternatives we have in their application to home and social uses for the elderly is of high priority (Jones, 1981; see also Hearing about High Technology and its Benefits for an Aging Population before the Select Committee on Aging, House of Representatives, May 22, 1984; Brickfield, 1984).

What is the minimal knowledge necessary to use the services and technologies? What are the necessary capabilities (i.e., search techniques)? How can the world's knowledge be indexed to facilitate its use by the common citizen? How should the market be organized so that certain groups are not excluded? Are there different communicative intents of the elderly concerning the ways of delivering televised instruction? How do they rely on the mental effort during learning and the learning outcomes (see Salomon, 1984)? These are some questions for research, development, and action for and with older adults. For "the electronic evolution of society is unassailable and unstoppable. However, the direction in which that evolution proceeds requires conscious planning if we are to influence and shape its impact on human beings and their society" (Jones, 1981, p. 32).

In a study about the future of telecommunication, the majority of experts estimated a significant share of new telecommunications services in the United States and other countries in the Organization for Economic Cooperation and Development (OECD) by the year 2000. For example, according to 55 percent of the experts, videotext will reach a market penetration of 5 to 10 percent in the OECD countries in the year 2000; 58 percent of the experts predicted that there will be home telecommunication centers in 25 percent of the Unites States homes (Pelton, 1981). A home communications center can be used for a variety of purposes. Education is one of them. With these techniques, new delivery systems for education of new groups of students become increasingly available. One of these groups may be the elderly. Even though their participation in adult education increased slightly from 4.5 percent of the age group 55 years and over in 1978 (National Center for Education Statistics, 1980) to 5.3 percent in 1981 (Grant and Snyder, n.d.), this portion is still far less than representative. In addition, this is only about a third of the percentage of younger age groups involved in this type of education.

Most adult education is now run by the private sector or by industry (Willis, 1985). Therefore, for certain subgroups of society such as the retired there is not the opportunity for this education, particularly since the retired elderly have little chance of receiving on-the-job training. *As we are shifting from an industrial to a postindustrial or information society there is an increasing social obligation to educate these elderly by using all available channels for disseminating education, both in general and specifically about these new services and potentials.* However, this education does not mean perfect accommodation to the changes of an information society. Another even more important aspect of this issue is that the educated become active participants in these advances "to ensure the continuing development of new technologies capable of meeting their evolving needs" (Jones, 1983, p. 155).

In the preceding paragraphs an optimistic picture about the future for the elderly was drawn. However, this is only one side of the picture. The information society is a *literacy-intensive society.* Basic reading and writing skills are needed more than ever before (Naisbitt, 1982). This must be realized, since as demonstrated in the recent report "A Nation at Risk" (National Commission on Excellence in Education, 1983), "some 23 million American adults are functionally illiterate by the simplest tests of everyday reading, writing, and comprehension" (National Commission on Excellence in Education, 1983, p. 8).

In other words, there is a danger that not all members of the society may participate in the progress and accrue the benefits of the information technology for daily, independent life. Considering that professional knowledge is necessary to master the information overload and to get access to the resources principally available via terminals and screens at home, it is possible that only a small proportion of the elderly (those well-educated and/or self-instructed during the lifelong learning process) might gain the increasing benefits and access the potential merits of the information technology. They might be far better able to satisfy their coping, expressive, contributive, influential, and transcendence needs (McClusky, 1971). On the other hand, probably this will not occur for the greater part of the elderly (see also National Commission on Excellence in Education, 1983). Therefore, the likelihood will increase of dividing the society as well as the subgroup of the elderly into a small elite group of beneficiaries and a majority excluded from the benefits of these innovations (see also Baldwin and McVoy, 1983; Elton and Carey, 1983).

Further, the assumption that *"high-tech leads to high-touch"* (Naisbitt, 1982) can be verified with many convincing examples, but the opposite is also possible. This is confirmed by self-reports of the target group. The majority complain that machines make life too impersonal, and half of them are confused and bothered by using the products of the information technology (Kerschner and Chelsvig Hart, 1984). The majority of the elderly still prefer to go shopping and banking without the use of telecommunication since these outings allow for face-to-face contacts. However, the advantages may meet the wants and needs of a certain subgroup of the elderly. For example, for the homebound and other persons with restricted mobility these innovations can contribute to a more independent lifestyle in a familiar environment.

Other questions concern the amount of time spent watching television. Will the amount of passive television consumption increase because of the time saved due to activities which can be realized now via two-way cable telecommunication? Will high-tech perhaps lead only to vicarious reinforcement (Bandura, 1977), and to an increasing isolation of certain subgroups of the elderly? These questions cannot yet be answered (see Bengtson, 1984; Black and Bengtson, 1977), but there are some indications that certain subgroups of heavy television viewers will increase their television consumption (Nielsen, 1984; Agostino, 1980).

Still unforeseen is the reaction of the educational system. Will they use the technologies to raise the quality of their services? Will they resist the information technology as the majority resisted instructional technology despite repeated proof that it better fit the learning conditions of the clientele (Heinrich, 1984)?

Research in instructional technology also reveals that

> media do not affect learning in and of themselves. Rather, some particular qualities of media may affect particular cognitions that are relevant for the learning of the knowledge or skill required by students with specific aptitude levels when learning some tasks. *These cognitive effects are not necessarily unique to one or another medium or attribute of a medium. The same cognitive effect may often be obtained by other means* (Clark and Salomon, in press, p. 45, emphasis added).

In other words, a decision concerning the pros and cons of broadcasting versus narrowcasting cannot be made with theoretical learning criteria alone. Additional criteria are to be considered in implementing and using telecommunication and its services. Perhaps the most important is the economic cost–benefit ratio. The dramatic falling off of prices for hardware is not equal to the price for the software. On the contrary, the production costs for software are still high. The price for professional work is more likely to increase instead of decrease. For an entrepreneur, this means that the risk for the return of investment is high, especially when the markets become increasingly smaller due to differentiation (Toffler, 1980).

There is still a lack of appropriate software for these new technologies (see Baldwin and McVoy, 1983). Jones (1983) reviews three public nonprofit experiments (WETA-TV, On-Line Computer Library Center, Green Thumb) and five commercial operations (Knight Rider, Times Mirror, Warner Amex Cable Communications Company, The Source, and CompuServe) with videotext, teletext, and home computer systems. "Their offerings vary between specialized information; a mixture of information, message, and transactional services; and entertainment" (Jones, 1983, p. 147), with limited interactivity. The actual software is far away from ladling out the possibilities of these technologies in order to create applications and services unimaginable now, but which will characterize the third wave of communication (Naisbitt, 1982; Toffler, 1980). Jones (1983, p. 153) concludes: "technically and economically these problems are on their way to solution. *The real problem is to identify and recognize the information needs of citizens today* and to develop the software to meet these needs."

Baldwin and McVoy (1983) point out "that cable companies are promising services beyond tested technical capabilities at the time of application" in order to get franchises. Who will feed the 24 public access channels, i.e., produce material for 576 daily hours of channel time available? Will the gap between professional and "home made" television programming (Rosenmayr, 1983) facilitate or hinder the feeding of these channels? PACE and READING are still the two most often mentioned examples of the successful use of the new telecommunication technology for and by the elderly. A later example is "Life at the Top," a public access cable television program for elders in Memphis, Tennessee (Winter, 1985). But are they representative? Can these experiences be transferred to the elderly in general? Will the private sector develop data banks which are geared toward the needs of the individual citizen and offer software which is especially directed to the sophistication levels and economic capabilities of the private nonindustrial user? Jones (1981, p. 49) doubts that. Thus, it seems that there are some dark clouds rising over the horizons of "Third Wave" telecommunication already (see also Postman, 1985).

CONCLUSION

In sum, an analysis and complete evaluation comparing the benefits for the elderly of narrowcasting to broadcasting is not possible at the present time. As was pointed out, not only must several criteria be considered in future research, but we must also consider how these criteria interrelate. Furthermore, it is an oversimplification to speak about the elderly and their relation to broad- or narrowcasting in general terms, especially when focusing on educational and educative purposes. A differentiation of elderly cohorts on the basis of personality characteristics as well as the potential services of narrowcasting (some of which are still unforeseen) must first be made. In regard to this research, one fruitful conception for future hypotheses in educational settings for older adult learning might be the *mastery learning concept*, initially developed in regard to school-age children (Bloom, 1971). More theory-oriented and differentiated hypotheses must be developed and empirically tested in order to close the gaps in current research and to move research past the speculation which is presently dominating the field of mass media, a field whose latest developments are of great concern to the elderly.

REFERENCES

AARP (American Association of Retired Persons) (1983). *You're on the air.*
ADAMS, M., and GROEN, R. (1974). *Reaching the retired: A survey of the media habits, preferences, and needs of senior citizens in Metro Toronto.* Ottawa: Information Canada. (Catalogue No. BC 92-9/1974).
AGOSTINO, D. (1980). Cable television's impact on the audience of public television. *Journal of Broadcasting, 24,* 347–365.
AMES, E., and FABRIKANT, G. (1985). The smorgasbord of how-to home videos. *Business Week, No. 2877, January 21, 1985,* 55, 58.
BALDWIN, T. F., GREENBERG, B. S., BLOCK, M. P., and STOYANOFF, N. (1978). Rockford, Ill.: Cognitive and affective outcomes. *Journal of Communication, 28,* 180–194.
BALDWIN, T. F., and McVOY, D. S. (1983). *Cable communication.* Englewood Cliffs, New Jersey: Prentice-Hall.
BANDURA, A. (1977). *Social learning theory.* Englewood Cliffs, New Jersey: Prentice-Hall.
BEARDSLEY, R. (Ed.). (1982). *The home video and cable yearbook 1982–83.* New York: Facts on File.
BENGTSON, V. L. (1984). Competence, aging, and social support systems: Implications of telecommunications technology. In R. E. Dunkle, M. R. Haug, and M. Rosenberg (Eds.), *Communications technology and the elderly. Issues and forecasts.* New York: Springer.
BLACK, K. E., and BENGTSON, V. L. (1977). Implications of telecommunications technology for old people, families, and bureaucracies. In E. Shanas and M. B. Sussman (Eds.), *Family, bureaucracies, and the elderly.* Durham, North Carolina: Duke.
BLOOM, B. S. (1971). Mastery learning. In J. H. Block (Ed.), *Mastery learning: Theory and practice.* New York: Holt, Rinehart & Winston.
BOTWINICK, R. (1978). *Aging and behavior, 2nd edition.* New York: Springer.
BOWER, R. T. (1973). *Television and the public.* New York: Holt, Rinehart, & Winston.
BRICKFIELD, C. F. (1984). Attitudes and perceptions of elder people. In P. K. Robinson, J. Livingston, and J. Birren (Eds.), *Aging and technological advances.* New York: Plenum.
BUREAU OF THE CENSUS (1983). *Statistical abstract of the United States 1984, 104th edition.* Washington, D.C.: U.S. Government Printing Office.
BURRUS-BAMMEL, L. L., and BAMMEL, G. (1985). Leisure and creation. In J. E. Birren and K. W. Schaie (Eds.), *Handbook of the psychology of aging, 2nd edition.* New York: Van Nostrand Reinhold Co., Inc.

CABLE VISION (a monthly magazine).

CARNEGIE COMMISSION ON HIGHER EDUCATION (1982). *The fourth revolution: Instructional technology in higher education.* New York: McGraw-Hill.

CHICKERING, A. W., and HAVIGHURST, R. J. (1981). The life cycle. In A. W. Chickering and associates, *The modern American college: Responding to the new realities of diverse students and a changing society.* San Francisco: Jossey-Bass.

CLARK, R. E., and SALOMON, G. (In press). Media in teaching. In M. Witrock (Ed.), *Handbook of research on teaching, Vol. III.* New York: Macmillan.

COHEN, E. S. (1984). Aging and technological advances in telecommunications. In P. K. Robinson, J. L. Livingston, and J. E. Birren (Eds.), *Aging and technological advances.* New York: Plenum.

COLLEGE OF EXTENDED STUDIES, SAN DIEGO STATE UNIVERSITY. *Televised educational growth opportunities.*

COMSTOCK, G., CHAFFEE, S., KATZMAN, N., McCOMBS, M., and ROBERTS, D. (1978). *Television and human behavior.* New York: Columbia University Press.

CROSS, P. K. (1981). *Adults as learners.* San Francisco: Jossey-Bass.

DALE, E. (1965). *Audiovisual methods in teaching, 3rd edition.* New York: Center for Applied Research in Education.

DANOWSKI, J. A. (1975). *Informational aging: Interpersonal and mass communication patterns in a retirement community.* Paper presented at the 28th annual meeting of the Gerontological Society. Louisville, Kentucky.

DANOWSKI, J. A., and HANNEMANN, G. J. (1980). Aging and preferences for interactive cable services. *Journal of Broadcasting, 24,* 337–345.

DAVIS, R. H. (1971). Television and the older adult. *Journal of Broadcasting, 15,* 153–159.

DAVIS, R. H. (1978). Advocacy: Using media to change attitude. *The Gerontologist, 18,* 408.

DAVIS, R. H. (1979). Understanding media as instructional aids in gerontology. *Educational Gerontology, 4,* 57–65.

DAVIS, R. H. (1980). *Television and the aging audience.* Los Angeles: The Ethel Percy Andrus Gerontology Center, University of Southern California.

DAVIS, R. H., and DAVIS, J. A. (1985). *TV's image of the elderly.* Lexington, Massachusetts: Lexington Books.

DAVIS, R. H., and FLEISHER, D. (1979). *The Prime Time film series.* Los Angeles: The Ethel Percy Andrus Gerontology Center, University of Southern California.

DAVIS, R. H., and MILLER, R. V. (1983). The acquisition of specialized information by older adults through utilization of new telecommunications technology. *Educational Gerontology, 9,* 217–232.

DeGRAZIA, S. (1961). The uses of time. In R. W. Kleemeier (Ed.), *Aging and leisure.* New York: Oxford University Press.

DOOLITTLE, J. C. (1979). News media use by older adults. *Journalism Quarterly, 56,* 311–317, 345.

EIGLER, G., and STRAKA, G. A. (1978). *Mastery learning—Lernerfolg fuer jeden?* Muenchen/Wien/Baltimore: Urban and Schwarzenberg.

ELLIOTT, J. (1984). The daytime television drama portrayal of older adults. *The Gerontologist, 24,* 628–633.

ELTON, M., and CAREY, J. (1983). Computerizing information: Consumer reactions to teletext. *Journal of Communication, 33*(1), 162–173.

FORMAN, D. C., and RICHARDSON, P. (1977). Open learning and guidelines for the designing of instructional materials. *Technological Horizons in Education, 4* (January 1977), 9–12, 18.

FRANKFURTER ALLGEMEINE (February 14, 1985). Auf Beta entfällt weniger als 20%.

GAGNÉ, R. M. (1977). *The conditions of learning, 3rd edition.* New York: Holt, Rinehart & Winston.

GRANT, W. V., and SNYDER, T. D. (n.d.). *Digest of education statistics 1983–84.* Washington, D.C.: National Center for Educational Statistics.

HAEFNER, K. (1982). Die neue Bildungskrise. Herausforderung der Informationstechnik an Bildung und Ausbildung. Basel: Bikhaeuser.

HARRINGTON, M. H. (1977). *A study of mass media use, preferences and needs of an elderly population in the San Diego area.* San Diego State University, M.A. thesis.

HARRIS, L., AND ASSOCIATES, INC. (1975). *The myth and reality of aging in America.* Washington, D.C.: The National Council on Aging.

HAVIGHURST, R. J. (1972). *Developmental tasks in education, 3rd edition.* New York: McKay.

HEARING BEFORE THE SELECT COMMITTEE ON AGING, HOUSE OF REPRESENTATIVES (May 22, 1984). *High technology and its benefits for an aging population.* Washington, D.C.: U.S. Government Printing Office (Comm. Pub. No. 98-459).

HEINRICH, R. (1984). The proper study of instructional technology. *ERIC/ECTJ Annual Review Paper, 32,* 67–68.

HOLBERG, B. (1975). *Distance education: Survey and bibliography.* New York: Nichols Publishing Co.

JONES, M. G. (1981). Telecommunications technologies: New approaches to consumer information dissemination. *The Information Society, 1* (1981–82), 31–52.

JONES, M. G. (1983). The challenge of the new information technologies: The need to respond to citizens' information needs. *The Information Society, 2* (1983–84), 145–156.

KAY, P., and GERENDASY, S. (1976). *Social services and cable TV.* Washington, D.C.: U.S. Government Printing Office.

KERSCHNER, P. A., and CHELSVIG HART, K. (1984). The aged user and technology. In R. E. Dunkle, M. R. Haug, and M. Rosenberg (Eds.), *Communications technology and the elderly. Issues and forecasts.* New York: Springer.

KORNBLUH, M. (1984). Computer and telecommunications applications to enhance the quality of life and of our elderly. In P. K. Robinson, J. E. Livingston, and J. E. Birren (Eds.), *Aging and technological advances.* New York: Plenum.

KUBEY, R. W. (1980). Television and aging: Past, present, and future. *The Gerontologist, 20,* 16–35.

LA BUDA, D. (1978). *Using instructional television in education for the elderly.* M.A. thesis. San Jose: California State University.

LEVY, M. L., and FINK, L. (1984). Home video recorders and the transience of television broadcasts. *Journal of Communication, 34*(2), 56–71.

LIEBERMAN RESEARCH, INC. (June 1977). *Summary and conclusions: The impact of the Getting On television program on people's attitudes toward and images of older people.* New York: Department of Aging.

LONG, H. B. (1983). *Adult learning–Research and practice.* New York: Cambridge.

McCLUSKY, H. Y. (1971). *Education: Background and issues.* Washington, D.C.: White House Conference on Aging.

MOSS, M. L. (Ed.). (1978). *Two-way cable television: An evaluation of community uses in Reading, Pennsylvania, Vol. 1.*

MOSS, M. L. (1978a.) Reading, Pa.: Research on community uses. *Journal of Communication, 28*(2), 160–167.

NAISBITT, J. (1982). *Megatrends.* New York: Warner.

NATIONAL CENTER FOR EDUCATION STATISTICS (Feb. 5, 1980). *Participation in adult education, 1978 report.* Washington, D.C.: Department of Health, Education, and Welfare.

NATIONAL COMMISSION ON EXCELLENCE IN EDUCATION (1983). *A nation at risk: The imperative for educational reform: A report to the nation and the Secretary of Education.* Washington, D.C.: United States Department of Education.

NIELSEN MEDIA RESEARCH (1982–84). *Nielsen report on television.* New York: A. C. Nielsen Company.

OFFICE OF COMMUNICATION RESEARCH (1981). *An evaluation of Over Easy, 2nd edition.* Washington, D.C.: Corporation of Public Broadcasting.

OLSON, D. (1977). Oral and written communication and the cognitive processing of children. *Journal of Communication, 27,* 10–26.

OLSON, D., and BRUNER, J. (1974). Learning through experience and learning through media. In D. Olson (Ed.), *Media and symbols: The forms of expression, communication, and education. 73rd Yearbook of the N.S.S.E.* Chicago: University of Chicago Press.

PAISLEY, W. (1983). Computerizing information: Lessons of a videotext trial. *Journal of Communication, 33*(1), 153–161.

PEARL, D., BOUTHILET, B., and LAZAR, J. (Eds.) (1982). *Television and behavior, Vol. II.* Rockville, Maryland: National Institute of Mental Health (DHHW Publication No. [ADM] 82-1196).

PELTON, J. N. (1981). The future of telecommunications: A delphi survey. *Journal of Communication, 31*(1), 177–189.

PETERSON, D. A. (1983). *Facilitating learning for older people.* San Francisco: Jossey-Bass.

POSTMAN, N. (1983). *The disappearance of childhood.* New York: Dell Pub.

POSTMAN, N. (1985). *Amusing ourselves to death.* New York: Viking-Penguin.

PRATT, J. D., and WOOD, L. E. (1984). Cognition and elderly people. *Ageing and Society, 4,* 273–304.

REAL, M., ANDERSON, H. L., and HARRINGTON, M. H. (1980). Television access for older adults. *Journal of Communication, 30,* 81–88.

RICHARDSON, P. (1980). Telecommunications and adult learning: What nine projects reveal. *New Directions for Continuing Education, 5,* 31–40.

RICHARDSON, P. (1983). Issues in television-centered instruction. In L. N. Purdy (Ed.), *Reaching new students through new technologies.* Dubuque: Kendall & Hunt.

RICHTER, J. (1984). Interactive television and the elderly. In R. E. Dunkle, M. R. Haug, and M. Rosenberg (Eds.), *Communications technology and the elderly: Issues and forecasts.* New York: Springer.

ROCKART, J. F., and MORTON, S.M.S. (1975). *Computers and the learning process in higher education.* A report prepared for the Carnegie Commission on Higher Education. New York: McGraw-Hill.

ROSENMAYR, L. (1983). *Die spaete Freiheit.* Berlin: Severin und Siedler.

RUBIN, A. M. (1982). Directions in television and aging research. *Journal of Broadcasting, 26,* 537–551.

SALOMON, G. (1981). *Communication and education.* Beverly Hills: Sage.

SALOMON, G. (1984). Television is "easy" and print is "tough": The differential investment of mental effort in learning as a function of perceptions and attributions. *Journal of Educational Psychology, 76,* 647–658.

SCHRAMM, W. (1969). Aging and mass communication. In M. Riley, J. Riley, and M. Johnson (Eds.), *Aging and society, Vol. 2. Aging and the professions.* New York: Russell Sage Foundation.

STRAKA, G. A. (1981). Zielerreichendes Lernen. In H. Schiefele and H. Krapp, (Eds.), *Handlexikon zur paedagogischen Psychologie.* Muenchen: Ehrenwirth.

STRAKA, G. A. (1983). Features of a form of didactics based upon teaching–learning theory. *Education, 28,* 56–58.

TOFFLER, A. (1980). *The third wave.* New York: Bantam.

WELFORD, A. T. (1981). Signal, noise, performance, and aging. *Human Factors, 23,* 97–109.

WIESNER, P. (1983). Some observations on telecourse research and practice. *Adult Education Quarterly, 33,* 215–221.

WILLIS, S. L. (1985). Towards an educational psychology of the older adult learner: Intellectual and cognitive bases. In J. E. Birren and K. W. Schaie (Eds.), *The handbook of the psychology of aging.* New York: Van Nostrand Reinhold Co., Inc. (pp. 818–847).

WINTER, R. (1985). Elders are video pioneers. *WGS (Western Gerontological Society) Connection, 6*(1), 7.

WIRTH, M. O., BALDWIN, T. F., and ZENATY, J. (1984). Demand for sex-oriented cable TV in the USA. *Telecommunication Policy, 8,* 314–320.

WOOLLEY, J. C. (1984). Videotext: A new way to communicate. In R. E. Dunkle, M. R. Haug, and M. Rosenberg (Eds.), *Communications technology and the elderly: Issues and forecasts.* New York: Springer.

5

LATE LIFE LEARNING IN THE INFORMATION SOCIETY

Harry R. Moody

The settled pessimism of so much of the culture of the late 20th century is in effect an absolute loss of the future: of any significant belief that it can be both different and better.

Raymond Williams, *The Year 2000*

INTRODUCTION

The closing decades of the 20th century are witnessing a dramatic transformation in the structure of the world economy and American society. New technologies, from microcomputers to satellite transmission, are creating a global communication network, a transnational information society, with far-reaching implications for the future. At the same time, the advent of an information society coincides with an-

The author is grateful for a Mina Shaughnessy Scholarship from the Fund for the Improvement of Post-Secondary Education (U.S. Dept. of Education), which provided sabbatical support during preparation of this chapter.

other historical watershed: the demographic aging of the populations in advanced industrial societies (Pifer and Bronte, 1986). Both developments—the information society and population aging—will interact in unforeseeable ways.

Will the coming of an information society enhance the learning environment for an aging population? There are signs that point in contradictory directions. An information society is in many ways inhospitable to old age. First, it is inhospitable because the centrality of information and abstract knowledge depreciates knowledge derived from life experience; for example, accelerating innovation in the economy tends toward skill obsolescence (Achenbaum, 1974). Second, the speed of manipulation and transmission of information by electronic technology induces habits of haste and impatience with the slower learning style of later life. And third, the instantaneous propagation of information through mass media accelerates the fashion, novelty and sensation of the present. Past and future become absorbed by sensate immediacy. Increasingly, the old feel left out. The result is a "new ageism" driven by technological change and reinforced by the political economy of the post-industrial world.

At the same time, the information society opens up new ways to offer more segments of the population access to information. Computers and microelectronics provide decentralized availability of information allowing enhanced control of the environment. For example, new technology will enable more homebound elderly to participate in society even when physical mobility is restricted. And, because productive tasks can now be performed with less stress and physical labor, there are, in principle, many more ways in which an aging population could become productive.

Here precisely is the contradiction. Lifelong learning and enhanced productivity are now made technologically feasible in an aging society (Bonham, 1980). Yet the system of politics and culture reinforces the obsolescence of old age and discourages older people from making effective use of the new tools for life enrichment. This contradiction stands at the center of dilemmas faced by an aging population in an information society.

In the discussion that follows, late-life learning is examined along several distinct lines: first, changes in the psychology of information processing over the life span; second, the economic shift toward a postindustrial society; third, the impact of an information society on different age groups and on the structure of the life course itself; fourth, the distinctions between information, knowledge, and wisdom, and the prospect for enriched learning in the later years. The chapter concludes with some suggestions for the design of late-life educational programs based on emerging trends in the information society.

THE PSYCHOLOGY OF INFORMATION PROCESSING IN LATE LIFE

The new information environment. There are age-related differences in learning and memory that are important in late-life learning (Willis, 1985). Many of these age-related differences are likely to put older people at a disadvantage in coping with the new environment of an information society. This new environment presents an unprecedented quantity, volatility, rapidity, and incoherence of information. It is not only more "information-rich" and dense with more differentiated kinds of information. The environment also moves toward ever higher speeds of information transmission and tends toward fragmentation and dissolution of enduring cultural forms through which one might make sense of new information. This quantity, rapidity, volatility, and incoherence places unprecedented demands on information-processing and learning capacities of older people.

Age-related changes in learning. The most important age-related changes in learning are those involving speed and short-term (recent) memory rather than memory of past events. Broadly speaking, older people perform worse on tasks demanding speed, as opposed to power or intrinsic capacity for learning. In real-life settings—for example, driving a car—losses of speed of reaction time can often be compensated for by perceptual and cognitive strategies. But the loss of speed is undeniable. Psychological research demonstrates that, individual differences aside, with age people become slower in their reaction time to stimuli. This fact does not mean the old are unable to learn. On the contrary, once the old have learned new material, they are likely to remember it as well as younger people. But their ability to learn new information is also influenced by whether the material is *meaningful* or not. For example, the elderly do far worse than younger persons in recalling nonsense syllables, just as they do much worse when tasks are presented with demands for speed of performance.

There remains vigorous debate about the extent and character of declines in intellectual capacity over the life span. There is further controversy about the cause of such changes, about whether such declines are reversible, and about the role of education as an intervention strategy for reversing declines (Peterson, 1983). But certain trends in the research findings are clear. Most studies do suggest that declines in performance are to be found in fluid rather than in crystallized intelligence (Horn, 1982). This distinction is an important one. What it means is that, with advancing age, people are more likely to retain intellectual capacities built on cumulative (crystallized) information learned through long experience.

What are the implications of these findings for late-life learning in an information society? First and foremost there is the contrast between optimal information-processing modes in late life and the demands of the new information environment. Crystallized intelligence becomes less valuable, while fluid intelligence becomes more so. An information society provides a vastly enlarged range of information through a multiplicity of channels. Just as the first industrial revolution brought an upsurge in available energy, so the postindustrial drive toward an information economy brings an upsurge in the sheer quantity of available information.

Emerging information technology offers a leap in the *speed* by which we are able to gain access to a vastly enlarged domain of information. For example, through "windowing" software on personal computers, one can simultaneously observe data drawn from an array of data sets and then reconfigure data according to rapidly shifting criteria. In this environment the need for psychological mnemonics or other recall strategies grows smaller since microelectronics makes information instantly available. Even elementary memory tasks seem suddenly obsolete: why learn the multiplication tables when a pocket calculator can do the job?

While eroding reliance on memory, the technology of an information society also cultivates ever higher rates of speed, and so encourages greater impatience with those who cannot keep up with high speed. Just as city-dwellers grow impatient with "country bumpkins" who don't drive fast enough, so the younger generation grows impatient with older people whose speed is not up to the enhanced power of information processing. In all of modern life, the habit of speed has accelerated. The information society reinforces that habit of speed on the mental and social plane. The result of this new environment is to put older people at a disadvantage because they are likely to perform worse on tasks demanding speed. The result is also to push aside a certain style of learning—for example, critical thinking or the cultivation of wisdom that might require time and slow reflection in order to flourish at all.

Just as the quantity of information has devalued memory, so the capacity to manipulate information has devalued certain skills and roles prized by traditional education. In an age of pocket calculators, why teach arithmetic in the traditional manner? In reality, however, the need for strategies of mnemonics, heuristics, and pattern recognition has never been greater than in an era of instant information. It is precisely *because* of ubiquitous pocket calculators that it is more necessary than ever to acquire skills for estimating numerical quantities in arithmetic. Estimation means having a "rough-and-ready" capacity to judge the plausibility of rule-governed solutions against a wider context. Estimation means being able to know whether a proposed solution "makes sense." Failing to learn strategies for estimation means being condemned to take the calculator's answer (or the computer's answer) at face value. It means failing to have any cognitive framework for *judging* truth-values or appraising their plausibility in the light of experience.

Gains of life experience.   It is important to recognize that the coming of an information society offers contradictory trends for late-life learning. The rise in sheer information density and differentiation in itself need not be a disadvantage for the elderly. The key factor will be whether life experience serves to promote late-life learning and thus help older people to cope with the new information environment. Here again the psychology of information processing helps illuminate the problem. Well-established findings in the psychology of learning underscore the importance of "chunking" strategies: that is, grouping bits of data into broader, more comprehensible units for learning. Many older people have well-developed cognitive strategies for "chunking" data (e.g., mnemonics, metaphors, associative patterning). But these cognitive strategies are generally applied to familiar domains of information, not necessarily to new, initially meaningless data.

Consider some simple examples. Long experience with a small-town college library would make it easier, not harder, for a person suddenly walking into the Library of Congress for the first time. In the same way, an older, seasoned world-traveller would probably find it easier to find the way around in a strange foreign city than would a younger person who had never travelled abroad before. To encounter an enormous library or a strange city is to be exposed to a bewildering flood of new stimuli. But to have learned "chunking" skills—strategies sometimes called "learning how to learn"—is a big step forward in knowing how to screen out irrelevant data under the threat of stimulus overload. Note, however, that in the examples offered here we are *not* describing older persons whose earlier experiences were "information-poor": that is, persons lacking education or other opportunities to develop "cognitive maps" allowing them to travel on unknown terrain.

The trip to the Library of Congress or to a foreign city represents only one type of example of an upsurge of available information. Another information upsurge would be the case of a rural villager from the Third World suddenly transported into Times Square. In this case, the rural villager is likely to be utterly lost and overwhelmed by new stimuli. Just as a sudden electrical surge can burn out a microcomputer, so an unexpected information surge can "burn out" our habitual information-processing capacity. Anthropological evidence suggests that the rural villager suddenly confronted with a modern environment is likely to be confused and demoralized by the bewildering variety of stimuli and information. The question for the future, then, is basically this: Which analogy best describes the situation of older people in an information society . . . the seasoned library-user or world traveller, on the one hand, or the bewildered rural villager, on the other?

Cognitive strategies and lifespan development.   The answer will depend on the effectiveness of cognitive strategies for learning from prior experience and transferring that experiential knowledge to novel situations. This observation points to the central question: How is it possible to learn cognitive strategies that are genuinely *developmental*—that is, progressive or cumulative—so that new information does not result in overload but is organized through patterns adaptable to new settings? At what points in the life course can one acquire these cognitive strategies? Specifically, how do we design educational interventions to enable people to derive from their own experience new strategies for coping with a complex information environment? If late-life learning is to draw on the gains of life experience, then these questions must move to the center of adult education in the information society.

The answer to these questions will be found in a deeper understanding of what it means to "learn from experience." Specifically, we need to look at the role of analogy in learning over the life span. Learning by analogy is very different from simply accumulating information or applying procedural rules from prior experience. Analogical learning is the capacity of human intelligence to recognize similarities and differences among infinitely varied categories of experience. Instead of responding to new information in terms of a fixed pattern of response, analogical learning involves a lawful transformation of earlier patterns according to some heuristic principle. It is to this process, found in a variety of fields from manual crafts and trades to the most advanced levels of theoretical physics, that Michael Polanyi gives the name "personal knowledge" (Polanyi, 1958).

This personal knowledge is what we call, for lack of a better name, "learning from life experience." Instead of the reinforcement of a fixed habit pattern, personal knowledge results in the acquisition of flexible responses to new stimuli. Learning from experience requires complex cognitive strategies for analogical reasoning in coping with different fields of information. It is a method of discovery (heuristics). Thinking by means of analogy or metaphor means employing a cognitive strategy drawn from *heuristic* rather than *algorithmic* (rule-governed) problem-solving.

It is common enough to see older people who have devoted years of life experience mastering algorithms that have been quickly rendered obsolete either by new circumstances or by sheer information overload. These people have indeed "learned from experience." But the result of their learning has only been deeper *habituation* ill-adapted to the new information society (Kastenbaum, 1984). All too often such rigid "learning from experience" is taken as a sign of "premature aging." The problem is that any set of fixed algorithms—rules of procedure—will be threatened by radical reconfiguration of the information environment. By contrast, those older people who also have "learned from experience" by acquiring skills of analogical thinking will find it possible to build on prior experience even in a radically new information environment. Those older people commonly judged "wise" are those who respond to genuinely novel situations by applying the lessons of experience in an entirely new context. They do not abandon past experience, but they apply their learning analogically (Clayton and Birren, 1980; Staude, 1981).

AGING AND POSTINDUSTRIAL SOCIETY

Changing structure of knowledge. Changes in information processing or cognitive strategy must be set against the background of a wider epistemological transformation evident with the coming of postindustrial society. The hallmark of the new information society is not only speed or quantity of information but a shift in the structure of knowledge itself. There is growing complexity, specialization, and multiple branching of interconnections among all fields of knowledge: molecular biology, cybernetics, neuropsychology, and so on (Bell, 1973). The result is to accelerate specialization while at the same time eroding the boundaries between theory and practice. Practical experience now becomes mediated by abstract forms of knowledge whose boundaries constantly recede. Flow charts and computer simulations replace certitudes derived from practical judgment. Age and experience offer no guideposts because ordinary experience is no longer intelligible on its own terms, and so the knowledge derived from experience is susceptible to obsolescence.

The most valuable commodity in a society becomes, not experiential knowledge, but technical knowledge: operations research, genetic engineering, software design, market forecasting, and so on. Each advance unleashes new *forces* of production, foremost among them being telecommunications technology and the computer. But the information society also exhibits new *relations* in the production and distribution of knowledge. These include shifting power relations among classes, new patterns of industrial growth or decline, a transformation of the educational system, and changing relations among age groups over the life course.

Historical choices. In order to assess prospects for late-life learning in the information society, the development of new forces of production must be clearly distinguished from new relations of production. It is a fundamental error to confuse these two, and it is precisely such confusion that gives rise to a feeling of technological determinism: a sense that advances in technology automatically dictate the social uses to which new technologies will be put. Yet any careful reading of the history of science and technology will refute such determinism. Williams (1983), for example, is particularly anxious to dispel the idea that some sort of technological determinism—for example, the power of new information technology—must dictate the configuration of postindustrial society. To forecast any such future, we need something more than a framework of technological determinism.

Both the *forces* and the *relations* of production must be grasped if we are to understand the new possibilities of learning over the life span. Without this distinction, there is a danger of reification and mystification of information technology (Dupuy, 1980). It is this danger that Williams refers to as "the unholy alliance of technological determinism with cultural pessimism" (Williams, 1983, p. 129). We imagine that the elderly are somehow "condemned" to live in a futuristic information society where their life experience becomes ever more alienated from the dominant forms of production and knowledge. But such a future is not determined at all. If the pessimistic scenario comes to pass, it will not be because of new forces of production or technology alone. Rather, it will be because we have not grasped the need to change those relations of production that prevent information technology from being used in the service of continued learning and lifespan development.

The information economy. The American economy today is undergoing a profound transformation as it moves toward an information economy (Porat, 1977). A generation ago it was already clear that the major shift in economic development would be a movement away from manufacturing industries and toward the enlargement of the tertiary or service sector. Indeed, that shift has already taken place. Today white-collar jobs in the service sector comprise 52% of the labor force. But the current wave of economic change represents something more profound: the rise of the information sector to a decisive role in the economy (Ginzberg, 1982).

What is included in the information sector of the economy? Defined broadly, it would include printing and publishing; telecommunications of all kinds; mass media; financial services and data processing; research and education; and those manufacturing and service corporations engaged in production and distribution of telecommunications products or services. In postindustrial society the use of such equipment, particularly computers, will be essential for efficiency in manufacturing and transportation, not to mention other service occupations such as retail trade, banking, and financial services.

The historical trend in employment is away from manufacturing toward information industries. The crest of employment in manufacturing came in 1920, when 53% of the work force was thus employed. In that year only 19% held jobs in information, knowledge, education, and other service enterprises. But by 1976, only 4% were employed in agriculture and 29% in manufacturing, while fully one half were employed in the information sector. Another 17% were in other service jobs (Molitor, 1981). It is estimated that by 1990 as many as 10 to 15 million manufacturing workers will no longer be needed in their current jobs. By the year 2000 as few as 2 or 3% of the labor force will be on the farm, while just over 20% will be in manufacturing. By that year nearly two thirds will work in the information sector.

Productivity and job displacement. The introduction of information technology will be the key to future productivity gains through computers, telecommunications, robotics, and automated manufacturing. The next industrial revolution—the transition to an information economy—will be based on an unlimited natural resource: namely, the production and distribution of knowledge (Hamrin, 1981). We are now seeing the substitution of information-intensive capital for energy-intensive capital: telecommunications instead of travel, automated control devices in transportation systems, fuel-efficiency in the heating and cooling of buildings, automated factories to reduce costs and improve productivity.

But productivity gains in manufacturing have already meant a displacement of the work force from traditional blue-collar jobs. The same displacement will occur in white-collar work as well, as word processing, data processing, and electronic communications revolutionize white-collar work and create the "office of the future." Indeed, job displacement *must* occur to achieve productivity gains in the service sector. The optimistic scenario—higher productivity—is simply the other side of a pessimistic scenario—rising unemployment. Many low-level service jobs—in supermarkets, gas stations, retail banking, car washes, and toll booths—will be altered, perhaps toward a "de-skilling" of the work force along the lines that Marxist critics have argued (Braverman, 1976).

There is considerable debate about whether the final result will be an increase or decrease in the total number of jobs and the performance of the economy as a whole. Some observers, like economist Wassily Leontief, predict massive unemployment. But the question about total jobs in the aggregate economy is only part of the problem. What is more certain is that ". . . above and beyond job destruction, the information revolution will bring about job shuffling on an intra-firm, inter-industry, and even inter-regional basis. Significant frictional dislocations can therefore be expected in all sectors of the economy" (Hamrin, 1981). But older workers, for a variety of reasons, are less able to cope with such "job shuffling" and its "frictional dislocations." Where does unemployment cease to be "frictional" and start being recognized as "structural"? In all these discussions, there has been little attention to the impact of information technology on older workers. What is needed today is a "postindustrial gerontology" to understand how the information economy will reshape the life cycle of workers.

Postindustrial gerontology.   The new information technology in the workplace puts a premium on innovation and speed of information transfer, not on the value of accumulated life experience. In an information economy, the experience of older workers decreases in value. What increases in value is speed, quick response time, and short-term memory: all mental functions where older workers are at a disadvantage. Perhaps for this reason, older workers tend to be far more threatened and fearful of computers in the workplace than younger workers are. This fact means that programs to retrain older workers will face a major challenge if older workers are to remain productive in a competitive economic environment. But retraining will be even more necessary because all forms of specialized expertise are susceptible to obsolescence in an economy built on innovation in the knowledge industries.

The real—and unanswered—question is whether we will see that expectation of retraining applied to older workers: not only to technical or professional workers but to the broad cross-section of workers who can be made more productive by continued reinvestment in their level of skills (Stearns, 1985). The assumption that older workers can't be retrained is refuted by the experience in other countries as well as our own (French, 1980; Belbin and Belbin, 1972). Retraining does have its costs, but the cost of failing to retrain workers may be even greater (Reich, 1983). As worker retraining becomes a routine fact of life throughout the adult life span, it may prove easier for such retraining to be continued into the later years.

The jobs for which older workers need retraining are by no means all in high technology areas. Some jobs where high demand is expected are precisely those where older, experienced workers could have an advantage from their life experience. For example, the Bureau of Labor Statistics projects substantial growth by 1990 in labor market demand for midwives, geriatric social workers, and employment interviewers—all fields where age and seasoned experience could be positive features. Substantial job growth of course is also expected in more exotic high technology fields such as genetic engineering, computer systems, or robotics. But these glamour fields should not blind us to the continued demand for services. The information economy will also see continued growth in service industries of all kinds. For example, consider a field such as sales, which has grown both in proportion to the total labor force as well as in workers over age 65. Sales training is a good example of a field where the life experience of older workers can easily be converted into an asset for productivity. But here, too, retraining in changing technical skills will be needed to adapt to the new environment.

For some older workers retraining may mean learning brand-new skills—word-processing or electronic appliance repair, for example. But other jobs make more extensive use of prior skills in new settings. In these jobs there is an important "value-added" component to retraining. Examples would be in learning to be an employment counselor, a midwife, or a real estate broker. "Value-added" jobs are those where prior experience can be reinforced by new technical knowledge. The total combination—life experience plus new training—is a strong one. These value-added jobs, ideal for older workers, take advantage of age and experience. They are jobs where technical knowledge and seasoned experience are complementary and not in opposition to one another.

In any forecast of the future we should avoid painting too rosy a picture. Some of the rapidly growing service jobs depend hardly at all on either prior experience or retraining: jobs such as fast-food workers, for example. Putting grandma or grandpa to work in McDonald's is hardly a cheerful picture of "human resource development" in an aging society. Indeed, the grim side of displacement of older workers is the "de-skilling" of jobs and the consignment of low-skill workers into dead-end jobs or unemployment. The 19th century poorhouse consigned vulnerable old people to institutionalized poverty and the workhouse. In the same fashion tomorrow's postindustrial economy may condemn older workers to de-skilled jobs. To forestall that scenario will demand greater priority for policies based on human development over the entire life span. Unfortunately, to date neither business nor government have shown much imagination in designing such policies for lifespan development and late-life learning (Morrison, 1983).

Lifelong learning in an information society. Many analysts have called for public policies committed to enlarging human capacities over the life span, including those of middle-aged and older adults (Wirtz, 1975; Barton, 1982). Some observers have argued optimistically that the practice of lifelong learning is bound to become increasingly common as our society shifts increasingly toward an information economy. The assumption seems to be that, throughout the life span, individuals will be challenged by the information economy to update skills and knowledge. In this optimistic forecast, the obsolescence of old age would appear as no more than a transitional problem generated by the transformation of the industrial economy towards a postindustrial age. The new technology and economy of the information society will make growth and change available to all age groups over the entire life course.

This new ideology of lifelong learning has become widespread in adult education today. It was articulated in the "Lifelong Learning Act" (1976), but it is actually embodied in thousands of adult education programs flourishing in both higher education and the world of business (Eurich, 1985). The new mood is captured well by W. D. Narr:

> Permanent qualifications, which were acquired over long periods of time and were characteristic of the classic model of the skilled worker, are less desirable today. What is stressed first and foremost in contemporary training is the performance attitude itself, irrespective of the nature of the specific performance. Flexibility and mobility are valued as central postulates . . . . Reschooling and training are the new watchwords (Narr, 1984, p. 37).

What we are witnessing today, he argues, is the fading of authoritarian pedagogies in favor of *pedagogies of flux,* of lifelong learning, or, as Narr puts it, "Process pedagogies (that) teach the art of permanent leave-taking" (Narr, 1984, p. 47). We take our leave with little regret; up-to-date information keeps us well prepared for any contingency. This version of "andragogy" (Knowles, 1980) is well-attuned to the needs of "minimal self" (Lasch, 1984), of "protean man" (Lifton, 1970) in the postindustrial world. As an ideology for lifelong learning, it expresses the interests of the well-educated, young professional who can dexterously redefine past qualifications in order to adapt to fast-changing circumstances. Instead of permanent qualifications, what is prized is just this attitude of infinite flexibility: a self without past or future, indeed with no final identity at all.

What does this ideology of lifelong learning contribute to our understanding of the older learner? Will learning and development in later life actually be enhanced by the transition to an information economy? There are reasons for doubt. The information society places a premium on the ceaseless flow of information. However, the instantaneous availability of information does bring all age groups together in a common present. As W. H. Auden put it, "Today we are all contemporaries." The result is an illusory sensation that the historical separation of old age has somehow been abolished. The information society abolishes generational time in the same way that mass communications over the globe have served to abolish geographical space. Of course, the actual barriers and distances remain, but the illusion of proximity is what captivates our imagination.

The obsolescence of old age. It is now commonplace to hear that, to avoid obsolescence, to "keep up with new ideas," everyone must keep learning while growing older. One of the great clichés of the information society is the idea that we must all keep ourselves informed, almost on a daily basis, about new trends in politics, art, entertainment, technology, and economics. To be caught "uninformed" is to risk embarrassment: one is more easily thought "old," with outdated ideas. Generations succeed each other at an ever faster rate. Increasingly, adults must become informed by their children about the latest trends in fashion, in music, or in electronic technology. All culture becomes "youth culture," and all age groups can participate in that culture, indeed must participate at the risk of becoming obsolete (Mead, 1978).

In this vision of the information society, everyone has a duty to keep on learning in a continual battle against premature aging. Just as cosmetics or plastic surgery promote the illusion of endless youth, so being up-to-date helps defeat the threat of obsolescence. This is a familiar picture of a population of "news junkies," of home computers and portable radios, a world where changing fashions and technology make information into the supreme commodity. The message of the information society is that we must keep consuming more and more of it. In the new commodity market of information exchange, the penalty for being too slow is to fall behind, to be uninformed. Maximizing the speed and flow of information becomes a criterion of youth and a magical antidote for aging. But the dizzying speed of electronic technology makes old age itself obsolete. As the speed and proliferation of information accelerates, we are simultaneously witnessing the disappearance of institutions that might help people make sense of information. The structure of the life course itself is being transformed.

AGE GROUPS IN THE INFORMATION SOCIETY

The modernized life cycle.   The advent of an information society has begun to change the structure of the human life course: the relations between youth, middle adulthood, and old age. The industrial age produced a distinctive, often rigid pattern of these "three boxes" or life-course stages (Bolles, 1978). In the modernized life course the activities of education, work, and leisure were assigned to each of these separate stages of life (Best, 1980). The rise of universal schooling and of a fixed retirement age were both instances of this modernization of the life cycle to conform to the industrial order (Gruman, 1978).

But the postindustrial society operates on a different logic and the information society demands new patterns for the life course. To begin with, the volatility of information shifts the power balance between youth and age in unpredictable ways: if power now depends on instantaneous access to information systems, then age loses many advantages over youth. We move from a hierarchical system to a horizontal "networking" approach to work and communication. Age, experience, and seniority lose their place in the hierarchy. For example, the experienced stockbroker no longer has an edge when the young broker can get a quick printout on the office computer terminal. In medicine, computer-assisted diagnosis makes the older physician's accumulated experience less and less important. Senior corporate management can no longer exercise centralized control of information while junior employees carry out orders. In this sense, the gaps between all age groups shrink.

An age-irrelevant society?   The culture of instantaneous information promotes an "age-irrelevant," present-oriented society where age-grades are progressively abolished (Neugarten, 1974). But age-irrelevance operates only in the realm of culture and information. While the culture promotes maximum flexibility, the economy is moving in the opposite direction: toward greater specialization and narrowing of functions (Bell, 1976). The channeling vehicle for this specialization is the educational system with its control of educational credentials. Here lies the contradiction. The culture of an information economy creates greater openness— to new ideas, to immediate information of all kinds. In this domain, age is irrelevant. But the economy channels human activity according to seniority rules, educational credentials, and other barriers that segment the life course more rigidly. As competition for jobs gets tighter, the economy and the labor market demand stronger enforcement of age-grades through credentialism.

The impact of an information economy is to segment the stages of the life course because knowledge and information, as commodities, become the new passport to success and power. Credentials and diplomas certify that the appropriate information has been acquired. Youth is increasingly dominated by the educational system and by credentialism; old age by the rapid obsolescence of earlier knowledge. In short, the three boxes of life—education, work, retirement— are not abolished, but the relationships between youth and age are disrupted. Instantaneous information erodes expectations and alters the relations between generations.

Credentialism and seniority: The new guild mentality.   An information economy means greater specialization and the ascendency of theoretical knowledge. This change too has implications for age-relations. Mastery of the environment becomes possible through knowledge and information, not life experience. The growth and "branching" of knowledge has contradictory effects on previous educational credentials. It devalues them through obsolescence but at the same time demands new credentials. The net effect is still to erode the claims of age and experience. Specialization finally consolidates the power of credentials but makes acquisition of credentials an endless process of "lifelong learning."

In this process, both the young and the old are pushed into new roles. The growth of specialized fields of knowledge delays or closes off access by younger people to specific fields of work if those young people lack the proper credentials (Berg, 1971). For example, without a high school diploma or a bachelor's degree, a secretarial job may not be open regardless of ability to learn or to perform. Earlier it was possible to become a lawyer through supervised apprenticeship; now law school becomes mandatory. Where in earlier generations it was possible to gain mastery, and social mobility, through direct experience, today increasingly credentialized information alone is the key. Credentialism acts as a screening device that keeps young people in school and reinforces a "youth ghetto." The final irony here is that the value of educational credentials themselves are eroded too. First, credentials are a "positional good" valued for comparative status claims. As more and more people graduate from college, the value of the degree becomes diminished. Second, schools and colleges are less successful today at conveying skills and knowledge previously acquired by credential holders. Since employers know this, young people holding credentials again lose comparative advantage (Freeman, 1976).

But growing specialization and credentialism also make career change in later life more difficult. Here middle-aged and older adults are disadvantaged. The psychological consequences of this condition have been labelled the "one life-one career" syndrome that links aging to a feeling of being trapped (Sarason, 1977). At the level of economic policy, specialization and credentialism have a more serious drawback: they limit the mobility of labor and weaken the total productivity of the work force in much the same way that any caste or guild system diminishes productivity. For example, the fifteen-year veteran of the police force may have many of the human relations skills to make a good social worker but he lacks an

M.S.W. and can't get hired. The woman who's been at home raising a family for a decade or more may find her credentials obsolete when she seeks reentry to the job market. The power of credentialism not only stifles human growth and development; it harms the economy by preventing the mobility of the work force. Seniority rules and credentialism constitute a new "guild mentality" increasingly at odds with the culture and technology of the information society.

Technology and self-directed learning. It is sometimes argued that the spread of new information technology will make possible forms of self-directed learning that serve to undercut the old monopoly power of credential-driven educational institutions. Some studies suggest that self-directed learning already plays a dominant role in adult learning projects (Tough, 1972). New technology will further accelerate that trend. The use of personal computers in the home vastly expands the amount of information available for purposes of lifelong learning. For example, with laser storage discs, it may soon be possible to store and have access to entire libraries on a home computer. In principle, many problems of access to centralized institutions—libraries, classrooms, college campuses—could be solved. Instead of bringing people to centralized learning institutions, knowledge is brought to people in their own homes. Enthusiasm for "distance learning" in many countries, both developing and industrialized, is evidence of the potential of telecommunications for lifelong learning (Bonham, 1980).

What is needed is a policy framework that would support such a technological base for lifelong learning in the postindustrial society. With such a base, older learners, in particular, could enjoy greater access to learning resources. Hamrin, for example, envisages the creation of a "national common-carrier information utility" which would be accessible to every home: "The greatest single potential of an information utility might be the opportunity to reduce the cost of education to the point where society could afford to provide open and equal access to learning opportunities for all members throughout their lives" (Hamrin, 1981, p. 68).

Other critics, however, have voiced doubts about this rosy forecast for the future. There is a fear that information-rich groups in society will grow more powerful, while those who are "information-poor"—and this could include many of the elderly—will be further disadvantaged. What has happened to date is that the elderly have been "plugged in" to the information society through the passive reception of mass media, primarily television. Active control of information technology—home computers, data bases, electronic communications—is largely the domain of the young, and here too only an elite group of the young segmented along lines of class and gender.

What is the solution? Some would urge efforts to promote "computer literacy" among the elderly so they would be less disenfranchised. Such compensatory approaches do have a role, and experiments to encourage access by older people to computers should be encouraged. But the problem of aging in an information society is deeper. The coming of an information society may mean a qualitative shift in modal forms of human communication. Walter Benjamin, writing a half century ago, recognized the coming shift. He observed that the language of information is now taking precedence over the language of experience (Benjamin in Arendt, 1968b). Here lies the true obsolescence of old age in an information society. Will the solution be found in an economy or social structure that cultivates obsolescence?

Acquiring more and more information is not the same thing as the cultivation of wisdom. The solution may not necessarily be to "plug in" the elderly to a new information utility. Instead of being a time to assimilate more and more information, old age may be the period of life to go in the opposite direction: to reduce the quantity and complexity of information in favor of what is deeper and more essential. Instead of encouraging elders to become more adept information junkies, we should encourage a complementary style of late life learning based on the strengths of age and experience.

The return of personal narrative.   John Naisbitt argues that high tech demands—and stimulates—high touch (Naisbitt, 1982). We can make the same point about communication in the information society. High tech information media need not drive out "high touch" approach. On the contrary, it may stimulate an even greater demand for it, just as the spread of mass-produced merchandise drives up the value and the price of antiques. As high tech information becomes more common, high touch communication will become rare and precious. Revived interest in oral history, family history, and autobiography are signs in this direction. Personal narrative and storytelling—the tale that is unique and irreplaceable—may have a distinctive, even treasured place in the information society of the future. The goal is not to absorb everyone—including the old folks—into a fast-paced, world-wide telecommunications network. On the contrary, the more the information society proliferates, the more there will be a need for irreplaceable personal narratives: the symbolic equivalent of one of the "high touch" activities that make life meaningful.

The new role for storytelling illuminates a crucial element in the psychology of aging: the search for meaning. But meaning must be based on some enduring sense of the place of an individual life in the human life cycle, in the cycle of generations (Erikson, 1982). For older adults, the great psychological task of late life is to establish a sense of self based on the knowledge gained from life experience. In earlier times and in more age-integrated societies, opportunities were more easily available for fulfilling this traditional role of "elders of the tribe" (Mergler and Goldstein, 1983). Today, for a variety of reasons, this is no longer the case. Worse still, in a world with barriers between the three boxes of life, children infrequently have daily contact with older people who could serve as custodians and witnesses of history. In the new environment, the voices of old are not heard. Deprived of a form with which to ensure the survival of the culture that shaped their lives, the voice of the storyteller now falls silent.

THE NARRATIVE STRUCTURE OF THE LIFE COURSE

The storyteller.   The value of personal narrative—of storytelling—reminds us that our sense of the meaning of life is inevitably tied to our capacity to tell a story, to make sense of the events that happen to us. And this narrative structure of the life course is today increasingly at risk. In a brilliant essay entitled "The Storyteller," Walter Benjamin writes: ". . . the art of storytelling is coming to an end. Less and less frequently do we encounter people with the ability to tell a tale properly. . . . It is as if something that seemed inalienable to us, the securest among our possessions, were taken from us: the ability to exchange experiences" (Benjamin, 1968b, p. 83).

This theme of the incommunicability of experience in the modern world is fundamental to Benjamin's message. It is a theme intimately tied to the meaning of wisdom and the integrity of the life cycle, including, of course, the meaning of old age. Is it possible for one generation to pass on to the next some fragment of practical wisdom, some understanding of what has been learned from life? If so, what status could such wisdom have in an information society?

For Benjamin, wisdom is above all *practical* knowledge of how to live. It is a knowledge that is intimately bound up with the shape of life experience: with what we may call *the narrative structure of the life course* (MacIntyre, 1982). The communicability of wisdom is tied to the communicability of a *life story*. In telling the tale, it is the storyteller who teaches us how to live:

> An orientation toward practical interests is characteristic of many born story-tellers . . . every real story . . . contains, openly or covertly, something useful. The usefulness may, in one case, consist in a moral; in another, in some practical advice; in a third, in a proverb or maxim. In every case the storyteller is a man who has counsel for his readers. But if today 'having counsel' is beginning to have an old-fashioned ring, this is because the communicability of experience is decreasing. After all, counsel is less an answer to a question than a proposal concerning the continuation of a story which is just unfolding. To seek this counsel one would first have to be able to tell the story . . . . Counsel woven into the fabric of real life is wisdom. The art of storytelling is reaching its end because the epic side of truth, wisdom, is dying out (Benjamin, 1968b, pp. 86–87).

Benjamin adds that "this is a process that has been going on for a long time" and he therefore resists any attempt to see it as a symptom of decay or of "modernism." Rather, he believes it results from the "secular productive forces of history" which have gradually "removed narrative from the realm of living speech." Writing in the 1930s, Benjamin had in mind the ascendancy of mass communications and mass culture: newspapers, radio, cinema, and the forces of propaganda and advertising. By the final decades of the 20th century, new productive forces of telecommunications technology would be pushing this process still farther.

In the information society we must reckon with on-line data bases, portable computers, electronic mail, and multimedia learning systems that bombard us with information from every direction. In such a world, the narrative structure of the life course is increasingly at risk. "If the art of storytelling has become rare, the dissemination of information has had a decisive share in this state of affairs," writes Benjamin (1968b, p. 89). He notes that it is the greater part of the art of storytelling to keep a story free from explanation as the story is being told. This is the "tacit dimension" of storytelling (Polanyi, 1958). But it is just this tacit dimension of experience that is rejected by an information society. Everything must be analyzed and explained in order to cope with the avalanche of information confronting us. Every fact is saturated with explanations that shape its significance for us. It is as if the very overload of information were expressly designed to keep our mentality as far as possible from silence and reflection.

Death and wisdom. This emerging information environment is one in which there is no real place for the wisdom of age or the awareness of finitude and death. Yet death and wisdom are intimately linked. In modern times the face of death has changed. Indeed, it is characteristic of modernized societies to "banish" death from everyday experience (Aries, 1974; Choron, 1963). The result is not merely to postpone the event by means of medical technology; it is also to eliminate the vividness of death from general consciousness (Becker, 1973).

The banishing of death from everyday life is closely tied to the disappearance of storytelling: "It is . . . characteristic that not only a man's knowledge or wisdom, but above all his real life—and this is the stuff that stories are made of—first assumes transmissible form at the moment of his death" (Benjamin, 1968b). It is death which creates that "authority" which is the very source of what a story is: "Death is the sanction of everything that the storyteller can tell. He has borrowed his authority from death" (Benjamin, 1968b, p. 94). It is the existential consciousness of death that gives a life story its sincerity and seriousness.

When the function of storytelling is conceived in this fashion, one recognizes immediately why storytelling must be bound up with wisdom—with our image of the Wise Old Man and Wise Old Woman (Weaver, 1964; Hillman, 1970). "Seen in this way, the storyteller joins the ranks of the teachers and sages. He has counsel—not for a few situations, as the proverb does, but for many, like the sage. For it is granted to him to reach back to a whole lifetime . . . . His gift is the ability to relate his life; his distinction, to be able to tell his entire life . . . . The storyteller is the figure in which the righteous man encounters himself" (Benjamin, 1968b, pp. 108-09).

A compelling image, but can storytelling serve as a model for the wisdom of old age in the postindustrial society? Doesn't it seem ludicrous for us to look to old people in order to receive "counsel" about what to do in life? The overwhelming fact about our historical position today is a discontinuity that ruptures and fragments the life experience of the older generation. Each generation is on its own. Experience has become incommunicable.

The incommunicability of experience. Benjamin has insisted on the incommunicability of experience. Yet it is not so much that the experience itself is incommunicable but that it is irrelevant. Like an early model of a transistor, it is simply out of date, obsolete, interesting perhaps only as a specimen of past history. This is the environment of modernity where "all that is solid melts into air" (Berman, 1982). In such a world we must wonder whether it makes any sense for the storyteller to retell a life story. Within the field of gerontology now for over twenty years there has been a persistent enthusiasm for the idea of "life-review" as a method for vindicating storytelling and reminiscence in old age (Butler, 1963, 1977; Merriam, 1980; Moody, 1984). We are entitled to wonder what inspires such fervent interest in life-review. Do we "believe" in life-review because we so desperately want the experience of old people to "make sense" to themselves or to us? Do we secretly hope for them to feel that their lives count, that life has meaning for us all (Moody, 1985)?

There is a certain "senselessness" that belongs to the fabric of experience today, that is well conveyed in the art and literature of "postmodern" culture. It is a feeling that sets the tone for so many of the dramas of Samuel Beckett. In "Waiting for Godot" and "End Game" Beckett has painted a stark landscape for the search for meaning. Beckett's plays are not naturalistic dramas; they are not set in "real life" but they do convey a kind of "counsel" which may be important, even if it is not the substance of wisdom. "While waiting I shall tell myself stories, if I can," writes Beckett ("Malone Dies"). It is this tentative hope ("If I can") that defines the present dilemma.

While insisting on the need for fashioning stories, Beckett, like Walter Benjamin, is passionate in his refusal of the saving power of memory. Memory, by itself, is too fragile and unreliable a power to redeem us. This, at least, is the implicit message of "Krapp's Last Tape," where the aged Krapp rummages around his tape recordings (memories?) of a bygone day but can never find the links (meanings?) that enable him to make sense of his life. We are drawn to storytelling, as we are drawn to life-review, seeking everywhere the saving power of memory.

But in the life stories of modern autobiography, we will find that the self has been "deconstructed" and has vanished from the scene (Olney, 1980). As we plunge deeper we fear that the stories we tell may turn out to be mere fictions, whistling in the dark in a world without continuity. Our literature reflects a dialectic of ego-integrity versus despair. But the polarity is not merely a dilemma of individual psychology; it reflects a collapse of shared meanings in postmodern culture. Our literature, then, reflects our life. The image of wisdom in old age represents a wish that the story might turn out with a happy ending or at least with an ending that makes sense. The poet Louise Bogan at the end of her own troubled life wrote, "In the beginning we want life to be romantic; later on, to be endurable; finally, to be understandable."

The map of knowledge: Information, knowledge, and wisdom. The new information environment puts traditional values and meanings into question. It overturns the saving power of memory without putting anything in its place, and so the ending of the story, old age itself, no longer makes sense. Can late-life learning be anything more than piling up new stimuli in a world where information technology makes life experience incommunicable? In order to respond to this new situation we need, as never before, to be clear about distinctions in the order of knowledge and the relationship of knowledge to lifespan development. We need, in short, an epistemology of lifespan development.

We are now in a position to understand the relationship between information, knowledge, and wisdom. Information is generated in numberless forms. It comes on the wire service, as a telephone book, a data-base, a ticker tape, a statistical compilation: all up-to-date, all soon obsolete. According to the mathematical theory of information, it can be given a precise measurement, can be transmitted, stored, and retrieved. The paradox of the information society is that as the quantity of available information expands, each bit of information becomes less valuable and less intelligible by itself. To find our way in this bewildering maze requires a cognitive map.

The map of knowledge is what enables us to recognize patterns in the field of information that surrounds us. The map of knowledge can be intuitive or discursive; in either case, it guides us through the maze. In past epochs, discursive knowledge, through reading and writing, was confined to a few. But knowledge gained through life experience was far more important. A farmer, a shoemaker, a sea captain all acquired their essential skills through experiential knowledge. The invention of the printing press and the spread of education changed the situation decisively. As literacy spread, that balance between symbolic and experiential knowledge became reversed: now it was symbolic knowledge that would confer power and prestige. But even with the advance of schooling, experiential knowledge still retained value in coping with a stable, predictable and complex environment. Today, the information society has changed the situation once again. With the explosion of information, literacy and symbolic knowledge, by themselves, have only a limited value. They, too, are vulnerable to obsolescence.

For older people, this shift has decisive implications. Both experiential and symbolic knowledge belong to crystallized intelligence. But now these gains of age and experience have less and less importance. In the information society, crystallized intelligence falls in value. Information of all kinds, whether conveyed in numerical, verbal, digital, or any other form, is abundantly available; and at the same time, all information is susceptible to rapid obsolescence. Theoretical knowledge, preeminently scientific knowledge, becomes the indispensable cognitive map.

At any point in history, theoretical knowledge confers a certain mastery on the explosive domain of information. By knowing the theory, we can "chunk" vastly more information. But knowledge and technology do not stand still. No sooner does theory gain a grip on the world than the grip begins to slip again. With each "paradigm shift" to a higher order of explanation, theoretical knowledge itself becomes obsolete (Kuhn, 1970).

With each advance the gains of experiential knowledge are lost. The problem is that theoretical knowledge diverges more and more from experiential knowledge. Theoretical principles are increasingly abstract and remote from everyday experience. Models drawn from experience no longer correct or modify theoretical principles. Where once symbolic knowledge and experiential knowledge corroborated one another, now they diverge. As theoretical knowledge becomes fragmented and remote, our "cognitive map" becomes frayed at the edges and finally becomes illegible.

Where is the wisdom we have lost in knowledge?
Where is the knowledge we have lost in information?

T. S. Eliot
The Four Quartets

Wisdom and meaning.   There is a story about Mulla Nasr Edin, the Middle Eastern folk hero. One evening a neighbor found the Mulla crawling around on the ground under a street lamp not far from his house. "What are you doing?" asked the neighbor. "Looking for my house key," replied Mulla. "Where did you lose it?" asked the neighbor, and Mulla answered, "Over there by the door." "Then why," asked his neighbor, "are you looking for it here under the street lamp?" "Because there's so much light out here!" responded Mulla Nasr Edin.

When Louise Bogan said that, finally, we want life to be "understandable," she was not referring to an "understanding" that might be found in a data-base or in a new theoretical paradigm. She was referring to a kind of understanding that has always been called *wisdom*. Just as the sheer accumulation of information in itself will never yield theoretical knowledge that *makes sense* of the facts, so the sheer refinement of theoretical knowledge will never yield the wisdom that makes sense of life experience. Information and knowledge belong to two incommensurable levels. Intensifying one level brings one no closer to the next level. In the same fashion, knowledge and wisdom belong to two incommensurable levels. More knowledge does not bring wisdom.

The information society encourages a presumption that every question has a quick answer. After all, we can find information and knowledge in many places in the information society. But where will we find wisdom? The traditional answer points to cultural sources concerned with the transmission of transcendent understanding of the meaning of life. These sources might include, for example, the Book of Ecclesiastes, the Bhagavad-Gita, Talmudic proverbs, folklore and folk sayings, the teaching stories of Zen Buddhism and Sufism. The new information environment has not made them obsolete since what they convey is at a level beyond either information or theoretical knowledge.

In these sources we find insight into the human condition. That insight is not formalizable in a hierarchical-explanatory symbol system, such as we find in theoretical knowledge. Nor does it consist in some new fact about the world, such as the information society supplies for us in abundance. Wisdom, rather, grows directly from lived experience. It is experiential knowledge: in Polanyi's terms, "tacit knowing," which is very far from saying that it is vague, emotive, or impractical. Wisdom, after all, is "counsel woven into the fabric of real life." At the practical level, wisdom is superior judgment concerning uncertain matters of practical life. Wisdom means knowing how to live. The fact that it is "tacit" means that wisdom belongs to an entirely different order from either information or theoretical knowledge. Wisdom cannot be reduced to theoretical knowledge because wisdom amounts to the exercise of judgment on questions that themselves cannot be reduced to a "problem-solution" (algorithmic) form of reasoning. Wisdom is concerned with an entirely different cognitive structure.

Depth perception of experience. The cognitive structure of wisdom is isomorphic with narrative form: with storytelling. What the storyteller speaks, the wise person knows. The true story is characterized by its simplicity, its numinous quality, its timelessness, and its multiple levels of meaning. Like a dream, the true story is incommensurable with ordinary life, and, for that very reason, it is what makes life intelligible to us. This element of incommensurability can sometimes be called surprise, humor, or incongruity. We find these qualities in folk tales, parables, Zen koans, or Sufi stories.

We see these same qualities in the Mulla Nasr Edin story cited earlier. To understand why that story conveys wisdom, one need only ask the question: "How would I 'explain' this story if someone heard it but didn't get the point?" The question sounds puzzling. We find the story funny because each of us recognizes himself in Mulla's ridiculous behavior. The story gives us a glimpse of ourselves doing the same thing that Mulla does. But unless one already possessed some degree of detachment and self-understanding, it would be impossible to convey the meaning of the story to someone who didn't get the point. Here, then, is the paradox of wisdom. It is immediately available yet cannot be communicated directly. The Mulla Nasr Edin story is immediately transparent and timeless; yet it contains multiple depths of meaning.

Wisdom is precisely this "depth perception" of human experience and its multiple meanings. While ordinary consciousness sees life in one-dimensional terms, wisdom sees life in its depths. We can characterize wisdom only by paradoxes. Though grounded in an individual narrative, wisdom generalizes far beyond the limited empirical field in which crystallized intelligence can operate. Like crystallized intelligence, it grows from experience. Like fluid intelligence, it is not bound by past experience. In terms of cognitive development, wisdom belongs to a level of "post-formal" operations. The paradoxes of wisdom are captured by dialectical operations that embrace opposites in a deeper unity (Riegel, 1976).

These characteristics of wisdom suggest why it is not easily recognized in an information society. The categories of the information society promise an abundance of data and a luminous refinement of theoretical knowledge. But in that dazzling light, wisdom is not to be found. Instead, like Mulla Nasr Edin, if we seek wisdom it must be in the darkness: in those obscure regions of personal knowledge that hold the key to the existential understanding. This conclusion should not be surprising. It simply restates, for the postindustrial age, what the mystics of every age and culture have insisted on (Parrinder, 1976).

Erik Erikson made the virtue of wisdom the capstone of his structure of life-span development (Erikson, 1980). Erikson was surely right in pointing to wisdom as the distinctive virtue of the last stage of life: an affirmation of meaning over and above the finality of death, an acceptance of the continuity of generations over and above the individual life cycle. But this understanding of wisdom—as existential, mystical, transformative—seems too remote from ordinary experience. Wisdom, in that lofty sense, may convey to us a conviction about "the meaning of life" (Moody, 1985). But in our day-to-day existence, we need something more tangible, more comprehensible, if wisdom is indeed the goal of late-life learning. We can find the key in a more everyday experience of self-knowledge.

The beginning and the end of wisdom.   I have spoken of experiential knowledge and symbolic knowledge, but not yet of self-knowledge. Here of course is the key to wisdom, as philosophers beginning with Socrates have insisted. The opposite of knowledge is ignorance or error. But the opposite of wisdom is foolishness, or being in the grip of an illusion. Thus, when one achieves a moment of wisdom, it is not because of new information or new evidence about the world. A different kind of transformation must occur (Needleman, 1982). An example of this process of insight is the case of Ebenezer Scrooge in Dickens' story "A Christmas Carol." When Scrooge finally realizes that he has been living wrongly, the world suddenly looks different (McKee, 1983). He awakes "as if from a dream" to see the world rightly. Wisdom means seeing through illusions (Meacham, 1982). But seeing through illusions requires living through those illusions and, hopefully, going beyond them. And this takes age and experience, though it does not come invariably with time.

Here, then, is the decisive point. Experiential knowledge in itself does not automatically result in wisdom—otherwise all those with long experience would be wise. Instead, experiential knowledge when understood and transformed can become wisdom. But experiential knowledge, including its refined version as wisdom, always remains something altogether different from theoretical knowledge. It is *personal* knowledge. One can *have* theoretical knowledge without any corresponding transformation of one's personal being. But one cannot "have" wisdom without *being* wise. It is this transformative process, finally, that must be the task of late-life learning. The coming of an information society cannot make that task any easier than it has ever been. But at least the abundance of information and the obsolescence of knowledge should remove from us the persistent illusion that the key is to be found in piling up more information, skills, or experience. If, finally, we want life to be understandable, the path lies in an altogether different direction. That discovery itself is the beginning of wisdom.

CONCLUSION: SOME IMPLICATIONS
FOR OLDER ADULT EDUCATION

The line of argument in this chapter has been philosophical. Yet, if the argument is sound, there are many practical implications of this discussion for the design of educational programs for older adults. Some of these implications may briefly be summarized as follows.

Autobiography and life-review. In the last stage of life the search for meaning and integration of the self often involves storytelling, both as an internal psychological process and as a social transaction across generations (Prado, 1983; Freeman, 1984). The art of storytelling assumes a special significance in autobiography, oral history, or other cultural forms of self-expression such as folk art. Gerontological practitioners have begun to explore new ways to incorporate these activities into programs for older people, and educators need to design programs that build on the narrative structure of life experience among older people. Education in late life is less concerned with information processing than with drawing on prior experience in order to "make sense" of information past and present.

Self-help groups. Knowledge drawn from life experience is not only a path toward self-integration; it can also be a means of acquiring practical coping skills. One of the best examples of this is the effectiveness of self-help groups for older people. In the last decade there has been a dramatic growth of mutual self-help groups, again a response to the demand for "high touch" options in an impersonal technological society (Borkman, 1982b; Gartner and Riessman, 1984). Self-help has proved to be an important means of meeting human needs in ways that go beyond what professionalized service delivery systems can accomplish. For older people a key feature of mutual self-help groups is the role of *experiential learning* in such groups (Borkman, 1982b). These groups not only provide services; they also provide education based on exchange of personal stories among members of the group. An unanswered question for the future will be how the professional care-givers and the formal education system can more effectively build on the experiential learning of mutual self-help groups.

Older worker retraining. Experiential learning has implications for employment and retraining of older workers. Employment policy for an aging work force is beginning to recognize the role of retraining, a function which will prove essential in the postindustrial information economy. But retraining for older workers must move toward a "value-added" concept of training and education over the life span. That is, instead of ignoring prior life experience or treating it as a factor of interference in acquiring new skills, our approach to worker retraining should seek to capitalize on skills and knowledge derived from earlier experience. Programs for older workers sponsored under the Job Training Partnership Act or the Senior Employment Program could demonstrate and evaluate such a value-added approach to older worker retraining.

Liberal arts and humanities.   The success of late-life learning enterprises such as Elderhostel or the Senior Center Humanities Program has drawn attention to the remarkable popularity of the liberal arts and humanities for older people (Kaplan, 1981). Indeed, national surveys repeatedly demonstrate that these subjects are the ones most frequently selected by older students, ironically at a time when enrollment by younger students in these fields has declined. The study of literature, philosophy, and history, more so than other fields, draws on accumulated life experience and thereby enlists the motivation of older learners. The liberal arts provide an interpretive framework in which each of us can see how an individual life story fits into the larger story of human culture. As faculty and program planners recognize this point, there should be more explicit attention to how humanistic learning builds on the narrative structure of experience and in this fashion offers an opportunity for older students to discover meaning in the last stage of life. Liberal arts education for the old can be potentially a far richer experience than at any other period of life.

Role of information technology.   New telecommunications technology opens up possibilities for *narrowcasting* rather than the conventional style of broadcasting historically tied to mass media (Straka, this volume; Toffler, 1980). Important innovations here include multiple cable TV channels, low-power TV, low-cost videocassette recorders, and cameras for home video production. Narrowcasting offers a far wider selection of options to correspond with personal preference and variations of life experience. On the positive side, individual playback control of videocassettes allows for self-paced learning and repeated review and reinforcement: both important elements for late-life learning. On the other hand, telecommunications technology cannot replace the need for socialization ("high touch") in old age.

The information society presents a challenge to traditional values and assumptions, including cultural patterns and meanings important to older people. Yet information technology can also offer new ways of integrating traditional social ties by strengthening so-called "mediating structures": e.g., families, churches, neighborhoods, and ethnic groups. For example, home video cameras and cassette players allow families to make "video postcards" to document treasured moments, including the reminiscences of older family members. Similarly, low-power television can allow even relatively small local neighborhood or ethnic groups to document their own heritage and transmit learning materials of direct interest to that small group alone. Such "tools of conviviality" help break up the massification of society and foster a deeper sense of personal meaning. Just as the long-distance telephone has promoted stronger family ties even at geographical distance, so new telecommunications can serve to strengthen intimate forms of human association.

Integrated delivery systems. The rapid and fragmented evolution of tele-communications technologies gives no guarantee that an integrated lifelong learning system will in fact emerge. Yet the need for such a system is clear. The experience of the British Open University points to the importance of integrated systems of telecommunications that make use of a whole range of means of communication, not only broadcasting on wide geographic scale, but lower-cost radio and print media (Perry, 1976). Effective adult learning requires more than one-way transmission of information to a passive audience. There must also be provision for *interactive* communication, not necessarily through television but through simpler devices, such as the telephone, the postal system, and the provision of books and materials. The rapid evolution of the U.S. telephone system, under the impact of deregulation, is already giving rise to new combinations of telephone and computer-mediated communication. For the isolated or homebound elderly, these new systems of telecommunications hold great promise for enhancing lifelong learning. But that promise will not be fulfilled automatically. The success of the Open University was dependent on heavy public investment on a centralized basis combined with flexible, decentralized operation allowing integrated use of appropriate technology at the local scale. This combination is what holds the key to the future.

This last point is an apt note on which to conclude. The coming of an aging society and an information society does not, in itself, point to either an optimistic or pessimistic forecast for the future. Rising education levels in the older population and the spread of self-help groups are positive signs for the future. New telecommunications technologies could capitalize on special strengths and aptitudes for late-life learning. An example is the potential of low-power television used for decentralized narrowcasting. Audiences such as elderly ethnic groups, that would otherwise be too small or unprofitable for mass market broadcasting, could come into their own. Audio and video technologies could vastly expand learning opportunities for the homebound and enrich their quality of life. But will such prospects for late-life learning actually come to pass?

Today there is a lack of leadership in exploiting information technology for lifespan development. Neither education nor government but private electronics or entertainment corporations are those who have provided the bulk of investment in the new technologies now shaping the information society of the future. Yet there is scant evidence that the private marketplace will adequately address the learning needs of the older population. For example, there are already indications that local neighborhood or ethnic groups will not be the ones to receive low-power TV licenses. Instead Sears and other big corporations are moving aggressively to control that new technology. Similarly, retraining for older workers under the recent Job Training Partnership Act has been meager, while the interest of business has been low. The value-added approach to older worker retraining remains unexplored.

These contradictory trends reinforce a point made earlier. The shape of the information society will not be determined by technology alone, and so the prospect for educational technology in the service of lifelong learning remains an open question. It is not the technology of an information society but the control and the relations of production that are the key to the future. The preferred path would be the development of a technological infrastructure supported by public policies to put new "tools of conviviality" in the hands of people in ways that would enhance, not erode, cultural autonomy. The most impressive innovations in older adult education—for example, Elderhostel and the Senior Center Humanities Program—have been achieved through coordinated investment at a national focal point combined with decentralized administration to enlist the energies of volunteers, including older people themselves, at the local level. Activities at the large and small scale are both equally needed. "Think globally, but act locally" will remain the watchword of those who have faith in an open future.

REFERENCES

ACHENBAUM, W. (1974). The obsolescence of old age in America: 1865-1974. *Journal of Social History, 8,* 48-62.

ARIES, P. (1974). *Western attitudes toward death* (Trans. P. M. Ranum). Baltimore: Johns Hopkins University Press.

BARTON, P. (1982). *Worklife transitions: The adult learning connection.* New York: McGraw-Hill.

BECKER, E. (1973). *The denial of death.* New York: Free Press.

BELBIN, E., and BELBIN, R. M. (1972). *Problems in adult retraining.* London: Heinemann Educational Books.

BELL, D. (1973). *The coming of post-industrial society.* New York: Basic Books.

BELL, D. (1976). *The cultural contradictions of capitalism.* New York: Basic Books.

BENJAMIN, W. (1968a). The work of art in the age of mechanical reproduction. In Hannah Arendt (Ed.), *Illuminations.* New York: Harcourt, Brace, & World.

BENJAMIN, W. (1968b). The storyteller. In Hannah Arendt (Ed.), *Illuminations.* New York: Harcourt, Brace, & World.

BERG, I. (1971). *Education and jobs: The great training robbery.* Boston: Beacon Press.

BERMAN, M. (1982). *All that is solid melts into air: The experience of modernity.* New York: Simon & Schuster.

BEST, F. (1980). *Flexible life scheduling: Breaking the education-work-retirement lockstep.* New York: Praeger.

BOLLES, R. (1978). *The three boxes of life.* New York: Ten Speed Press.

BONHAM, G. (1980). *The communications revolution and the education of Americans.* New Rochelle, New York: Council on Learning.

BORKMAN, T. (1982a). Experiential knowledge: A new concept for the analysis of self-help groups. *Social Service Review, 50,* 445-456.

BORKMAN, T. (1982b). Where are older persons in mutual self-help groups? In A. Kolker and P. I. Ahmed (Eds.), *Aging.* New York: Elsevier.

BRAVERMAN, H. (1976). *Labor and monopoly capital: The degradation of work in the twentieth century.* New York: Monthly Review Press.

BUTLER, R. N. (1963). The life review: An interpretation of reminiscence in the aged. *Psychiatry, 26.*

BUTLER, R. N. (1982). Successful aging and the role of the life review. In S. H. Zarit (Ed.), *Readings in aging and death.* New York: Harper and Row.

CHORON, J. (1963). *Death and western thought.* New York: Collier Books.

CLAYTON, V. (1982). Wisdom and intelligence: The nature and function of knowledge in the later years. *International Journal of Aging and Human Development, 15,* 315-323.

CLAYTON, V., and BIRREN, J. (1980). The development of wisdom across the lifespan: A reexamination of an ancient topic. In P. B. Baltes and O. G. Brim, Jr. (Eds.), *Lifespan development and behavior.* New York: Academic Press.

DUPUY, J. (1980). Myths of the information society. In K. Woodward, *The myths of information: Technology and postindustrial culture.* Madison, Wisconsin: Coda Press.

ERIKSON, E. (1980). *Identity and the life cycle.* New York: Norton.

ERIKSON, E. (1982). *The life cycle completed: A review.* New York: Norton.

EURICH, N. P. (1985). *Corporate classrooms: The learning business.* New York: Carnegie Foundation for the Advancement of Teaching.

FREEMAN, M. (1984). History, narrative, and life-span developmental knowledge. *Human Development, 27,* 1–19.

FREEMAN, R. (1976). *The overeducated American.* New York: Academic Press.

FRENCH, J. R. (1980). *Education and training for middle-aged and older workers: Policy issues and options.* Washington, D.C.: National Institute for Work and Learning.

GARTNER, A., and RIESSMAN, F. (1984). *The self-help revolution.* New York: Human Sciences Press.

GINZBERG, E. (1982). Mechanization of work. *Scientific American,* September, 1982, 66–75.

GRUMAN, G. J. (1978). Cultural origins of present-day "age-ism": The modernization of the life cycle. In S. F. Spicker, K. M. Woodward, and D. Van Tassed (Eds.), *Aging and the elderly: Humanistic perspectives in gerontology.* Atlantic Highlands, New Jersey: Humanities Press.

HAMRIN, R. D. (1981). The information economy: Exploiting an infinite resource. *The Futurist,* August, 1981.

HILLMAN, J. (1970). On senex consciousness. *An Annual of Archetypal Psychology.* Dallas, Texas: Spring.

HORN, J. L. (1982). The theory of fluid and crystallized intelligence in relation to concepts of cognitive psychology and aging. In F. Craik and S. Trehub (Eds.), *Aging and cognitive processes.* New York: Plenum Press.

KAPLAN, M. (1981). Elderhostel: Using a lifetime of learning and experience. *Change, 13,* 38–41.

KASTENBAUM, R. (1984). When aging begins. *Research in Aging.*

KNOWLES, M. (1980). *The modern practice of adult education.* New York: Association Press.

KUHN, T. (1970). *The structure of scientific revolutions.* Chicago: University of Chicago Press.

LASCH, C. (1984). *The minimal self: Psychic survival in troubled times.* New York: Norton.

LIFELONG LEARNING ACT (1976).

LIFTON, R. J. (1970). Protean man. In R. J. Lifton (Ed.), *History and human survival.* New York: Random House.

LONG, H. (1983). *Adult and continuing education: Responding to change.* New York: Teachers College Press.

MacINTYRE, A. (1982). *After virtue.* Notre Dame, Indiana: University of Notre Dame Press.

McKEE, P. (November, 1983). Epistemology and old age. Paper presented at Symposium on Wisdom in Old Age, 36th annual meeting of Gerontological Society. San Francisco, California.

MEACHAM, J. A. (1982). Wisdom and the context of knowledge: Knowing that one doesn't know. In T. Kuhn and J. A. Meacham (Eds.), *On the development of developmental psychology.* Basel: Karger.

MEAD, M. (1978). *Culture and commitment: The new relationship between the generations in the 1970s.* New York: Columbia University Press.

MERGLER, N., and GOLDSTEIN, M. (1983). Why there are old people: Senescence as biological and cultural preparedness for the transmission of information. *Human Development, 26,* 72–90.

MERRIAM, S. (1980). The concept and function of reminiscence: A review of the research. *The Gerontologist, 20,* 604–609.

MOLITOR, G. T. (1981). The information society: The path to post-industrial growth. *The Futurist,* April, 1981.

MOODY, H. R. (1984). Bibliography on life-review. In M. Kaminsky (Ed.), *The uses of reminiscence.* New York: Haworth Press.

MOODY, H. R. (1985). The meaning of old age and the meaning of life. In T. Cole and S. Gadow (Eds.), *Aging and meaning: Views from the humanities.* Durham, North Carolina: Duke University Press.

MORRISON, M. (1983). The aging of the U.S. population: Human resource implications. *Monthly Labor Review, 106*(5), 13–19.

NAISBITT, J. (1982). *Megatrends: Ten new directions transforming our lives.* New York: Warner Books.

NARR, W. (1984). Toward a society of conditioned reflexes. In J. Habermas (Ed.), *Observations on "the spiritual situation of the age."* (Trans. A. Buchwalter). Cambridge, Massachusetts: MIT Press.

NEEDLEMAN, J. (1982). *The heart of philosophy.* New York: Knopf.

NEUGARTEN, B. (1974). Age groups in American society and the rise of the young-old. *Annals of the American Academy of Political and Social Science, 320,* 187–198.

NEUGARTEN, B. (1983). *Age or need?* Beverly Hills, California: Sage.

NEUGARTEN, B. (1985). Age in an aging society. *Daedelus* (Winter), Special issue on the aging society.

OLNEY, J. (1980). *Autobiography: Essays theoretical and critical.* Princeton, New Jersey: Princeton University Press.

PARRINDER, G. (1976). *Mysticism in the world's religions.* Oxford: Oxford University Press.

PERRY, W. (1976). *Open university: History and evaluation of a dynamic innovation in higher education.* Great Britain: Open University.

PETERSON, D. (1983). *Facilitating learning for older adults.* San Francisco: Jossey-Bass.

PIFER, A., and BRONTE, L. (Eds.) (1986). *The aging society.* New York: W. W. Norton.

POLANYI, M. (1958). *Personal knowledge: Toward a post-critical philosophy.* Chicago: University of Chicago Press.

PORAT, M. (1977). *The information economy.* Washington, D.C.: U.S. Department of Commerce.

PRADO, C. G. (Spring, 1983). Ageing and narrative. *International Journal of Applied Philosophy, 1,* 3.

REICH, R. (1983). *The next American frontier.* New York: Times Books.

RIEGEL, K. F. (1976). Toward a dialectical theory of development. *Human Development, American Psychologist, 31,* 689–700.

SARASON, S. (1977). *Work, aging and social change: Professionals and the one-life/one-career imperative.* New York: Free Press.

SHUMACHER, E. F. (1973). *Small is beautiful: Economics as if people mattered.* New York: Harper & Row.

STAUDE, J. (1981). *Wisdom and age.* Berkeley, California: Ross Books.

STEARNS, H. (1985). Training and retraining adult and older adult workers. In P. Robinson, J. Livingston, and J. Birren (Eds.), *Age, health and employment.* Englewood Cliffs, New Jersey: Prentice-Hall.

TOFFLER, A. (1980). *The third wave.* New York: William Morrow.

TOUGH, A. (1972). *The adult's learning projects.* Toronto, Ontario: Institute for Studies in Education.

WEAVER, R. (1964). *The wise old woman: A study of active imagination.* London: Vincent Stuart Ltd.

WILLIAMS, R. (1983). *The year 2000.* New York: Pantheon.

WILLIS, S. L. (1985). Towards an educational psychology of the older adult learner: Intellectual and cognitive bases. In J. E. Birren and K. W. Schaie (Eds.), *Handbook of the psychology of aging.* New York: Van Nostrand Reinhold.

WIRTZ, W. (1975). *The boundless resource: A prospect for an education-work policy.* Washington, D.C.: New Republic Books.

6

EDUCATION, LIFESTYLE, AND THE HEALTH OF THE AGING

James P. Henry and John McCallum

INTRODUCTION

Culture is, by definition, the act of developing by education. Hence, the cultural canon of the individual has acquired aspects which can be modified. With this in mind, the present chapter explores the relationship between different cultures and the health of older adults, focusing on health and social effects on the education of the aging. It is concerned with the possibility of modifying the lifestyle of the individual as it has been assimilated during exposure to the culture. Evidence is discussed that the culture adopted by any particular group involves a lifestyle that has well-defined effects upon the health of those living and aging within it. Since this lifestyle is acquired through formal education or informal socialization, we are concerned in this chapter with the direction of educational changes that a society might take in order to improve the health of its aging citizens. It is through the timely, early promotion of mental as well as physical health that late-life health can be improved.

This topic is vast. It includes choices of diet, with its many variants of fat, sugar, and fiber; the habitual use of stimulants like nicotine and caffeine; and the use of drugs such as alcohol and marijuana. Lifestyle varies from the workaholism of the Protestant ethic to the inertia of those Polynesians whose culture, overwhelmed by our technocracy, ceased to provide them with convincing norms

(Henry and Stephens, 1977). It involves physical exertion ranging from obsessive excess to a generalized flabby obesity. However, these will not be discussed; rather, the focus of this chapter will be the influence of psychosocial variables on the health of the aging, particularly the cardiovascular system. Much is coming to be known about the current pandemics of heart disease and high blood pressure and their consequences in the "young-old," i.e., those aged 60 to 75 years. The findings demonstrate that psychosocial responses can have powerful effects on the incidence of cardiovascular disease (Berkman and Syme, 1979; Friedman and Ulmer, 1984; Henry and Stephens, 1977; Marmot, 1982; Ruberman et al., 1984; Waldron et al., 1982).

These are controversial matters and the authors' expressions of opinion can be discriminated from the statements of experts by the citation given for the latter. Statements of fact based on experimental evidence can be recognized by reference to the title of the publication and, on occasion, by the citation of statistical probability.

CULTURE AND BLOOD PRESSURE

Previous work has discussed the influence of chronic emotional arousal on the incidence of hypertension and coronary heart disease (Henry, 1982, 1985; Henry and Meehan, 1981). Together, these two conditions account for a large proportion of the premature mortality of "young-old" men and women in technologically advanced societies. The evidence that hypertension is related to suppressed anger and that coronary heart disease involves the addition of a component of depression (Henry and Meehan, 1981) with a sense of helplessness has been presented in Henry's (1985) review of "Psychosocial Factors in Disease and Aging." In that review, the recent work of Waldron, Nowoiarski, Freimer, Henry, Post, and Witten (1982), a comprehensive survey of observations of the blood pressure of various cultures throughout the world, was summarized. The Waldron et al. survey reexamined the questions raised by the extraordinary range that is found in the rates of increased blood pressure as individuals age.

Figure 6-1, from an earlier study by Henry and Cassel (1969), contrasts three groups—each from one of six different ethnic backgrounds. These data demonstrated that various groups of Caucasians, blacks, and Orientals included some individuals whose blood pressure remained unchanged with increased age, even up into the sixties. These individuals coexisted with others of different lifestyles whose pressure rose with age until the mean at age 60 was well into the hypertensive range of 160 ± 20 mm Hg.

Henry and Cassel concluded that the mean blood pressure of the population is lower when the culture is stable, traditional forms are honored, and group members are adapted to their roles by early experience and are secure in them (Henry and Cassel, 1969). Similarly, the analysis by Waldron et al. (1982) showed that the rise of blood pressure with age was greater in groups that had greater involvement in a money economy, more economic competition, more contact with persons of different cultures or beliefs, and more unfulfilled aspirations for a return to traditional values and beliefs. They concluded that chronic emotional arousal due to cultural disruption of cooperative relationships and traditional patterns may have

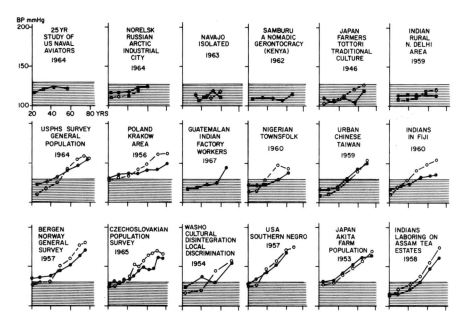

FIGURE 6-1 Contrasting rates of change in blood pressure with age can be found in all races. In general, blood pressure is lower where the culture is stable, tradition forms are honored, and the group members are secure in their roles and adapted to them by early experience.

Source: Henry and Cassel, 1969.

resulted from cultural changes that characterize the modern industrial state (Waldron et al., 1982).

The dangers imposed by contemporary technocracies on the cardiovascular health of their members can be differentiated into two separate neuroendocrine patterns driven by different emotional states. Chronic hypertension is found where the aging individual is denied the expectations of his childhood as a result of life in a changing, crowded, and competitive society which, nevertheless, retains a strong traditional cultural canon (Henry and Stephens, 1977). For example, this would be the case in those societies which adhere to the tenets of a major religion. The mechanism of the hypertensive tendency is believed to be a suppression of awareness of this frustration of expectancies, associated with an anger which does not find outward expression (Diamond, 1982). In older persons this emotional suppression may result in a low-renin hypertension. In some cases salt intake has an effect on blood pressure and a reduction in intake will help to control it (Laragh and Pecker, 1983). However, salt is not a factor in a majority of hypertensives who experience repeated psychosocial arousal: They develop a renin-dependent hypertension which is not salt sensitive. There is growing evidence that there are psychological differences between these renin-dependent hypertensives and those with low-renin hypertension (Thailer et al., 1985). On neuroendocrine grounds it might be suggested that, while the renin-dependent high blood pressure is primarily associated with suppressed anger, the low-renin hypertension may also involve elements of alexithymia and a *forme fruste* of depression (Henry, in press; Henry and Stephens, 1977).

It is proposed further that the development of the atherosclerosis typical of coronary heart disease requires a cultural lifestyle that adds another set of factors. Indeed, the individual may escape hypertension to fall prey to lethal blocks of the coronary vessels by atheromatous plaques. A combination of a high fat diet with ambitious workaholism (Henry, 1983; Henry and Stephens, 1977), together with the hostility which often develops in those competing without traditional social supports, leads to depressive emotions fostering the development of obstruction of the coronary vessels (Bruhn et al., 1974; Friedman and Ulmer, 1984). Atherosclerosis is decreased but still develops when fat is eliminated from the diet of socially stressed animals (Kaplan et al., 1983; Kaplan et al., 1985). Unlike the case of high blood pressure, women of the same middle-age as the vulnerable men remain relatively free from this obstructive disease of the coronary vessels (Atherosclerosis Study Group, 1984). But they still develop high blood pressure (Waldron et al., 1982), suggesting that the two diseases originate from different mechanisms. Perhaps women are spared the atherosclerosis because the culture and their genetic and hormonal constitution make the drive to control less marked, and their social skills and attachment behavior better developed (Eaker et al., 1983). Thus, in one culture there may be much hypertension in both sexes but little coronary heart disease while in another culture both diseases may be rampant in the males but only hypertension in the females. And in still other cultures there may be very little hypertension or coronary heart disease (Henry, 1983; Henry and Meehan, 1981).

SOCIAL CHANGE AND CHANGES
IN BLOOD PRESSURE

The social differences which distinguish these various cultures can now be considered. A classical situation in which blood pressure does not rise with age and there is little coronary heart disease was described by Donnison, an English physician who worked for several years in the 1920s in a tribal reservation on the shores of Lake Victoria in the then British colony of Kenya (Donnison, 1929). Donnison realized to his surprise that he could find no case of hypertension in 1,800 consecutive hospital admissions. Considering a possible cause, he observed that the cultural patterns of the tribes living on reservations had not been seriously disturbed for generations despite their loss of sovereignty and subjection to British rule. Struck by the difference between their time-honored methods of child-rearing and those of his native England, he wrote a book presenting the hypothesis that successful childhood integration of inborn drives into patterns acceptable to the surrounding society was the critical factor in the development of a culture free from high blood pressure (Donnison, 1938).

Similarly, the effect of psychoemotional influences has been cited by Folkow in his classical review of the physiological aspects of primary hypertension (Folkow, 1982). He regards these influences as the primary environmental factors inducing this condition. The other possible predisposing element is the amount of salt in the diet. However, recent work by Laragh's group has shown that salt only plays a role in low-renin hypertension which, as noted earlier, represents a minority of the cases of hypertension (Laragh and Pecker, 1983).

A study by Graham provides further impressive evidence of the role of environmental stimuli on hypertension. Graham found extraordinarily high blood pressure (> 180 mm Hg) in one out of three members of a victorious tank batallion resting on the beaches in Tunisia after two years of continuous mobile warfare in the Lybian desert (Graham, 1945). Although this was a fixed pressure at the time of initial measurement, it gradually subsided after a few weeks, presumably because of the structural adaptation of the media of the arterioles and a return of sympathetic drive mechanisms to normal. Likewise, Miasnikov, a Russian hypertensiologist, observed a similar epidemic of high blood pressure during the two-year siege and bombardment of Leningrad (Miasnikov, 1962). These findings are comparable in that both populations had faced strong and repeated sympathetic arousal due to unpleasant and threatening conditions which the subjects had no means of avoiding.

It may be argued that these studies are not convincing because they were short-term from the viewpoint of human disease. However, in some recent studies repeated blood pressure surveys have been made over a period of years. For example, on the South Pacific Islands of Palau and Ponape in the Carolines, blood pressure measurements were accompanied by careful observation by anthropologists. Since the end of World War II it has been shown that the "sleepy" island of Ponape with a twelve-mile diameter and a population of 15,000 did not modernize very quickly, largely retaining its traditional ways of life (Henry and Stephens, 1977). Furthermore, as Figure 6-2 shows, in 1947 the mean blood pressure of the men was not only low but did not rise significantly with age. During the past

FIGURE 6-2

Contrasting the rise in blood pressure with age in 1968 in Koror, the capital of the Palau Islands, Western Carolines (Micronesia) with that of the general population of the more traditional South Sea island of Ponape in 1948 and also in 1971. The curve for 1948 represents conditions before the American occupation had started to take effect after World War II. The 1971 curve represents a survey taken after 23 years of American administration.

Source: Henry and Stephens, 1977.

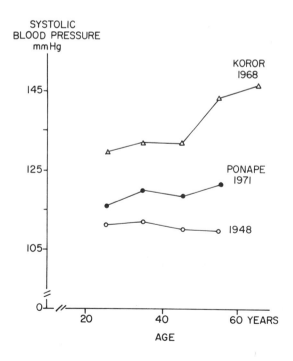

twenty-five years some social changes have altered the culture, as a result of the islanders' closer contact with the West and its lifestyle following incorporation of the Carolines into the U.S. Trust Territory of the Pacific (Henry and Stephens, 1977).

Sociocultural interviews have shown that those living in Kolonia, the administrative center and capital of Ponape, are becoming acculturated into Western habits and values. As Figure 6-2 shows, a 1971 blood pressure survey recorded slightly higher blood pressures than those taken some twenty-five years before. Subsequently, a very detailed analysis of the socioeconomic picture was matched with individual blood pressures for the males.

There was a significant increase in the blood pressure of men living in Kolonia and intermediate areas. Only the most traditional regions showed no change. This occurred despite controlling for body mass, i.e., allowing for increasing obesity. In 1983, Patrick et al. speculated that these blood pressure increases are progressive changes that will become still more extensive as Western contact with this traditional culture continues.

As Figure 6-3 shows, the higher the modernity score, the higher the blood pressure in Kolonia. The score was measured in terms of the subject's segment of the economy, source of income, English proficiency, occupation, and education. Patrick et al. found that, for the extremes on the scale, systolic blood pressure increased from 116 mm Hg to 123 mm Hg (P<0.01) and diastolic pressure from 60 mm Hg to 76 mm Hg (P<0.01) (Patrick et al., 1983).

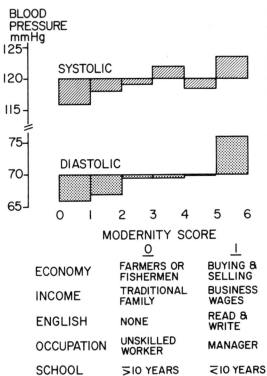

FIGURE 6-3

Average systolic and diastolic blood pressures adjusted for age and body weight in Kolonia, the capital of Ponape Island, for various scores indicating the degree of modernization of each individual.

Source: Patrick, Prior, and Smith, 1983. Reprinted by permission.

In nearby islands more affected by technocracy the hypertension is still more marked. Evidence has been presented elsewhere concerning the degree of modernization of Koror, the capital city of Palau (Henry and Stephens, 1977). In 1968 it was already far more Westernized and changed in its values than Kolonia. The history of Koror and Palau, the record of heavy colonization by Japan between the 1920s and 40s, and the urbanization that occurred could explain the sharp change in blood pressure with age shown in Figures 6-2 and 6-3.

There is further recent evidence of the effects of the sociocultural milieu on blood pressure. In a paper published in 1983, Joseph et al. reported on a remarkable prospective study of the blood pressure of those forced to migrate from the hurricane-devastated Polynesian Tokelau atolls to New Zealand in 1975–77. The data garnered by this government project is particularly compelling since response rates were 97–99% and the immigrants were carefully examined before leaving.

The difference between male immigrants after years of exposure to New Zealand and those males who stayed behind was 7.2 mm Hg systolic pressure (P<0.001) and 8.1 mm Hg diastolic pressure (P<0.001). Among females the rise in adjusted systolic pressure was 1.8 mm Hg (P<0.065), and in diastolic pressure, 3.0 mm Hg (P<0.00) (see Figure 6-4).

Differences in body mass explain only a small proportion of the observed immigrant–nonimmigrant differential in blood pressure. Joseph et al. emphasized that before they left their atolls, the blood pressure of those who eventually emi-

FIGURE 6-4

Comparing male and female blood pressures of Tokelauans who migrated to New Zealand with those who stayed on the atolls. The effect is highly significant after correction for any changes in body weight.

Source: Joseph, Prior, Salmond, and Stanley, 1983. Reprinted by permission.

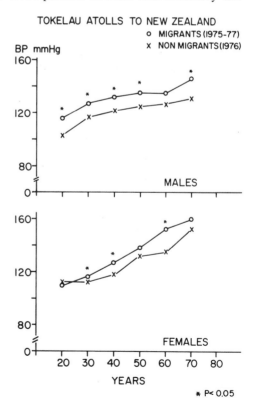

grated did not differ from that of those who stayed behind. Salt intake was carefully studied, especially in view of earlier observations which suggested that a greatly differing blood pressure in primitive Polynesian Puka Puka and more urban Roratanga may have been due to their difference in salt intake (Prior, 1968). However, despite detailed analysis, the salt data did not yield sufficiently compelling differences even to be considered as a factor in the analysis of variance. The authors concluded that whatever the reason, salt or no salt, the Tokelauan study provides "compelling evidence linking Westernization and the development of chronic disease" (Joseph et al., 1983).

Blood pressure changes are not restricted to increases due to modernization; it is also possible for the blood pressure of a group to decrease below that normally found in that particular social system for persons of that age. An example is given in Figure 6-5.

In the 1920s a number of American doctors and nurses went to work in China in mission hospitals. Their blood pressures while still in the United States were significantly higher than those measured after some years of work in China. This study took place prior to the great revolutionary upheaval in China and, at that time, the populace served by those missions still regarded their thousand-year-old, stable cultural tradition as the "natural order of things." It was the opinion

FIGURE 6-5 A majority of American nurses and doctors working in two Chinese mission hospitals in the 1920s showed a decrease of casual systolic blood pressure below stateside values. Possible reasons for this in terms of changes in psychosocial stimulation are presented in the text.

Source: Henry and Cassel, 1969.

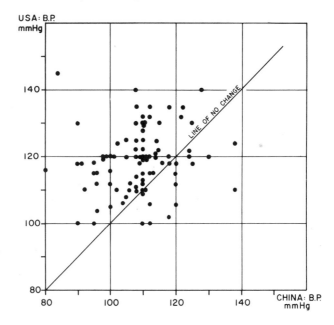

of the American physicians who reported on this drop in blood pressure that the favorable stable social ambiance in China had played a part in leading to "relaxation" on the part of the Americans (Foster, 1930).

The explanation these physicians proposed is compatible with contemporary medical experience. Current work in hypertension using relaxation as a nondrug intervention is producing blood pressure decreases of the same order as those observed at the aforementioned missions (Lehmann and Benson, 1983). It may be that the friendly acceptance by the Chinese of much needed Western medical skills, together with their own Christian traditions, led to a reduction of the anxiety level of these highly respected and locally privileged American men and women. This, in turn, may have increased their sense of "control" and allowed for a corresponding reduction of sympathetic arousal.

Migration has also been associated with a lower than expected blood pressure in the Falkland Islands, a British Crown colony in the South Atlantic. In 1984, King and Bleaney reported that the Falkland Island men enjoyed such an advantage over their agemates in the mother country (King and Bleaney, 1984). However, as Figure 6-6 shows, colony women of postmenopausal age had higher blood pressure than those living in Great Britain.

These findings were based on health survey data obtained just before the invasion of the Falklands by Argentina and the ensuing war to liberate these loyal frontiersmen living on the warmer fringes of British Antarctica. The total population of the Falkland Islands is only 2,000. A thousand of them live in the capital and the only town, Stanley, with a preponderance of women; the rest are scattered in homesteads devoted to sheep farming on the two approximately 1,000-square-

FIGURE 6-6   Comparing the prevalence of hypertension per 1000 population in the Falkland Islands in 1979 with males and females of the same age groups in Great Britain. Total number examined in Falkland Islands: males, 992; females, 821.

Source: King and Bleaney, 1984. Reprinted by permission.

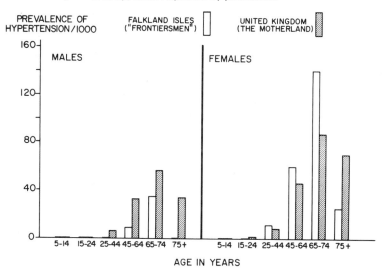

mile groups of islands. A crown colony, the Falklands are the gateway to British holdings in Antarctica. The colony is said to be "101%" loyal, and is well run by a highly sophisticated civil service (Anon, 1969). The rigorous climate is dominated by constant cold winds blowing over endless, treeless, rolling grasslands similar to those of Northern Scotland (Strange, 1972). The men either work on the sheep farms or for the government, which is a carefully tailored miniature facsimile of the parliament and government of Great Britain. Approximately 10% of the population return to England every year, some on leave and some with no thought of returning to the Islands. As A. B. Hadden has expressed it "there is a strong urge to see for themselves the bright lights and discos, the fast cars, the television and what have you that they have heard so much of" (Hadden, 1976). But having travelled 8,000 miles to see these wonders, they gradually find out about the drawbacks and learn to prize the peace and tranquility of their frontier colony. As Fox (1982) says, they miss the freedom of life and the time to think, for, as Strange (1972) comments, the settlements where the sheep are farmed are not concerned with clock-watching. Wool production is the island's only industry and all work is done in a tight, communal spirit. There is no competitive free enterprise; neither is there unemployment, however. And there is time, and indeed need, for every man to engage in healthy activities like cutting the peat that heats their homes or working in the yard to produce vegetables. There is even energy left over for amateur music and painting (Strange, 1972).

The population is ethnically homogeneous, derived from the British Isles including Scotland, and there is a treasuring of that culture which is supported by the church and the civil service (Anon, 1969). As the newly arrived governor of the colony said to the legislative council: "Everything that I have experienced has confirmed my concept of the colony as a genuinely unique achievement—I still marvel that so civilized a community should have been created in so remote a corner of the world—the phenomenon, I believe, is largely explicable in terms of the British genius" (for government). Later he commented on "the island's blessed insulation from so much of pollution and stress that beset most of the developed world" (French, 1975).

The fall of blood pressure in the doctors and nurses who migrated from the United States to China in the 1920s was attributed to a more favorable social ambience. Likewise, the above précis of conditions for men in the Falkland Islands in the late 1970s would indicate that it was strongly socially supportive, serving as a focus for what remained of the "spirit of the British Empire." It was preserving for its essentially British population a culture that for the men, but perhaps not for the women, reduced emotional arousal along with its neuroendocrine accompaniments of chronic hostility and insecurity and consequent high blood pressure. Finally, since about 10% of the population returned to or emigrated from Great Britain every year, it is possible that "there was self selection going on. Those who elected not to leave the Islands had adapted to the relaxed lifestyle and consequently experienced less of hypertension." To attribute the low blood pressure to plenty of exercise and less obesity is perhaps to say the same thing but in other words (King and Bleaney, 1984).

In his discussion of inhibited power motivation and high blood pressure in men, McClelland (1979) has analyzed the effect of challenges to the assertiveness of an individual and his competence to control his environment. McClelland supports the suppressed hostility hypothesis of the development of hypertension and points to three factors at work: A strong need for power or control, a disposition to check the overt expression of this need, and a social situation in which the individual experiences repeated challenges to the capacity to control access to needs. Animal studies have shown that if the defense-alarm fight-flight response is repeatedly alerted it will cause prolonged sympathetic arousal and sustained renin-dependent high blood pressure (Henry and Stephens, 1977; Henry, Stephens, and Larson, 1985). This is also what occurs when persons are living in a culture with which they do not have the skills to cope as a result of various influences such as advances in technology (Henry and Stephens, 1977).

Figure 6-7 presents the results from a survey of the mortality from hypertension in various cities. These studies indicate that the death rate is far higher in some South American cities than in San Francisco or Bristol, England. The data support a relation between hypertension and the rate at which the cities are growing. Henry and Cassel (1969) argue that a high growth rate can be taken to imply a probability of inadequate housing, and a need for facilities such as public transportation, schools, hospitals, and even stores. In addition, there is often a high influx of immigrants unused to the demands and expectations of city life. Strong and repeated threatening stimuli may result from such competitive and unfavorably disordered situations. The aged frequently suffer in the competition. A significant percentage of the aged in the "exploding" populations of such cities will fail to achieve the goals they desire in spite of all their striving and effort. The stimulation of the sympathetic system that they will experience may well be sustained and intense, and may lead to high blood pressure. An individual living in a traditional, stable

FIGURE 6-7

Preliminary observations suggest that the rate of growth of a city may be related to the incidence of hypertension in the general population.

Source: Henry and Cassel, 1969.

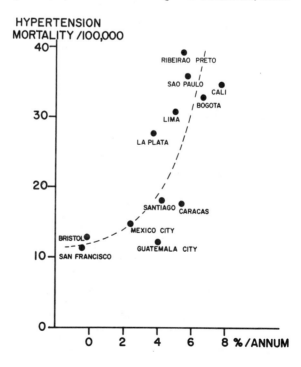

society is better equipped by the culture which he espouses to deal with the familiar world around him (Henry and Stephens, 1977). As a consequence, he may suffer less chronic arousal of his neuroendocrine system by sustained emotional states. When the changes introduced by the technical revolution or by invasion by another culture disrupt the individual's familiar environment, the individual is then faced with a new set of demands for which past experience has left him or her unprepared (Henry and Cassel, 1969; Henry and Stephens, 1977; Joseph et al., 1983; Patrick et al., 1983; Tyroler and Cassel, 1964).

CULTURES WITH HYPERTENSION
BUT NOT CORONARY DISEASE

Thus, it is proposed that certain characteristics of a changing society lead to a change in the prevalence of high blood pressure but not necessarily coronary heart disease. The ensuing lifestyle differences can be seen from the reports of various social scientists. These differences result in differences between the psychophysiology of the emotional traits and states of certain populations and those of the surrounding society (Henry, 1986a). Along these lines, two remarkable studies have been carried out on social groups in the United States (Bruhn and Wolf, 1979; Marmot and Syme, 1976). In both it was found that although men and women had a high prevalence of high blood pressure neither suffered from the expected coronary heart disease (see also Eaker et al., 1983). By contrast, the expected large proportion of "young-old" males in the surrounding United States society did suffer from the condition. What then protected men in these societies from coronary heart disease but not high blood pressure?

The Marmot-Syme Japanese-American Study

The first of these studies, by Marmot and Syme (1976), contrasted the behavioral patterns with the incidence of coronary heart disease in northern Californian Japanese-Americans. This population living in the San Francisco area constitutes a group of people who can be divided into those who have adopted the competitive and individual style of the "White Anglo-Saxon Protestant" and those who have remained closely tied to a traditional Japanese culture. The hypothesis of the Marmot-Syme study is that the social support provided by the Japanese culture is important in preventing a chronic arousal of the neuroendocrine system by helpless-hopeless feelings. The study began by confirming Gordon's (1967) observations that the gradient in morbidity from coronary heart disease per 1000 rises from 1.8 in Japanese individuals to 3.2 in Hawaiian-Japanese to 9.8 in Caucasian-Americans. This gradient held for each of the complications associated with coronary heart disease, such as angina and myocardial infarction. In addition, these individuals show more of the hostile, cynical aspects of the so-called type A behavior pattern which characterizes the attempt to achieve a dominant social position (Williams et al., 1980; Williams et al., in press). The pattern involves an increased pace of activity and covert hostility and despair when the lifestyle is seen as leading to a loss of social support and impeding attainment of goals (Henry and Meehan, 1981).

The social changes to which Japanese-Americans have been exposed include those of the dominant culture. For example, in a similar study Tyroler and Cassel

(1964) demonstrated that persons living in the hills of Carolina who moved to the city to work in factories had an increased incidence of coronary heart disease. They contrasted this industrial culture with that of the hill society, with its traditional nineteenth-century religious patterns and social support system rooted in a cultural set of norms with which the men had been familiar since infancy. Not only did the factory society which these men joined differ in its values from the hill society, but the men themselves were in transition. They were confronted by the challenge of discontinuity and/or incongruity due to rapid sociocultural changes. The authors argued that the observed increase in coronary disease was in part due to the psychosocial stimulation. Like the Carolinian "hillbillies" who had permanently abandoned their mountain culture, those Japanese-Americans who reject tradition undergo a change in the level of psychosocial stress. In contrast, the Japanese-Americans who stay traditional may be exposed to rapid changes at work in the American scene but, at home, may enjoy important protection as they are surrounded by a stable traditional group who provide emotional support. It is proposed that it is in this difference that the aforementioned differential increase in coronary heart disease is rooted.

Characteristics of the Japanese culture.   The social support in Japanese culture forms the core of a theoretical thesis by Matsumoto which sought to explain the lower incidence of coronary heart disease in Japan, which is one-eighth that of Americans in the San Francisco area (Matsumoto, 1970). His hypothesis, which later influenced Marmot and Syme in their experimental design, argued that it is the absence of certain types of social stimulation and not diet that accounts for the low Japanese coronary heart disease rates. Japan is a fully modern urbanized and industrialized state by Western standards. It is not a simple traditional hunter-gatherer or pastoral society, illiterate and without money. As a matter of fact, Japan has as high an incidence of high blood pressure in both men and women as any Western country, indicating similar effects of modern technocracy. For example, Ueda et al. (1983) report that in 1978 in the town of Hisayama the prevalence of hypertension in males was 17% and in females, 20%, with cases of borderline hypertension, i.e., systolic blood pressure 140-159 mm Hg, running at an additional 23% in both sexes. Thus a formidable four out of ten persons had some degree of high blood pressure. Despite this, coronary heart disease in Japan is at a far lower level than in the West (Marmot and Syme, 1976); this suggests that even in technologically highly developed societies it is possible to maintain certain types of emotion, i.e., helplessness, at a low level despite a generally high level of anxiety and tension with its accompanying high blood pressure.

Matsumoto (1970) notes that in the West persons are regarded as individuals to a greater degree than in Japan, where there is more attachment and interdependence among the various members of society. Not only do Japanese children receive more emotional support from their parents but, in general, the culture encourages attachment behavior between persons of the same sex. For example, once a large company hires the Japanese man he is rarely dismissed. Seniority is the major criterion for advancement and changing jobs from company to company is rare. Their high degree of commercial enterprise is relatively recent; work is still influenced by feudal tradition. As a result it is paternalistic, providing supportive company stores, worship, and sports facilities. Unlike his American counterpart, the Japanese employee takes his leisure with his fellow workers; his relationship with them is clearly differentiated from that with his family. He spends less time with the latter than the American, and this pattern forms an essential part of the culture (Matsumoto, 1970). The success of the Japanese workplace is due to its capacity to mobilize the energies of workers by making the workplace a "quasi-community" (Okamoto, 1985).

On the way home from work Japanese men chat with one another in tea shops in a relaxed atmosphere designed for releasing tension and regaining composure and serenity. Group cohesion goes a step further at various drinking places where female company is provided. At home, full acceptance of this pattern has been provided by a nonworking wife who does not allow domestic concerns to intervene in this male commitment to his work community (Okamoto, 1985). Finally, as Ruth Benedict (1946) notes, bathhouses permit the expression of a fine art of passive indulgence which is hard to duplicate in the bathing habits of the rest of the world.

Commitment of the individual to the group is a dominant feature of Japanese society. Personal obligation and duty are regarded as more important than individual fulfillment. The community is the focus of value, and the various officeholders in the social hierarchy culminating with the emperor have an especially important place in their symbolic value system (Matsumoto, 1970). The company, replacing the feudal aristocracy which lasted until the early nineteenth century in modern industrial Japan, is now responsible for major portions of social and commercial life and succeeds in providing powerful emotinal support. Individuals stay with the company for life: their commitment to superiors and coworker/friends is very important to them. They report their careers in terms of links to others, and advances in careers as a consequence of these links rather than of their individual efforts and abilities (Hamaguchi, 1985). These companies offer security, a familiar situation, and guaranteed job advancement (Henry and Stephens, 1977).

There are important differences between this highly structured Japanese society, with its reliance on order and hierarchy, and Western society's faith in freedom and equality. The Japanese person is more concerned with taking his proper station in life than the American and his goals are sought in cooperation with his peer group. The social structure protects the male Japanese against the challenges, such as loss of employment, which a changing technology will otherwise thrust upon the individual unless supported by the culture (Matsumoto, 1970).

As noted, in Japan advancement is along socially prescribed lines, and a lack of competition within the group differs from the hostility and mistrust of others' motives and from the highly individualized striving, ambition, and competitiveness typical of the West (Williams et al., 1980; Williams, in press). It is this difference which has raised the question of whether Euro-American culture might promote more heart disease than the Japanese culture (Marmot, 1982). In this regard, it can be argued that for any particular subgroup of Japanese-Americans the greater their exposure to Western culture the greater their chance of having coronary heart disease. Conversely, the more the subgroup clings to the traditional Japanese values of loyalty and commitment to the group, the less the risk. Thus this type of group orientation might provide stability and cut down on the competitiveness between group members despite industrialization and a rapidly changing advanced technology.

Historians report that the original Japanese settlers in California formed tightly knit enclaves both by choice and to protect themselves against the external pressures of racial prejudice. Close and supportive, as well as committed to group values, the already emigrated provided much help in settling any new arrivals. This segregated community preserved the Japanese family structure prior to World War II. Children had a strong sense of duty to the older generation because of their family backgrounds. The Buddhist and Christian churches were also an important focus of Japanese community life: providing education, social groups, and meeting places (Henry and Stephens, 1977).

After World War II the American-born Japanese worked hard and gained success in the wider American middle-class society; but even then they supported strong family unity. Despite the recent economic achievements of the Japanese-Americans the two cultures still differ. The contemporary American middle class of predominantly competitive and untrusting personalities sets a high value on efficiency, output, and productivity in contrast to the Japanese traditionalist emphasis on style and mode of interaction. It is said that even today, although the traditional Japanese-Americans have discarded their native language and many of their old customs, they still seek the ethnic structure and cradle-to-grave service offered by their culture (Henry and Stephens, 1977).

The study. In a classic example of objective epidemiologic investigation, Marmot and Syme (1976) made a study of 3,800 Japanese-Americans living in eight San Francisco Bay Area counties. Each subject completed medical, demographic, and cultural questionnaires from which four indices of acculturation were compiled to measure cultural upbringing, cultural assimilation, social assimilation, and social and cultural attitudes. Laboratory procedures such as plasma cholesterol levels and electrocardiograms were included.

When classified according to cultural upbringing, the most acculturated group of Japanese-Americans was shown to have 2.5 times more coronary heart disease than the most traditional group. These differences in disease rates are not explained by differences in coronary risk factors, for this value was undiminished by controlling successively for Westernization of diet, smoking, serum lipids, blood pressure, relative weight, or serum glucose. Figure 6-8 shows how culture overrides the effects of diet.

FIGURE 6-8
Prevalence of definitive coronary heart disease (CHD) in men according to their cultural upbringing and social assimilation, controlling for risk factors. Japanese (open columns) and Western (shaded columns) cultures show a highly significant difference regardless of dietary preference.

Source: Marmot, 1975. Reprinted by permission.

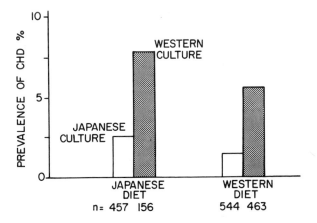

The least acculturated group had a prevalence comparable to the low rates observed in Japan, and the most acculturated group approximated the high rates observed in Caucasian-Americans. Marmot and Syme conclude that although the differences in dietary habits in Japan and the United States may be importantly related to the differences in the incidence of disease, they alone do not explain them. The evidence suggests that closely-knit stable subgroups whose members enjoy the support of their fellow men may be protected against otherwise highly socially-stimulating situations in a rapidly changing society (Marmot, 1982).

The prevalence of raised systemic arterial pressure in the Japanese is not lower than in Western society (Ueda et al., 1983). In a recent survey of the relation between psychosocial factors and blood pressure in Michigan, Cottington et al. pointed out that there were a number of reliable predictors (Cottington et al., 1985) including a difficulty in expressing emotions, along with anger and the harboring of grudges and aggressive impulses. But coronary heart disease involves an extra factor which the results of the Marmot-Syme study would suggest is associated with a sense of social support. Lacking this, the less traditional, more individualistic Japanese-Americans were perhaps vulnerable to a suppressed feeling of helplessness and depression (Henry, 1983) in addition to the anger typical of hypertension (Diamond, 1982). There is growing evidence of the negative effect of this combination of isolation and depression with suppressed anger as the following account of the Italian-American community of Roseto, Pennsylvania will suggest (Bruhn and Wolf, 1979; Bruhn et al., 1982).

The Roseto Study

The Rosetan community which nestles in the hills seventy-five miles north of Philadelphia is about 700 feet above sea level. The town, which is terraced, covers no more than one-half square mile. The houses are close together and near the street so that residents sitting on the porches can chat readily with neighbors and passersby. The lots are deep and narrow with lawn and garden space behind the houses. First settled in 1893 by Catholics of peasant stock from a small town of the same name in Southern Italy, the founders were not accepted socially by their nearby Anglo-Saxon Protestant neighbors (Bruhn and Wolf, 1979). The population was approximately 1,500 and, from the beginning, until it was fully formed and incorporated in 1912, the town's fortunes were guided by an exceptionally cultured and sophisticated Italian priest named Father Pasquale de Nisco. Father de Nisco acted as the civic as well as spiritual leader of his flock. Although offered an urban parish he elected to stay in the little village, ending his days there in 1911. The resulting well-organized, well-schooled, industrious community was for the most part composed of cohesive patriarchal Italian-American Catholic families (Bruhn and Wolf, 1979).

A mile away, in the neighboring town of Bangor, lives an ethnic mixture of English, Germans, and Italians. Here the family is more individualistic, the religion Protestant, and male and female roles overlapped (Bruhn and Wolf, 1979). In December, 1961, a preliminary medical survey of Roseto was made by a group of physicians, technicians, and dietitians from the University of Oklahoma. They were headed by the physician Dr. Stewart Wolf, psychosomatist and former collaborator of the Cornell psychophysiologist Dr. Harold Wolff, and by Dr. John Bruhn, a sociologist who thereafter dedicated his energies to the project. The study had been prompted by the observation of Dr. Benjamin Falcone, who had practiced medicine for 17 years in the vicinity, that heart attacks were rare among Rosetans in the 40-to-50-year age group. The team's observations confirmed that during a seven-year period from 1955 to 1961 there had been no "coronary" deaths of individuals below age 47 in Roseto, while in surrounding communities, such as Bangor, the deaths in each decade of life closely matched the average figures for the United States (Figure 6-9). A careful and detailed investigation demonstrated that diet was not responsible. Briefly, 41% of the 2,700 calories diet came from lard and both men and women were about 20 pounds overweight (Bruhn and Wolf, 1979).

Writing in the early 1970s, the anthropologist Carla Bianco perceived the crucial difference between the Rosetans and their neighbors in Bangor as their reinforcement of mutual trust and cohesion upon arrival from Italy (Bianco, 1974). Guided by the gifted Father de Nisco and perceiving themselves as culturally isolated in an alien land, the Rosetans wholeheartedly followed his orthodox Catholic leadership. He encouraged his parishoners to secure American citizenship, send their children to school, form sports clubs, initiate a circulating library, and form specific Catholic organizations to meet the emotional needs of each age group, i.e., adults, boys, girls, mothers, and wives (Bruhn and Wolf, 1979). Thus, they reinforced those elements of their traditional religious culture that gave them a sense of security and self-appreciation. These values persisted for a full generation after de Nisco's death. Indeed, in the late 1960s, Rosetans still retained highly traditional values toward

FIGURE 6-9   An unusually low death rate from myocardial infarction was observed in Roseto, a traditional Italian-American community in Pennsylvania, between 1955 and 1961. Its inhabitants, who derive from Roseto (province of Foggia) in southern Italy, eat a high-fat diet. The ethnic mixture of residents in Bangor, Pennsylvania, a town of the same size only a mile away, was not considered traditional. The difference between death rates (both sexes) in both towns was significant ($p < 0.001$); the authors considered it compatible with the difference between the life styles of the two communities.

Source: Stout, Morrow, Brandt, and Wolf, 1964. Reprinted by permission.

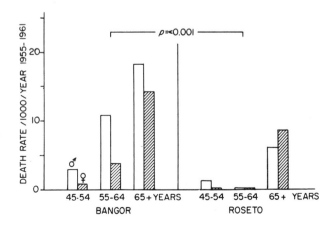

family, education, work, law, and authority. Strong leadership initiated these attitudes and, as in the case of the Japanese-Americans, the Rosetans' values were perpetuated during the earlier years because of hostile neighbors. The upshot was that the community of Roseto, Pennsylvania was actually more homogeneous and traditional than the parent village of Roseto in Foggia, Italy (Bruhn and Wolf, 1979).

Such was the state of affairs in the early 1960s when Wolf and Bruhn started their studies. Twenty years later, in 1982, they reported on the lessons from Roseto as seen from the perspective of "twenty years later" (Bruhn, Philips, and Wolf, 1982). First they reviewed the ties that bound the original community together. With the benefit of the hindsight of their prolonged study, they noted the extraordinary ethnic solidarity that had created an atmosphere of common understanding about values and about what was acceptable behavior. In the early days, the families of the first generation rallied to the aid of the bereaved, sick, or financially strapped. Prominent in this support were older single women who also nursed the elderly. The women were encouraged in this by the respected community leaders. It is relevant that the incidence of senile dementia, which imposes a great burden on nursing staff, was found to be very low in Roseto (Bruhn et al., 1982).

The practice of their religion was important to Rosetans and there was a strict rule of attendance at church and the meetings of church organizations. Families gathered to eat and drink on the occasion of weddings, confirmations, baptisms, and funerals. Social clubs were a means for the community to remain cohesive and, for the women, the almost universal practice of working from 8 A.M. to 3:30 P.M. at one of the several family-owned blouse mills was socially as well as economically rewarding. There was camaraderie at work and the extra money brought the income of the family up to the American middle-class level needed for sending the children to college (Bruhn et al., 1982).

However, the Rosetans soon learned that education would enable their children to have the "good life" of the America which surrounded their little enclave, and they struggled hard to meet these demands. Changes occurred because, in contrast with the traditional simple Italian lifestyle of the original village of Roseto, material acquisition and a different lifestyle, including social mobility, were traditional in the surrounding American society (Bruhn and Wolf, 1979). Preserving Rosetan ethnic and occupational exclusivity meant working at the same job in the same geographic area and relinquishing personal goals for the sake of the care of the elderly. All this precludes the mobility needed for the lifestyle of the United States. Also, the Rosetans who attended college realized they could not return to their hometown to work. There were no jobs in the village for the college-educated. The young Rosetans on their way to becoming middle-class Americans returned home less often. They had small families, attended church less often, worked long hours, and had little or no time for getting together after work. They smoked cigarettes and drank more than their fathers, ignored wise sleep and nutritional traditions, and focused on a better job, a better car, and a "house with a swimming pool." They rejected the old traditional life for the new: often at the strong encouragement of relatives and under pressure from loved ones (Bruhn and Wolf, 1979).

Roseto revisited twenty years later.   According to Bruhn and Wolf the results have become clear: The change in the values that were chosen as the new generation of Rosetans acculturated had repercussions on individual, family, and community life. A cohesive social structure with sharp sanctions for deviation from the norm had characterized the immigrants whose tenure lasted from the turn of the century to the 1940s. But by the time the grandchildren of the immigrants had grown up, these cultural patterns were declining. Rosetans had drifted from the traditional Roman Catholic values of Father de Nisco's founding group. Roseto had become more and more "American" and the family, the church, and the workplace had lost some of their emotionally supportive valence. Some of the security, stability, and direction to life goals had been lost (Bruhn and Wolf, 1979; Bruhn et al., 1982).

Social support serves as a buffer against the deleterious effects of excessive demands, inadequate decision latitude at work, bereavement, and other life changes (Broadhead et al., 1983; Bruhn and Philips, 1984). The early Rosetans had enjoyed excellent social support, and their family and community clannishness made use of each person's skills. This satisfied individual and collective needs and gave a sense of belonging and pride which was reflected in the low mortality and morbidity rate from coronary heart disease. Today Roseto no longer differs from the surrounding villages.

When first published in the 1960s (Stout et al., 1964) the work of Wolf's group was skeptically reviewed by the famous lipid specialist Keys (Keys, 1966a; 1966b). He questioned the diagnostic accuracy of the mortality data, raised the possibility of differential migration, and questioned whether the saturated fatty acid intake may not have been lower in Roseto. More recently Bruhn and Wolf's *The Roseto Story: An Anatomy of Health* has been unenthusiastically reviewed by Kannel, the director of the equally famous Framingham study concerning development of heart disease. His objections focused on the statistical difficulties presented by the small numbers involved in the study (Kannel, 1980).

Over the past two decades these and other criticisms have largely been answered by skilled and persistent in-depth studies. The fact that the community of 1,500 persons was small for convincing statistics meant that the investigators could make a clinical appraisal and deal with their subjects as individuals at the clinical level. Working out of a laboratory at nearby Totts Gap for two decades, Wolf and his team have watched over this community which has served them as an epidemiological laboratory. Peer review studies have been made of the various features of the original study that were challenged. This holds for details of the diet and for the original diagnoses, each of which has been confirmed in office and hospital records; as well as for the mental states, as contrasted with nearby Nazareth and Bangor (Bruhn et al., 1982). Most importantly the study became predictive and, as the years went on, it was convincingly demonstrated that the coronary artery morbidity for Roseto did in fact rise to the norm for the rest of the country. This occurred in confirmation of the hypothesis that as their culture gradually lost its protective social supports it would come to approximate the culture of the surrounding towns. Today, the work stands firm as evidence of the importance of social support and close family ties in countering the deleterious effects of emotional arousal and life changes on the occurrence of myocardial infarction and cardiac arrest.

In summary, Wolf et al. (1973) reported that for the years 1955 to 1961 the myocardial infarction mortality rate in Roseto for men under 65 was a small fraction of that in nearby Bangor and Nazareth. But by 1965 to 1970, for predictable reasons, the mortality had risen to two-thirds the nearby rate (Bruhn and Wolf, 1979; Wolf, Grace, Bruhn, and Stout, 1973). Today, in accordance with their hypothesis, they are finding that nearly 10% of males in the coronary age groups of 40 to 60 have received bypass operations (Wolf, personal communication, 1985). Very importantly, the rate of hypertension does not differ significantly from the national average (Bruhn and Wolf, 1979). Thus, the picture is very similar to that found by Marmot and Syme in the Japanese-Americans. In both cases a group holding onto an old established traditional lifestyle was being constantly challenged by an alien culture whose control over the environment and material success was seen as formidable yet desirable.

PERSONALITY VARIABLES
AND HYPERTENSION: A SUMMARY

Previous papers have reviewed the personality of persons with high blood pressure as reported in various studies during the past twenty years (Diamond, 1982; Esler, Julius, Zweifler, Randall, Harburg, Gardiner, and DeQuattro, 1977; McClelland, 1979). Blood pressure is higher in groups which are well socialized with strong suppression of emotion. Suppressed anger and suspicion, together with a sense of insufficient control, are reported (Cottington, Brock, House, and Hawthorne, 1985). There is less hypertension where traditional cooperative relations, beliefs, and patterns have persisted (Henry and Cassel, 1969). In general, high blood pressure is associated with a level of social achievement which does not satisfy the individual (Cottington, Brock, House, and Hawthorne, 1985; Waldron, Nowoiarski, Freimer, Henry, Post, and Witten, 1982) and there is suppressed anger at lack of successful environmental control with its resulting frustration in attaining goals (Theorell, Hjemdahl, Ericson, Kollner, Knox, Perski, Svenisa, Tidgren, and Walker, 1985).

Cynicism and the Type A Personality

A recent editorial in a leading medical journal asked whether a disease (such as hypertension) can indeed be a reflection of psyche (Angell, 1985). The occasion was the failure of Cassileth et al. (1985) to find that social and psychological factors influenced the survival time of persons with advanced malignant disease and of Case et al. (1985) and several other groups to find a correlation between what was originally called Type A personality (Friedman and Ulmer, 1984) and the recurrence of acute myocardial infarction. Angell raised the question of whether mental state is indeed an important cause of disease except insofar as our health is affected by what we decide to eat or drink, or by the drugs we take. In the author's opinion the now overwhelming evidence that social support and health are intimately linked (Berkman and Syme, 1979; Broadhead et al., 1983; Bruhn and Philips, 1984) and the solid connections between disease and chronic disorders of neuroendocrine regulation (Henry, 1982) make a viewpoint such as Angell's highly controversial.

Indeed, behavioral physician Williams whose group has already demonstrated the strong correlation between hostility and coronary heart disease (Williams et al., 1982), has recently foreseen Angell's question (Angell, 1985). In a subtle discussion of the behavioral aspects of the Type A personality, he explains researchers' failure to find that high risk groups undergoing coronary angiography have statistically significant global Type A personality relationships (Williams, in press). He concludes it is the result of the subjects' inability to compensate. There are certain crucial domains within the global Type A concept such as mistrust and anger, which constitute their coping style and allow for this compensation. He explains the intriguing failure of one group to find a correlation between high scores on the Medley Hostility NMPI scale, as filled in by physicians when they were medical school applicants, and the mortality rate from coronary heart disease of these same physicians twenty-five years later (Williams, in press). These applicants' scores were very significantly lower (P<0.0001) than those of medical students studied by his own group who were completing the same scale during psychiatric training (Barefoot et al., 1983). He concludes that suspicious, cynical, untrusting applicants will be likely to dissemble and conceal their true feelings when taking a test they perceive could affect their chances of admission into school; once in school the motive to conceal vanishes.

Similar consideration of the effects of subjective viewpoints caused Case et al. (1985) to question whether subfactors in the global Type A personality might become subdued after myocardial infarction. Indeed, subjects' left ventricular dysfunction may have led to postinfarction cardiovascular readjustments that indirectly affected the subjects' competitive drives. For example, left ventricular dysfunction is often associated with a fall in blood pressure and a rise in central venous pressure during effort (Morris et al., 1982). This would be associated with vasoconstriction from changes in the input from low and high pressure cardiovascular receptors into the locus ceruleus (Elam et al., 1984). This critical brainstem center and the nearby raphe may perceive the information as signifying loss of control and respond to the challenge of effort with less arousal (Jones et al., 1983); i.e., those with left ventricular dysfunction may no longer experience the appropriate feelings of arousal and may fail to respond with the classic Type A workaholic frenzy. As they slip into exhaustion, defeat and frustration develop and they perceive the control that is so important to them slipping away (Henry, 1983; 1984; 1985). At the same time the set of their brainstem centers shifts to depression with elevated corticoids.

To recapitulate the differences in emotional state in the two diseases, in the hypertensive individual there is suppression of anger with dissatisfaction with the role in life (Diamond, 1982). By contrast, in coronary heart disease the almost paranoid sense of being on one's own, alone, and the belief that others are not to be trusted gives a potential for alienation that leads to despairing frustration (Bruhn et al., 1974; Friedman and Ulmer, 1984; Henry, 1983; Williams, Haney Jr., Lee, Kong, Blumenthal, and Whalen, 1980). The traditional Japanese-American and the Rosetan Italian-American can be hypertensive and sense a pressure for more achievement while suppressing any feelings of anger. But in addition, their traditional lifestyle and their cohesive social network protect them from the chronic despair and depression which appear responsible for the progression of atheromatous obstruction of the coronary arteries (Henry, 1983).

TRADITION VERSUS CULTURAL INSTABILITY

Waldron's extensive work with data from various hypertensive groups has drawn attention to the need of those confronted by economic modernization, for example because of migration, to learn new behavior. One feature of these hypertensive groups is their increasing involvement with money in a cash economy, with buying and selling, as opposed to the barter of groups like pastoralists or hunter-gatherers (Waldron, Nowoiarski, Freimer, Henry, Post, and Witten, 1982). We would speculate that this substitution of money, with its numbers, for the process of bartering may mean the development of a more abstract "left hemispheric" evaluation of items. The nature of the object being bought for money instead of being exchanged for another item may become less important than the monetary transaction itself, as the latter becomes more complex and abstract.

Shils has discussed matters along these lines in his treatise on tradition (Shils, 1981). In it he argues that the idea of progress—with a focus on rationality and expediency—and of improving things as they exist and replacing them with more efficient items, is at odds with tradition as the normative mode of action and belief. Those attached to institutions, practices, and beliefs designated as traditional are called reactionary. He discusses the attitude of the eighteenth-century enlightenment and nineteenth-century liberal scientism and their hope that reason and scientific knowledge would free man from enslavement to the "dead weight" of tradition.

In a long and cogent discussion Shils refutes the above view. He points to the role of tradition in science itself. Nobody starts *de novo*: The body of established knowledge must first be mastered and, with this knowledge, science grows ever greater. The first conception of an unsolved problem in this received tradition and the generation of an idea about its solution both depend on the availability of the tradition and its mastery. According to Shil's argument, new knowledge would be impossible without old knowledge.

Shil goes on to discuss in detail the need for stability, the need to live in an ordered world marked by a framework and rules. He describes the immigrants' loss of the sense of affinity as they abandon culinary traditions, convivial customs, proverbial sayings, and celebratory ceremonies as they become assimilated. There is a loss of much that "centers" the individual and that serves to give Antonovsky and Kobasa's sense of coherence and meaning (Birren and Livingston, 1985). The move to rationalization and freedom from traditional norms which are not based on demonstrable fact thus threatens a destabilization and loss of normative value systems. According to Shils, an excessive rationalism can be associated with an individualism that ignores consideration of family and group, and loses interest in civility and an ordered hierarchy. There is a vunerability to social conflict and to gullible belief in unstable, apparently charismatic individuals.

Shils argues that although traditions have been shaken they cannot be obliterated as long as human beings are born to human beings to whom they become attached, and as long as parental care is necessary for the healthy growth of children. As long as the universe remains mysterious and humans seek order in it they, in Shils' view, will create and form and attach themselves to tradition. For Shils, as long as rules and categories and institutions are needed, and as long as they cannot be created just when the occasion arises and for that occasion only, humans will cling to tradition even when they proudly think they are not doing so. However, he concedes that although traditions are necessary for mankind, they are not immutable. They can change their peculiar configuration and the impact of many persons gradually affects the course of tradition and the policies of institutions. For example, since 1953 Japan has shown a continued move towards new, rational opinions and away from traditional opinions with important exceptions in "value of work," "man and nature," "importance of benefactors," and a growing belief in the superiority of the Japanese over Westerners (Sakamoto, 1975, p. 6). However, it has been shown by social epidemiology that health suffers in the groups that lose social supports due to too-rapid culture change (Berkman and Syme, 1979; Broadhead et al., 1983; Henry and Stephens, 1977; Tyroler and Cassel, 1974).

Traditional Religion, Social Supports, and Health

Peter Berger, whose ground breaking book *The Sacred Canopy* presents the elements of a sociological theory of religion, strongly endorses Shils' careful study of the role of tradition in human societies (Berger, 1967). He agrees that tradition is not just reactionary sterile conservatism. According to Berger, each generation hands down its culture to the next, and the enduring weight of the past in human affairs is not just a nuisance to be cleared away as mankind breaks new ground. In his view, matters are quite to the contrary; he views tradition as indispensable to human society.

Thus in exercising their traditional cultural canon, including their religious beliefs, the Japanese-Americans and the Rosetan Italian-Americans were providing themselves with strong social support systems. These supports would protect them from an excessive stimulation of the neuroendocrine system with corresponding damaging levels of activation of the sympathetic adrenal medullary and pituitary adrenal cortical systems. In *The Sacred Canopy,* Berger discusses moments of intense emotional arousal that accompany the making and breaking of attachment bonds—as occurs at birth, death, divorce, marriage, or the success or failure of human enterprises as in wars for national survival or triumphs over natural obstacles like mountains, oceans, or exploration of the moon. Berger accepts theologian Otto's (1952) classic description of the numinous or sacred occasion as one where the reality of everyday life dramatically loses its primacy. He speaks of "awe" in the sense that Astronaut Cernan has recently used it. Describing the United States Space Program as the "greatest of human endeavors" and his own feelings on the sterile moon far from the nurturant biosphere of "Mother" Earth, Cernan writes:

> When I was the last man to walk on the moon in December 1972 I stood in the blue darkness and looked in awe at the earth from the lunar surface. What I saw was almost too beautiful to grasp. There was too much logic, too much purpose. It was just too beautiful to have happened by accident. It does not matter how you choose to worship God or by whatever name you call him but he has to exist to have created what I was privileged to see (Cernan, 1985).

This Otto would describe as an experience of the holy or numinous (Otto, 1952).

Jungian psychiatrist Bolen (1984), in her recent book on the psychology of women, describes her wedding experience in a similar vein. Brought up as a middle-of-the-road Protestant, no mystery or magic had accompanied its rituals. But she too was overwhelmed by Otto's "awe" as she found herself swept by the marriage ceremony into the feeling that she was participating in something sacred (Bolen,

1984). There was a sense, as in the case of the astronaut, of experiencing something beyond ordinary reality—something numinous (Otto, 1952).

For Berger religion has the role of keeping this emotional "other" dimension of human experience within bounds. The "sacred canopy" controls the numinous with ritual so the emotions surrounding birth, marriage, death, and our other "passages" are kept within bounds. We live in the ordinary but on special occasions we have the ordinary breached. Eventually we return to the ordinary (Berger, 1967). We would propose that for the adherent of an established traditional religion, such as a Rosetan, ordinary social life is held in place by the rituals. For these Roman Catholics, the disruptive aspects of the other reality were muted and held in proportion by the ancient cultural canon which they unquestioningly accepted. The religion not only domesticated the ecstasies of success and love channelling them into socially acceptable "moral conduct": it also protected against the despair that so often accompanies the hostile-aggressive potential coronary victim as he meets with failure and rejection while in pursuit of his solitary ambitions (Williams et al., 1980).

Presumably neither the Japanese-American nor the Italian-American culture protected their adherents from the suppressed hostility (Diamond, 1982), the sense of insecurity and lack of control that the rapidly changing culture of today's technocracy induces in so many of us (Bruhn and Wolf, 1979; Karasek et al., 1982; Marmot and Syme, 1976; Ruberman et al., 1984). Both sexes of both groups suffered from the same high blood pressure as the rest of Western society; but the men in both groups were remarkably free from coronary heart disease, especially in late maturity from 45 to 65 years. We believe that the mechanism of this protection is connected with the strong social supports provided by both cultures. These supports did not prevent a hypertensiogenic, suppressed, irritated disappointment with the contrast between the reality of the society around them and their early beliefs and expectations (Waldron et al., 1982). Nevertheless, the social network and the established traditional beliefs protected them from depression in their day-to-day routine search for the basic desiderata such as food, drink, and companionable safe harborage for the family.

At the same time, the cultural canon harnesses the capacity to experience the numinous as myths that teach a successful social interaction. We speculate that the long experience of established religious traditions has developed skillful use of myth and ritual to keep a control over raw emotions of rage, fear, and despair (Berger, 1967; Henry and Stephens, 1977; Otto, 1952). Both the crude fight-flight drive to control and the strong emotions engendered during the bonding of men and women, as well as parents and children, are kept in proper proportion. The belief systems of the traditional society, with their long established balanced intuitive appreciation and respect for the facts of human nature, support the members in controlling the emotional arousal induced by the everyday life of their society.

The Japanese-American and Rosetan data suggest that when there are great changes afoot and there is much instability, as in the present time, diseases of adaptation such as hypertension appear, but that nevertheless the workaholic drive— *Joyless Sisyphus* (Bruhn, Paredes, Adsett, and Wolf, 1974)—the exhaustion, and the covert depression typical of the victim of fatal coronary heart disease can still be avoided in the culture that can retain a measure of traditional social support (Henry, 1983; 1985).

Shifts in the Cultural Canon

Thus, we would speculate that the declining power of some of our traditional beliefs, especially in the area of gender and family mores, may be in part responsible for the current epidemic of coronary heart disease. The work with Japanese-Americans shows that belief is not a matter of intellectual conviction alone. It is the lifestyle that is critical. Aging Trappist monks living in monasteries in the United States in the 1960s had highly elevated blood pressure (Henry and Cassel, 1969). But those in Germany over a generation before did not (Seile, 1930). Was this because there had been some change in the beliefs of a devout modern Catholic? Probably not, for the Benedictine priests who work in the competitive, hard-driving milieu of the parishes and seminaries of the United States have a high incidence of coronary heart disease. Yet they are devout and have the same beliefs and follow the same catechism as those working in monastic calm who do not suffer from heart disease (Caffrey, 1966). Conscious beliefs apart, Shils (1981) presents evidence that the traditions that used to provide the Roman Catholic church with its great strength are losing their deep emotional conviction. Likewise, Friedman and Ulmer (1984) comment on the growing restlessness with their traditional lifestyle, as witness the well-known defections of clergy and of nuns. On family issues, such as that of birth control, the church has continued to take the side of the instinct of attached men and women to raise families of several children. Yet today's medical skills in preserving infant lives dictate to the technologically advanced states that man must sharply control population. The fact that the Rosetans and the Japanese-Americans developed less heart disease may be because, despite considerable cultural changes in other areas, their traditional beliefs were still able to dictate an emotionally protective lifestyle which, whether biologically right or wrong in the long run, successfully kept emotional arousal in hand for the time being.

STRESS AS A MATTER OF CONTROL VERSUS DEMAND

In a stimulating diagrammatic presentation, Karasek, Schwaitz, and Pieper (1982) have contrasted the demands of various work situations in modern society with the sense of control enjoyed by the individual. In Figure 6-10 we have combined their ideas with a similar but physiologically-based approach presented in the essay on psychosocial factors, disease, and aging cited above (Henry, 1985).

Figure 6-10 presents two axes: a corticoid one for control, depicted here as ranging from a prevailing sense of security and freedom to make decisions to distressed helplessness; and a catecholamine axis for demand, which ranges from a situation where the individual is generally relaxed and at ease to one in which he or she is aroused into defensive coping with the fight-flight response. We propose that the traditional slow-paced society of the hunter-gatherer and pastoralist, where there is neither hypertension nor coronary heart disease, is most closely simulated in contemporary society in the quadrant of the Karasek et al. diagram where the forester, the book binder, and the monk are located. Changes fostered by technocracy increase the demand on the individual. Part of this stems from the communication and transportation revolutions: the car, plane, and telephone, and the

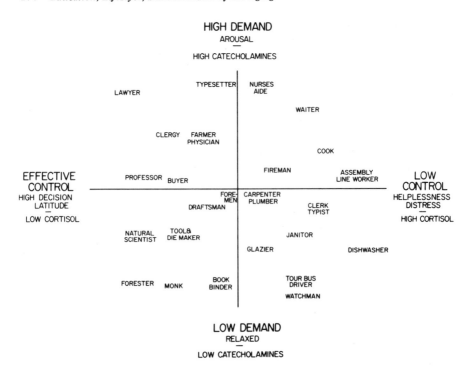

FIGURE 6-10   Mean job characteristics scores by 1970 Census Occupational Codes and U.S. Quality of Working Life Surveys. *Abscissa:* Work Load, i.e.,: Demands *Ordinate:* Extent of Control, i.e., Decision Latitude. Jobs that are in the high control lower left quadrant are associated with lower rates of cardiovascular disease than those in the upper right quadrant which are associated with high demand and low control. Note the modern tendency for demand to become higher and control less, as in the production lines of technocracy. In contrast, the arts and crafts have changed little over the centuries: lower demand and more control.

Source: Karasek, Schivaitz, and Pieper, 1982. Reprinted by permission.

rapid pace demanded by the social changes of industrial and postindustrial society have all moved most of us upward on the demand axis so that we all find more to do and less time in which to do it. Our sense of security has decreased.

Other psychological changes noted in this section may be implicit in the type of thinking needed for a money economy. This may explain why even in protected Roseto and the monasteries of today's Catholic church the incidence of hypertension has risen. The freedom from this disease that was enjoyed by the hunter-gatherers and the pastoralists of Waldron (Waldron, Nowoiarski, Freimer, Henry, Post, and Witten, 1982) and Donnison (Donnison, 1929) has been lost. Nevertheless, the majority in Roseto still perceived that taking care of the pressing tasks of each day followed the dictates of their traditional belief system. Like the lawyers and professors in the upper-left-hand box of Figure 6-10, they perceived themselves as being to some degree in harmony with the order of things and, therefore, in some sense still "in control."

As in the case of the upper-right-hand quadrant of Figure 6-10, we speculate that it is not only when there is much to be done and little time to do it, as in the case of the cook or waiter, but also when there is a feeling that your input does not count and that the order of things pays no attention to your needs, that the depression and helplessness leading to coronary heart disease are encouraged. There are data to support this differentiation. Marmot, Rose, Shipley, and Hamilton (1978) have shown that high-level civil servants in England who enjoy both control of their work pace and great job security, have a far lower incidence of coronary heart disease than the helpless messengers in the same service who are at the beck and call of everyone.

In a beautifully solid study, Ruberman, Weinblatt, Goldberg, and Chaudhary (1984) have recently shown that in our technocracy those with poor education who have a low status job with little decision latitude and who, unlike the Rosetans, lack a supporting social network and experience high levels of isolation, have more than four times the risk of sudden death after recovery from a myocardial infarction than men with better social status. They thus associated high stress and social isolation with those with the least education. Berkman and Syme (1979), discussing social networks and overall mortality, describe the recent work of Joseph who reexamined Marmot and Syme's Japanese-American data. Joseph concluded that over and above any risks such as serum cholesterol, systolic blood pressure, smoking or lack of physical activity, loss of social affiliation created a three- to four-fold extra risk (Berkman and Syme, 1979). It is important that the educational level of the original Rosetan group was as modest as that of the vulnerable subjects of Ruberman et al. (1984). This suggests that it was the Rosetan tradition and social affiliation that were the critical factors protecting them.

Reviewing these and other results, Graboys (1984) writes "of an Orwellian recipe in which the estranged worker beseiged from above and below mixes internal rage and incessant frustration into a fatal brew." In an editorial, he comments on "the need for us to elicit a social history from our patients with ischaemic heart disease before we proceed to the technologic forms of diagnostic evaluation that characterize the contemporary practice of cardiology." He states that we should explore the psychosocial causes of stress that may be impairing a patient's ability to resist the adversity of heart disease and may ultimately lead to a chronic and debilitating sense of despair and futility" (Graboys, 1984).

The 1974 study of Bruhn, Paredes, Adsett, and Wolf (1974) on psychological predictors of sudden death in myocardial infarction has pointed to the role of depression and joyless striving in susceptibility to ischaemic heart disease (i.e., *Joyless Sisyphus*). It is these supposed unhappy characteristics of the world of the coronary-prone that are not found in the description in Bruhn and Wolf's (1979) *The Roseto Story: An Anatomy of Health*. They write:

> We found that family relationships were extremely close and mutually supportive. This cohesive quality extended to neighbors and the community as a whole. There was a well defined man-woman relationship in Roseto where the man was uncontested head of the family. The elderly were cherished and respected and they retained their authority throughout life. The atmosphere of Roseto was gay and friendly and reflected an enthusiastic and optimistic attitude toward life.

Their book proposes that the Rosetan way of life and its social pattern may have contributed significantly to the healthy state of the community. As traditional values are gradually being abandoned by the rising generation, the death rate from heart attack in Roseto appears to be climbing toward the American norm. In 1985 the death rate was within 20% of the rate of the surrounding communities; and, as noted above, out of 350 males of the 40-to-60-year age groups no less than 25 had the telltale scar of coronary bypass surgery (Wolf, personal communication, 1985).

PREVENTION OF CARDIOVASCULAR DISEASE
BY PSYCHOSOCIAL INTERVENTION

Two groups out of the many who are now exploring behavioral methods of improving health may be cited. Both report considerable success: one with coronary heart disease; the other with the behavioral treatment of hypertension. In a ten-year follow-up to the Friedman and Rosenman book *Type A Behavior and Your Heart,* Friedman and Ulmer report on the findings of a four-year study aimed at learning whether Type A behavior could be modified and whether such modification will reduce the risk of heart attack. Not only did most of those receiving "Type A avoidance" counseling succeed in changing their behavior pattern but by doing so they cut their heart attack rate in half. The new book discusses the background causes of Type A behavior: the hidden insecurity and damaged self-esteem that generally precede the more obvious free-floating hostility and sense of time urgency, and the drive toward self destruction. In a mood reminiscent of the Alcoholics Anonymous literature, they discuss teaching a number of "freedoms" including that to overcome insecurity and repair self-esteem, to give and receive love, to mature, to listen, to play, and to enjoy family and friends and tranquility (Friedman and Ulmer, 1984).

Friedman and Ulmer stress the need for coping by managing to match inner resources to outside demands. In their view, a person is in trouble when demands exceed resources. At home the demands can be those of spouse, friends, or children, or those arising from owning a home and property. At work the demands include those of supervisors, of meeting deadlines, and of distress from interpersonal relationships with co-workers. In the community the demands can be problems with neighbors, irritation at waiting in line at stores and banks, and so on.

Patients were asked to review their ties with intimate others and to seriously evaluate how these ties were being nurtured. They were asked to review the stability of their lifestyle and their closeness to their children. They were encouraged to have something to love including, if possible, an affectionate pet. Patients were trained to avoid hurry especially in driving; to avoid irritating line-ups, perhaps by spending a little more money or avoiding "bargain" stores; to reduce intake of alcohol, caffeine, and nicotine; to relax regularly in a quiet place with adequate space; to listen actively to others, carefully appreciating what they say; to express love and affection; and to love self by being less self-critical and more accepting of the beauty of being average in most things.

Another remarkably successful set of studies has been conducted since 1975 by Dr. Chandra Patel in England. Combining yoga with a biofeedback method, her patients were first taught to relax on a couch in a quiet room. Breathing was to be smooth and regular. They were instructed in progressive physical relaxation by a method with similarities to Jacobson's (1938) but originating from "Hatha Yoga." Simultaneous tensing of protagonist and antagonist muscle groups was avoided. Instead, at each session patients relaxed each group of muscles sequentially, progressing at each session to involve the whole body. After a few weeks during which they learned to relax physically, they had to progress to the more difficult achievement of mental relaxation. With this accomplishment they found that they became less aware of both the outside world and of their limbs. In order to progress beyond a mere conscious voluntary control of breathing, yoga methods were used. The patients were instructed that while focusing attention on breathing they were to repeat a phrase or word (mantra) with every expiration. Patients were free to select their own object or idea for this concentration. Training in how to relax while at home, while going about town, and while at work accompanied this more personal instruction.

In repeated tests over the years Patel and her associates have reported a reduction of systolic blood pressure by approximately 20 ± 11 mm Hg (Patel, Marmot, and Terry, 1981; Patel and North, 1975). There was a sharp reduction in the amount of drugs required to keep the pressure at the desired level. In the group's most recent observations involving a five-year follow-up of patients who were no longer attending relaxation sessions, there has been a significant diminution in electrocardiographic abnormalities, as well as confirmation of already reported evidence of a fall in risk factors such as cholesterol and plasma renin levels (Patel, personal communication, 1985). Patel's results with blood pressure have been reproduced by others and the use of behavioral techniques for aiding in the drug control of mild hypertension is becoming acceptable medical practice (McCaffrey and Blanchard, 1985). It is especially valuable in younger people with renin-dependent hypertension who are not helped by reduction of salt intake and who otherwise face a lifetime of taking drugs for a slowly progressive condition which will only "surface" and become symptomatic in later life.

Religion and Education for Health

Religion has always been an essential feature of human culture even in cultures that shy away from use of the word. To the sociologist Berger, religion is an educational system that teaches the members of a culture how to link the experience of symbols, myths, fantasies, and emotional insights to the everyday world (Berger, 1967). Religion seeks to integrate everyday life with the "other" of the basic experiences of love and hate, depression and euphoria. From this sociological viewpoint a religion involves learned behavior and is the result of the education of its adherents. We speculate that its critical function is the connection of everyday life with the profoundly moving "other" without which the individual remains vulnerable to anomia—is without conviction as to the worth of things, and without motivation. The development of the relatedness necessary for the attachment and bonding of a society such as the Rosetans depends on proper access to myths and rituals. Religion keeps the right balance between raw emotions and a sterile intellectualism which cuts the individual off from symbolic, emotionally meaningful material. It could be proposed that religious education that has such a balanced approach is an expression of a culture that has the good fortune to be neither too pragmatic nor too wrapped up in myths and dreams (Henry, 1986b).

In a recent analysis of the importance of religion in old age it was found that the best predictor that any one religious style would turn out to be important in guiding one's life was the particular tradition that the individual had been taught (McCallum, 1984). In Australia, Irish Catholicism was found to give the most satisfaction in old age. But it also involves a traditional culture which produces the high friendship satisfaction and volunteerism of strong social bonding. The similarity to the Italian-Catholic Rosetan behavior suggests that in the corresponding Australian situation the Irish Catholic tradition could be shown to be protective of physical as well as psychosocial health. It appears that culture plays a very critical part in determining the amount of psychosocial arousal that is experienced by a society. But culture *is* learned behavior; *the product of education* (Henry and Stephens, 1977; Shils, 1981). In animal studies chronic adverse psychosocial arousal has been demonstrated to be a powerful mechanism for the production of chronic heart disease (Kaplan, Manuck, Clarkson, Lusso, Taub, and Miller, 1983; Kaplan, Manuck, Clarkson, and Pritchard, 1985). In a recent review of the objectives of preventive medicine, Dole (1985) has discussed the mechanisms with which any further improvement in the incidence of disease will necessarily be involved. To raise the median age of death in our society any further than the present 80+ years would require a substantial reduction in mortality from heart disease. If the Roseto story is accepted, cultures that emphasize attachment behavior and group welfare as opposed to an intense striving for achievement and individual accomplishment will experience lower rates of ischaemic heart disease.

It remains to be seen what changes will occur in the future in our education and in our culture. The current rationalized world that seeks individual affluence lacks the emphasis on attachment that a traditional education provided. The works cited above (Friedman and Ulmer, 1984; Patel, Marmot, and Terry, 1981) indicate that those who are treating chronic cardiovascular disease are coming to realize there is a need to change our current normative synthesis. Their approach puts interesting emphasis on teaching the acquisition of patterns of attachment behavior and social integration.

There are a number of examples of positive effects brought about by the emotions associated with the old normative synthesis of traditional religion. The now fading Catholic faith of the Rosetans and their health have been discussed above (Friedman and Ulmer, 1984). The basic text of "Alcoholics Anonymous" acknowledges a debt to their traditional religious mentor and "wonderful friend" Catholic Father Edward Dowling. The book, which avoids the subject of denominational religion, makes a point of drawing attention to the role of "spiritual experience" in the personality change involved in recovering from alcoholism. The authors state that with few exceptions these people find they have tapped an unsuspected inner resource which they personally identify with their own conception of a "power greater than themselves" (Anon, 1979). Likewise, Friedman and Ulmer's book on the successful Recurrent Coronary Prevention Project was dedicated to their mentor Father James Gill. They comment that "50-to-60-year-old men and women can and do recover their religious beliefs (particularly if they have been believing Catholics) and in doing so lose some of their most troublesome Type A traits" (Friedman and Ulmer, 1984). Similarly, it is the theme of Herbert Benson's carefully nondenominational *Beyond the Relaxation Response* that "for whatever reason, faith in the sense of deepest personal belief or religion when combined with a meditation program does make a difference in the attempt to control blood pressure" by the relaxation technique (Benson, 1984). The nature of such an experience has been discussed elsewhere. It has been suggested that it involves serene mental states which may be difficult to achieve when the individual is in an "uptight" alert coping mood (Henry, 1982; 1985; Henry and Stephens, 1977).

SUMMARY

The lifestyle peculiar to each culture has its own special effect on those aging within it: a determining factor being the level and type of chronic emotional arousal that prevails in that particular society. Since culture involves education, changes in the lifestyle of older adults can be achieved by reacculturation, thereby mitigating or even avoiding certain diseases of older adulthood.

Modern industrial states have tended to neglect tradition as they accept the new cultural patterns developing out of the discoveries of science and technology. Their social and educative systems emphasize power, i.e., production and competition in the workplace, and put less weight on the affiliation of the earlier traditional family and the emotional rewards of the close interaction of members of a bonded group. Epidemiological evidence of the effects of such a bias on the health of the aged includes the Marmot-Syme study of Japanese-Americans showing the vulnerability to heart disease of those who abandon traditional aspects of Japanese culture. The story of Roseto is also relevant. As long as the immigrants to this Pennsylvania town still followed their Roman Catholic, southern Italian cultural patterns they enjoyed a great health advantage. In recent years their distinctive culture has become assimilated into that of the surrounding society, and their incidence of heart disease has risen to the same level. A related finding is the observation of Waldron et al. (1982) that the blood pressure in social groups living in industrialized society is higher than in the societies of traditional agriculturalists, pastoralists, or hunter-gatherers. Traditional cultures may enjoy less chronic cardiovascular disease because there is less intense striving for achievement, and because they do not neglect attachment behavior and feeling-oriented prayer and meditation to the same degree as modern industrialized societies. Cardiologist Friedman's group has recently trained older persons, known to be vulnerable to coronary heart disease, to exhibit a more relaxed, more loving, and more friendly behavior. They present evidence that there is less coronary heart disease in those adopting this pattern which emphasizes the affiliative behaviors of the old traditional cultures.

REFERENCES

ANGELL, M. (1985). Disease as a reflection of psyche. *New England Journal of Medicine, 312,* 1570–1572.

ANON, B. (1969). Falkland Islands and dependencies. *Report of Foreign and Commonwealth Office for Years 1966 and 1967.* London: H. M. Stationary Office.

ANON, B. (1976). *Alcoholics Anonymous.* New York: Alcoholics Anonymous World Services, Inc.

ATHEROSCLEROSIS STUDY GROUP (1984). Optimal resources for primary prevention of atherosclerotic diseases. *Circulation, 70,* 157–195.

ASTON, J. G., FOOTE, S. L., and BLOOM, F. E. (1983). Anatomy and physiology of locus coeruleus neurons: Functional implications. In M. B. Leyler and R. C. Lake (Eds.), *Frontiers of clinical neuroscience, Vol. 2, Norepinephrine.* New York: Balt Williams (pp. 92–116).

BAREFOOT, J. C., DAHLSTROM, W. G., and WILLIAMS, R. B. (1983). Hostility, CHD incidence and total mortality: A 25-year follow-up study of 255 physicians. *Psychosomatic Medicine, 45,* 59.

BENEDICT, R. (1946). *The chrysanthemum and the sword: Patterns of Japanese culture.* Boston: Haughton.

BENSON, H. (1984). *Beyond the relaxation response.* New York: Berkeley Books.

BERGER, P. L. (1967). *The sacred canopy: Elements of a sociological theory of religion.* Garden City, New York: Doubleday.

BERKMAN, L. F., and SYME, L. (1979). Social networks, host resistance, and mortality: A nine-year follow-up study of Alameda County residents. *American Journal of Epidemiology, 109,* 186–204.

BIANCO, C. (1974). *The two Rosetos.* Bloomington, Indiana: Indiana University Press.

BIRREN, J. E., and LIVINGSTON, J. E. (Eds.) (1985). *Cognition, stress, and aging.* Englewood Cliffs, New Jersey: Prentice-Hall, Inc.

BOLEN, J. S. (1984). *Goddesses in everywoman.* San Francisco: Harper and Row.

BROADHEAD, W. E., KAPLAN, B., JAMES, S., WAGNER, E. H., SCHOENBACH, V. J., GREIVSON, R., HEYDEN, S., TIBBLEN, G., and GEHLBACH, S. (1983). The evidence for a relationship between social support and health. *American Journal of Epidemiology, 117,* 521–537.

BRUHN, J. G. PAREDES, A., ADSETT, A., and WOLF, S. (1974). Psychological predictors of sudden death in myocardial infarction. *Journal of Psychosomatic Responses, 18,* 187–191.

BRUHN, J. G., and PHILIPS, B. U., JR. (1984). Measuring social support: A synthesis of current approaches. *Journal of Behavioral Medicine, 7,* 151–169.

BRUHN, J. G., PHILIPS, B. U., JR., and WOLF, S. (1982). Lessons from Roseto twenty years later: A community study of heart disease. *Southern Medical Journal, 75,* 575–580.

BRUHN, J. G., and WOLF, S. (1979). *The Roseto story: An anatomy of health.* Norman, Oklahoma: University of Oklahoma Press.

CAFFREY, C. B. (1966). Behavior patterns and personality characteristics as related to prevalence rates of coronary heart disease in Trappist and Benedictine Monks. Ph.D. dissertation: (Clinical Psychology). Catholic University of America, Washington, D.C./Ann Arbor, Michigan: University Microfilms Inc. (pp. 67–1830).

CASE, R. B., HELLER, S. S., and CASE, N. B. (1985). Type A behavior and survival after acute myocardial infarction. *New England Journal of Medicine, 312,* 737–741.

CASSILETH, B. R., RUSH, E. J., MILLER, D. S., BROWN, C., and MILLER, C. (1985). Psychosocial correlates of survival in advanced malignant disease. *New England Journal of Medicine, 312,* 1551–1555.

CERNAN, E. (1985). The price of being a space hero. *TV Guide, 33*(15), 4–7.

COTTINGTON, E. M., BROCK, B. M., HOUSE, J. S., and HAWTHORNE, V. M. (1985). Psychosocial factors and blood pressure in the Michigan Statewide Blood Pressure Survey. *American Journal of Epidemiology, 121,* 15–29.

DIAMOND, E. L. (1982). The role of anger and hostility in essential hypertension and coronary heart disease. *Psychological Bulletin, 92*(2), 410–433.

DOLE, R. (1985). Preventive medicine: The objectives in the value of preventive medicine. *Ciba Foundation Symposium #110.* Pitman, London: Ciba Foundation (pp. 3-21).

DONNISON, C. P. (1929). Blood pressure in the African native, its bearing on the etiology of hyperpiesia and artheriosclerosis. *Lancet, 1,* 6-7.

DONNISON, C. P. (1938). *Civilization and disease.* Baltimore, Maryland: William Wood & Co.

EAKER, E. D., HAYNES, S. G., and FEINLAUB, M. (1983). Spouse behavior and coronary heart disease in men: Prospective results from the Framingham Study. *American Journal of Epidemiology, 118,* 23-41.

ELAM, M., YAO, T., SVENSSON, T. H., and THOREN, P. (1984). Regulation of locus coeruleus neurons and splanchnic sympathetic nerves by cardiovascular afferents. *Brain Research, 290,* 281-287.

ESLER, M., JULIUS, S., ZWEIFLER, A., RANDALL, O., HARBURG, E., GARDINER, H., and DeQUATTRO, V. (1977). Mild high-renin essential hypertension: Neurogenic human hypertension. *New England Journal of Medicine, 296,* 405-411.

FOLKOW, B. (1982). Physiological aspects of primary hypertension. *Physiological Review, 62,* 347-504.

FOSTER, J. H. (1930). Practice of medicine in China and New England with observation on hypertension. *New England Journal of Medicine, 203,* 1073-1076.

FOX, R. (1982). *Eyewitness Falklands,* Chapter 10: *These quiet little islands of ours, past, present, and future.* London: Mathews.

FRENCH. N. A. (1975). Governor's speech: June 10-12 meeting of the Legislative Council. *Falkland Islands Gazette, 84*(8), 1.

FRIEDMAN, N. M., and ULMER, D. (1984). *Treating Type A behavior and your heart.* New York: A. A. Knopf.

GORDON, T. (1967). Further mortality experience among Japanese Americans. *Public Health Report, 82,* 973-984.

GRABOYS, T. B. (1984). Stress and the aching heart. *New England Journal of Medicine, 311,* 594-595.

GRAHAM, J. D. (1945). High blood pressure after battle. *Lancet, 1,* 239-240.

HADDEN, A. B. (1976). June 25 meeting of the Legislative Council. *Falkland Islands Gazette, 85*(8), 20.

HAMAGUCHI, E. (1985). The career patterns of the Japanese. In K. Morioka (Ed.), *Family and lifecourse in middle-aged men.* Tokyo: The Family and Lifecourse Study Group.

HENRY, J. P. (1982). The relation of social and biological processes in disease. *Social Science and Medicine, 16*(4), 369-380.

HENRY, J. P. (1983). Coronary heart disease and arousal of the adrenal cortical axis. In T. M. Dembrowski, T. Schmidt, and G. Blumchen (Eds.), *Biobehavioral basis of coronary prone behavior.* Basel, Switzerland: S. Karger A. G.

HENRY, J. P. (1984). Stress in today's managers and executives. In K. Holmer (Ed.), *Newspaper publishers handbook.* Norwich: Adprint (pp. 43-46).

HENRY, J. P. (1985). Psychosocial factors in disease and aging. In J. E. Birren and J. Livingston (Eds.), *Cognition, stress, and aging.* Englewood Cliffs, New Jersey: Prentice-Hall, Inc.

HENRY, J. P. (1986a). Relation of psychosocial factors to the epidemiology of senile dementia. In M.L.M. Gilhooly, S. H. Zarit, and J. E. Birren (Eds.), *The dementias: Policy and management.* Englewood Cliffs, New Jersey: Prentice-Hall, Inc.

HENRY, J. P. (1986b). Religious experience: Archetypes and the neurophysiology of emotion. *Zygon, 21,* 47-74.

HENRY, J. P. (In press). Neuroendocrine patterns of emotional response. In R. Plutchik (Ed.), *Biological foundations of emotion.* New York: Academic Press.

HENRY, J. P., and CASSEL, J. C. (1969). Psychosocial factors in essential hypertension: Recent epidemiologic and animal experimental evidence. *American Journal of Epidemiology, 90,* 1–200.

HENRY, J. P., and MEEHAN, J. P. (1981). Psychosocial stimuli, physiological specificity, and cardiovascular disease. In H. Weiner, M. A. Hofer, and A. J. Stunkard (Eds.), *Brain, behavior, and body disease.* New York: Raven Press (pp. 305–333).

HENRY, J. P., and STEPHENS, P. M. (1977). *Stress, health and the social environment: A sociobiologic approach to medicine.* New York: Springer-Verlag.

HENRY, J. P., STEPHENS, P. M., and LARSON, P. (1985). Specific effects of stress on disease processes. In G. P. Moberg (Ed.), *Animal stress.* Bethesda, Maryland: American Physiological Society (pp. 161–171).

JACOBSON, E. (1938). *Progressive relaxation: A physiological and clinical investigation of muscular states and significance in psychology and medical practice.* Chicago: University of Chicago Press.

JOSEPH, J. G., PRIOR, I. A., SALMOND, C. E., and STANLEY, D. (1983). Elevation of systolic and diastolic blood pressure associated with migration: The Tokelau Island Study. *Journal of Chronic Disease, 36,* 507–516.

KANNEL, W. B. (1980). The Roseto story: A review. *Social Science and Medicine, 144,* 253–254.

KAPLAN, J. R., MANUCK, S. B., CLARKSON, T. B., LUSSO, F. M., TAUB, D. M., and MILLER, E. W. (1983). Social stress and atherosclerosis in normocholesterolemic monkeys. *Science, 220,* 73–75.

KAPLAN, J. R., MANUCK, S. B., CLARKSON, T. B., and PRITCHARD, R. W. (1985). Animal models of behavioral influences on atherogenesis. In E. Kaplan and S. B. Manuck (Eds.), *Advances in behavioral medicine.* Greenwich, New York: JAI, Inc. (pp. 115–164).

KARASEK, R. A., SCHWAITZ, J. E., and PIEPER, C. (1982). *A job title-based system for analysis of psychosocial effects of job content, part I.* Department of Industrial Engineering and Operations Research, Columbia University, Room 302, Southwest Mudd Building, New York, New York 10027.

KEYS, A. (1966a). Arteriosclerotic heart disease in Roseto, Pennsylvania. *Journal of the American Medical Association, 195,* 93–95.

KEYS, A. (1966b). Arteriosclerotic heart disease in a favored community. *Journal of Chronic Diseases, 19,* 245–254.

KING, H. O., and BLEANEY, A. A. (1984). The low prevalence of hypertension in Falkland Island men. *Journal for General Practitioners, 34,* 95–96.

KRYSTAL, H. (1978). Trauma and affect. *The Psychoanalytic Study of the Child, 33,* 81–116.

KRYSTAL, H. (1979). Alexithymia and psychotherapy. *American Journal of Psychotherapy, 33,* 17–31.

LARAGH, J. H., and PECKER, M. S. (1983). Dietary sodium and essential hypertension: Some myths, hopes, and truths. *Annals of Internal Medicine, 98* (Part 2), 735–743.

LEHMANN, J. W., and BENSON, H. (1983). The nonpharmacologic treatment of hypertension. In J. Genest et al. (Eds.), *Hypertension: Physiopathology and treatment.* New York: McGraw-Hill.

MARMOT, M. G. (1982). Socioeconomic and cultural factors in ischaemic heart disease. *Advances in Cardiology, 29,* 68–76.

MARMOT, M. G., ROSE, G., SHIPLEY, M., and HAMILTON, P.J.S. (1978). Employment grade and coronary heart disease in British civil servants. *Journal of Epidemiological Community Health, 32,* 244-249.

MARMOT, M. G., and SYME, S. L. (1976). Acculturation and coronary heart disease in Japanese-Americans. *American Journal of Epidemiology, 104,* 225-247.

MATSUMOTO, Y. S. (1970). Social stress and coronary heart disease in Japan: A hypothesis. *Milbank Memorial Fund Quarterly, 68,* 9-36.

McCAFFREY, R. J., and BLANCHARD, E. B. (1985). Stress management approaches to the treatment of essential hypertension. *Annals of Behavior Medicine, 7,* 5-11.

McCALLUM, J. (1984). The importance of religion in old age: An exploration of Australian evidence. Working Paper #68. Statistical Services Section, School of Social Sciences, Australian National University: Canberra Act 2601.

McCLELLAND, D. C. (1979). Inhibited power motivation and high blood pressure in men. *Journal of Abnormal Psychology, 88,* 182-190.

McCLELLAND, D. C., and PELON, D. A. (1983). Sources of adult motives in patterns of parent behavior in early childhood. *Journal of Personality and Social Psychology, 44,* 564-574.

MIASNIKOV, A. L. (1962). Significance of disturbances of higher nervous activity in the pathogenesis of hypertensive disease. In J. H. Cort, V. Fencl, Z. Hejl, and J. Jirka (Eds.), *The pathogenesis of essential hypertension.* New York: Pergamon Press, Macmillan Co. (pp. 153-162).

MORRIS, S. N., PHILLIPS, J. F., JORDAN, J. W., and McHENRY, P. L. (1978). Incidence and significance of decreases in systolic blood pressure during graded treadmill exercise testing. *American Journal of Cardiology, 41,* 221-227.

MURPHY, M. R., MacLEAN, P. D., and HAMILTON, S. C. (1981). Species-typical behavior of hamsters deprived from birth of neocortex. *Science, 213,* 459-461.

OKAMOTO, H. (1985). Corporations and social change. *Japan Echo, 12*(2), 64-67.

OTTO, R. (1952). *The idea of the holy: An inquiry into the non-rational factor in the idea of the divine and its relation to the rational.* London: Oxford University Press.

PATEL, C. H., and NORTH, W.R.S. (1975). Randomized controlled trial of yoga and biofeedback in management of hypertension. *Lancet, 2,* 93-95.

PATEL, D., MARMOT, M. G., and TERRY, D. J. (1981). Controlled trial of biofeedback-aided behavioral methods in reducing mild hypertension. *British Medical Journal, 282,* 2005-2008.

PATRICK, R. C., PRIOR, I. A., and SMITH, A. H. (1983). Relationships between blood pressure and modernity among Ponapeans. *International Journal of Epidemiology, 12,* 36-44.

PRIOR, I. A., EVANS, J. G. HARVEY, H. P., DAVIDSON, F., and LINDSEY, M. (1968). Sodium intake and blood pressure in two Polynesian populations. *New England Journal of Medicine, 279,* 515-520.

RUBERMAN, W., WEINBLATT, E., GOLDBERG, J. D., and CHAUDHARY, B. S. (1984). Psychosocial influences on mortality after myocardial infarction. *New England Journal of Medicine, 311,* 552-559.

SAKAMOTO, Y. (1975). A study of the Japanese national character: Fifth nationwide survey. In C. Hayashi, H. Aoyama, S. Nisihira, T. Suzuki, and Y. Sakamoto (Eds.), *Nipponzin no kokuminsei (3).* Tokyo: Shisêdô.

SEILE, F. (1930). Uber den Einfluss der vegetarischen Ernahrung auf den Blutdruk. *Medizinsche, Klink, 26,* 929-931.

SHILS, E. (1981). *Tradition.* Chicago: University of Chicago Press.

SHIPKO, S., WILLIAM, A. A., and NICHOLAS, N. (1983). Towards a teleological model of alexithymia and post-traumatic stress disorder. *Psychotherapeutics and Psychosomatics, 39,* 122–126.

STOUT, C., MORROW, J., BRANDT, E., and WOLF, S. (1964). Unusually low incidence of death from myocardial infarction in an Italian-American community in Pennsylvania. *Journal of the American Medical Association, 188,* 845–849.

STRANGE, I. (1972). *The Falkland Islands.* Harrisburg, Pennsylvania: Stackpole Books.

THAILER, S. A., FREEDMAN, R., HARSHFIELD, G. A., and PICKERING, T. G. (1985). Psychological differences between high-normal and low-renin hypertensives. *Psychosomatic Medicine, 47,* 294–297.

THEORELL, T., HJEMDAHL, P., ERICSON, F., KOLLNER, A., KNOX, S., PERSKI, A., SVENISA, J., TIDGREN, B., and WALKER, D. (1985). Psychosocial and psychological factors in relation to blood pressure at rest: A study of Swedish men in their upper twenties. *Psychosomatic Medicine, 47,* 90.

TYROLER, H. A., and CASSEL, J. (1964). Health consequences of culture change II: The effect of urbanization on coronary heart mortality in rural residents. *Journal of Chronic Disability, 17,* 167–177.

UEDA, K., OMAE, T., FUJII, I., and YANAI, T. (1983). Natural history of borderline hypertension in a community: An epidemiological aspect. *Japanese Circulation Journal, 47,* 199–206.

WALDRON, I., NOWOIARSKI, M., FREIMER, M., HENRY, J. P., POST, N., and WITTEN, C. (1982). Cross-cultural variation in blood pressure: A quantitative analysis of the relationships of blood pressure to cultural characteristics, salt consumption and body weight. *Social Science and Medicine, 16,* 419–430.

WALLETSCHEK, H., and RAAB, A. (1982). Spontaneous activity of dorsal raphe neurons during defensive and offensive encounters in the tree shrew. *Physiology and Behavior, 28,* 697–705.

WILLIAMS, R. B. (In press). Psychological factors in coronary heart disease: Epidemiological evidence. *Circulation.*

WILLIAMS, R. B., HANEY, T. L., JR., LEE, K. L., KONG, Y. H., BLUMENTHAL, J. A., and WHALEN, R. E. (1980). Type A behavior, hostility, and coronary atherosclerosis. *Psychosomatic Medicine, 42,* 539–558.

WOLF, S., GRACE, L. K., BRUHN, J. G., and STOUT, C. (1973). Roseto revisited: Further data on the incidence of myocardial infarction in Roseto and neighboring Pennsylvanian communities. *Transactions of American Clinical and Climatological Association, 85,* 100–108.

7

APPLICATION OF CLASSROOM HEALTH EDUCATION TO HEALTH BEHAVIOR IN DAILY LIFE

Gwen C. Uman and Penelope L. Richardson

INTRODUCTION

Harriet, a 76-year-old gray-haired woman who wore loose-fitting slacks and oversized flowered blouses, had arthritis in her right knee for ten years or more. It came on slowly at first, and she made minor adjustments, such as buying more supportive shoes, selecting straight-backed firm chairs to sit in, and standing and walking just a little less each year. Last year she fell on her knee, suddenly increasing her pain and disability. Her walking deteriorated. Sometimes she used a cane. Many nights she couldn't sleep because the pain was so severe.

Harriet's doctor reassured her that she just had osteoarthritis and gave her popular anti-inflammatory medications which she was unable to take because they caused stomach upset. By the time she began the six-week Arthritis Self-Help Course she was feeling desperate.

The first tactic she adopted during the class was relaxation, finding that she could fall asleep easily for the first time in months by listening to a relaxation tape recording made available in the class. She faithfully attempted the stretching, strengthening, and endurance exercises taught in the class, but quickly discovered that they worsened her pain and caused unbearable muscle spasms. She went back to using her exercise bicycle and rowing machine as she had before her fall, finding that these exercises, along with one taught to her by another student in the class, were better for her than the "official" exercises.

The *Arthritis Helpbook* (required reading for the class) chapter on medication (Lorig and Fries, 1980) gave her many ideas about how to take aspirin more effectively and with fewer side effects. Over the months after the class ended, she developed a routine of taking aspirin or Ascriptin with meals to reduce daytime pain, and taking it in the middle of the night to cut down on morning stiffness.

Harriet discovered how much better she felt when she got out of the house and went to the ASH course. She began to reinterpret her pain as "manageable" rather than as a sign of some underlying, more severe disease such as cancer or as a symptom so severe that she might die from it.

In spite of her new-found ability to control her pain, Harriet's disability progressed slowly during and after the class, and she pined for access to a specialist who would take an interest in her and reverse the course of her problem. She vacillated between bravely believing that she was "making a comeback" and feeling discouraged about having to stay home taking care of her sick husband. She failed to take the steps she knew would help her— getting out of the house.

Six to eight months after the class ended she began to attend an arthritis support group once a month. She was quiet in the group, but enjoyed socializing before and after the meeting.

The foregoing is a vignette from the life of one member of an Arthritis Self-Help class. This class was observed for the purposes of understanding how and to what extent older learners apply what is taught in a classroom to their daily lives, and to identify factors which influence this application. In the realm of health education, application of what is taught (also thought of as health behavior change or *compliance*) is one of the most important instructional outcomes. Sometimes application is life-saving. More often, it offers improved function and lessened symptoms, as in the case of Harriet finally getting some sleep at night, or prevents new problems or complications. Sometimes, applying what is taught in class may worsen a problem, as in the case of the effect of the exercises on Harriet.

In the present chapter, in order to examine older learners' application of classroom learning to daily life, first the traditional transfer of learning theory will be presented. Theoretical perspectives more closely related to Harriet's experience (problem solving, self-help, and change) will then be reviewed. Finally, the chapter will examine application from the learners' viewpoint, summarizing the results of a qualitative study of an Arthritis Self-Help class (Uman, 1985).

The purpose of this chapter is to analyze differences between the traditional view of transfer of learning and older learners' actual experiences applying classroom learning in their daily lives.

TRADITIONAL VIEW

Harriet took a class two hours a week for six weeks on how to help herself cope with her arthritis. How much of what was taught in the classroom was *transferred* into her everyday life? Did she transfer relaxation techniques, exercises, and medication use exactly as taught?

Royer (1979), in his review of research, defined *transfer of learning* as the extent to which a learning event contributes to or detracts from subsequent learning or problem-solving. He argued that educators need to arrange instruction so that (1) relevant previous learning can facilitate the acquisition of new learning; and (2) material acquired in the classroom can be used to solve or deal with everyday problems and events. The former instructional challenge represents issues of *near* transfer (Mayer, 1977), most of the work in transfer of learning to date. The latter instructional challenge represents issues of *far* transfer, the primary subject matter of the present chapter.

Royer (1979) defined far transfer as the situation in which information learned in school is applied to a daily life problem or learning situation. The importance of examining far transfer of learning was validated by Willis (1984) who noted that acquisition was the primary mode of learning in youth, while learning in adulthood increasingly involved application, synthesis, and integration of new learning with prior knowledge as well as the inhibition of irrelevant or obsolete prior knowledge.

Royer (1979) reviewed two sets of theories relevant to transfer problems. Theories emphasizing environmental events, which are associated with the behaviorist tradition, are concerned with such external events as the stimulus and the response. Theories emphasizing internal events, based on cognitive psychology, use an information processing model in which the critical step is retrieving a relevant skill or bit of knowledge when a problem is encountered.

External Events

Ellis' (1965) transfer of learning theory, largely an identical-elements theory, emphasized that (1) the more similar the stimuli of the initial and criterion tasks, the greater the transfer of learning will be (stimulus generalization); (2) the more similar the responses demanded by the two tasks, the greater the transfer will be (response generalization); (3) if the responses of the two tasks are to be different, the greater the similarity of the stimuli, the less the transfer and vice versa (interference); (4) the more practice, the greater the transfer (because of better initial learning and because practice provides the opportunity to develop strategies for performing the task); and (5) the more recently the subject has practiced, the greater the transfer (a "warm-up" effect). In addition, Birren, Cunningham, and Yamamoto (1983) noted that the familiarity or meaningfulness of a task is important in attaining maximal performance from older subjects.

Ellis (1965) also suggested the following practical guidelines for teachers which emphasize manipulating initial instruction to enhance transfer: maximizing similarity between teaching and testing, providing adequate experience with the original task, providing a variety of examples, labeling important features of the task (differentiating), and ensuring that general principles are learned before expecting transfer.

Royer (1979) and Clark and Voogel (1985) held that external event theories apply only to near transfer of learning. However, Goldstein (1973) devised a behaviorist instructional approach, Structured Learning Therapy (SLT), for inexperienced learners which specifies *far* transfer as the desired outcome. This approach uses real-world practice, self-report of practice experiences, and feedback, as the means of achieving far transfer and has been successful in improving social function in the chronically mentally ill. Thus, Goldstein's work calls into question the idea that external event theories cannot provide guidance for far transfer.

Internal Events

In contrast to external event theories, cognitive theory emphasizes that the key to transfer is the integration of new material into the pre-existing cognitive structure. Far transfer might be thought of as decoding or recalling appropriate content (knowledge of *what is*) or procedures (knowledge of *how to*) to be used in a novel situation. Here, transfer involves searching for additional cues in the novel situation, and then modifying the pre-existing content or procedure to respond most appropriately. In this regard, Arenberg and Robertson-Tchabo (1977) concluded in their review that there is an age-related difficulty in retrieving stored information and an age-related difference in the nature of potential retrieval cues used. Ineffective and infrequent use of organizing strategies means that retrieval cues are minimal.

Mayer (1974, 1977) has shown that instructional strategies designed to activate cognitive structure affect transfer performance on learning concepts and tasks. Cognitive theories, however, have not developed to the point of delineating principles of transfer of learning. Royer (1979) concluded that cognitive transfer theories needed to be better developed so that they could be used to facilitate far transfer. Many internal-events researchers have suggested instructional strategies to enhance far transfer. These strategies focus on manipulating initial instruction in the following ways: practicing with a great variety of examples to enhance far transfer (Gagné, 1970); helping students improve their questioning behavior (identifying what questions need to be asked in a novel situation), improving initial learning, and optimizing the perceived demand characteristics of the situation so that the learner will pay better attention and invest more effort in the task (Bransford, Nitsch, and Franks, 1981); teaching by analogy (Clark and Bovy, 1982; Rumelhart and Norman, 1981); and using prompting [that is, suggesting to the learner how he or she might think of the new situation (Salomon, 1981)]. Internal event theories also emphasize learner characteristics of prior general and specific knowledge and ability as determinants of learning and transfer (Clark and Voogel, 1985).

Summary. Whether the educator adopts an internal or an external event theory, teaching for transfer of learning usually involves attention to initial learning/instruction, including practice and experience with examples, and teaching cognitive processes (to differentiate features of the task or to organize knowledge for easy retrieval). Research on aging suggests that the latter technique is especially crucial for older learners (Arenberg and Robertson-Tchabo, 1977). In addition, prior knowledge and experience are considered by internal event theorists to be important in planning instruction.

However, in fact, Harriet and her classmates were not in dire need of instruction related to initial learning. They were not only experienced in living with the problems of arthritis, but most availed themselves of a myriad of scientific and lay information about arthritis on an ongoing basis. Harriet didn't waste time practicing tactics if they didn't work. She *did* reinterpret the meaning of her pain and develop a new understanding of how to control it. Harriet's life at home was different from the classroom situation. Even though care was taken to teach simple tactics, she adapted most of what was taught to fit her prior patterns of behavior. She, along with two thirds of her classmates, transferred what they had learned into their daily lives *only* if transfer is redefined as adaptation rather than rote application of what is learned. Transfer as adaptation had little apparent relationship to initial learning/ instruction.

ALTERNATIVE THEORETICAL VIEWS

Problem Solving

Harriet's arthritis was clearly a problem to her, and she took the Arthritis Self-Help Course in hopes of solving that problem.

Frederiksen (1984) identified three different types of problems. *Well-structured problems* are clearly formulated, have only one answer, and can be solved using a known algorithm (such as arithmetic problems). *Structured problems requiring productive thinking* are the same as well-structured problems except that the algorithm is not known to the learner and has to be generated (e.g., learning that adding $3+3+3$ is the same as multiplying 3×3). *Ill-structured problems* lack clear formulation, lack an algorithm, and might have more than one answer (e.g., most political, social, and some scientific problems). There might be different theories and different instructional methods appropriate for these three different types of problems.

Problem solving procedures such as means-end analysis (Bhaskar and Simon, 1977), algorithms, general strategies, heuristics, plans (Sacerdoti, 1977), hypothesis testing (Simon, 1980), and pattern recognition (deGroot, 1966) have been taught to students in order to enhance problem solving ability. However, it is possible that the solution of unstructured problems, which may be devoid of patterns, cannot be taught at all.

In 1980, Yinger suggested that an inordinate amount of research effort was being directed toward enhancing intellectual skills and strategies, which are mainly procedural, and cautioned that the problems of daily life, which are practical rather than theoretical and uncertain rather than procedural, may not be solvable by traditional means. Focusing on the procedural aspects is to delude students into believing that most problems have solutions. Yinger supported the work of researchers such as Reid (1979), who noted the characteristics of practical problems:

1. They have to be answered even if the answer is to do nothing.
2. The grounds on which to base the solution are generally uncertain.
3. Existing states of affairs must be taken into account.
4. They are unique and the "knowns" or "givens" cannot be fully described.
5. They require compromise between competing goals and values.
6. The outcome of a solution cannot be predicted, nor can we ever know the exact outcomes of solutions not chosen.

Thus, the hallmark of practical problems is uncertainty. Yinger recommended that greater emphasis be placed on revealing the nature of practical problems and developing knowledge, skill, and appropriate attitudes to improve problem solving.

There is controversy among problem solving researchers and theorists about whether problem solving skills should be taught (Frederiksen, 1984). Some believe that specific knowledge and "practice, practice, practice" are the ingredients of a future expert. There is also controversy about whether these skills can be taught so that solving of ill-structured problems is really enhanced. However, very little research has been done in this regard.

In addition to teaching problem solving procedures and practicing, instructional implications are as follows: teach the specific knowledge needed (Norman, 1980; Simon and Hayes, 1976); teach cognitive processes of acquisition and retrieval (Glaser, 1976; Resnick, 1976); teach analogical processes (Norman, 1980); and teach by the discovery method because learning by discovery reorganizes knowledge hierarchies, whereas learning by rules just adds onto knowledge structures (Greeno, 1980).

Salthouse (1982) reviewed age changes in primary abilities and characteristics thought to be contributory to problem solving and decision making. He proposed that when older adults were compared with young adults, they:

1. were less likely to produce unusual solutions to problems;
2. experienced more difficulty in shifting from one type of problem to another;
3. tended to form primitive organization of items;
4. had greater difficulty ignoring irrelevant information;
5. were less systematic in progress toward a solution;
6. required more information to make logical deductions; and
7. operated less effectively at abstract as opposed to concrete levels of thought.

The role of experience in compensating for these age-related declines in basic skills is unclear due to the scanty amount of research done (see Charness, 1981). Interestingly, Moshman (1979), in studying the hypothesis-test problem solving procedure, showed that there was a strong bias toward overvaluing confirmatory evidence and undervaluing disconfirming and neutral evidence in laboratory situations. However, when Christensen-Szalanski and Bushyhead (1981) studied experienced physicians as opposed to medical students and residents, they found that real-life experiences tended to overcome the biased use of information which was demonstrated in laboratory studies. This suggests that experience may positively influence problem solving rather than increasing automaticity or rigidity. It also reflects the likelihood that experts will use pattern recognition to solve problems, since experienced physicians in the study could more easily discern patterns of typical illnesses from random signs and symptoms than could residents.

Summary. Instructional techniques which may enhance problem solving overlap with techniques derived from transfer of learning theories in three important areas: initial learning (content and procedural knowledge), practice, and cognitive processes (ways of structuring and integrating new knowledge into long-term memory for easy retrieval). In addition, there are specific important techniques to be taught such as problem solving procedures and pattern recognition. Beyond initial learning, attitude is considered a learner characteristic important to problem solving success. Characteristics of the novel situation (outside the classroom) are also important—the true nature of the practical problem to be solved.

Returning to our case example, Harriet probably would not benefit from being taught problem solving procedures since she already had a competent pattern of behavior which included active problem solving attempts. In fact, the revelation of the ill-structured nature of her problem mitigated against any known instructional technique assisting her in improving her problem solving. In the class she learned that there was no cure for arthritis, and no exact treatment for her type of arthritis. This information was equivalent to revealing the real uncertainty involved in finding a solution to her problem, and hence the need to employ multiple and ever-changing solutions. It actually cut down on Harriet's discouragement by removing the expectation that there was a single solution.

Self-Help

The goal of Harriet's self-help class was to increase her control over her condition. How well did the self-help approach work?

Froland, Pancoast, Chapman, and Kimboko (1981) distinguish between two worlds of care: the world of informal, private caring relationships arising out of family, community, and other social ties; and the world of professional, governmentally-financed services. Unruh (1983) reviewed past work on social integration of the elderly (the alternative to disengagement) and found, in addition to the conventional forms of social organization such as clubs and families, another form which he called *social worlds*. These worlds had weak authority structures, and people could readily move in and out of them. Social roles were very informal and the dominant mode of communication was through various media, making these social worlds frequently invisible—membership not being immediately evident. Identification with a social world was primarily cognitive, so they did not have to be concrete in the here and now. Unruh found that social worlds might be vestiges of the past with which a person still identifies, such as the world of work or the outdoor world, even after retirement or disability prevents active participation in that world.

Unruh's informants were continuously involved in maintaining ongoing social worlds, which required a great deal of physical and mental effort in the face of increasing age and disability; and in abandoning some social worlds because of disinterest, relocation, or diminished resources, as well as seeking out new social worlds of greater interest. He found four progressive stages of belonging to social worlds: stranger, tourist, regular, and insider. *Strangers* in a new social world experienced naiveté, disorientation, superficiality, and detachment. *Tourists* exhibited curiosity, learning, transiency, and entertainment in the social world. Finally, *regulars* and *insiders* were more knowledgeable, permanent, and comfortable in the social world.

Pancoast, Froland, and Parker (1983) explored the interface between the formal world and the informal (self-help) world. Characteristics of self-help groups include self-awareness, self-determination, conscious objectives, strategies, philosophies, and organizational structures. The goals of the group are the grounds for meeting; any other gains, such as social satisfaction, are secondary. One's membership in the group lasts only as long as one's interest in its purposes is sustained. Self-help groups are more often face-to-face experiences than are Unruh's social worlds. They may serve more specifically as a means for individuals and small groups to deal with their own problems and struggles in the world. The role of a self-help group or social world vis-à-vis the formal sector may be explicitly decided by professionals within the formal system. This is often the case if group members' problems are serious enough to bring them to the attention of the formal system, suggesting that they need help because their own social resources have been depleted. In this context, self-help is not seen as a replacement for the formal services of professionals. This type of self-help group is likely to lobby actively for *more* formal services for its members. Simultaneously, group members can meet and deal with *negative* consequences of formal system actions and attitudes. Thus, a tension exists between the formal and informal worlds.

Summary. Instructional methods in self-help groups vary from none at all (rap groups), to guest lecturing (providing information from the formal world to members), to planned learning experiences involving information, discussion, practice, and sharing of members' reactions. In some manner, the formal and informal worlds of the topic of interest are brought together to increase self-awareness and actualize self-determination.

Harriet did gain more control over her arthritis after experiencing the self-help approach. She slept better. She changed her belief that she couldn't tolerate any pain-relieving medicine. She maintained her belief that resistive exercises were good for her, even though the formal world discouraged that. And, ultimately, she found a way to get out of the house, if only once a month, to engage in socializing and find support.

Change

How did all these changes occur in Harriet, and how much change can be expected? Salomon (1981) and Watzlawick, Weakland, and Fisch (1974) have described useful types and principles of change which help explain Harriet's experience.

Salomon (1981) defined three types of change: naive change, epistemic change, and drip-effect change. *Naive change* is the most powerful and takes place when a person is inexperienced and is suddenly exposed to something new, stimulating an unguided and uncritical search and acceptance of what is being presented.

Epistemic change is the weakest kind of change, in which the person is very experienced, but not sufficiently to deal with novel events. This invokes a guided search for facts and a weighing of their validity.

Drip-effect change, based on repeated passive exposure to an experience and resulting in a gradual change over time, is similar to Stein's (1971) concept of adult learning. According to Stein, ". . . a considerable part of adult learning occurs in the daily processes of living, of adjusting to changing conditions, frequently without conscious consideration. The adult seeks new learning only when that learning offers more than he can get without learning." Stein refers to the stereotypic rigidity of the older learner, offering an alternative conception that this apparent rigidity represents a well-functioning pattern of competence. The instructor's job, in the case of the experientially-expert older learner who is motivated by some level of need to attend a course of this type, would be to make clear how new ideas, facts, skills, and insights can be easily integrated into that already well-functioning pattern.

Salomon (1981) also hypothesized predictors of change: the larger the discrepancy between pre-existing knowledge and beliefs and the new exposure, the greater the potential for change; the weaker the pre-existing knowledge and beliefs, the greater the potential for change; the less general and encompassing the pre-existing knowledge and beliefs, the greater the potential for change; and the more meaningful social reinforcement available, the greater the potential for change.

Watzlawick, Weakland, and Fisch (1974) defined difficult behaviors as those which create serious obstacles to accomplishing a mutual task, such as the task of health care personnel working with patients to achieve compliance. They believe that mistakes in management of these problems are made because the problem is seen as individual, residing within the patient, rather than as interactional, residing between the health care provider and the patient. Solutions are usually restricted to explanations and urgings about diet, exercise, and medications. In this regard, Watzlawick et al. suggest three important change principles for breaking out of this unsuccessful cycle. The first principle is to *discontinue strategies which do not work.* If the usual urgings are not working, as frequently occurs in chronic diseases like hypertension and arthritis, one must discontinue them and try something completely different.

The second principle is to *reframe the situation.* Reframing means moving from a specific way of viewing the problem to a way which is more general or at a higher level of abstraction than the original way. For example, one would most likely think of arthritis as a disease to be cured or treated, as we think of most diseases. If instead we think of arthritis as a problem consisting of pain which results in stress and depression that worsen the perception of pain, then different treatments and a greater variety of treatments can be thought of to mitigate the problem. Furthermore, in this view the solution does not reside solely with the physician, but can be shared by both physician and patient.

The third principle is to *use paradox.* Do or suggest the opposite of what one would expect to solve the problem. Paradox has the potential for provoking change; and bringing together the formal and informal worlds of care in a self-help group creates just such a paradox and becomes a springboard for change. It may be a vehicle for seeing the situation from a new perspective.

Summary. The change theories discussed suggest thoughtful consideration of learner characteristics and of the novel situation in the context of daily life. Salomon's classifications of change direct the instructor to think about how much change is possible based on the learner's background and experience. The principles of Watzlawick et al. (1974) stimulate the instructor to think and teach creatively about the situation or problem to be solved.

Harriet had been exposed to the drip-effect change of arthritis for ten years. She had adapted to her arthritis experiences unconsciously, and it was upon this baseline which the self-help course had to build. Harriet was susceptible to naive change because she had never before been exposed to an adult education experience. The reframing of the meaning and characteristics of arthritis, as described above, created the greatest amount of change for her. With regard to specific techniques for dealing with arthritis, Harriet engaged more in epistemic change, critically and carefully selecting the techniques which helped her and avoiding those which harmed her even if they were encouraged by the leaders.

Conclusions About Views from the Literature

The traditional and alternative views of how adults might apply classroom learning in their daily lives can be summarized in the comparative recommendations shown in Table 7-1. Together these recommendations suggest an oversimplified instructional model depicting the components of learning and application. The model, as shown in Figure 7-1, is composed of *learner characteristics* (prior knowledge, experience, and attitude); *instructional approaches* (e.g., providing for practice, teaching cognitive strategies, and training in pattern recognition); and *the application situation* (exposing the true nature of the problem, reframing it). Learner characteristics combine with instructional approaches to result in application (by way of initial learning). Application might be thought of as transfer of learning, problem solving, self-help, and/or behavior change. The latter involves application of learning through demonstrated performance.

Older learners' experiences in an Arthritis Self-Help (ASH) course will now

TABLE 7-1   A Comparison of Instructional Recommendations

TRANSFER	PROBLEM SOLVING	SELF HELP	CHANGE
Maximize similarity between initial cues and transfer cues.	Provide practice and experience.	Expose members to others with the problem.	Consider learner experience and knowledge.
Provide experience with a variety of examples.	Teach specific knowledge needed.	Expose members to the formal world.	Define nature of the prior experience.
Differentiate features of a task.	Teach analogical processes.	Develop self-awareness.	Discontinue strategies which do not work.
Ensure initial learning.	Teach cognitive processes.	Develop self-determination	Reframe the situation.
Improve questioning behavior.	Teach problem solving procedures.	Develop strategies.	Use paradox.
Optimize perceived demand characteristics.	Use discovery learning.		Teach how to integrate new skills into pre-existing competent patterns of behavior.
Teach by analogy.	Teach pattern recognition.		
Use prompting.	Consider learner attitudes.		
Teach cognitive organization strategies.	Consider type of problem.		
Consider pre-existing learner ability, knowledge, and experience.			

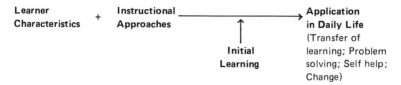

FIGURE 7-1 Simplified instructional model based on traditional and alternative views.

be examined more closely to reveal a learner-generated model of application. Differences between the simplified model from the literature (described above) and the learners' model will be discussed. Finally, implications for teaching, research, and policy will be presented.

EXPERIENTIAL VIEWS

The recent field investigation (Uman, 1985) of one six-week Arthritis Self-Help course, using participant observation of class sessions and in-depth interviews of the class members four to six months after the course ended, was designed specifically to elicit learners' perceptions of the factors influencing classroom application in daily life. There were 15 students in the class. The students ranged in age from 50 to 85 and most of them had osteoarthritis. Two students may have had rheumatoid arthritis, but the diagnoses in these cases were unclear. Only one of the students was formally employed, the others being retired and/or homemakers. Three fourths of the students were of working-class or blue-collar economic backgrounds, one fourth were of professional or white-collar economic backgrounds. All of the students were living at home, either alone or with spouses and sometimes with young adult children.

The overall purpose of the Arthritis Self-Help course was to teach the knowledge and skills students needed to reduce their pain and disability (Lorig and Fries, 1980). Lecture, discussion, and demonstration/practice were the predominant instructional methods. Content included the anatomy of a joint; differential diagnosis of several types of arthritis; stretching, strengthening, and endurance exercises; relaxation techniques; the relationship between stress, pain, and mood (depression); medications; diet; communication with the health care team; relationship problems caused by arthritis; energy conservation and joint protection; and pain control.

Four processes were found to influence behavior change or application: using tactics, gathering information, carrying out life activities, and reformulating perceptions of the problem. These factors can be looked at as phases in an ongoing cycle of strategizing to overcome an obstacle (see Figure 7-2). The students in the class shared a common obstacle to freely carrying out their life activities. This obstacle, arthritis, and its attendant pain and disability, activated *using tactics* for dealing with arthritis so the person could *carry out life activities*. Choice of tactics was influenced by *gathering information. Reformulating perceptions of the problem* was influenced by and, in turn, influenced gathering information and using tactics. It is clear that while the traditional view on classroom application to daily life concentrated on microscopic features of learning and instruction, students concen-

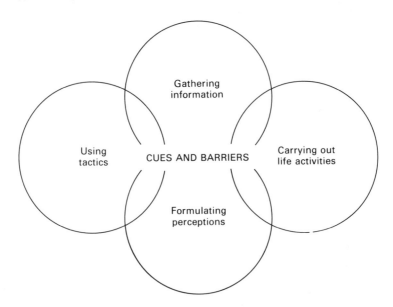

FIGURE 7-2 Cycle of strategizing to overcome obstacles.

trated on broader aspects of living. The ASH course was one small aspect of their overall lives and of their "careers" as people with arthritis. Each of the four processes will now be described and interrelated below.

Using Tactics

By using tactics to overcome the obstacle of arthritis, learners were able to carry out their life activities. Thus, using tactics was a vehicle for getting things done. It was both a factor influencing application and an outcome measure of how much application took place. Specific tactics or techniques taught in the course were said to reduce pain and disability if used correctly. The criterion for successful application was using these tactics in the home environment or in daily life several months after the course ended.

Tactics included any techniques used by learners or believed to be of value (advised for others) in decreasing the pain or disability of arthritis, such as seeking social support, protecting joints, conserving energy, exercising, interacting with the doctor, taking medications, using relaxation techniques, altering dietary habits, controlling other health problems, keeping active, using heat, cold, or massage, and using mental control (thus accepting arthritis, fighting it, and/or denying it).

Many of these tactics were taught in the class, which emphasized the specifics of how to apply them. Ten of the 15 students added new tactics or changed tactics during and after the class. Interestingly, the greatest increases were in the relatively underemphasized tactic of social support and the outcome of mental control, the latter not being part of the intended curriculum. There were small increases in the most emphasized tactics of exercise and relaxation techniques. Tactics taught in the class were not adopted exactly as taught, however. Almost all applications were *adaptations* created to fit the person's pre-existing patterns of behavior.

Thus, the measure of transference might be not how much the learner uses that which was taught in the classroom in daily life, but whether and how much the learner adapted or changed for his or her own life purposes the tactics taught in the classroom.

Four types of learners could be differentiated based on the way they used tactics. The *collectors* saved up information about tactics for use at a later time, "when they really needed it." The *creators* used many tactics and adapted them widely, making every effort to prevent their symptoms from altering their lives. The *acceptors* apparently had discovered their limits and selected primarily passive tactics (e.g., rest, relaxation, narcotic medications). The *rejectors* resisted most suggestions for using tactics and angrily held on to the unrealistic hope that some powerful other (usually a doctor) would rescue them. Members of this latter group were frequently newly diagnosed rheumatoid arthritics or were those with very painful osteoarthritis who couldn't fulfill the roles they expected of themselves.

As well as being an outcome measure, using tactics also influenced application in daily life. Those who were already using many tactics prior to the class tended to make the most changes. The practice of using tactics stimulated experimentation with new tactics and modification of prior tactics. Learners were cued to adopt tactics if they obtained benefit (reduced pain, increased activity) after practicing them and to abandon tactics which, upon practice, increased pain or failed to fit into their life activities.

Gathering Information

Information was gathered from sources both within and among persons with arthritis (cognitive, attitudinal, and experiential sources) and from outside sources (the formal and the informal worlds of health care, the media, and significant others). The learners in this study could be classified as *arthritis experts,* experientially and cognitively, rather than as novices needing to learn basic knowledge and skills. For example, Harriet wanted to confirm her prior knowledge and beliefs and the information she read in the *National Enquirer.* She also wanted to be sure she was getting the right medical advice. The level of interest expressed by these arthritis experts was related to the recurrent and intractable nature of their problem and the extreme effect it had on their lives (e.g., cutting down on their working years; preventing engagement in desired activities).

Except for dietary beliefs there were no major discrepancies between formal and informal world knowledge and beliefs. Seven students enjoyed the class, felt it was pleasurable and/or worthwhile. Nine students said they enjoyed other class members and valued the camaraderie which developed. Specific perceived benefits of the class included mutual support, pain control, and assertiveness with doctors. Specific learnings attributed to the class included learning about assistive devices; using cold to decrease pain; and learning how to take medicines, do exercises, protect joints, conserve energy, and define arthritis. Three students bought extra books to share with friends, and two wished the class had lasted much longer than six weeks.

Three students didn't like the class, found it stressful because it focused on the negative (let people talk about their symptoms), or said they learned nothing new from it. Two of them were attending at the request of their spouses, while one used denial as a predominant mental tactic to deal with arthritis.

In gathering information, students weighed its value according to how they felt about the information source and the power attributed to the source. Formal world sources had more power than informal sources; more credence was given to fellow sufferers than to those sources who did not have arthritis.

Gathering information from the class most frequently involved epistemic change (searching for and evaluating new knowledge; then applying, accepting, rejecting, or modifying it). Like using tactics, gathering information from a wide variety of sources was another important factor influencing application of classroom learning.

Carrying Out Life Activities

Strauss (1974) observed that people's chronic illnesses and their regimens only complicate, and are secondary to, the management of daily existence which all of us perform. Carrying out life activities is the third phase in the cycle of strategizing to overcome obstacles. The learners in this study engaged in mental, physical, and/or social activities which ranged from boredom (not enough activity) to memories and plans (passive activities) and actual pastimes. Work (or memories of work) and family life were the most frequently engaged-in life activities, followed by creative activities and recreation, wishing, reminiscing, being entertained, and relaxing. Taking classes (including health, art, and exercise classes as well as Bible study) either was presently or had been a frequent adult activity for all of the learners except Harriet.

Six of the eight socially-isolated learners made changes in their behaviors during and after the class, whereas only four out of the seven socially integrated learners made changes. This suggests the possible special importance of the Arthritis Self-Help class in creating a climate of acceptance so that people with few social contacts can capitalize on the experience of others. Stein (1971) observed that new opinions are normally acquired through the influence of an associate with sound knowledge and strong views. In this regard, socially-isolated people may not otherwise have had access to such people without taking the class.

While there were basic temporal problems related to life activities, such as too much time, too little time, and inappropriate scheduling of activities, sometimes interfering with using tactics, the issues of timing seemed secondary to the larger issue of the meaning that life activities had in the learners' lives. Life activities were tied to self-esteem and quality of life, confirming their importance as motivators to using tactics and gathering more information. Thus, life activities were important factors influencing classroom application in daily life.

Reformulating Perceptions of the Problem

Reformulating perceptions of the problem of arthritis involved a blending of the learners' views on disease severity, general health, duration of illness, health care experiences, and emotional responses (including the responses of significant others). In terms of general health, as expected in the age group of learners studied, the class members all had multiple chronic illnesses. Severity of their arthritis was expressed by the learners as a combination of amount and persistence of pain, number of joints involved, limitations on desired activities, disease duration, and trajectory (how rapidly arthritis came upon them). Two learners had mild arthritis, five had moderate arthritis, and six had severe arthritis based on these subjective indicators (two learners were spouses who did not have arthritis). A larger proportion of the severely afflicted learners made changes than did those in the mild and moderate categories.

Negative health care experiences outweighed positive experiences among these learners. Examples of negative experiences included too little care, delayed care, lack of care, incorrect care, provider disinterest, and excessively expensive care. If, as Becker and Maiman (1975) suggested, negative health care experiences result in poor compliance, then the Arthritis Self-Help class may have been a positive health care experience which resulted in good compliance, or changing tactics.

Based on the foregoing perceptions about their bodies and their doctors, and also what they learned from significant others, learners responded emotionally to their problem, most commonly with fear, depression and sadness, or acceptance. Denial, suffering, complaining, feelings of guilt, embarrassment, and anger were emotional responses noted less frequently. Significant others also expressed worry, sympathy, feelings of helplessness, and anger at the arthritic person's choice of tactics. Strauss (1974) noted a similar range of responses people might have to their symptoms. Fear of serious illness and impending death were less prominent than the larger fear of total dependence and institutionalization which was a real possibility for some of the participants in the foreseeable future. The general lack of visibility of their problem (most participants did not have marked physical deformity), combined with the non-life-threatening nature of the problem and its intermittent occurrence (good days and bad days), created important discrepancies between the meaning of their symptoms to these learners and the meaning to outside parties, especially doctors and signficant others. The larger the discrepancy, the greater the emotional distress associated with it.

The overall perception of the problem as characterized by these participants was very much like Yinger's (1980) description of a practical problem, with the hallmark of uncertainty of solution.

In summary, a nondebilitating emotional response to the problem and a reframing of the problem combine to reformulate perceptions of the problem. The process of reformulating perceptions of the problem is ongoing and is a factor influencing application, as well as a phase influenced by the three other phases of the cycle of strategizing to overcome a problem.

Summary of the Experiential View

The results of the field study of the Arthritis Self-Help course suggest that people with arthritis are engaged in a continuous cycle of strategizing to overcome obstacles. The cycle includes using tactics, gathering information, carrying out life activities, and reformulating perceptions of the problem. As the cycle continues the tactics are fine-tuned; information is evaluated in light of prior knowledge and legitimacy of source, being accepted, rejected, or modified; life activities are abandoned, maintained, or added to; and perceptions of the magnitude, meaning, and nature of the problem are reformulated. Throughout the cycle, in each of the four phases, there are cues and barriers which push learners toward or pull them away from certain actions. While patterns of strategizing could be discerned in the learners, the relationship between all of the factors involved was much more complex and idiosyncratic than what was suggested in the traditional transfer-of-learning literature. Learners were confirmed to have well-functioning patterns of competence (Stein, 1971) and carried out a guided search for information when they needed it to solve more difficult problems, such as when they decided to take the class. The class succeeded in reframing or exposing the true nature of the problem and in making clear how ideas, facts, skills, and insights could fit into their already existing (and primarily successful) patterns or habits. Social reinforcers were life activities; physical reinforcers were biofeedback (increases or decreases in pain); and interactional reinforcers (input from significant others and health care providers) tended to be negative, adversely affecting emotional response to the problem and hence problem perception.

In larger sense it is plausible that, when the teacher comes in contact with them, all adult learners are poised in the midst of a continuous strategizing cycle to overcome problems. The teacher enters the learners' usual cycle at the point of gathering information. Adult learners evaluate what is taught in a classroom in light of all their other information sources and filter it through their own perceptions of the problem. The adult learner will adapt and select tactics to use in carrying out the many life activities he or she is involved with, only a small segment of which is the class being attended. What the learner learns may look very different from what the teacher intended the outcome to be, but may be equally or more important for the learner. Under these circumstances measurement and evaluation of outcome is difficult. Learners themselves may not be able to articulate the benefits of a class. The best the teacher can offer the adult learner might be a framework for viewing the material and perceptions which the learner did not have access to before, and a straightforward presentation of the background knowledge and skills needed to implement desired tactics.

Comparison of the Traditional View and the Experiential View

Whereas the traditional view concentrated primarily on initial learning, the experiential view offered by these expert learners concentrated on global aspects of daily life representing application as opposed to initial learning.

Whereas the traditional view recommended an extensive list of instructional methods, the class methods were limited primarily to lecture, discussion, and demonstration/practice. Cognitive structuring methods, extensive practice with feedback, and attending directly to attitudes and beliefs were not used, while clear presentation of basic knowledge and skills was accomplished. Reframing the nature of the problem did take place and, although not directly referred to in this regard by course developers, it was an important cognitive structuring method, stimulating much change among learners.

Overall, while actual determinants of application are much more complex than the literature reviewed would suggest, the teacher's influence on application can be characterized much more simply than the elaborate initial learning recommendations which the traditional view would suggest. The final section of the chapter will present implications for the enhancement of classroom application to daily life in teaching, research, and policy.

IMPLICATIONS

Teaching

Given a well-constructed class based on a thorough needs assessment of the target population, teachers might be successful instructing older adults using lecture, discussion, and demonstration/practice. The lecture should include reformulating or revealing the true nature of the problem for learners. Discussion should center specifically on helping learners fit new techniques into their pre-existing successful patterns of behavior. For application to be achieved, it may be necessary for learners to share information concerning their usual life activities. From that base, specific suggestions in regard to application can be made both by the teacher and by all members of the class.

Teacher anxiety about lack of time to communicate all of the required facts to learners should be allayed by remembering that older learners in a health education class are likely to have a wealth of experiential knowledge about their health problems and to continually seek out and receive information from many sources.

Since learners' perceptions of their problems as hopeless interfere with applying new and more desirable health behaviors to everyday life, teachers should take steps which will increase learners' feelings of being understood and which will decrease fear and depression. This can be done by promoting long-term interaction between learners, and by teaching better communication patterns between learners and the formal system of care. Promoting the dual concepts of self-acceptance and a fighting spirit were the most effective communications the leaders and learners provided each other in the observed ASH class.

Research

Although implications for teaching were outlined above, they must be considered tentative. It must be remembered that the cycle of strategizing to overcome obstacles is a model based on the study of only one example of older adult health education and, as such, cannot be assumed to be generalizable. The history of adult education is littered with such descriptive theories which slip into prescriptive mythology, bypassing the important step of confirmatory research. Confirmatory experiments or quasi-experiments that could more clearly elucidate the predictive power (or lack thereof) of such descriptive theories are needed. Before embarking on experimental studies, several follow-up descriptive studies might be conducted to confirm or modify the proposed processes which seem to most directly influence application of classroom learning. Other types of older learners in health education and general education classes might be studied using more structured observational tools and interview schedules. Younger adults, perhaps in the context of on-the-job training, human resource development, and continuing professional education, might also be studied in comparison to older learners in order to identify any possible differences.

Due to the importance and frequency of unintended outcomes, careful attention should be paid to measuring learning and application in experimental designs. Phased studies might be constructed in which the first phase is qualitative to determine the range of outcomes and reveal any new influencing factors. The second phase could be quantitative, using measuring instruments constructed from the first phase.

Policy

The exploration of learners' views of application in this study strongly suggests that a large percentage of older learners may be applying in their daily lives that which they learn in health education classes. This finding is important because it means that older adults are willing and able to make changes which may enhance their health and decrease the likelihood of illness complications. Older adults may be overcoming their own cohort effects by making these changes. For example, when today's eighty-year-olds were growing up it was considered healthful to eat plenty of good red meat and potatoes and whole milk; smoking was considered a social activity; and it was a sign of success to be able to become more sedentary with advancing years. What is remarkable is the flexibility with which older adults have learned and accepted today's health principles of exercise and diets low in animal fat and high in fiber; and the numbers who are willing to at least seriously attempt changes in spite of physical limitations.

The experiential view suggests, although it does not confirm, that health education can be beneficial to older adults and to the society which contributes to their support, as they once supported society during their own working years. Rather than to cynically despair of promoting health behavior change in anybody, especially older people, the experiential view suggests that we need to look more closely in order to see change and that we need to redefine change as *adapting* rather than mimicking prescribed health behavior, especially in the case of chronic diseases.

Thus, from a policy standpoint, health education for older adults should be promoted, funded, and underwritten. Furthermore, resources should be devoted to upgrading teachers' abilities to promote application and to carry out the research needed to confirm and modify the understanding of factors which promote application.

REFERENCES

ARENBERG, D., and ROBERTSON-TCHABO, E. A. (1977). Learning and aging. In J. E. Birren and K. W. Schaie (Eds.), *Handbook of the psychology of aging.* New York: Van Nostrand Reinhold.

BECKER, M. H., and MAIMAN, L. A. (1975). Sociobehavioral determinants of compliance with health and medical care recommendations. *Medical Care, XIII,* 10–24.

BHASKAR, R., and SIMON, H. A. (1977). Problem solving in semantically rich domains: An example from engineering thermodynamics. *Cognitive Science, 1,* 193–215.

BIRREN, J. E., CUNNINGHAM, W. R., and YAMAMOTO, K. (1983). Psychology of adult development and aging. *Annual Review of Psychology, 34,* 543–575.

BRANSFORD, J. D., NITSCH, K. E., and FRANKS, J. J. (1981). Schooling and the facilitation of knowing. In J. R. Anderson, R. J. Spiro, and W. E. Montague (Eds.), *Schooling and the acquisition of knowledge.* Hillsdale, New Jersey: Erlbaum.

CHARNESS, N. (1981). Visual short-term memory and aging in chess players. *Journal of Gerontology, 36,* 615–619.

CHRISTENSEN-SZALANSKI, J. J., and BUSHYHEAD, J. B. (1981). Physicians' use of probabilistic information in a real clinical setting. *Journal of Experimental Psychology: Human Perception and Performance, 7,* 928–935.

CLARK, R. E., and BOVY, R. C. (March 1982). *Instructional methods.* Paper presented at the meeting of the American Educational Research Association, New York, New York.

CLARK, R. E., and VOOGEL, A. (1985). Transfer of training principles for instructional design. *Educational Communication and Technology Journal, 33,* 113–123.

de GROOT, A. D. (1966). Perception and memory versus thought. In B. Kleinmuntz (Ed.), *Problem solving: Research, method and theory.* New York: Wiley.

ELLIS, H. C. (1965). *The transfer of learning.* New York: The Macmillan Company.

FREDERIKSEN, N. (1984). Implications of cognitive theory for instruction in problem solving. *Review of Educational Research, 54,* 363–407.

FROLAND, C., PANCOAST, D., CHAPMAN, N., and KIMBOKO, P. (1981). *Helping networks in human services.* Beverly Hills, California: Sage.

GAGNÉ, R. M. (1970). *The conditions of learning, 2nd edition.* New York: Holt, Rinehart & Winston, Inc.

GLASER, R. (1976). Cognitive psychology and instructional design. In D. Klahr (Ed.), *Cognition and instruction.* Hillsdale, New Jersey: Erlbaum.

GOLDSTEIN, A. (1973). *Structured learning therapy.* New York: Academic Press.

GREENO, J. G. (1980). Some examples of cognitive task analysis with instructional implications. In R. E. Snow, P. A. Federico, and W. E. Montague (Eds.), *Aptitude, learning and instruction. Vol. 2: Cognitive process analyses of learning and problem solving.* Hillsdale, New Jersey: Erlbaum.

LORIG, K., and FRIES, J. F. (1980). *The arthritis helpbook.* Reading, Massachusetts: Addison-Wesley.

MAYER, R. E. (1974). Acquisition processes and resilience under varying testing conditions of structurally different problem-solving procedures. *Journal of Educational Psychology, 66,* 644–656.

MAYER, R. E. (1977). Different rule systems for counting behavior acquired in meaningful and rote contexts of learning. *Journal of Educational Psychology, 69,* 537–546.

MERRILL, M. D., KOWALLIS, T., and WILSON, B. G. (1980). Instructional design in transition. In F. H. Farley and N. J. Gordon (Eds.), *New perspectives in educational psychology.* Chicago: National Society for the Study of Education.

MOSHMAN, D. (1979). Development of formal hypothesis testing ability. *Developmental Psychology, 15,* 104–112.

NORMAN, D. A. (1980). Cognitive engineering in education. In D. T. Tuma and F. Reif (Eds.), *Problem solving and education: Issues in teaching and research.* Hillsdale, New Jersey: Erlbaum.

PANCOAST, D. L., PARKER, P., and FROLAND, C. (1983). *Rediscovering self-help.* Beverly Hills, California: Sage.

REID, W. A. (1979). Practical reasoning and curriculum theory: In search of a new paradigm. *Curriculum Inquiry, 9,* 187–207.

RESNICK, L. B. (1976). Task analysis in instructional design: Some cases from mathematics. In D. Klahr (Ed.), *Cognition and instruction.* Hillsdale, New Jersey: Erlbaum.

ROYER, J. M. (1979). Theories of transfer of learning. *Educational Psychologist, 14,* 53–69.

RUMELHART, D. E., and NORMAN, D. A. (1981). Analogical processes in learning. In J. R. Anderson (Ed.), *Cognitive skills and acquisition.* Hillsdale, New Jersey: Erlbaum.

SACERDOTI, E. G. (1977). *A structure for plans and behavior.* New York: Elsevier.

SALOMON, G. (1981). *Communication and education: Social and psychological interactions.* Beverly Hills, California: Sage.

SALTHOUSE, T. A. (1982). *Adult cognition.* New York: Springer-Verlag.

SIMON, H. A. (1980). Problem solving and education. In D. T. Tuma and F. Reif (Eds.), *Problem solving and education: Issues in teaching and research.* Hillsdale, New Jersey: Erlbaum.

SIMON, H. A., and HAYES, J. R. (1976). Understanding complex task instructions. In D. Klahr (Ed.), *Cognition and instruction.* Hillsdale, New Jersey: Erlbaum.

STEIN, L. S. (1971). Adult learning principles, the individual curriculum, and nursing leadership. *The Journal of Continuing Education in Nursing, 2,* 7–13.

STRAUSS, A. L. (1974). *Chronic illness and the quality of life.* St. Louis: C. V. Mosby Company.

UMAN, G. C. (1985). *A multi-case study of the relationship between formal health education and subsequent health behavior.* Doctoral dissertation. Los Angeles: University of Southern California.

UNRUH, D. R. (1983). *Invisible lives.* Beverly Hills, California: Sage.

WATZLAWICK, P., WEAKLAND, J., and FISCH, R. (1974). *Change.* New York: Norton.

WILLIS, S. L. (1984). Towards an educational psychology of the older adult learner: Intellectual and cognitive bases. In J. E. Birren and K. W. Schaie (Eds.), *The handbook of the psychology of aging.* New York: Van Nostrand Reinhold Co., Inc.

YINGER, R. J. (1980). Can we really teach them to think? In R. E. Young (Ed.), *New directions for teaching and learning. Number 3: Fostering critical thinking.* San Francisco: Jossey-Bass.

8

THE EFFECTS OF PHYSICAL ACTIVITY ON THE PHYSIOLOGICAL AND PSYCHOLOGICAL HEALTH OF THE OLDER ADULT

Implications for Education

Priscilla Gilliam MacRae

INTRODUCTION

There has been a tendency for health care professionals and physical educators to view health education as an "innoculation" that need only be given once. It is assumed that, following the "innoculation" in early life, the individual will henceforth make healthy lifestyle choices and will not need further education in this area. However, the reality is that promoting healthy lifestyles must be continued throughout the life span.

One lifestyle choice that appears to be important in health promotion and disease prevention is regular physical activity. While vigorous physical activity has been recommended for the young adult as a way of enhancing health both physiologically and psychologically, the traditional emphasis for the older adult has focused on light, nonvigorous activity. The older adult is often represented as frail, disease-ridden, and unable to take part in vigorous physical activity. Our society has encouraged the older person to "slow down and take it easy." These societal expectations as well as the increase in mechanization have promoted a sedentary lifestyle among the majority of older adults.

The sedentary lifestyle of many older people may also be due to a lack of awareness of what is appropriate and essential activity for promoting health and preventing disease. Warnings about the problems associated with exercise and the recommendation that a doctor's permission be obtained before beginning an exercise program increase many older adults' apprehensions about physical activity. Many older people believe they are too old to participate in vigorous physical activity, or that they cannot derive benefits from participation in such activity (Conrad, 1976; Ostrow, 1980; 1984). However, it has recently become apparent that the potential for older people to gain benefits from participation in vigorous physical activity has been greatly underestimated.

Personal testimonies and record-book examples demonstrate that age need not necessarily be a limiting factor for physical performance. For example, Clarence De Mar, a famous marathon runner, normally ran 12 miles a day and was still running marathons at 65 years of age (deVries, 1984). Other examples of outstanding performance by older people include a 77-year-old man who ran 6 miles in 50:36 (approximately 8 minutes per mile) (Webb, Urner, and McDaniels, 1977); a 60-year-old man who ran a mile in 5:19 (Pollock, Miller, and Wilmore, 1974); and a 70-year-old cyclist who completed a 3,400 mile cross-country bicycle journey (Faria and Frankel, 1977). While these are examples of exceptional people, they provide some indication of the upper limits of strenuous exercise for older persons and serve to modify our expectations.

Many older adults do not begin their physical activity until later in life. Biegel (1984) relates the story of an 87-year-old woman who began a regular program of physical activity at the age of 81:

> Only five feet three inches tall and weighing 100 pounds for the past 40 years, she had developed cardiovascular disease and was treated for angina at age 67. At age 75 she was hospitalized with a severe heart attack; by age 81, she had developed an arthritic limp and had congestive heart failure, hypertension, and angina. When she began a regimen of dieting and walking at age 81, her limp limited her walking to 100 feet; the circulation in her hands was so impaired that she wore gloves in the summer to keep her hands warm. Gradually increasing her walking, she was able, by age 82, to be free of drugs and her previous symptoms. After four years of increased activity, she participated in the Senior Olympics in Irvine, California, where she won gold medals in the half mile and mile running events. The following year, at age 86½, she repeated those runs for another two gold medals. Each morning she runs a mile and rides her stationary bicycle 10–15 miles; three times weekly she works out in a gymnasium; and she follows her diet strictly (p. 31).

Another older adult celebrated his 90th birthday by walking 10 miles, bringing his postretirement walking total to 135,000 miles. He is currently vigorous and young in spirit, but was not always so. He retired at age 55, flabby, lame, and lethargic. His son's challenge to "straighten up and fly right" caused him to begin a regular program of physical activity (Biegel, 1984, p. 34).

Only in the last 15 years has it been clearly documented that older adults can benefit from a lifestyle incorporating physical activity. In fact, older adults are more in need of guidance about the type, frequency, intensity, and duration of physical activity than the younger adults who have been the usual focus of teaching efforts. It is now known that most of the physiological benefits associated with a regular program of physical activity for younger people also apply to older people, even those who have been inactive for many years.

The purpose of this chapter is to link the topics of physical activity, aging, and health by reviewing the relevant research literature and suggesting how physical activity may benefit the physiological and psychological health of the older individual. The physiological changes associated with the aging process will be discussed, as well as the effects of regular physical activity on these changes. The effects of physical activity on various psychological aspects of the older adult will also be examined. The final section of this chapter will discuss the implications these findings have for the present educational system.

AGING

Aging is a complex process that influences the biological, psychological, and sociological functioning of the organism. *Biological aging* has been defined as

> the process of change in the organism, which over time lowers the probability of survival and reduces the physiological capacity for self-regulation, repair, and adaptation to environmental demands (Birren and Zarit, 1984, p. 9).

Biological aging is most often associated with decrements in physiological function. *Psychological aging* refers to changes that occur in the organism's ability to adapt to alterations in the social and physical environment, as well as within the organism itself, which occur with the passage of time (Birren and Zarit, 1984). Both biological and psychological aging are influenced by genetic, environmental, and lifestyle factors. This chapter will examine the effects of one aspect of lifestyle, physical activity, on the biological and psychological aspects of the aging organism.

How we define the *older person* is always a dilemma in any discussion of aging. Many gerontologists, such as Brocklehurst (1973), make a distinction between middle age (40 to 65 years), old age (65 to 75 years), very old age (75 to 85 years), and extreme old age (over 85 years). However, most of the existing research concerning physical activity and aging has been conducted with individuals 50 to 75 years of age. Therefore, this age group will be the general focus of the present chapter. A great deal more research is needed with the very old, who more often have some functional impairment. It is more difficult, however, to conduct this type of research with appropriate controls.

PHYSICAL ACTIVITY

Physical activity or *exercise* can refer to a variety of movement activities. For the purposes of this chapter, physical activity will be defined as any activity that involves the movement of large muscle groups, can be maintained continuously, and is rhythmical and aerobic in nature: e.g., walking, jogging, bicycling, swimming, rowing, cross-country skiing, aerobic dancing, and rope jumping. Most physical activity programs, for any age group, attempt to develop and maintain cardiorespiratory function and body composition by following the American College of Sports Medicine Guidelines for Quantity and Quality of Exercise for Healthy Adults (1978). These guidelines recommend continuous aerobic-type activity performed

3 to 5 days per week at an intensity of 50 to 85% of a person's maximum oxygen consumption for 15 to 60 minutes. Maximum oxygen consumption (VO_2) is defined as the maximal amount of oxygen the body can consume at a maximal workload. This measure is considered the best single measure of physical fitness (Shephard, 1968).

HEALTH

Health may be defined in several ways. It has most often been defined as the absence of disease or as the organism's ability to perform its vital functions normally. In this chapter, however, health is defined as the functional process of identifying one's changing needs and taking appropriate actions to meet those needs in order to maximize one's potentials in the physical, psychological, intellectual, and spiritual domains (Warner-Reitz, 1981). This functional definition of health emphasizes the role of personal responsibility and choice in obtaining and maintaining optimal health. Choice may be defined as the "voluntary and purposive action of selecting from two or more alternatives that which is superior" (*Webster's Dictionary*, 1976). Thus, it is important for people to be aware of the many alternatives available to them in the areas of health promotion and disease prevention.

CONTEMPORARY ISSUES OF HEALTH, PHYSICAL ACTIVITY, AND AGING

Due to a lower birthrate and an increase in life expectancy, the United States is currently witnessing demographic changes which have enormous social, political, and economic implications. In 1900 there were only 3 million people aged 65 and older, making up 4% of the United States' population. In 1980 there were nearly 25 million people aged 65 and older, composing 11% of the total United States' population (Soldo, 1980). This dramatic increase in the number of older people is focusing the nation's attention on the living conditions, health status, and medical costs of the older individual.

During this century not only has there been a demographic shift but there has also been a shift in the major disease processes, from infectious diseases—such as tuberculosis, cholera, typhoid, and polio—to chronic degenerative diseases—such as cardiovascular disease, cancer, degenerative joint disease, and strokes. Butler (1975) pointed out that 86% of the older population suffers from at least one chronic degenerative disease. In most cases, death of the older individual is attributed to one or more of these diseases. The 1979 Surgeon General's Report (*Healthy People*) on health promotion and disease prevention stated that at least 50% of the deaths in the United States resulted from a chosen lifestyle of unhealthy behavior, while only 10% of the deaths were due to inadequate health care, 20% due to biological factors, and 20% due to environmental factors. It was further reported that the greatest potential for reducing premature deaths and avoiding disability lies in the assumption of personal responsibility for health. The goals specified by this 1979 Surgeon General's Report included improved control of hypertension, decreased rates of cigarette smoking, and increased physical activity.

It is becoming evident that the practice of health care for older people is generally directed toward acute care or long term care for the already ill, while little emphasis is placed on the equally important area of health promotion and disease prevention. The epidemic proportions of degenerative disease to a large extent are due to an individual's personal health habits and lifestyle choices. Smoking, improper diet (which in the United States frequently consists of excessive sugar, salt, fats, and alcohol intake), and a lack of regular physical activity are lifestyle choices that contribute to the onset and severity of these degenerative diseases (Belloc, 1973; Belloc and Breslow, 1972).

The issue of the effects of aging and physical activity on physiological functioning is complicated by the fact that changes in physiological functioning may result from a combination of at least three factors: true aging, disease processes, and an increasingly sedentary lifestyle. Bortz (1982) challenged the concept that aging *per se* is the cause of the decline in physical and mental functioning. He detailed the similarities between aging and physical inactivity and suggested that "at least a portion of the changes that are commonly attributed to aging is in reality caused by disuse, and as such, is subject to correction" (p. 203). Furthermore, it has been suggested that a lifetime of physical exercise holds the greatest promise for sustained health (Bortz, 1982; Butler, 1975; deVries, 1984).

PHYSIOLOGICAL FUNCTIONING, AGING, AND PHYSICAL ACTIVITY

Several different systems are involved in the physiological functioning of the body, all of which appear to be affected to some extent by the aging process (see Table 8-1). These systems include the cardiovascular and circulatory system, the respiratory system, the musculoskeletal system, and the nervous system. Table 8-1 summarizes the relationships between age, physical activity, and various aspects of physiological functioning.

Methods of examining the effects of physical activity on the physiological functioning of the older adult include epidemiological, cross-sectional, and longitudinal studies. For example, epidemiologists have examined the effects of the level of physical activity on mortality due to coronary heart disease (Paffenbarger, Hyde, Wing, and Steinmetz, 1984; Paffenbarger, Wing, and Hyde, 1978). Paffenbarger et al. (1984) examined this relationship in a longitudinal study of 17,000 Harvard alumni. They found that sports participation in college did not have a significant benefit in reducing the lifelong risk of coronary heart disease. However, the alumni who participated in regular vigorous activity throughout their lifetimes had a 50% lower risk of coronary heart disease than their sedentary classmates. Furthermore, the benefit of exercise in affecting the incidence of coronary heart disease was independent of contrary lifestyle elements, such as smoking, obesity, weight gain, hypertension, and adverse parental disease history.

Using cross-sectional techniques, researchers have taken physiological measurements of master athletes who were competitors in the World Master's Championships, and compared these measurements with those of the general population in the same age groups (Kavanagh and Shephard, 1977; Pollock, Miller, and Wilmore, 1974). They found that age-related changes—such as maximum oxygen consumption, blood pressure, blood lipids, pulmonary ventilation, and percentage of body fat—are not as great in these individuals as in the general population of the same age.

Thus, both the cross-sectional and the epidemiological data demonstrate that there is a clear relationship between physical activity and physiological functioning. However, these data do not definitively prove that this relationship is causal. For example, the general population used for comparison purposes most likely included more individuals with chronic degenerative disease than included in the group of master athletes. It is also true that athletic groups contain a much lower percentage of smokers and obese individuals than the general population. Hence, the master

TABLE 8-1.   The Effects of Age and Physical Activity on Physiological Function in Older Adults: ↑ Increase, ↓ Decrease, 0 No Change.

PHYSIOLOGICAL CHANGES WITH AGE	PHYSICAL ACTIVITY EFFECTS	SOURCE
Cardiovascular/Circulatory Systems		
↓ in maximal oxygen consumption	↑	Adams & deVries, 1973; Barry et al., 1966a; Buccola & Stone, 1975; Dehn & Bruce, 1972; deVries, 1970, 1971; Niinimaa & Shephard, 1978; Seals et al., 1984b; Sidney & Shephard, 1978; Suominen et al., 1977a, 1977b
↓ in maximal arteriovenous oxygen difference	↑	Seals et al., 1984b; Suominen et al., 1977a, 1977b
↓ in stroke volume, heart rate and therefore ↓ in cardiac output	↑ 0	Hartley et al., 1969; Hagberg et al., 1985 deVries, 1970; Seals et al., 1984b
↑ in resting blood pressure	↓	Barry et al., 1966a; Buccola & Stone, 1975; deVries, 1970, 1971; Stamford, 1972
	0	Adams & deVries, 1973; Seals et al., 1984b
↑ in ECG abnormalities	↓	Barry et al., 1966a; Sidney & Shephard, 1977b
↑ in atherosclerosis		
↑ in blood lipids	↓	Holloszy et al., 1984
↓ in glucose tolerance	↑	Seals, 1984a; Holloszy et al., 1984
↓ in insulin clearance	↑	Holloszy et al., 1984
Respiratory System		
↓ in vital capacity	↑	deVries, 1970, 1972; Chebotarev et al., 1974
	0	Adams & deVries, 1973; Barry et al., 1966a; Buccola & Stone, 1975; Niinamaa & Shephard, 1978
↑ in thoracic compliance		
↓ maximal ventilation rate during exercise	↑	deVries, 1972; Barry et al., 1966a; Seals et al., 1984b

TABLE 8-1. (continued)

PHYSIOLOGICAL CHANGES WITH AGE	PHYSICAL ACTIVITY EFFECTS	SOURCE
Musculoskeletal System		
↓ in maximal strength	↑	Chapman et al., 1972; deVries, 1971; Perkins & Kaiser, 1962; Suominen et al., 1977a, 1977b; Dummer et al., 1985
↓ in muscular endurance	↑	deVries, 1971; Perkins & Kaiser, 1962; Dummer et al., 1985
↓ in joint flexibility	↑	Chapman et al., 1972
↓ in bone mass	↑	Aloia et al., 1978; Novak, 1972; Smith & Reddan, 1975; Smith, 1982; Oyster et al., 1984
↓ in lean body mass	↑	Sidney et al., 1977; Hagberg et al., 1985
↑ in body fat	↓	Barry et al., 1966a; deVries, 1970; Hagberg et al., 1985; Seals et al., 1984b; Sidney et al., 1977a, 1977b, 1977c
Nervous System		
↓ in brain glucose utilization	0	Farrar et al., 1983
↓ brain cell number and brain weight		
↓ in neurotransmitter content and receptor number in the CNS	↑	Gilliam et al., 1984; Gilliam-MacRae et al., in progress
↑ in abnormal EEG waves		

athletes may be a self-selected group who have chosen to be physically active because they have fewer health problems than the general population.

Be that as it may, the generalizability of the data from the master athletes *is* substantiated in other research. For example, Morrison, Van Malsen, and Noakes (1984) examined physical activity levels and other coronary risk factors in over 1,000 men and reported that individuals in their fifth to seventh decade who participated in vigorous activity three or more times a week had maximal oxygen consumption values equivalent to equally-active individuals 20 years younger. Furthermore, these values were significantly higher than those of their sedentary age-matched counterparts. These results support the hypothesis that the decrease in maximal oxygen consumption associated with age is due to a decrease in amount and intensity of physical activity and not to aging *per se.*

The effects of physical activity on the physiological function of the older adult can also be examined by conducting longitudinal training studies. In longitudinal studies, individuals are assessed initially, placed on a physical activity program for a certain interval of time, and then reevaluated at the conclusion of the training period. Longitudinal studies are to be preferred to the epidemiological or cross-sectional studies. However, they are expensive to conduct and usually involve small numbers of subjects. Most of the longitudinal studies have shown that exercise programs undertaken by older adults later in life, even if these adults have not been active previously, can produce benefits in cardiovascular, circulatory, respiratory, and central nervous system function (see Table 8-1).

Cardiovascular/Circulatory Systems

Many aspects of the cardiovascular and circulatory systems' functioning decline with age. Maximum oxygen consumption, which measures the efficiency of the lungs, heart, and muscles in supplying oxygen to the body and using the oxygen that is supplied, has been shown to decline at a rate of 1% per year after the midtwenties (Astrand, 1960). This represents as much as a 50% loss in maximum oxygen consumption by 75 years of age. The decline in maximum oxygen consumption is due to a decline in central functioning, i.e., maximum heart rate, stroke volume, and cardiac output, as well as a decline in peripheral functioning, i.e., arteriovenous oxygen (deVries, 1984; Shephard, 1978).

Typically, blood pressure rises with age, thereby putting a greater strain on the heart and circulatory system (Anderson and Cowan, 1972; Siconolfi et al., 1985). An increase in atherosclerosis (clogging of the coronary arteries with fatty deposits) is also more evident with advancing years. This is due in part to higher circulating levels of blood lipids, i.e., total cholesterol and triglycerides (Saltin and Grimby, 1968). The increase in atherosclerosis causes a decrease in blood flow to the heart and brain which, if severe enough, can cause heart damage (heart attack) or brain damage (stroke).

Older individuals also have a lower tolerance for glucose and a decreased insulin sensitivity (Fitzgerald et al., 1961), which often result in such diseases as adult-onset diabetes. Diabetes increases the individual's risk of developing peripheral vascular disease, hypertension, and atherosclerosis.

There is substantial evidence that regular aerobic exercise can bring about positive changes in many aspects of cardiovascular and circulatory function in the older adult. Changes in cardiovascular functions with exercise include increases in maximal oxygen consumption (Adams and deVries, 1973; Barry et al., 1966a; Buccola and Stone, 1975; deVries, 1970, 1971; Niinimaa and Shephard, 1978; Seals et al., 1984b; Sidney and Shephard, 1978; Suominen, Heikkinen, Liesen, Michel, and Hollman, 1977a; Suominen, Heikkinen, and Parketti, 1977b). This increase in maximum oxygen consumption is due mainly to increases in peripheral adaptations in the muscle, such as increases in capillarization and oxidative enzyme levels (Seals et al., 1984b; Suominen, Heikkinen, Liesen, Michel, and Hollman, 1977a; Suominen, Heikkinen, and Parketti, 1977b). Two studies, however, have also reported exercise-induced improvements in central adaptations such as stroke volume (Hagberg, Allen, Seals, Hurley, Ehsani, and Holloszy, 1985; Hartley et al., 1969).

Decreases in resting blood pressure and electrocardiogram abnormalities were found after older adults participated in a vigorous program of physical activity (Barry et al., 1966a; deVries, 1970, 1971; Stamford, 1972). Improvements in blood lipid levels, glucose tolerance, and insulin sensitivity have also been reported in physically active experimental groups when compared with sedentary control groups (Barry et al., 1966a; Holloszy et al., 1984; Seals et al., 1984a).

Some recent research (Holloszy et al., 1984; Seals et al., 1984b) examined the effects of a one-year endurance exercise program to determine the effects of low-intensity and high-intensity exercise on various parameters of cardiovascular and respiratory function, body composition, blood lipids, and glucose tolerance of a group of older adults (mean age of 63). A battery of physiological tests was given before the program began, again after 6 months of low-intensity exercise (walking for 20–30 minutes at a moderate intensity, 40% of maximum oxygen consumption, for three times per week), and again 12 months later, after 6 months of high-intensity exercise (jogging for 30–45 minutes at a high intensity, 75% of maximum oxygen consumption, for three times per week). Significant improvement in maximal oxygen consumption was found in the experimental group after 6 months of exercise (12% improvement), while the 6 additional months of high-intensity exercise produced a further and more marked increase of 18%. Ventilation during maximal exercise was improved 7% and 22% after 6 and 12 months of exercise, respectively. These improvements are of much greater magnitude than those obtained in previous studies and appear to be due to the higher intensity (up to 85% of VO_2) and longer duration (12 months vs. 2 to 3 months) of the exercise program. The subjects also showed significant decreases in body weight and body fat after the 12 months of exercise, but not after the 6 months of exercise. Blood lipid levels (cholesterol and triglycerides) and glucose tolerance tests were also improved after 12 months of exercise with no significant changes in these parameters after 6 months of the low-intensity exercise.

It appears that the higher intensity of exercise and longer duration (12 months vs. 6 months) are necessary requirements for exercise to influence factors such as body composition, blood lipids, and glucose tolerance. These results document the ability of the older asymptomatic adult to respond with significant physiological improvements to a regular individualized program of physical activity. In a position statement, the American College of Sports Medicine (1978) stated this view when it reported that "age in itself does not appear to be a deterrent to endurance training" (p. viii).

Respiratory System

Respiratory changes with age include a reduction in vital capacity and an increase in residual volume, thereby decreasing the efficiency of ventilatory function (Chebotarev, Korkushko, and Ivanov, 1974; Norris, Shock, Landowne, and Falzone, 1956). The decrease in vital capacity of the lungs is due to loss of elasticity of lung tissue, rigidity of the chest wall (increase in thoracic compliance), and decreased strength of the respiratory muscles (Chebotarev et al., 1974). The increase in residual volume, due to a decrease in the elasticity of lung tissue with age, results in a decrease in the amount of air involved in ventilation and, hence, less efficient ventilation. These changes in respiratory function lead to a decrease in the oxygen content of the arterial blood which may in turn cause hypoxic conditions that can affect functioning of the brain, heart, and muscles in the older adult.

It has also been reported that the older person is not able to reach the same maximal ventilation rate as the younger individual due to the stiffening of the thorax and decreased strength of the respiratory muscles (Mittman, Edelman, Norris, and Shock, 1965; Rizzato and Marazzini, 1970; Turner, Mead, and Wohl,

1968). This is particularly detrimental to the functioning of older adults when they are placed under conditions of increasing workloads (deVries, 1972).

Studies that have examined the effects of physical activity on respiratory function have reported equivocal results. Some investigators have reported little change in vital capacity and thoracic compliance (Adams and deVries, 1973; Barry et al., 1966a; Buccola and Stone, 1975; Niinamaa and Shephard, 1978), while other researchers have found significant improvements in vital capacity after chronic physical activity (Chebotarev et al., 1974; deVries, 1970, 1972). These inconsistent results may be due to the different measurement techniques used or to variations in intensity, duration, and frequency of the physical activity program employed. However, maximal ventilation rate during exercise has been shown consistently to increase significantly after several weeks of regular vigorous activity (Barry et al., 1966a; deVries, 1970, 1971; Seals et al., 1984b).

Musculoskeletal System

Proper functioning of the musculoskeletal system, which includes the muscles, the bones, and the joints, is essential to optimal health and physiological function. Musculoskeletal function can be examined by measuring muscular strength, muscular endurance, flexibility, and bone density. Muscular strength refers to the amount of force the muscle can produce in a single maximum contraction. Age changes in muscular strength are generally manifested by a slow loss of strength with age. Men usually experience a 10 to 20% loss of strength from 20 to 60 years of age while women usually exhibit somewhat greater age-related strength loss (Montoye and Lamphiear, 1977; Petrofsky and Lind, 1975).

Muscular endurance, the capacity of the muscle to perform continuous submaximal contractions, shows greater decreases with age than muscular strength (Dummer, Clarke, Vaccaro, Welden, Goldfarb, and Sockler, 1985; Larson, 1978). Animal studies have shown that these losses in muscular strength and endurance are due to changes that occur at the cellular level, with a loss in contractile elements and muscle fiber number (Gutman, Hanzlikova, and Jakoubek, 1968) as well as a reduction in respiratory enzymes of the muscle (Ermini, 1976).

The decline in muscular endurance is also associated with changes in body composition, i.e., a decrease in lean body mass and an increase in body fat (Forbes and Reina, 1970; Parizkova, 1963; Shephard, 1978). As the body loses lean muscle mass, there is a concomitant reduction in its basal and resting metabolic rate causing a decrease in caloric expenditure. Frequently, food intake is not reduced in proportion to the decrease in caloric expenditure and therefore increases in fat stores result. These increases in body fat place a greater load on the already weakened muscular system, often leading to functional problems that affect walking, lifting, carrying, and other daily activities.

A decrease in muscular strength and endurance, particularly in the abdominal muscles, is often the cause of chronic lower back pain. In 1974, insurance companies reported more claims for back disability than for any other cause (Massachusetts Mutual Insurance Company, 1975). Lower back pain and other musculoskeletal disorders are the result of inadequate muscle strength and flexibility and are the cause of discomfort, losses in income, increased disability, and premature retirement (Pollock, Wilmore, and Fox, 1984).

The effects of age on flexibility are more difficult to evaluate and quantify than muscular changes. Flexibility simply refers to the range of motion around a particular joint. Age is usually associated with a decline in joint flexibility, accompanied by a decrease in stability, mobility, and power, and an increase in deformity (Adrian, 1981). Decreased flexibility with age is probably the result of combined histological and morphological changes in the components of the joint, including cartilage, ligaments, and tendons.

In addition to proper functioning of joints and muscles, the strength of the bones is an important aspect of the musculoskeletal system. Osteoporosis, a decrease in bone density of sufficient magnitude to result in fractures as a result of minimal stress, is a major problem of older adults, particularly women. The rate of bone loss in men is 0.4% per year after age 50, but it usually is not a problem until the eighth decade. Women begin to lose bone mass at the rate of 0.75 to 1.0% per year between the ages of 30 and 35. Higher bone mineral loss (2 to 3%) may occur with menopause and continue for an additional five years (Smith, 1982). It has been shown that levels of estrogen and dietary intake of calcium and vitamin D, as well as physical activity, affect the rate of bone mineral loss (Aloia, Cohn, Ostuni, Cane, and Ellis, 1978; Recker, Saville, and Heaney, 1977; Weiss, Ure, Ballard, Williams, and Daling, 1980).

Exercise-induced improvements in the musculoskeletal system include increases in maximal strength, muscular endurance, joint flexibility, and lean body mass, and a decrease in percentage of body fat (Barry et al., 1966a; Chapman et al., 1972; deVries, 1970, 1971; Dummer et al., 1985; Holloszy et al., 1984; Novak, 1972; Perkins and Kaiser, 1962; Sidney et al., 1977; Suominen et al., 1977a, 1977b). It is important, however, to note that the exercise-induced improvements in musculoskeletal function are specific to the type of exercise performed during the training sessions. Decreases in body fat and improvements in bone density are most often found when the participants have performed moderately strenuous aerobic exercise for 30 to 45 minutes, three to four times per week (Aloia et al., 1978; Holloszy et al., 1984; Smith et al., 1981). The greatest increases in muscular strength and muscular endurance are found when weight training or aerobic training programs are used (Dummer et al., 1985; Perkins and Kaiser, 1962; Suominen et al., 1977a, 1977b). Improvements in flexibility have been found in participants who were involved in a nonstrenuous progressive program and in those involved in a more strenuous jogging and cycling program (Bassett, McClamrock, and Schelzer, 1982; Buccola and Stone, 1975; Frekany and Leslie, 1975; Lesser, 1978).

There is increasing evidence that physical activity is a definite factor in the retardation of osteoporosis in the older adult, particularly in older women (Aloia, 1982; Aloia, Cohn, Ostuni, Cane, and Ellis, 1978; Oyster, Morton, and Linnell, 1984; Smith, 1982; Smith and Reddan, 1975; Smith, Reddan, and Smith, 1981). For example, research by Smith et al. (1981) indicates that improvement in bone mineral content in older adults with severe bone loss is possible with a three-day-a-week exercise program. This improvement in bone mineral content is of particular importance since osteoporosis is the most common disorder of the human skeleton, affecting at least 6 million older men and women in the United States (Oyster et al., 1984). Also, osteoporosis is the cause of many accidents leading to enormous medical bills and loss of independent functioning in many older adults.

Nervous System

Disturbances in central nervous system function also occur with age. Although cerebral blood flow appears to remain stable in normal healthy older adults (Dastur, Lane, Hansen, Kety, Butler, Perlin, and Sokoloff, 1963), there is evidence of a decrease in glucose utilization in brain structures associated with vision, audition, and sensorimotor function (Farrar et al., 1983; Smith, Goochee, Rapoport, and Sokoloff, 1980). Age-related morphological changes, which include degeneration of cells in specific brain areas such as the cerebral cortex and limbic system (Brody, 1955; Scheibel et al., 1975, 1976, 1977) also occur. In addition, aging is associated with decreases in brain neurotransmitter levels and receptor number, particularly in the nigrostriatal dopamine system and other catecholamine systems (Finch, 1973; McGeer and McGeer, 1976). Finally, disturbances in EEG patterns have also been associated with the aging process (Wang and Busse, 1969).

Though cardiovascular, respiratory, and musculoskeletal adaptations to chronic physical activity are documented, little is known concerning the effects of chronic physical activity upon central nervous system function, particularly in the older individual. The effects of physical activity on the functioning of the nervous system has only recently been examined. One study reported no effects of chronic exercise training on glucose utilization in the caudate, cerebellum, and motor cortex of young and old male rats (Farrar, Ardies, Gilliam, Dodd, and Spirduso, 1983). However, other data suggest that chronic exercise may ameliorate some of the loss in dopamine receptors usually associated with the aging process in male rodents (Gilliam-MacRae, Wilcox, Farrar, and Spirduso, in progress; Spirduso, 1983). Further investigation is needed in this area before well-documented conclusions can be stated.

Summary: Effects of Physical Activity on the Physiological Functioning of the Older Adult

Although aging is most often associated with declining physiological functioning, there is evidence that older adults benefit from programs of regular vigorous physical activity. Improvements in physiological functioning are due to adaptations of the cardiovascular, circulatory, respiratory, musculoskeletal, and nervous systems. Beneficial changes in maximum oxygen consumption, electrocardiograms, blood pressure, blood lipids, glucose tolerance, and ventilatory function have been associated with regular physical activity. Improvements in muscular strength and endurance, body composition, joint flexibility, and bone density have also been found.

Very little research examining the effects of exercise on central nervous system function has been conducted. There is, however, some evidence that exercise affects neurotransmitter function in certain brain nuclei of rodents. The extent of physiological gains probably depends upon personal factors such as initial level of fitness, motivation, attitudes, and personality as well as program factors such as type, intensity, frequency, and duration of physical activity.

There is good evidence that moderate physical activity promotes the functional integrity of many of the physiological systems. This enables the individual to maintain proper physiological functioning over a longer period of time, thereby slowing some of the deterioration processes often associated with aging. Controlled longitudinal studies are needed to examine the effects of regularly-performed exercise of different types (aerobic, strength, or flexibility) on the rate of age-related declines in cardiovascular, respiratory, musculoskeletal, and nervous system functioning. The precise type, intensity, frequency, and duration of physical activity needed to elicit optimal gains in the physiological health of the older adult have yet to be established. It also must be determined if older adults with chronic disease can benefit from some type of moderate physical activity.

THE EFFECTS OF PHYSICAL ACTIVITY ON THE PSYCHOLOGICAL FUNCTIONING OF THE OLDER ADULT

Most research in the area of aging and physical activity has focused on the effects of activity on the physical health of the older adult. An equally important consideration is the extent to which physical activity influences mental health. Most individuals report that they "feel good" or "feel better" following vigorous physical activity. Attempts to quantify these subjective reports have measured such constructs as behavioral slowing, cognition, self-concept, body image, depression, and anxiety.

However, few of these studies have used correct methodology, and older adults have seldom been the focus of the study. A recent review of over 1,000 articles on the psychological effects of habitual exercise found only 12 studies that met the criterion of a randomized, controlled experiment with at least 10 subjects and exercise programs of sufficient intensity, duration, and frequency to induce physiological changes (Hughes, 1984). The majority of the studies reviewed suffered from a limited number of subjects, no control group, or nonrandom assignment to the control group. Other common shortcomings included poor choices of psychological construct measures, experimentor/subject biases, failure to document physiological changes that resulted from participation in the exercise program, and inadequate descriptions of methods. In addition to these methodological problems, it is difficult to analyze the effects of physical activity on the psychological function of the older adult when it is not clear what psychological changes occur in "normal aging."

The few well-controlled studies which have examined the effects of physical activity on the psychological functioning of the older adult have yielded equivocal results. Some have reported improved physiological functioning with no change in cognitive, depression, or anxiety constructs (Barry et al., 1966b; Stamford, 1972; Tredway, 1978), while others have shown improvements in both physiological and psychological function (Dustman et al., 1984; Powell, 1974; Sidney and Shephard, 1977a, 1977c). What follows is a brief review of those constructs in which the effects of physical activity have been researched adequately enough to draw some conclusions.

Behavioral Slowing

One of the best-documented psychological changes that occur with age is a slowing in behavioral functioning. Older people consistently perform more slowly on tasks requiring response speed, such as reaction-time and movement-time tasks, as well as tapping and copying tasks (Birren and Botwinick, 1955; Hodgkins, 1962; Spirduso, 1975; Spirduso and Clifford, 1978; Suci, 1960; Welford, 1977). Of these motor responses, reaction time is purportedly one of the best behavioral measures of central nervous system integrity (Birren, Woods, and Williams, 1979).

Spirduso (1980) reviewed the literature on the effects of physical activity on psychomotor speed. She suggested that physical activity may, by its trophic effect on the central nervous system, to some extent retard the age-related declines in psychomotor speed and neuromuscular efficiency. Studies have also shown that older men and women who have maintained a physically-active lifestyle have faster reaction and movement times than their sedentary counterparts (Clarkson and Kroll, 1978; Hart, 1981; Sherwood and Selder, 1979; Spirduso, 1975; Spirduso and Clifford, 1978; Woods, 1981). In fact, these older, active individuals responded as quickly as inactive men and women who were 40 years younger.

In order to determine whether the faster behavioral responses of physically-active older individuals reflects a genetic predisposition for superiority in response speed or if exercise *per se* has a beneficial effect on central nervous system function, Dustman et al. (1984) examined the effects of a four-month exercise program (three one-hour sessions per week) on various aspects of neuropsychological and physiological function. They recruited older, healthy, sedentary adults (55 to 70 years). They then randomly assigned the subjects to three different groups: a control group (N=15) that performed no exercise, an exercise group (N=13) that performed a regular aerobic exercise program involving walking and jogging, and an exercise control group (N=15) that performed a regular exercise program of strength and flexibility exercises with no aerobic exercise. Those in the aerobic exercise group significantly improved their maximal oxygen consumption and performance on most neuropsychological measures such as simple reaction time, critical flicker fusion, digit symbol, and Stroop tests. The control and exercise control groups showed no significant changes in these same measures. These findings strongly support the concepts that physically inactive older adults can participate in a program of regular exercise at an intensity sufficient to improve their physical fitness level significantly, and that regular aerobic exercise can also improve their neuropsychological functioning.

Cognitive Functioning

The only well-controlled study concerned with the effects of physical activity on cognitive function examined the effect of a 12-week exercise program (walking and calisthenics) on the memory and intellectual abilities of 30 geriatric institutionalized patients (Powell, 1974). Subjects were grouped by age, sex, and ward residence and randomly assigned to either a mild-exercise group, an attention-control group, or a noncontact control group. The exercise group improved on two of the three memory tests with no change found in other measures of intellectual abilities. These results, however, can only be generalized to clinical geriatric populations.

Self-Concept, Body Image, Depression, and Anxiety

Several well-controlled experiments have examined the effects of physical activity on self-concept in young and middle-aged adults (Gary and Guthrie, 1972; Hilyer, Dillon, Caro, Jenkins, Spencer, Meadows, and Brookes, 1982; Hilyer and

Mitchell, 1979; McGowan, Jarman, and Pedersen, 1974). The results of these studies support regular physical activity as a way to improve self-concept. These positive effects may result from the fact that the subjects studied had self-concept problems: McGowan et al. (1974) chose boys low in self-esteem; Gary and Guthrie (1972) studied alcoholics; and Hilyer et al. (1982) studied juvenile delinquents. This possibility is supported by the research of Hilyer and Mitchell (1979) who found that exercise only improved the self-esteem of men who were initially low in self-esteem but not in men initially high in self-esteem.

Perri and Templer (1984–85) investigated the effects of a fourteen-week aerobic exercise program on depression, anxiety, self-concept, locus of control, and short-term memory in older adults. The exercise group showed a significant increase over the control group in self-concept and locus of control. These results would seem to indicate that the exercise participants had an increase in self-confidence and sense of mastery over their environment.

Other studies have examined the effects of physical activity on the body image of older adult subjects. *Body image* may be defined as one's attitude toward the aesthetic and functional dimensions of one's body. Self-concept and body image appear to be related concepts. Kreitler and Kreitler (1970) suggest that physically inactive older people have distorted body images; they often perceive their bodies to be broader and heavier than they really are. Older women appear to have greater discrepancies between their ideal and their perceived body images than older men (Sidney and Shephard, 1977c). A vicious cycle is often created: a distorted body image produces feelings of clumsiness, anxiety, and insecurity, which lead to less interest and participation in physical activity, which in turn leads to physical deterioration and a further distortion in body image (Kreitler and Kreitler, 1970).

Two studies examined the effects of a walking/jogging program on body image in a group of older adults. Stamford (1972) studied institutionalized geriatric men and found no change in body image after 12 weeks of a walking program. Sidney and Shephard (1977a, 1977c) examined the effects of an exercise program on various psychological measures in a group of healthy adult volunteers (mean age 66). The latter subjects were involved in a walking/jogging program for 1 hour per day, 4 days per week for 14 weeks. They found significant posttest improvements in body image only among those older adults classified as high-frequency, high-intensity participants. These same participants also exhibited improvements in mood scores (McPherson's The Real Me scores) and attitudes toward physical activity. The subjects classified as less-frequent and/or less-intense exercise participants showed no posttest improvements in body image or on the mood scales. Eighty-three percent of all the subjects reported improvements in "well-being" and showed a decrease in scores on the Taylor Manifest Anxiety Scale. Additional scientific evidence that a regular program of physical activity decreases anxiety and depression in older adults could not be located.

Summary: Effects of Physical Activity on Psychological Functioning of the Older Adult

The effects of regular physical activity on the response speed (behavioral slowing) of the older adult is well-documented. Cross-sectional studies of young and old, active and inactive individuals have demonstrated that the older active individual is able to exhibit reaction times very similar to young, inactive individuals and significantly faster than his or her sedentary counterpart. In a longitudinal study, it was also found that regular aerobic exercise in an older adult population improved simple reaction time and other neuropsychological parameters; while in the control group and in the exercise control group, whose members did strength and flexibility exercises, no significant improvements in these measures were shown.

The effects of physical activity on cognitive function, self-concept, body image, depression, and anxiety have been encouraging but not overwhelming. Some studies have used institutionalized geriatric subjects, who are at a lower initial functioning level than the average older adult. Studies conducted with normal healthy adults reported significant improvements in self-concept, body image, locus of control, and decreases in anxiety levels only in the subjects who exercised consistently and at a high level of intensity. These results are similar to those in the physiological literature reported in this chapter: greater physiological benefits are gained by groups that perform the greatest amount of physical activity over the longest period of time.

Well-controlled research in the area of aging, physical activity, and psychological function is greatly needed to determine if physical activity can improve aspects of psychological function. Carefully designed and controlled physical activity programs with thorough and appropriate measures of physiological and psychological functioning should lead to greater understanding in this area.

IMPLICATIONS FOR EDUCATION

As noted earlier, more research is needed to elucidate the effects of regular physical activity on the physiological and psychological functioning of the older adult. However, there is already sufficient evidence that participation in a regular program of physical activity results in improved physiological functioning in the older, healthy adult. On the other hand, although the results concerning the psychological effects of exercise are provocative, they are not sufficiently documented to justify major conclusions. What then can be stated about the role of the educator, the physical educator, the gerontologist, and those in the health and medical professions involved in the movement toward a healthier older population? Should educators be involved in promoting health and preventing disease?

Education has been defined as "the deliberate, systematic, and sustained effort to transmit, evoke, or acquire knowledge, attitudes, values, skills, or sensibilities, as well as any outcomes of that effort" (Cremin, 1976, p. 27). If education is deliberately designed to transmit knowledge, attitudes, values, and skills, then it is of the utmost importance that the educational curricula, the research efforts, and the community services of health care professionals, physical educators, and gerontologists include the areas of health promotion and disease prevention.

Educational Curricula

One way to obtain information about the level of university training in a particular field of study is to examine the educational curricula. Historically, medical education has not included geriatrics or health promotion/disease prevention as a formal part of the curriculum (Nelson, 1983; Smith, Marcy, Mast, and Ham, 1984).

Recently, the number of medical schools responding to the need for training in these areas has increased considerably. Most medical school curricula do include learning experiences that increase the students' cognitive knowledge of geriatrics; these activities, however, have not been as effective in developing clinical skills and positively influencing students' attitudes toward the older patient (Smith et al., 1984).

It has been reported that 84% of United States medical schools require some hours in preventive medicine in their curricula (Nelson, 1983). However, concepts of risk assessment, behavior change, exercise physiology, and nutrition are still visibly absent from medical school curricula (Dismuke and Miller, 1983). Even if physicians were taught many of these concepts, few clinical models for implementation now exist. Thus, physicians are well trained in the treatment of those already ill, but prevention has been largely ignored in their academic training.

College and university curricula in physical education have changed dramatically over the last 15 years from a teacher-education emphasis to an emphasis on the scientific basis of human movement. Most undergraduate and graduate programs in physical education and exercise science include courses on the physiology of exercise, the motor control system, and the anatomical and biomechanical bases of human movement. However, very few programs include any course work related to the physiology or psychology of the older adult and how exercise can affect his or her functioning. Educational curricula in this area should include basic scientific knowledge in exercise and movement, the knowledge of how to develop safe and effective physical activity programs for all ages and populations with special difficulties, and the knowledge of how to motivate individuals to incorporate regular physical activity into their lifestyles.

Research

Another indicator of the level of university research and training activity in a particular field of study is to examine the number and type of dissertations written. During the most recent seven-year period analyzed, i.e., 1976 to 1982, there was more than a doubling of the number of dissertations written on various aspects of aging as compared to the prior seven-year period. However, the number of dissertations on aging remains small. Relative to the number of dissertations on all subjects, only one percent of all dissertations listed focused on aging (Moore, Mueller, and Birren, submitted). Over the 15-year period from 1969 to 1983 the number of dissertations addressing the topics of aging and exercise has remained fairly constant, averaging about two dissertations per year. The number of dissertations on health and aging has increased over that same time period from approximately five per year in 1969 to approximately 27 per year in 1983 (Moore and Birren, 1972; Mueller and Birren, 1974; Mueller and Birren, 1979; Mueller and Kronauer, 1978; Mueller, Longo, and Kronauer, 1982; Mueller, Moore, and Birren, 1976). It may thus be inferred that health and aging have become of increasing interest to educators. On the other hand, the effects of exercise on aging have not been given the same increased interest. This area of research would appear to be a fruitful topic for further research.

Torrens, Breslow, and Fielding (1982) examined the role of universities in personal health improvement. They recommended that the university of the future have two major programs of activities in the health area: one devoted to research, teaching, and treatment services to patients, examples of which currently exist in university hospitals; and one devoted to research, teaching, and preventive services to the public in the form of a new health-promotion laboratory. The universities' involvement would include policy-making, education, and research in the area of health promotion.

Another role for the university would be the creation of opportunities for bringing together experts from many disciplines to review current findings and to develop appropriate guidelines for public policy. This must be followed by mechanisms for dissemination of the results of the reviews and deliberations so that the findings are easily and readily available to policy-makers as well as the general public. Health science curricula need to emphasize the processes that lead to chronic disease, not just the treatment of symptoms and episodes. There should also be an emphasis on the development of healthful lifestyle patterns for students, clinicians, and educators in the health sciences. The university should conduct research in disease prevention as actively as it currently conducts research in disease treatments. Only then can more appropriate programs in health promotion and prevention for the older adult be established.

Finally, if the greatest potential for reducing premature deaths and avoiding disability lies in the assumption of personal responsibility for health, then the educator should be a facilitator in encouraging older adults to assume personal responsibility for their health. Part of this role as a facilitator involves becoming aware of what types of programs and options are available for the older adult and making these options known to the older adult community.

Community Service

Educators may also be involved in offering older adults opportunities in health-enhancing activities such as supervised physical activity classes. Some community colleges now have Emeritus Institutes designed specifically to serve the educational needs of older students. Many physical activity courses, such as swimming, dancing, walking, jogging, weight training, and yoga are offered. These courses are often scheduled in local community centers and schools because these places are more readily accessible to the older adult than college or university campuses. These courses overcome many of the older adult's barriers to exercise because they are conveniently located, inexpensive, and taught by exercise leaders knowledgeable in the areas of exercise and aging.

Conclusion

At least two paths can be taken in discussing the health care system. These two paths might be termed the hard path and the soft path. The hard path advocates the growth of medical-industrial complexes with emphasis upon centralized, monetized systems of health care. The soft path, on the other hand, promotes the holistic approach to health care based on nonmonetized services such as self-help, volunteers, and peer counseling. The hard path encourages high technology to extend the quantity of life at all costs, while the soft path advocates appropriate technology to improve the quality of life as well as the quantity. The hard path is disease-based, with the emphasis on curing the disease; while the soft path emphasizes health promotion in an attempt to prevent disease or, in the case of existing disease, provides caring and coping strategies for the individual. Finally, the hard path is service delivery-oriented, while the soft path is education-oriented with the emphasis on individual responsibility for health. The emphasis of our present health care system is on the hard path. It is clear, however, that as medical costs continue to increase, composing an ever larger percentage of the United States' gross national product, an alternative to this path is necessary.

REFERENCES

ADAMS, G. M., and deVRIES, H. A. (1973). Physiological effects of an exercise training regimen on women aged 52 to 79. *Journal of Gerontology, 28,* 50–55.

ADRIAN, M. J. (1981). Flexibility in the aging adult. In E. L. Smith and R. C. Cerfass (Eds.), *Exercise and aging.* Hillside, New Jersey: Enslow Publishers.

ALOIA, J. F. (1982). Estrogen and exercise in prevention and treatment of osteoporosis. *Geriatrics, 37,* 81–85.

ALOIA, J. F., COHN, S. H., OSTUNI, H., CANE, R., and ELLIS, K. (1978). Prevention of involutional bone loss by exercise. *Annals of Internal Medicine, 89,* 356–358.

AMERICAN COLLEGE OF SPORTS MEDICINE (1978). Position statement on the recommended quantity and quality of exercise for developing and maintaining fitness in healthy adults. *Medicine and Science in Sports, 10,* 7–10.

ANDERSON, W. F., and COWAN, N. R. (1972). Arterial blood pressure in healthy older people. *Gerontologia Clinica, 14,* 129.

ASTRAND, I. (1960). Aerobic work capacity in men and women with special reference to age. *Acta Physiologie Scandinavica, 49* (suppl. 169), 1–92.

BARRY, A. J., DALY, J. W., PRUETT, E.D.R., STEINMETZ, J. R., PAGE, H. F., BIRKHEAD, N. C., and RODAHL, K. (1966a). The effects of physical conditioning on older individuals. I: Work capacity, circulatory-respiratory function, and work electrocardiogram. *Journal of Gerontology, 21,* 182–191.

BARRY, A. J., STEINMETZ, J. R., PAGE, H. F., RODAHL, K. (1966b). The effects of physical conditioning on older individuals. II: Motor performance and cognitive function. *Journal of Gerontology, 21,* 192–197.

BASSETT, C., McCLAMROCK, E., and SCHELZER, M. (1982). A 10-week exercise program for senior citizens. *Geriatric Nursing, 3,* 103–107.

BELLOC, N. B. (1973). Relationship of health practices and mortality. *Preventive Medicine, 2,* 67–81.

BELLOC, N. B., and BRESLOW, L. (1972). Relationship of physical health status and health practices. *Preventive Medicine, 1,* 409–421.

BIEGEL, L. (1984). *Physical fitness and the older person.* Rockville, Maryland: Aspen Systems Corporation.

BIRREN, J. E., and BOTWINICK, J. (1955). Age differences in finger, jaw, and foot reaction to auditory stimuli. *Journal of Gerontology, 10,* 429–432.

BIRREN, J. E., WOODS, A. M., and WILLIAMS, M. V. (1979). Speed of behavior as an indicator of age changes and the integrity of the nervous system. In F. Hoffmeister, C. Muller, and H. P. Krause (Eds.), *Brain function in old age.* New York: Springer-Verlag.

BIRREN, J. E., and ZARIT, J. M. (1984). Concepts of health, behavior and aging. In J. E. Birren and J. Livingston (Eds.), *Cognition, stress, and aging.* Englewood Cliffs, New Jersey: Prentice-Hall, Inc.

BORTZ, W. M. (1982). Disuse and aging. *Journal of the American Medical Association, 248*, 1203–1208.

BROCKLEHURST, J. C. (1973). Geriatric services and the day hospital. In J. C. Brocklehurst (Ed.), *Textbook of geriatric medicine and gerontology*. London: Churchill-Livingstone.

BRODY, H. (1955). Organization of the cerebral cortex. III: A study of aging in the human cerebral cortex. *Journal of Comparative Neurology, 102*, 511–520.

BUCCOLA, V. A., and STONE, W. J. (1975). Effects of jogging and cycling programs in physiological and personality variables in aged men. *Research Quarterly, 46*, 134–138.

BUTLER, R. N. (1975). *Why survive? Being old in America*. New York: Harper and Row Publishers.

CHAPMAN, E. A., deVRIES, H. A., and SWEZEY, R. (1972). Joint stiffness: Effects of exercise on old and young men. *Journal of Gerontology, 27*, 218–221.

CHEBOTAREV, D. F., KORKUSHKO, O. V., and IVANOV, L. A. (1974). Mechanisms of hypoxemia in the elderly. *Journal of Gerontology, 29*, 393–400.

CLARKSON, P. M., and KROLL, W. P. (1978). Age and level of physical activity as related to practice effects of variability of fractionated reaction time and movement time. *Journal of Motor Behavior, 10*, 275–286.

CONRAD, C. C. (1976). When you're young at heart. *Aging, 258*, 11–13.

CORRE, K. A., CHO, H., and BARNARD, R. J. (1976). Maximum exercise heart rate reduction with maturation in the rat. *Journal of Applied Psychology, 40*, 741–744.

CREMIN, L. (1976). *Public education*. New York: Basic Books, Inc.

DASTUR, D. K., LANE, M. H., HANSEN, D. B., KETY, S. S., BUTLER, R. N., PERLIN, S., and SOKOLOFF, L. (1963). Effects of aging on cerebral circulation and metabolism in man. In *Human aging: A biological and behavioral study*. PHS Publication #986. Washington, D.C.: U.S. Government Printing Office.

DEHN, M., and BRUCE, R. (1972). Longitudinal variations in maximal oxygen intake with age and activity. *Journal of Applied Physiology, 33*, 805–807.

deVRIES, H. A. (1970). Physiological effects of an exercise training regimen upon men aged 52 to 88. *Journal of Gerontology, 25*, 325–326.

deVRIES, H. A. (1971). Exercise intensity threshold for improvement of cardio-vascular-respiratory function in older men. *Geriatrics, 26*, 94–101.

deVRIES, H. A. (1972). Comparison of exercise responses in old and young men. II: Ventilatory mechanics. *Journal of Gerontology, 27*, 349–352.

deVRIES, H. A. (1984). Exercise and the physiology of aging. In H. M. Eckert and H. J. Montoye (Eds.), *Exercise and health*. Champaign, Illinois: Human Kinetics Publishers, Inc.

deVRIES, H. A., and ADAMS, G. M. (1972). Electromyographic comparison of single doses of exercise and meprobamate as to effects on muscular relaxation. *American Journal of Physical Medicine, 3*, 130–141.

DISMUKE, S. E., and MILLER, S. T. (1983). Why not share the secrets of good health? *Journal of the American Medical Association, 249*, 3181–3183.

DUMMER, G. M., CLARKE, D. H., VACCARO, P., WELDEN, L. V., GOLDFARB, A. H., and SOCKLER, J. M. (1985). Age-related differences in muscular strength and muscular endurance among female masters swimmers. *Research Quarterly for Exercise and Sport, 56*(2), 96–110.

DUSTMAN, R. E., RUHLING, R. O., RUSSELL, E. M., SHEARER, D. E., BONE-

KAT, W., SHIGEOKA, J. W., WOOD, J. S., and BRADFORD, D. C. (1984). Aerobic exercise training and improved neuropsychological function of older individuals. *Neurobiology of Aging, 5,* 35-42.

ERMINI, M. (1976). Aging changes in mammalian skeletal muscle. *Gerontology* (Basel), *22,* 301-316.

FARIA, I., and FRANKEL, M. (1977). Anthropometric and physiologic profile of a cyclist—age 70. *Medicine and Science in Sports, 9,* 118-121.

FARRAR, R. P., ARDIES, C. M., GILLIAM, P. E., DODD, H. L., and SPIRDUSO, W. W. (1983). The effects of aging and exercise upon regional blood glucose oxidation. *Society for Neuroscience, 9,* 931.

FINCH, C. E. (1973). Catecholamine metabolism in the brains of aging male mice. *Brain Research, 52,* 261-276.

FITZGERALD, M. G., MALINS, J. M., O'SULLIVAN, D. J., and WALL, M. (1961). The effect of sex and parity on the incidence of diabetes mellitus. *Quarterly Journal of Medicine, 15,* 57-70.

FORBES, G. B., and REINA, J. C. (1970). Adult lean body mass declines with age. Some longitudinal observations. *Metabolism, 19,* 653-663.

FREKANY, G. A., and LESLIE, D. K. (1975). Effects of an exercise program on selected flexibility measurements of senior citizens. *Gerontologist, 15,* 182-183.

GARY, V., and GUTHRIE, D. (1972). The effect of jogging on physical fitness and self-concept in hospitalized alcoholics. *Quarterly Journal Studying Alcohol, 33,* 1073-1078.

GILLIAM, P. E., SPIRDUSO, W. W., MARTIN, T. P., WALTERS, T. J., WILCOX, R. E., and FARRAR, R. P. (1984). The effects of exercise training on [3H]-spiperone binding in rat striatum. *Pharmacology, Biochemistry, and Behavior, 20,* 863-867.

GILLIAM-MACRAE, P. E., WILCOX, R. E., FARRAR, R. P., and SPIRDUSO, W. W. (In progress.) Endurance training effects on striated D_2 dopamine receptor binding and striated dopamine metabolites in young and old rats.

GUTMAN, E., HANZLIKOVA, V., and JAKOUBEK, B. (1968). Changes in the neuromuscular system during old age. *Experimental Gerontology, 3,* 141-146.

HAGBERG, J. M., ALLEN, W. K., SEALS, D. R., HURLEY, B. F., EHSANI, A. A., and HOLLOSZY, J. O. (1985). A hemodynamic comparison of young and older endurance athletes during exercise. *Journal of Applied Physiology, 58*(6), 2041-2046.

HART, B. A. (1981). The effect of age and habitual activity on the fractionated components of resisted and unresisted response time. *Medicine and Science in Sports and Exercise, 13,* 78.

HARTLEY, L. H., GRIMBY, G., KILBOM, A., NILSSON, N. J., ASTRAND, I., BJURE, J., EKBLOM, B., and SALTIN, B. (1969). Physical training in sedentary middle-aged and older men. 3: Cardiac output and gas exchange at submaximal and maximal exercise. *Scandinavia Journal of Clinical Laboratory Investigation, 24,* 335-344.

HEALTHY PEOPLE: THE SURGEON GENERAL'S REPORT ON HEALTH PROMOTION AND DISEASE PREVENTION (1979). Washington, D.C.: U.S. Department of Health, Education and Welfare.

HILYER, J. C., and MITCHELL, W. (1979). Effect of systematic physical fitness training combined with counseling on the self-concept of college students. *Journal of Counseling Psychology, 26,* 427-436.

HILYER, J. C., WILSON, D. G., DILLON, C., CARO, L., JENKINS, C., SPENCER,

W. A., MEADOWS, M. E., and BROOKES, W. (1982). Physical fitness training and counseling as treatment for youthful offenders. *Journal of Counseling Psychology, 29,* 292–303.

HODGKINS, J. (1962). Influence of age on the speed of reaction and movement in females. *Journal of Gerontology, 17,* 385–389.

HODGSON, J. L., and BUSKIRK, E. R. (1977). Physical fitness and age, with emphasis on cardiovascular function in the elderly. *Journal of the American Geriatrics Society, 25,* 385–392.

HOLLOSZY, J. O. (1983). Exercise, health, and aging: A need for more information. *Medicine and Science in Sports and Exercise, 15,* 1–5.

HOLLOSZY, J. O., HAGBERG, J. M., and EHSANI, A. A. (1984). Exercise, health and aging. *Gerontologist, 24,* 131.

HUGHES, J. R. (1984). Psychological effects of habitual aerobic exercise: A critical review. *Preventive Medicine, 13,* 66–78.

KAVANAGH, T., and SHEPHARD, R. J. (1977). The effects of continued training on the aging process. *Annals of the New York Academy of Science, 301,* 656–670.

KREITLER, H., and KREITLER, S. (1970). Movement and aging: A psychological approach. In D. Brunner and E. Jokl (Eds.), *Physical activity and aging.* Baltimore: University Park Press.

LARSON, L. (1978). Morphological and functional characteristics of the ageing skeletal muscle in man. A cross-sectional study. *Acta Physiologica Scandinavica Supplement, 457,* 1–36.

LESSER, M. (1978). The effects of rhythmic exercise on the range of motion in older adults. *American Corrective Therapy Journal, 32,* 118–122.

MASSACHUSETTS MUTUAL INSURANCE COMPANY (June 1975). Disability income protection approved claims, 1974, *World Supplement.*

McGEER, P. L., and McGEER, E. G. (1976). Enzymes associated with the metabolism of catecholamines, acetylcholine, and GABA in human controls and patients with Parkinson's disease and Huntington's chorea. *Journal of Neurochemistry, 26,* 65–70.

McGOWAN, R. W., JARMAN, B. O., and PEDERSEN, D. M. (1974). Effects of a competitive endurance training program on self-concept and peer approval. *Journal of Psychology, 86,* 57–60.

McKEOWN, T. (1976). *The role of medicine: Dream, mirage or nemesis?* London: Nuffield Provincial Hospitals Trust.

MITTMAN, C., EDELMAN, N. H., NORRIS, A. H., and SHOCK, N. W. (1965). Relationship between chest wall and pulmonary compliance and age. *Journal of Applied Physiology, 20,* 1211–1216.

MONTOYE, H. J., and LAMPHIEAR, D. E. (1977). Grip and arm strength in males and females, age 10–69. *Research Quarterly, 48,* 109–120.

MOORE, J. L., and BIRREN, J. E. (1972). A bibliography of doctoral dissertations on aging from American institutions of higher learning, 1969–71. *Journal of Gerontology, 27*(3), 399–402.

MOORE, J. L., MUELLER, J. E., and BIRREN, J. E. (Submitted). Analysis of doctoral dissertations on aging written in institutions of higher learning in the United States, 1976–1982.

MORGAN, W. P. (1984). Physical activity and mental health. In H. M. Eckert and H. J. Montoye (Eds.), *Exercise and health.* Champaign, Illinois: Human Kinetics Publishers, Inc.

MORGAN, W. P. (1985). Affective beneficience of vigorous physical activity. *Medicine and Science in Sports and Exercise, 17,* 94–100.

MORRISON, J. F., VAN MALSEN, S., and NOAKES, T. D. (1984). Leisure-time physical activity levels, cardiovascular fitness and coronary risk factors in 1015 white Zinbabweans. *South African Medical Journal, 65,* 250–256.

MUELLER, J. E., and BIRREN, J. E. (1974). A bibliography of doctoral dissertations on aging from American institutions of higher learning, 1971 to 1973. *Journal of Gerontology, 29,* 459–467.

MUELLER, J. E., and KRONAUER, M. L. (1978). A bibliography of doctoral dissertations on aging from American institutions of higher learning, 1975 to 1977. *Journal of Gerontology, 33,* 605–615.

MUELLER, J. E., and KRONAUER, M. L. (1980). A bibliography of doctoral dissertations on aging from American institutions of higher learning, 1977 to 1979. *Journal of Gerontology, 35,* 603–617.

MUELLER, J. L., LONGO, M., and KRONAUER, M. L. (1982). A bibliography of doctoral dissertations on aging from American institutions of higher learning, 1979 to 1981. *Journal of Gerontology, 37,* 496–512.

MUELLER, J. E., MOORE, J. L., and BIRREN, J. E. (1976). A bibliography of doctoral dissertations on aging from American institutions of higher learning, 1973 to 1975. *Journal of Gerontology, 31,* 471–483.

A NATIONAL RESEARCH PLAN FOR RESEARCH ON AGING (1982). NIH Publication No. 82-2453. Washington, D.C.: U.S. Department of Health and Human Services.

NELSON, M. E. (1983). Public health and preventive medicine in the curricula of osteopathic medical schools. *Journal of Medical Education, 58,* 662–664.

NIINIMAA, V., and SHEPHARD, R. J. (1978). Training and oxygen conductance in the elderly. I: The respiratory system. II: The cardiovascular system. *Journal of Gerontology, 33,* 362–367.

NORRIS, A. H., SHOCK, N. W., LANDOWNE, M., and FALZONE, J. A. (1956). Pulmonary function studies: Age differences in lung volumes and bellows function. *Journal of Gerontology, 11,* 379–387.

NOVAK, L. P. (1972). Aging, total body potassium, fat-free mass, and cell mass in males and females between 18 and 85 years. *Journal of Gerontology, 27,* 438–443.

OSTROW, A. C. (1980). Physical activity as it relates to the health of the aged. In N. Datan and N. Lohmann (Eds.), *Transitions of aging.* New York: Academic Press.

OSTROW, A. C. (1984). *Physical activity and the older adult: Psychological perspectives.* Princeton, New Jersey: Princeton Book Company, Publishers.

OYSTER, N., MORTON, M., and LINNELL, S. (1984). Physical activity and osteoporosis in post-menopausal women. *Medicine and Science in Sports and Exercise, 16*(1), 44–50.

PAFFENBARGER, R. S. JR., HYDE, R. T., WING, A. L., and STEINMETZ, C. H. (1984). A natural history of athleticism and cardiovascular health. *Journal of the American Medical Association, 252,* 491–495.

PAFFENBARGER, R. S. JR., WING, A. L., and HYDE, R. T. (1978). Physical activity as an index of heart attack risk in college alumni. *American Journal of Epidemiology, 108,* 161–175.

PARIZKOVA, J. (1963). Impact of age, diet, and exercise on man's body composition. *Annals of the New York Academy of Sciences, 110,* 661–674.

PERKINS, L. C., and KAISER, H. L. (1962). Results of short term isotonic and isometric exercise programs in persons over sixty. *Physical Therapy Review, 41,* 633–635.

PERRI, S., and TEMPLER, D. I. (1984–85). The effects of an aerobic exercise program on psychological variables in older adults. *International Journal of Aging and Human Development, 20,* 167–172.

PETROFSKY, J. S., and LIND, A. R. (1975). Aging, isometric strength and endurance, and cardiovascular responses to static effort. *Journal of Applied Physiology, 38,* 91–95.

POLLOCK, M. L., MILLER, H. S. JR., and WILMORE, J. (1974). A profile of a champion distance runner: Age 60. *Medicine and Science in Sports, 6,* 118–121.

POLLOCK, M. L., WILMORE, J. H., and FOX, S. M. (1984). *Exercise in health and disease.* Philadelphia: W. B. Saunders Company.

POWELL, R. R. (1974). Psychological effects of exercise therapy upon institutionalized geriatric mental patients. *Journal of Gerontology, 29,* 157–161.

RECKER, R. R., SAVILLE, P. D., and HEANEY, R. P. (1977). Effect of estrogens and calcium carbonate on bone loss on postmenopausal women. *Annals of Internal Medicine, 87,* 649–655.

RIZZATO, G., and MARAZZINI, L. (1970). Thoracoabdominal mechanics in elderly men. *Journal of Applied Physiology, 28,* 457–460.

SALTIN, B., and GRIMBY, G. (1968). Physiological analysis of middle-aged and old former athletes. Comparison with still active athletes of the same ages. *Circulation, 38,* 1104–1115.

SCHEIBEL, M. E., LINDSAY, R. D., TOMIYASU, U., and SCHEIBEL, A. B. (1975). Progressive dendritic changes in aging human cortex. *Experimental Neurology, 47,* 392–403.

SCHEIBEL, M. E., LINDSAY, R. D., TOMIYASU, U., and SCHEIBEL, A. B. (1976). Progressive dendritic changes in the aging human limbic system. *Experimental Neurology, 53,* 420–430.

SCHEIBEL, M. E., TOMIYASU, U., and SCHEIBEL, A. B. (1977). The aging human Betz cell. *Experimental Neurology, 56,* 598–609.

SCHMID, L. (1975). Malignant tumors as causes of death of former athletes. In H. Howarld and J. R. Poortmans (Eds.), *Metabolic adaptations to prolonged physical exercise.* Basel: Birkhauser Verlag.

SEALS, D. R., HAGBERG, J. M., ALLEN, W. K., HURLEY, B. F., DALSKY, G. P., EHSANI, A. A., and HOLLOSZY, J. O. (1984a). Glucose tolerance in young and older athletes and sedentary men. *Journal of Applied Physiology: Respiratory, Environmental, and Exercise Physiology, 56*(6), 1521–1525.

SEALS, D. R., HAGBERG, J. M., HURLEY, B. F., EHSANI, A. A., and HOLLOSZY, J. O. (1984b). Endurance training in older men and women, I. Cardiovascular responses to exercise. *Journal of Applied Physiology: Respiratory, Environmental, and Exercise Physiology, 57*(4), 1024–1029.

SHEPHARD, R. J. (1968). World standards of cardiorespiratory performance. *Archives of Environmental Health, 13,* 664–672.

SHEPHARD, R. J. (1978). *Physical activity and aging.* London: Croom Helm Limited.

SHERWOOD, D. E., and SELDER, D. J. (1979). Cardiorespiratory health, reaction time, and aging. *Medicine and Science in Sports, 11,* 186–189.

SICONOLFI, S. F., LASATER, T. M., McKINLAY, S., BOGGIA, P., and CARLETON, R. A. (1985). Physical fitness and blood pressure: The role of age. *American Journal of Epidemiology, 122,* 452–457.

SIDNEY, K. H., and SHEPHARD, R. J. (1976). Attitudes toward health and physical activity in the elderly: Effects of a physical training program. *Medicine and Science in Sports, 8,* 246–252.

SIDNEY, K. H., and SHEPHARD, R. J. (1977a). Activity patterns of elderly men and women. *Journal of Gerontology, 32,* 25–32.

SIDNEY, K. H., and SHEPHARD, R. J. (1977b). Training and electrocardiographic abnormalities in the elderly. *British Heart Journal, 39,* 1114–1120.

SIDNEY, K. H., and SHEPHARD, R. J. (1977c). Perception of exertion in the elderly, effects of aging, mode of exercise and physical training. *Perceptual and Motor Skills, 44,* 999–1010.

SIDNEY, K. H., and SHEPHARD, R. J. (1978). Frequency and intensity of exercise training for elderly subjects. *Medicine and Science in Sports, 10,* 125–131.

SIDNEY, K. H., SHEPHARD, R. J., and HARRISON, J. (1977). Endurance training and body composition of the elderly. *American Journal of Clinical Nutrition, 30,* 326–333.

SMITH, C. B., GOOCHEE, C., RAPOPORT, S. I., and SOKOLOFF, L. (1980). Effects of aging on local rates of cerebral glucose utilization in rats. *Brain, 103,* 351–365.

SMITH, E. L. (1982). Exercise for prevention of osteoporosis: A review. *Physician and Sports Medicine, 10*(3), 72–80.

SMITH, E. L., and REDDAN, W. G. (1975). Effects of physical activity on bone in the aged. *Medicine and Science in Sports, 7,* 84.

SMITH, E. L., REDDAN, W. G., and SMITH, P. E. (1981). Physical activity and calcium modalities for bone mineral increase in aged women. *Medicine and Science in Sports and Exercise, 13*(1), 60–64.

SMITH, M. R., MARCY, M. L., MAST, T. A., and HAM, R. J. (1984). Implementation and evaluation of a model geriatrics curriculum. *Journal of Medical Education, 59,* 416–424.

SOLDO, B. J. (1980). America's elderly in the 1980's. *Population Bulletin, 35*(4), 3–48.

SPIRDUSO, W. W. (1975). Reaction and movement time as a function of age and physical activity level. *Journal of Gerontology, 30,* 435–440.

SPIRDUSO, W. W. (1980). Physical fitness, aging, and psychomotor speed: A review. *Journal of Gerontology, 35*(6), 850–865.

SPIRDUSO, W. W. (1983). Exercise and the aging brain. *Research Quarterly for Exercise and Sport, 54,* 208–218.

SPIRDUSO, W. W., and CLIFFORD, P. (1978). Neuromuscular speed and consistency of performance as a function of age, physical activity level and type of activity. *Journal of Gerontology, 33,* 26–30.

STAMFORD, B. A. (1972). Physiological effects of training upon institutionalized geriatric men. *Journal of Gerontology, 27,* 451–455.

SUCI, G. J. (1960). Reaction time as a function of stimulus information and age. *Journal of Experimental Psychology, 60,* 242–244.

SUOMINEN, H., HEIKKINEN, E., LIESEN, H., MICHEL, D., and HOLLMAN, W. (1977a). Effects of 8 weeks' endurance training on skeletal muscle metabolism in 56- to 70-year-old sedentary men. *European Journal of Applied Physiology and Occupational Physiology, 37,* 173–180.

SUOMINEN, H., HEIKKINEN, E., and PARKATTI, I. (1977b). Effect of eight weeks' physical training on muscle and connective tissue of the M. vastus lateralis in 69-year-old men and women. *Journal of Gerontology, 32,* 33–37.

TORRENS, P. R., BRESLOW, L., and FIELDING, J. E. (1982). The role of universities in personal health improvement. *Preventive Medicine, 11*(4), 477–484.

TREDWAY, V. A. (1978). Mood and exercise in older adults. Unpublished doctoral dissertation. University of Southern California.

TURNER, J. M., MEAD, J., and WOHL, M. E. (1968). Elasticity of human lungs in relation to age. *Journal of Applied Physiology, 25,* 664–671.

WANG, H., and BUSSE, E. (1969). EEG of healthy older persons: A longitudinal study. A: Dominant background activity and occipital rhythm. *Journal of Gerontology, 24,* 419–426.

WARNER-REITZ, A. (1981). *Healthy lifestyle for seniors.* New York: Meals for Millions/Freedom from Hunger Foundation.

WEBB, J. L., URNER, S. C., and McDANIELS, J. (1977). Physiological characteristics of a champion runner: Age 77. *Journal of Gerontology, 32,* 286–290.

WEBSTER'S THIRD NEW INTERNATIONAL DICTIONARY OF THE ENGLISH LANGUAGE, UNABRIDGED. (1976). Gove, P. B., and Merriam-Webster Editorial Staff, (Eds.). Springfield, Massachusetts: G. & C. Merriam Company.

WEISS, N. S., URE, C. L., BALLARD, J. H., WILLIAMS, A. R., and DALING, J. R. (1980). Decreased risk of fractures of the hip and lower forearm with postmenopausal use of estrogen. *New England Journal of Medicine, 303,* 1195–1202.

WELFORD, A. T. (1977). Serial reaction times, continuity of task, single-channel effects, and age. In S. Dornic (Ed.), *Attention and performance VI.* Hillsdale, New Jersey: Lawrence Erlbaum.

WOODS, A. M. (1981). Age differences in the effect of physical activity and postural changes on information processing speed. Unpublished doctoral dissertation, University of Southern California.

YATES, A., LEEHEY, K., and SHESSLAK. C. M. (1983). Running—An analogue of anorexia? *New England Journal of Medicine, 308,* 251–255.

INDEXES

AUTHOR INDEX

SUBJECT INDEX